a **modern** introduction to **theology**

Most existing undergraduate textbooks of theology begin from basically
traditional positions on the Bible, doctrine, authority, interpretation and
God. It is very difficult to find a satisfactory survey of what theology is
really about, and how it has developed historically, unless one shares the
assumption that these traditional positions are normative. It is hardly
surprising therefore that many people from outside the theological guild,
or the Church, dismiss theology as an anachronistic and self-absorbed
discipline of little relevance to modern life. What makes Philip Kennedy's
book both singularly important and uniquely different is that it has a
completely new starting point. The author contends that traditional
Christian theology must extensively overhaul many of its theses because of
a multitude of modern social, historical and intellectual revolutions. Offering
a grand historical sweep of the genesis of the modern age, and writing with
great panache and a magisterial grasp of the relevant debates, conflicts
and controversies, *A Modern Introduction to Theology* moves a tired and
increasingly incoherent discipline in genuinely fresh and exciting directions.

PHILIP KENNEDY is a member of the Faculty of Theology in the University
of Oxford and is the Senior Tutor and a Fellow of Mansfield College. He is the
author of a much-praised volume on the theology of Edward Schillebeeckx.

'What a delight to discover in Kennedy's book a comprehensive resource for theological educators and inquirers! Researchers and students will engage vigorously with the spectrum of ideas and the depths of analysis of "intellectual revolutions in geography, astronomy, scientific method, critical philosophy, biblical studies, historical Jesus research, biology, physics and hermeneutics" developed in the text. Kennedy's theology is immediately accessible to all who share his concern for the crucial conflict between humankind and the ecosystem of the planet. His courage and competence in formulating "a language about God that does not expect God to rectify what humans are so systematically destroying" invites those who may have given up on Christianity to reassess their position. Deceptively simple in the clarity of expression, the book opens the reader to a rich panorama of complex ideas.'

Maryanne Confoy,
Professor of Pastoral Theology, Melbourne College of Divinity

'Philip Kennedy's book will make a fine introductory text in a variety of undergraduate classes. It contains excellent chapters on such standard topics as the challenges posed by the Enlightenment and the rise of biblical criticism, but it also offers the beginning student useful roadmaps to such subjects as globalism and economic justice, feminism, and recent developments in physical cosmology. Perhaps most striking are the interspersed text-boxes in which the author explains, in ordinary language, terms and concepts that the undergraduate student is likely to be encountering for the first time – a fine addition to a book that is sure to be widely used.'

Terry F. Godlove,
Professor of Philosophy and Religion, Hofstra University

'Some Christian readers will find this book challenging and disturbing, but if they value their faith, they should persevere. Kennedy has a genuine passion to discover a Christianity which can proclaim truth, and he is unflinching in his surgery of obstacles to that proclamation. Anyone seeking an adult faith will benefit from reading what he has written. *A Modern Introduction to Theology* can also serve as principal textbook for introductory student courses in theology and doctrine, the history of Christianity, Church history and philosophy of religion.'

Diarmaid N.J. MacCulloch,
Professor of the History of the Church, University of Oxford

'It is one of the unfortunate facts of our time that few books about theology manage to communicate beyond the circle of professional theologians. Even fewer are those that convey a sense of academic theology itself as an important, exciting, and challenging venture of human thought. Kennedy's book does just this. As he depicts it, theology is not just the defence or reinterpretation of ancient dogmas but a totally engaging effort to face the implications of the gospel for contemporary living. As such, theology will lead us to radical and critical positions vis-à-vis the institutional Church, and Kennedy does not shrink from being crystal-clear about just where the fault lines are to be found. Vigorous, punchy, and fast-moving, this book will excite, instruct, disturb and provoke. Accessible to students from sixth-form level upwards, it also contains much that calls for a response from academic colleagues and, no less importantly, the Churches themselves.'

George Pattison,
Lady Margaret Professor of Divinity, University of Oxford

a **modern** introduction to **theology**

new questions for old beliefs

PHILIP KENNEDY

I.B. TAURIS

LONDON · NEW YORK

Published in 2006 by
I.B.Tauris & Co. Ltd
6 Salem Rd, London W2 4BU
175 Fifth Avenue, New York NY 10010
www.ibtauris.com

In the United States and Canada distributed by Palgrave Macmillan,
a division of St. Martin's Press, 175 Fifth Avenue, New York, NY 10010

ISBN   1 84511 009 9 (Hb)
ISBN   1 84511 010 2 (Pb)
EAN   978 1 84511 009 3 (Hb)
EAN   978 1 84511 010 9 (Pb)

A full CIP record for this book is available from the British Library
A full CIP record for this book is available from the Library of Congress
Library of Congress catalog card: available

Typeset in Van Dijck by illuminati, Grosmont,
www.illuminatibooks.co.uk
Printed and bound in Great Britain by TJ International Ltd, Padstow, Cornwall

contents

orientation

Christianity was born in the agrarian societies of the ancient Middle East when the Empire of Rome was strong and the civilization of Greece pervasive. It survives in a vastly transformed world of slums and super-cities; in high-rise, high-tech, multimedia cultures; and in countries enthralled by computerized transnational money markets. Five hundred years ago, Christianity dominated the artistic, political and intellectual life of Europe. Its theology buttressed the power of monarchs, directed universities and commanded the allegiance of the populace. Its missionaries dispersed its doctrines to the far reaches of the globe. Today, Christianity's condition depends on where and how it is implanted. In some areas it flourishes or enjoys vigorous revivals. In others it is ignored as moribund and meaningless, or dismissed as an old-fashioned carry-over from a peasant past. In China it is a carefully monitored minority. Throughout Brazil it is more prevalent than any other faith-system. Around Morocco it hardly matters. For the United States of America it has a very public face. In general, though, and especially since the eighteenth century, Christianity has gradually lost its former ability to captivate western cultures. For many people, traditional Christian theology is a Humpty-Dumpty: it has tumbled from its perch and can't be put together again.

In short, Christian theology is a time-honoured enterprise mired in profoundly troubling circumstances. This book explores the way such a situation arose. It probes what has happened to Christianity and its solemnly taught theology since the advent of the modern era; introduces its readers to challenges and dilemmas currently confronting Christian life and thought; considers the attempts of various theologians to guarantee that Christianity continues; describes the genesis of modernity and the quandaries it poses for esteemed theologies; and charts the evolution of a chain of historical, political, social and intellectual revolutions that now cumulatively question the credibility of many aspects of traditional Christian teaching.

The presumed novelty or distinctiveness of this book rests with two factors. First, the text recoils from the assumptions that traditional theologies received from the past are unquestionable; that what has been formerly laid down doctrinally is absolutely normative for the present; and that an introduction to theology should confine itself to a reverential exposition of teachings conceived in bygone eras. Bluntly stated, the Christian tradition is not only a conduit of wisdom; it has also promoted disturbing dehumanizing prejudices. It proposes much that is helpful to people today, and a good deal that needs to be reconsidered or rejected. As such, it is a mixture of sense and nonsense. Theology would fail to convince at present were it to be practised with inattention to events and ideas peculiar to contemporary cultures. What is the point of addressing people by ignoring what is new and distinctive about their experiences and knowledge? The second facet of the book's novelty lies in the particular constellation of relatively recent historical transformations and intellectual discoveries that it broaches. The major part of the book considers ideas and events that were never encountered by pre-modern generations. In brief, new science, new experiences and new knowledge coalesce to invite new considerations of theology's primary tasks and taxing dilemmas.

Anyone observing Christians today will soon discover that they are adept at disagreement. Despite their commonalities they often dispute one another. Since its beginnings, Christianity has been a movement of creative discussions, rival voices, diverse opinions and varied tastes. Over the course of their history Christians have split into several thousand rival denominations. The questions they debate vary widely, but one in particular stands out – what is the best way to ensure that Christianity endures? Many Christians are greatly troubled by this question because over roughly the past two hundred years a long-standing culture of Christendom has been collapsing ignominiously, especially in Europe. Christendom was a civilization in which religious and civil authorities governed societies in concert. It began noticeably in 312 when the Emperor Constantine adopted Christianity as the religion of the Roman Empire. It insisted that Christian beliefs are true, and upheld them by political fiat. It kept the loyalty of by far the majority of Europe's inhabitants until it began to decline, notably during the nineteenth century. Its vestiges remain around the world, but it has lost the widespread political support it previously enjoyed.

Christianity is not Christendom. The former might survive without the latter. But how? For numerous Christians at present, the ideal strategy for advancing Christianity is repetition: to rehearse and reaffirm the grand account of human destiny that is taught by traditional Christian theology. Others disagree. For them, Christianity will languish as an irrelevant cultural sideshow unless it develops new theologies that are informed by knowledge that was unavailable to previous generations.

A dominant strand of conventional Christian theology tells a sober story of a Fall, Redemption and Judgement. It teaches that a primordial human couple, Adam and Eve, disobeyed God, and thereby fell from divine favour in paradise. All human beings – so the story goes – as descendants of Adam and Eve are estranged from God from birth, because they have inherited the debilitating after-effects of the first parents' original sin. No mere human could ever repair the damage of the first disobedience. So God's son became incarnate in history in the man Jesus, and sacrificed himself on a cross to redeem humanity by reconciling it with God. After his execution, Jesus was raised upward by God to a glorified heavenly mode of existence whence, one day, he will return downward to earth to judge the living and the dead. Whether one accepts or rejects him will decide one's everlasting fate. Those deemed unworthy of proceeding to heaven will be consigned to the miseries of hell for eternity. In sum, the three pillars of Christianity's conventional account of human destiny in relation to God are the doctrines of humanity's Fall, engineered by Adam and Eve; Redemption wrought by the self-sacrificing death of Jesus Christ; and his future Judgement of the entire human race. The entire lattice of traditional Christian doctrine can be condensed into a slogan of two words: 'Jesus saves'.

The sketch of the drama of perdition and salvation just outlined is not a caricature. It is a theological paradigm that has been preached and believed in Christian circles for the major part of Christian history. It was eloquently articulated about 1500 years ago by Aurelius Augustinus, otherwise known as St Augustine of Hippo (354–430). He recounts the story of the Fall in his massive book *The City of God*, which was produced in instalments between 416 and 422. His view of humanity's fate entered the lifeblood of Christendom and remains the official teaching of many major Churches. It was widely believed in the west during the Middle Ages. Despite their passionate debates, it united Catholics and Protestants throughout the sixteenth-century Reformation. Members of both groups fretted about what they took to be the real possibility of languishing in hell, and of being tormented by demons. Eventually, like Humpty-Dumpty, the story of the Fall began its own fall, as it met significant trouble in the form of growing incredulity. Its difficulties arose in the wake of a string of modern revolutions in a host of human fields of enquiry. The classical Christian drama of sin and salvation presupposes that the earth is the centre of the universe and that its age can be counted in thousands of years. It avers that the cosmos is vertically ordered with heaven above earth and hell. With major discoveries and advances in disciplines such as geography, astronomy, physics, biology and philosophy, the time-honoured edifice of Christian doctrine began to teeter as its underlying assumptions were more frequently questioned. Its power to convince was sapped and its ability to inspire diminished. The end result is that a homogenous Christian Europe is a phenomenon of the past. The populations of most European countries today are far from monochromatic and comprise at least three different groups: those who are indifferent to religion in general and Christianity in particular; those who profess religious creeds apart from Christianity; and those who are involved with Christian churches. How and why such a situation arose will be pondered at length below. Hereinafter, the expression 'traditional Christian theology' refers mainly to the long-standing Augustinian account of the Fall and its doctrine of a Father–Creator God.

The twelve chapters of this book are divided into four parts. The first considers the nature of theology, traditional Christian doctrines, and Christianity's current predicament. The second charts the evolution of modernity, the Enlightenment, and the gradual secularization of nineteenth-century Europe. The third considers aftershocks for traditional theology generated by the rise of the modern age. It focuses on modern biblical studies, the historical investigation of the identity of Jesus, and hermeneutics, or the theory of how to interpret language. The fourth part attends to acute dilemmas that have arisen for traditional theology since the advent of

> Throughout the book, the body of the text is occasionally interspersed with boxes that either explain expressions that might not be immediately intelligible, or furnish further information.

modernity. It discusses such topics as talk about God in relation to debilitating human poverty, women and Christianity, the interplay between theology and science, and religious diversity in a globalized era. The book ends with an estimation of theology's paramount task today and Christianity's greatest challenge.

A Modern Introduction to Theology is based on lectures I gave before undergraduates in the University of Oxford over the past ten years. The lectures were largely devoted to the history of modern Christian life and thought, and aimed to illustrate the peculiar challenges encountered by theologians in the modern era. My students were not always aware they were being used as guinea pigs to test new modes of probing ancient issues. Experiments complete, this book has been thoroughly recast to address a much wider and far more diverse audience. Importantly, it is not the fruit of sustained and contemplative sabbatical research. On the contrary, it was devised during a standard rota of university teaching and faculty business. That is not an excuse for its limitations, but an explanation for its final form and general tone.

This book is intended for a spectrum of readers. In the first place, it is addressed to any interested inquirer struggling to reconcile traditional religious language of angels and devils, heaven and hell, with the current human condition which knows of space probes, jet travel, digital television, pulsars, and mitochondrial DNA. Second, it is aimed at students of theology and religion who are keen to consider how modern intellectual, historical and cultural developments might relate to, or call into question, pre-modern styles of speaking about divinity. Third, it is offered as a compendium of thoughts and observations for adults who have lost the religious faith of their childhood. Often a perceived loss of faith is no more than the abandonment of a naive or misguided understanding that could easily be replaced by a more constructive religious world-view. Fourth, it is directed to people who feel denigrated by the champions of so-called theological orthodoxy, or who are regularly denounced by Churches that call themselves Christian. Religiously emboldened decriers of sinners and reprobates are frequently all too prone to confuse their own misinformed biases with an imagined divine authority. Fifth, it is meant for people who are unnerved by Christianity's cozy alliance with western wealth in many parts of the world, and are unable to see a relation between Jesus and the hierarchical Churches that followed him. Finally, it is intended for readers who labour to reconcile belief in God with a world of violence, inequality, war, ecological destruction, hunger and hatred.

I have written this book with the conviction that jargon is unnecessary. Theology has no language of its own. It uses the linguistic patterns shared by all human beings. It does possess a specialized terminology that it has accrued over time, but this can easily be translated into the plainest of terms. There is no need for theologians to drown their readers in an ocean of abstruse phraseology.

Even though most of this text discusses Christianity and the theologies it has produced, a great deal of what is said in these pages about historical change and intellectual discoveries impinges on other religious traditions to an equal extent. I do not presuppose that theology is the preserve of Christians, or even of theists. Some of the most sophisticated theologies of the twentieth century were written by atheists such as J.L. Mackie (1917–1981) and Anthony Flew (b. 1923).

I have discussed the contents of this book with many people, and I now need to acknowledge my debt to them. They are by no means universally enthusiastic about my conclusions and none of them can be blamed for the oversights and drawbacks of this book. In particular, I acknowledge my immense gratitude to my father Stephen, my stepmother Margaret, and my sisters and brothers. My mother, were she alive, would no doubt engage in lively debate about many of my conclusions. Many friends, students and colleagues have enlightened and encouraged me recently as I worked on this project, including Joël-Alexis Iseli,

Robert Gilbert, Guy Tourlamain, Jennifer Cooper, Dennis Kehrberg, Robert Wilson, Madeleine and Edwina Scanlon, Chris Ward, Daphne Hampson, Nathaniel Hannan, Alan Faulkner, Kevin Watson, John Heaton-Armstrong, Ian van Every and Steve Riley. I am very grateful to Jonathan Yonan and Alec Jarvis for reading and correcting large sections of the manuscript, and to George Pattison and Pamela Sue Anderson for commenting on the entire text. Finally, I wish to thank the members of Mansfield College in the University of Oxford for a lively academic home over the past five years.

This book would never have appeared without the advice and decisive intervention of Diarmaid MacCulloch, coupled with the expert judgement, considerable patience and constant support of my editor at I.B. Tauris, Alex Wright. I am exceptionally grateful to them both.

Throughout the text quotations from Hebrew and Christian Scriptures are taken from *The Holy Bible*, New Revised Standard Version, Anglicized Edition (Oxford: Oxford University Press, 1996).

Tellingly, the chapters of this book are not solely or even principally the product of university-based lecturing. They have also been decisively shaped by the fate of friends. I have encountered many people whose lives are profoundly sustained and nourished by Christian faith. For them, Christianity promises sanity amid despair and chaos. It provides purpose for the labour of living, and it celebrates meaning, truth and beauty in a world of murder and mayhem. Nevertheless, over the past three decades, a number of my friends and academic colleagues have either abandoned Christianity in disgust or resigned from ordained Christian ministry in depressed frustration. Many of them now dismiss Christianity as a hard-nosed, embarrassingly backward and overly repressive community. Some regard it as a silly and laughable anachronism. Others have become bored by it, or impatient with its perceived reluctance to change comprehensively. A few have become incensed by what they regard as its obsessive, prurient and wrong-headed denunciations of sexual excitements. For them, Christians are dyed-in-the-wool pleasure-haters. One of my closest companions is a Jew who loathes the Christian religion for its past pogroms of other Jews. Another is a talented physicist who avers that contemporary astronomers and cosmologists, rather than Christian preachers, are best equipped to explain how things are. An assertive graduate student of mine proffers the view that studying new ideas in the nineteenth century obliges one, as a matter of intellectual honesty and integrity, to jettison Christian beliefs. Two friends who were once Catholic priests in the same city now live together as a couple and pursue quite different work, abjuring any contact whatsoever with the Catholic Church. Other confidants are skilled musicians who regard Church music as aesthetically seductive, though regrettably based on doctrinal texts that form a farrago of nonsense. Additional companions and academic associates have never had any commitment to Christianity. They teasingly accuse me of squandering my time when I bother to comment on Christian life and thought. Several women – and men – I know, in far-flung places, are angrily disenthralled by prominent Christian hierarchs whom they deem to be scandalously demeaning of women. A number of bookish friends have judged on scholarly grounds that Christian creeds proclaim falsehoods.

And so it is that the following pages stem largely from my endeavours to decide whether or not my friends are right.

part I

quibbles with tradition

I

theology ancient and modern

If a creature were to comprehend, understand and experience God, he would
have to be drawn beyond himself into God and so comprehend God with God.
Whoever, then, might know what God is and so inquire into this would do
something forbidden and would go mad.

Jan van Ruusbroec (1293–1381)

A Modern Introduction to Theology is a study of opportunities and quandaries
confronting Christianity in the modern era. Its main aim is to discuss the way
relatively recent intellectual and social sea changes have colluded to question
the credibility and liveability of many aspects of traditional orthodox Christian
thought and religious customs. It is not so much a systematic survey of what this
or that modern theologian has said, but a probing of major modern currents of
thought and historical movements that challenge, and in several cases gainsay,
traditional theology. The taxing ideas, brilliant individuals and tumultuous cultural transitions encountered in these pages will all be pondered by scrutinizing
their specific and constantly altering historical contexts.

This chapter undertakes three tasks. First, it considers the nature of theology.
Second, it describes what distinguishes a *modern* introduction to theology from
any other kind of introduction. Third, it sketches core beliefs of the Christian
tradition before subsequent chapters explore new questions and challenges posed
for the beliefs by modernity.

the nature of theology

What, then, is theology? When did it begin? How is it produced? Can it be practised today with intellectual rigour and integrity? In effect, theology is a human

orthodoxy/orthodox/church/churches The word 'orthodoxy' in current religious discourse is potentially misleading. In one sense it can connote a self-styled right or correct ecclesiastical teaching, in counterpoise to a heterodox, or false, doctrine. In other circumstances, 'orthodoxy' can refer to a cluster of Christian denominations called 'Orthodoxy', or 'Orthodox Churches'. Such churches tend to be nationalistically self-conscious, such as the Greek Orthodox or the Russian Orthodox Churches. In any case, they distinguish themselves from Protestant, Catholic and Anglican Churches. In this book, Orthodoxy spelt with a capital 'O' will designate a specific ecclesial community, such as the Georgian Orthodox–Apostolic Church, rather than a teaching that is regarded by some as correct. William Warburton (1698–1779) is recorded as quipping, 'Orthodoxy is my doxy; heterodoxy is another man's doxy'! The word 'Church' is capitalized in this book when referring to an international community of devotees of Jesus, or to a denomination of Christians, like 'the Coptic Church'. When not capitalized, 'church' refers to a community or building in a particular place, as in 'The church in Iffley village'.

struggle to stammer about God and God's putative relation with all there is. As such, it sets itself an impossible task – to speak of the unspeakable.

Not everyone would agree with such a depiction of theology. Professional God-talkers – theologians – do not concur on how best to define theology. Anselm of Canterbury (*c.* 1033–1209) famously described theology as 'faith seeking understanding' (Latin: *fides querens intellectum*). His description of theology is timeworn. It is also open to the charge of being overly abstract. Whose faith is in question? What constitutes faith? And what does it mean to understand? Nowadays, theologians define theology in quite diverse ways. For David Ford, 'Theology at its broadest is thinking about questions raised by and about the religions.' According to Keith Ward, 'Theology is an enquiry into the being of God and the relation of God to the universe.'[1] Whatever else it might be, theology is at least a discourse about God and God's professed relation with all there is.

Theology's apparent success or evident failure depends on what is meant by God. The word 'God' is one of the most used and abused terms in human discourse. Contemporary English conversations are regularly peppered with expressions like 'God help me', 'God damn you', 'God be praised', 'God willing', 'Thank God', 'for God's sake', 'God save the Queen', 'God only knows', 'God bless America', 'Oh my God', or 'God no!' Yet, when people are pressed as to what they mean when they say 'God', they are not always able to present a coherent and credible account of who or what the monosyllabic word 'God' might designate.

Among humans today, there is no agreement as to who or what God might be, or to whether or not there is a God, or several Gods. The word 'God' is polyvalent and protean. It has accrued different meanings over time. In Old English, the term 'God' denoted a worshipped superhuman being, or deity. The term is also found in Old Frisian, Old Saxon, Old Norse, Old High German, and Old Dutch.[2] The Latin word for God is *Deus* (which descends into French as *Dieu*) and it is related to *dies*, a Latin noun for 'day'.[3] Light marks a day. So, in a Latin–French linguistic schema, God is light – the source of life. The monosyllable 'God' can operate either as a proper noun – that is, as a name – or a common noun referring to the category of a deity. In both instances, the noun 'God' as it has evolved over several centuries is like a rope with intertwined threads. The threads represent distinct understandings of the divine that eventually became tessellated with each other.[4] Within the rambling history of Christianity a particular concept of God eventually became regnant, namely the doctrine of the Trinity (see below). As such, God is also designated as timeless, perfectly powerful, utterly unchangeable, completely good, and incapable of suffering.[5]

It is advisable for Christians nowadays not to equate an understanding of God with the doctrine of the Trinity. Trinitarian theology is one among several possible ways of speaking about God. There is a questionable trend in contemporary anglophone theology to overlook that in Abrahamic religions – that is, in Judaism, Christianity and Islam – God is conceived fundamentally as the free Creator of all that is. When Christians replaced the Jewish celebration of the Sabbath with a celebration of the Resurrection of Jesus Christ, they unwittingly deflected attention from a Creator God, to a Triune God involved in the drama of human redemption.[6] The Sabbath is a festival during which Jews refrain for a day from doing any work to improve their immediate world. They thereby remind each other that God, not human beings, is the Creator and sustainer of the earth. A fixation on the Trinity, and a neglect of the theology of God the Creator, are amply evident in the recently published *Blackwell Companion to Modern Theology*. This publication has a chapter devoted to the Trinity, but is devoid of a chapter on creation, even though creation is discussed in various subdivisions of the book. Revealingly, the word 'God' does not even appear in the book's index.[7]

The attributes of God, according to which God is completely powerful and unchanging, stem principally from ancient Greek philosophy in the fifth century BCE. Earlier characterizations of the Gods, represented in the works ascribed to Homer and Hesiod, portray the Gods as badly behaved human beings writ large. According to the earlier tradition, the Gods are mischievous, malevolent, playful, and sexually rapacious. However, from the sixth to the fifth century, Greek thinkers began to describe the Gods in less anthropomorphic and more abstract ways.[8] Hence the more philosophically advanced tradition of depicting God as perfect, unchanging, and all-powerful. The Roman politician Cicero transmitted developed Hellenistic understandings of deities to a Roman audience with his treatise, *De natura deorum* (*The Nature of the Gods*), which was composed around 45–44 BCE.[9] Greek philosophical concepts of God, whether anthropomorphic or abstract, represent just one thread in the rope, so to speak, of the concept of God. Another strand comes from the Hebrew Bible where God is proclaimed as a fatherly Creator who intervenes in history to kill the enemies of the Israelites, to punish the wicked, and to comfort the downtrodden. A third filament in the God-concept is represented by a style of God-talk that is entirely negative, or, in technical language, apophatic. This thread is clearly represented by the Christian thinker Dionysius the Pseudo-Areopagite (*c.* 500 CE), who quite rightly rejected all concepts and images of God. For apophatic theologians, one can only say what God is not.

Other enmeshed threads constituting the concept of God emerged during the modern era, and will be encountered in subsequent chapters. All the threads, however, emerged at an extremely late stage of human evolution. Monotheism, the belief that there is only one God, did not evolve in any notable way before the middle Bronze Age (2000–1550 BCE).[10] Its evolution was preceded during the Paleolithic Age (100,000–30,000 BCE) by what appear to have been human beliefs in animal spirits; and during the Neolithic Age (*c.* 8,000–3,000 BCE) by forms of polytheism, the belief that there are several Gods; as well as by types of henotheism, the acceptance of one God as paramount among several Gods.

The concept of God as a Creator that is common to Judaism, Christianity and Islam is no older than roughly four thousand years. Before the advent of monotheism, language about Gods, in the form of polytheism and henotheism, was evident in several late Neolithic cultures. The people of Sumer in that era venerated a father God called An. He was envisaged as a great bull. His divine female mate was Ki, and his son was called Enlil.[11]

A study of ancient texts soon reveals that language about divinity is not a Christian or monotheistic invention. Stone tablets discovered since 1929 at Ras Shamra, on the Syrian coast, date from the second half of the second millennium BCE, and reveal a colourful pantheon of deities. These Ugaritic texts speak of the God El, an elderly patriarch; Asherah, a mother-goddess and consort of El; Baal, a young divine warrior; and Anat, the consort of Baal.[12] Pharaonic Egypt could also boast a large pantheon of deities such as Ammut, Aten, Geb, Isis, Osiris, Seth and Tefnut.[13]

As for the word 'theology', it comes from Greek philosophy. Plato deploys the original Greek term in his dialogue *The Republic*. In the course of a conversation in this work, Socrates and Plato's brother Adeimantus agree that founders of communities need to give guidelines to poets about the appropriate way to talk about the attributes of the Gods. At one point Adeimantus asks: 'What are these guidelines for talking about the gods?' To which Socrates replies: 'Whatever the type of poetry — epic, lyric, or tragic — God must always be portrayed as he really is.'[14] During the ensuing dialogue Plato provides his understanding that God is good, perfect and unchanging. The term Plato deploys for 'talking about the gods' is *theologias* — the Greek equivalent of the English word 'theologies'. The term he uses for God is *ho theos*, which means literally 'the God'. Plato uses a capital theta, the eighth letter of the Greek alphabet, for both words, 'theologies' and 'God'. In this book, I follow his custom of capitalizing the words 'God' and 'Gods', not wishing to imply that God-talk outside the confines of Christianity is specious.[15]

It is easy to overlook that theology is a surprisingly recent invention. For most of their existence human beings did not write theologies. There is an obvious reason for this: writing was only devised around five thousand years ago, towards the end of the Neolithic Age. It was invented in the land of the people of Kengir, which was later called Sumer (contemporary southern Iraq), by their conquerors. If history can be said to commence when sources document concepts and data for subsequent generations to read, then 'prehistory ended and history began in Sumer'.[16] When it was first invented, writing was logographic. A logograph is a sign or symbol that when inscribed, for instance, on a clay tablet represents a thing, word or concept. By the year 3000 BCE, there were about six logographic systems in use around the Near East. From Mesopotamia, writing spread to Egypt and the fertile lands of the Indus Valley. Logographic writing was later independently invented again in China and Mesoamerica.[17] With the invention of logographic writing, the history of theology was born.

Since *Homo sapiens* is a species that has survived for at least a hundred thousand years, and because the earth is about four and a half billion years old,

> **before the common era/ the common era**   The calendar currently used by most human beings was drawn up in the sixth century of the Common Era by Dionysius Exiguus (Denis the Dwarf), a monk living in Rome. Dionysius divided human history into two major epochs: (1) Before Christ (BC) and In the Year of Our Lord (*Anno Domini*, AD). This book adopts a recent academic convention according to which the phrases 'Before Christ' and 'In the Year of Our Lord' are replaced with the expressions 'Before the Common Era' (BCE) and 'The Common Era' (CE). Such a convention does not require people who disavow Christianity to designate dates by referring to Jesus Christ as their Lord.

the story of theology is exceptionally brief. Moreover, today there are many people, religious and otherwise, who are uninterested in God and talking about God. The lives of numerous Buddhists, for instance, are not focused on God. In short, God-talk is not an ever-present phenomenon in human history, ancient or recent. Even the major religions of the world only emerged in the very late stages of human evolution – over the past three or four thousand years; and not all of them are theistic. So the question of why people began to speak of God so latterly, and why they continue to do so, becomes all the more intriguing.

The contemporary zoologist Richard Dawkins memorably illustrates just how recently human beings emerged during the vastly extended historical process of biological evolution. He makes his point by engaging the analogy of outstretched arms:

> Fling your arms wide in an expansive gesture to span all of evolution from its origins at your left fingertip to today at your right fingertip. All the way across your midline to well past your right shoulder, life consists of nothing but bacteria. Many-celled, invertebrate life flowers somewhere around your right elbow. The dinosaurs originate in the middle of your right palm, and go extinct around your last finger joint. The whole story of *Homo sapiens* and our predecessor *Homo erectus* is contained in the thickness of one nail-clipping. As for recorded history; as for the Sumerians, the Babylonians, the Jewish patriarchs, the dynasties of Pharaohs, the legions of Rome, the Christian Fathers, the Laws of the Medes and Persians which never change; as for Troy and the Greeks, Helen and Achilles and Agamemnon dead; as for Napoleon and Hitler, the Beatles and Bill Clinton, they and everyone that knew them are blown away in the dust from one light stroke of a nail-file.[18]

Clearly, then, the enterprise of theology was unknown for by far the greater part of the existence of *Homo sapiens*. Before the invention of writing, there were no documented theologies as such. Archeological evidence of the hominid species *Homo neanderthalis* (Neanderthals) reveals that animal remains and plants were sometimes placed in their graves.[19] This may be an indication that Neanderthals entertained religious beliefs, but even by the time the species became extinct around 27,000 years ago theologies had still not been written.

This book is an introduction to theology and its many current challenges. It is not about religion and religious behaviour. Religion is not theology. People often behave religiously without being in the slightest way taxed or bothered by theology. This text refers to God frequently, but is not primarily about God. It concerns human attempts to talk about God today. Theology is a human, not a divine product. As such, it needs to be carefully distinguished from God. There is no guarantee that what people say about God in any way corresponds to, or confirms that there is, a God.

beliefs concerning gods and god

Polytheism	The belief that there are several Gods.
Henotheism	The belief that among several Gods one is supreme.
Kathenotheism	The belief that among several Gods one is supreme at a particular time, and that different Gods can be supreme in succession at other times.
Hecastotheism	The belief that all objects have sacred power.
Ditheism	The belief in two Gods.
Dualism	The belief that cosmic history is a battle between the two great powers of divine goodness and malicious evil.
Myriotheism	The belief that the number of Gods cannot be counted.
Zootheism	The belief in animal Gods.
Herotheism	The belief in deified men.
Anthropotheism	The belief that Gods are basically human in nature.
Autotheism	The belief that one is oneself divine.
Pantheism	The belief that God is in all things.
Panentheism	The belief that all things are in God.
Emanationism	The belief that all things are outgrowths of, or emanations from, God.
Theism	The belief that there is a God.
Monotheism	The belief that there is only one God.
Trinitarianism	The belief that there are three Persons in one God.
Creationism	The belief that each human soul is created individually by God, or that God created the world in six days.
Deism	The belief that God created the world, but does not act within it.
Atheism	The belief that there is no God.
Agnosticism	The belief that one lacks the means of knowing whether or not there is a God or many Gods or no deities at all.
Fideism	The belief that religious faith confirms that there is a God without recourse to reason.
Rationalism	The belief that human reason is the High Court in which to decide what counts as knowledge (of God) or superstition.

While it is a straightforward matter to declare that theology is human discourse about God or deities, it is a much more taxing affair to settle what the sources of theology are or should be. Many theologians view the Bible as a repository of knowledge about God and hence the primary resource for theology. The twentieth-century Swiss theologian Karl Barth insisted that theology, or 'dogmatics' as he termed it, ought to confine its deliberations to problems presented by the Bible.[20] During the Reformation, theologians such as Martin Luther and John Calvin similarly esteemed the Bible as the principal resource for theology. Others then and now defer much more to human reason as the most assured way of discoursing intelligibly about God. Some theologians have decided that theology is an exercise of poetic imagination. After all, the very word 'theology' was coined in the context of Plato's discussion about advice that needs to be given to poets so that they can talk about God responsibly. As we shall see in later chapters, debates about the nature, sources and methods of theology raged throughout modern times and continue unimpeded today.

dogmatic theology   For most of Christian history theologies were usually written according to a dogmatic method. A dogma is a teaching that is solemnly laid down as binding on believers by the leaders of a church. Councils of bishops have proclaimed dogmas for hundreds of years, notably since the third century of the Common Era.[21] A dogmatic theological method is one that accepts as its starting point the conviction that dogmas are true. A dogmatic theologian attempts to talk about human beings in relation to God, first, by explaining what he or she interprets as the principal meaning of a dogma, and second, by trying to relate the dogma to the lives of a contemporary audience. Dogmatic theology has long been complemented by other theological methods. Medieval theologians were fond of engaging Greek philosophies, and occasionally Islamic thought, to articulate their theological visions.

Premodern dogmatic and biblically based theologies rest on a principle of authority. They regard dogmas and biblical texts as objects to be received, revered and interpreted, not questioned or contradicted. The history of dogmatic, biblical and philosophical theologies endured a purgative time in the modern age, when numerous intellectuals advocated the use of their analytical reason, rather than submissive deference to dogmas or the Bible, as the exclusive means of enunciating theologies.

systematic theology   From the beginning of the eighteenth century the term 'systematic theology' was often used in Europe as a complement to dogmatic theology. As its name suggests, a systematic theology seeks to articulate a coherent and comprehensive, hence systematic, discourse about God and Christian doctrines. In 1727, Johann Franz Buddeus explained the term 'systematic theology' by observing that a theological discourse can be termed systematic if it meets two conditions. The first is that it must offer a comprehensive account of its subject matter. The second is that it ought to explain, confirm and prove its content in detail.[22] In the twentieth century, theologians often rendered their theologies systematic by interrelating all of their topics, or by harnessing a particular philosophical vision to elaborate theological themes. Paul Tillich's tripartite *Systematic Theology*, published 1951–57, relies on existentialist philosophy to interpret Christian faith systematically.[23] Existentialist philosophy, by the way, is a way of thinking focused on the question of what it means *to exist* as a human being today.

contemporary theology   Among contemporary theologians, there are basically five contrasting views of how theology ought to be practised. The British theologian David Ford, drawing on the work of Hans Frei, instructively arranges these views according to their methods. He aligns the methods on a spectrum of one extreme to another, depending on whether or not, and to what extent, the practitioner of each method regards the classical Christian theological tradition as compatible with distinctively modern and new patterns of thought. He describes the first perspective thus:

> Imagine a line punctuated by five types of theology. At one end, the first type is simply the attempt to repeat a traditional theology or version of Christianity and see all reality in its own terms, with no recognition of the significance for it of other perspectives or of all that has happened in recent centuries. At the other extreme, the fifth type gives complete priority to some secular philosophy or worldview, and Christianity in its own terms is only valid in so far as it fits in with that. So, for this fifth type, parts of Christian faith and practice may be found true or acceptable, but the assessment is always made according to criteria which are external to faith and which claim superiority to it.[24]

The five types of modern Christian theology are illustrated schematically and in the broadest of terms in the accompanying figure. The five most basic divisions

TYPE 1	TYPE 2	TYPE 3	TYPE 4	TYPE 5
Method: To repeat and defend classic dogmatic theological traditions with little or no attempt to appropriate new knowledge	*Method*: Primacy is accorded to the Christian Gospel and/or tradition in theology, but new thinking is by no means neglected	*Method*: Draws on two loci, past and present experiences, in order to interpret the Gospel and theological tradition	*Method*: Relies mostly on a particular philosophy or world-view in order to reinterpret the Gospel or classical doctrines	*Method*: Priority in theology is accorded to non-traditional and extra-biblical world-views to which the Christian Gospel is made to conform

among Christian theologians today should not obscure a much larger variety of theological styles that have contested for public attention over the past two centuries.

introducing theology in a modern way

It is entirely possible to study and write theology as if the past four centuries never transpired. Many Jewish, Christian, and Islamic scholars prefer to talk about God either by focusing exclusively on interpreting scriptures venerated as ancient, sacred and divinely inspired, or by combining an interest in sacred texts with orthodox dogmas. This book differs from such an approach by concluding that too much new knowledge has been accumulated by human beings since the advent of modernity (the focus of Chapter 3) for it to be ignored by students and teachers of theology. The new knowledge has produced novel questions and hiccups for pre-modern theological traditions, and it is precisely these questions and problems that preoccupy this book. It is vital that the questions be met because they can challenge or undermine the authority of the Bible and Church teachers by contradicting the way ecclesiastical leaders and scriptural writers have depicted the reality of the world for most of Christian history.

For example, for a hundred thousand years human beings could only see eight to nine thousand stars in the Milky Way galaxy on a moonless night. These stars, moreover, seemed, before the seventeenth century, to be permanently affixed to a great sphere that rotated around the earth. Only five planets were visible. Before the 1920s, the overwhelming assumption of human civilizations was that the Milky Way galaxy constituted the entire universe. The Bible and the complex body of pre-modern Christian doctrines have no knowledge of galaxies apart from the stars visible with the naked eye. In 1912, however, the North American astronomer Edwin Hubble discovered that the Great Nebula in the Andromeda constellation is a galaxy separate from the Milky Way that 'corrals hundreds and billions of stars in its huge spiral shape, which is 150,000 light-years in diameter'.[25] Humans now know that the universe is much more vast than anyone before the twentieth century was able to confirm.

Gone are the days when any relation between the universe and God can be discussed as a parochial earth-bound affair. A *modern* introduction to theology is simply an attempt, first, to underscore the implications and challenges of new knowledge for traditional theologies and, second, to argue that endeavouring to speak about God by bypassing new modern knowledge will only reach an intellectually and socially ghettoized subculture vulnerable to the accusation of being a mistaken, superstitious sect.

The crucial difference between modern and pre-modern thought, to speak very generally, concerns the human sensate perception of reality. Before the rise of modern science in the seventeenth century, inhabitants of the west generally assumed that their physical senses furnished them with reliable knowledge of the nature of the material world. Reality for them was as it appeared to them. Informed by new science, modern thought is marked by a new kind of distinction between *reality* and *appearance*. Modern thinkers know that reality can differ from the way it is perceived by physical senses. For example, a table appears to be solid, stationary and brown. Contemporary physics, however, instructs that it is nothing of the kind. In reality it is a flux of microscopic and submicroscopic particles, fields of matter, or waves. The table's particles are not wooden, but more rudimentary. They are not brown, but invisible. And, far from being stationary, they are whirling about at exceptionally high speed.[26]

Modern thought insists that reality is unveiled not to the casual observer, but to the scientific expert. But if that is so, then modernity witnessed a shift from the Church informing the inhabitants of the west about the nature of reality to scientists teaching that there is a fundamental distinction between the reality and the appearance of things. A modern introduction to theology needs to consider the multiple ways in which the pre-modern authority of the Church was challenged as physical sciences informed people about the nature of reality in previously unknown terms.

core beliefs of the christian tradition

As for Christianity's core traditional doctrines, they are codified in several texts and contexts. They can be studied in a variety of catechisms, synodical decrees and conciliar proclamations. Expressed at its simplest, classical Christian faith is built on two equiprimordial doctrines: (1) a teaching about God; and (2) an instruction about Jesus Christ. In the first place, over many centuries Christianity has professed that God is first and foremost a Creator of all there is. Throughout Christianity's long and turbulent history, its devotees have fought and hurled abuse at each other over the identity of Jesus, the nature of the Church, and the means of ultimate salvation. Nonetheless, they have never been seriously and fatefully divided over their cardinal conviction that God is a free, benign and powerful Creator of the universe. Over time, Christians developed a sophisticated Trinitarian doctrine about God.

the trinity   According to traditional Christian theology, God is triune. That is, God is a unity of three persons: Father, Son and Holy Spirit. The Father is God, the Son is God, and the Holy Spirit is God, but there are not three Gods, only one. According to the Athanasian Creed – a profession of Christian faith dating from either the fourth or the fifth century CE – the Father, the Son and the Holy Spirit are co-eternal and co-equal: none is before or after the other, and none is less or greater than the other.

The very word 'Trinity' means three-in-one. The 'one' mentioned here refers to a single divine essence or nature called *ousia* in Greek and *substantia* in Latin. The 'three' designates a triplicity of persons termed *hypostases* in Greek or *personae* in Latin. It is important to register that the Christian doctrine of the Trinity, when teaching that there are three persons in one God, does not advance the blatantly nonsensical case that three persons are one person or that one nature can be three natures. All of which is to observe that, above all, the doctrine of the Trinity is a teaching about God's nature, essence, substance or being. Thus, for traditional Latin theology, God is a single divine substance. When Father, Son and Holy Spirit are called God, it is because each is understood to enjoy a unique divine essence. The three persons share a single divine nature. That of which there are three in God relates to relations between Father, Son and Spirit, and not to three divine beings.[27]

The doctrine of the Trinity is nowhere to be found in the Bible. There are multiple references to Father, Son or *Logos* (Word), and Spirit in the Bible, but what is missing is any sustained articulation of the precise relations between the three. Is the Father greater than the Son as a parent is stronger than an infant? Are the Son and Spirit both subordinate to the Father? Trinitarian doctrine is the end product of a complex history of reflection on Jesus (the focus of Chapter 7). Early Christians struggled over hundreds of years in attempting to elaborate the relation of the man Jesus to the God who created the world. In Christian theology, the Greek word *trias*, the state of being triple, is not to be found before the second century of the Common Era. It first appeared in the writings of Theophilus of Antioch (later second century CE), an early apologist for Christianity. The equivalent Latin term, *trinitas*, the base of the English term 'Trinity', was coined in the third century by the African theologian Quintus Septimus Florens Tertullianus (160–222), commonly known as Tertullian. What has long been regarded as the classical doctrine of the Trinity emerged clearly in the latter half of the fourth century, principally among three Greek-speaking eastern theologians, Basil of Caesarea (*c.* 330–379), Gregory of Nyssa (*c.* 330–395), the younger brother of Basil, and Gregory Nazianzus (330–389). In 362, Athanasius (*c.* 296–373), the Bishop of Alexandria, presided over a council of bishops in Alexandria who spoke of God as one *ousia* (substance) and three *hypostases* (persons). Their formula has remained a yardstick of Christian orthodoxy ever since.

god incarnate   A clear distinctiveness of Trinitarian doctrine is the notion that a man, Jesus, is included in the identity of God. Such an idea is alien to Judaism and Islam. It leads directly to the second primordial doctrine of Christian faith, which concerns the identity and significance of Jesus Christ. John Hick summarizes conventional Christian assertions about Jesus in a lapidary fashion:

> The Traditional Christian understanding of Jesus of Nazareth is that he was God incarnate, who became a man to die for the sins of the world and who founded the church to proclaim this. If he was indeed God incarnate, Christianity is the only religion founded by God in person, and must as such be uniquely superior to all other religions.[28]

A long-standing teaching of historic Christianity asserts that the Christian religion is solely true and therefore inherently superior to each and every other religion. The dissipation of that teaching only began in earnest about thirty years ago. Many Christians still defend it passionately.

Of Jesus Christ, Christian churches have affirmed over nearly two millennia that:

- he was born of a virgin mother without the agency of a man;
- he existed before time began;
- he wrought wondrous signs, healings and miracles;
- he chose disciples to establish and promote a new religion over and above the religion of the Hebrews;
- he never sinned at any stage in his life;
- he forsook marriage;
- he died an agonizing sacrificial death to atone or make up for human depravity;
- after his death he descended into hell;
- he was then raised from death by God to enable him to return to heaven;
- before returning to heaven he visited former disciples on earth;
- he then ascended into heaven where he remains;
- he will one day return to earth to judge the living and the dead.

the creed of constantinople I

In the history of the Christian Church, there have been several noteworthy gatherings of bishops, who codified what they regarded as the essential content of Christian faith in the form of creeds, or formal professions of belief. One of the more significant of these meetings was the First Council of Constantinople, or

---

virgin birth and immaculate conception   The Creed of Constantinople I teaches that Jesus became incarnate 'from the holy Spirit and the virgin Mary'. The Christian doctrine of Jesus' birth to a virgin mother is often confused with the doctrine of the Immaculate Conception. The latter teaching refers to Mary, the mother of Jesus. The former concerns Jesus himself. According to the doctrine of the Immaculate Conception, Mary was conceived by her parents in such a way that she was not stained, as it were, by sin. As is well known, the Bible recounts a story of two primordial parents, Adam and Eve, rebelling against God. Premodern theologians frequently designated the effect of that rebellion as Original Sin. Within such a scheme, all subsequent human beings were thought to inherit aboriginal sin from the two first parents. For the doctrine of the Immaculate Conception, Mary did not. By contrast, the teaching of the Virgin Birth avers that Jesus was born to a virgin. That is, his mother conceived him while (physically) remaining a virgin. The doctrine of the Immaculate Conception was promulgated by Pope Pius IX in 1854 in exactly the same year as Nathaniel Pringsheim microscopically observed for the first time human sperm entering an ovum. The doctrines of the Virgin Birth and Immaculate Conception are not as central to Christian faith as those concerning the Trinity and God Incarnate. The medieval theologians Thomas Aquinas and Bonaventure both denied the Immaculate Conception, but still count as Christians.

Constantinople I, which was convened in 381 CE. A very good way of grasping the heart of what Christians have believed over many centuries is to examine the creed of Constantinople I. It is a significant profession of faith for two reasons. First, it incorporates and modifies the creed of Nicaea I (325), and was itself adopted by the Council of Chalcedon in 451. In the second place, it 'remains today, almost word for word, the basic creed of most Christian churches and is widely used in the liturgy'.[29]

The text of this major doctrinal decree is as follows:

We believe in one God the Father all powerful, maker of heaven and of earth, and of all things both seen and unseen. And in one Lord Jesus Christ, the only-begotten Son of God, begotten from the Father before all the ages, light from light, true God from true God, begotten not made, consubstantial with the Father, through whom all things came to be; for us humans and for our salvation he came down from the heavens and became incarnate from the holy Spirit and the virgin Mary, became human and was crucified on our behalf under Pontius Pilate; he suffered and was buried and rose up on the third day in accordance with the scriptures; he is coming again with glory to judge the living and the dead; his kingdom will have no end. And in the Spirit, the holy, the lordly and life-giving one, proceeding forth from the Father, co-worshipped and co-glorified with Father and Son, the one who spoke through the prophets; in one holy, catholic and apostolic church. We confess one baptism for the forgiving of sins. We look forward to a resurrection of the dead and life in the age to come. Amen.[30]

The spatial references of descent and assent assumed by these doctrines ('he came down from the heavens'/'he rose up') are highly significant because they belie the fact that a great deal of conventional Christian doctrine is parasitic upon a medieval, static, and hierarchically ordered cosmos with earth below, heaven above earth, and hell within the earth. One of western civilization's greatest extended poems, Dante's *Divine Comedy*, graphically depicts its author's journey through hell to paradise. Catholic theology complements language about Christ's descent and ascent by proclaiming that after her death, his mother's body was assumed by divine agency upwards into heaven.

Contemporary scientific cosmology renders a great deal of classical Christian doctrinal and liturgical language decidedly quaint. It is now known, not assumed, that the earth is not the pivot of the cosmos. As intimated earlier, the known scale of the observable universe was never even remotely envisaged by ancient and medieval humans. The scale of the mappable universe is staggeringly vast. To illustrate, the Hercules galaxy cluster involves around twenty thousand galaxies. The Hydra galaxy cluster is moving away from other clusters of galaxies at a speed of 250 million kilometres per hour.[31] And the Milky Way galaxy includes at least a hundred billion stars.[32] The earth is just one puny planet among others revolving around a single star amid a local family of a hundred and more billion other stars. 'The most important thing that science has taught us about our place in the Universe is that we are not special.'[33]

In the light of which, can it really be credibly maintained that Jesus Christ's descent to earth is the key event and place in cosmic history? Such is but one of several disturbing quandaries with which modern theology, unlike many pre-modern theologies, strives to grapple.

Many other doctrines flow from the three already mentioned dealing with God, Jesus Christ, and reconciliation, salvation or redemption. Several of them will be met in the pages of this book.

Considered as a whole, classical Christian theology is an attempt to provide an answer to what is frequently called the question of the meaning of life. For the philosopher Julian Young,

From about the fourth to the eighteenth century Western thinking was Christian thinking. This meant that throughout this period the question of the meaning of life was a non-issue; a non-issue because the answer was *obvious*, self-evident, the topic completely sewn up by Christianity's version of Platonism. And if perchance, one did threaten the prevailing meaning-giving story, then one got persecuted. Hence Schopenhauer's sardonic remark that Christianity's single greatest argument has always been the stake.[34]

The point is, something has happened in modern times to render the question of the meaning of life less obvious, more disputed, less certain, and certainly more perplexing. The brilliant German philosopher Friedrich Nietzsche once observed that when people begin to talk incessantly about 'values', we can be confident that values are in trouble. As Julian Young points out,

> The same is true of the meaning of life. That we talk, make nervous, Woody Allen-ish jokes, write and read books such as this one about it suggests we are troubled by the topic. Such talk, however, is a relatively recent phenomenon. For most of our Western history we have not talked about the meaning of life. This is because we used to be quite certain that we knew what it was. We were certain about it because we thought we knew that over and above this world of doubtful virtue and happiness is another world: a world Nietzsche calls (somewhat ironically) the 'true world' or, alternatively expressed, 'God'.[35]

What Nietzsche calls the 'true world' has been envisaged in a variety of philosophies and religions as an ultimate destiny. According to such a view, the manifest, visible, tangible setting called earth is not the real world. It is a temporary, transitory habitat. By contrast, the real world is currently unseen. It is a destination to be reached. It is the end-point of a journey. The real world is heaven or paradise. It involves a utopian existence. Philosophies and religions that esteem a real world have a far-reaching global scope. They see the entirety of cosmic history, with human beings in it, as a great journey towards final reward and destination.

One of the more famous real-world philosophers was Plato (*c.* 428–347 BCE), an Athenian thinker and cavalry officer in the circle of Socrates (469–399 BCE). Plato wrote over twenty works called dialogues. Two of them, the *Phaedrus* and the *Phaedo*, enunciated his celebrated doctrine of souls that have fallen from a pristine state and have to journey back to an ideal real world. A similar doctrine of the soul appears in the work of Augustine, who turned out to be used as an unquestionable authority for later Christian theologians.

Conventional, classical, traditional or orthodox Christian theology is a real-world world-view. Expressed in a nutshell, the meaning of life for a Christian is found in pilgrimage. Christians are on a journey. Their final destiny will be either heaven or hell. Classical Christian theology, to be sure, is a story about the real world created and governed by God and Christ, who are able to save people from everything and everyone that bedevils them and stymies their well-being.

In this grand doctrinal scheme of God, Christ and salvation, it is crucial to note a great deal of spatial imagery. God is *above* in Heaven. Jesus Christ *descends* to earth and then *ascends* into Heaven just after *descending* into Hell. Heaven and Hell are conceived as places somewhere.

The real-world world-view came to be challenged and questioned intensely as the modern era began to gestate. At the beginning of modernity, 'the birth and success of experimental science presented the severest of challenges to traditional Christian belief. For it became clear that on the map of the cosmos as drawn by Copernicus, Galileo and Newton no plausible place remained at which to locate the Christian heaven and its inhabitants.'[36]

Merely the briefest sketch of the nature and origins of theology, and of the heart of classical Christian doctrine, has been undertaken above. Subsequent chapters will return frequently to a host of interrelated doctrines in the light of newly acquired knowledge and recently established cultures.

2

christianity's current predicament

> What has been is what will be,
> and what has been done is what will be done;
> there is nothing new under the sun.
> Is there such a thing of which it is said,
> 'See, this is new'?
> It has already been,
> in the ages before us.
>
> *Ecclesiastes 1.9–10*

Is there such a thing as progress in knowledge? Obviously so, or assuredly not? More specifically, should conventional Christianity radically modify its doctrines and practices in the light of advanced knowledge generated in modern times? Or ought it to perpetuate itself in contemporary settings by recapitulating ancient wisdoms? Answering such questions is the burden of this book.

For many Christians today, all sublime knowledge about God, the world, Jesus Christ and human beings was formulated in a distant past. Several regard the Bible and the extensive body of Christian doctrines codified over hundreds of years as divinely inspired, and therefore ineluctably binding on present-day Christians. For these Christians belief is unchanging, and the past imperfectable. For others, contemporary humans are party to novel and sophisticated information that renders ancient and medieval religious visions of reality decidedly defunct. A more resolute view lampoons religious dogma as ballast that must be consigned to oblivion.

modern sea changes and traditional christianity

In many parts of the world at present, Christian Churches have become much more enfeebled than they used to be. Their current state allows for a nebula of explanations. Even so, a cardinal reason they are declining in numbers and social influence in disparate cultures recently might well reside in a 'general loss of public confidence in the objective truth of the major Christian beliefs'.[1] During the Middle Ages, the very notion of God was simply taken for granted by most westerners. However, after the seventeenth-century wars of religion in central Europe, and following the Enlightenment in the eighteenth century, monotheistic religions and their understandings of God became far more widely regarded as products of human imagination. The writings of modern totemic intellectual figures such as Ludwig Feuerbach, Karl Marx, Friedrich Nietzsche, Sigmund Freud and Émile Durkheim fell into line to 'put belief in God first in jeopardy and then in flight before an increasingly secular Western culture'.[2] Hence the suspicion that especially since the Second World War a collapse of religious meaning has been taking place in several settings around the world, but spectacularly so in the west.[3] The forces that are debilitating churches today did not gestate overnight. They were born centuries ago when a medieval religious world-view began to cede ground to a peculiarly modern, sceptical and secular one. These forces and the questions they generated for old beliefs will be investigated in subsequent chapters. In this chapter Christianity's recently acquired and uncertain historical predicament in the west is outlined in an impressionistic and general way. *The Concise Oxford Dictionary of Current English* instructs that a predicament is 'a difficult, unpleasant, or embarrassing situation'.[4] Hence, to speak of Christianity's current predicament is to refer to the crisis, dilemma, embarrassment, emergency and impasse in which it now finds itself.

The difficulty that Christianity presently faces is multifaceted, but a major part of its troubles can be summed up in a word – hybridization. By the early third millennium, the Christian Church has become a hybrid. It is composed of two large incongruous elements. Both parts are moving in markedly diverse ways. And both face uncertain futures.

The contemporary divide between two major parts of latter-day Christianity does not revolve around a bifurcation between Catholic and Protestants; liberals and conservatives; radicals and fundamentalists; heretics and Bible-bashers; or priests overseeing lay people. It is of a very different order. One Christian world is extremely wealthy, highly educated, and largely unenthused by age-old ecclesiastical teachings and customs. This is the world of the west. It can boast an exceptionally sophisticated university-based tradition of learning that has scrutinized Christian history and texts over hundreds of years. Nonetheless, in this literate, occasionally urbane, mobile, wealthy and educated world of mainly European civilization, Churches are losing adherents at a rapid rate. Untold numbers of contemporary human beings in the industrialized, commercialized and digitalized Occident now prefer to spend Sunday mornings in gymnasiums rather than churches. Why? The United States of America tells a different story. Christianity is popular there, but principally as an expression of private belief. The Church is not supposed to direct the State. The USA has never known the culture of Christendom in the same way as Europe.

The increasingly weakened state of conventional Christianity in Europe stands in stark contrast to the fate of another Christian world found in Latin America, Africa and Asia. In those regions, Christian Churches appear to be thriving and growing. Many of them involve masses of people who are dreadfully poor, ill-educated and afflicted by preventable diseases. A major ambition of this book is to probe why conventional Christianity appears to be collapsing or radically mutating in those parts of the world where it scrutinized its doctrines and practices at the highest levels of university research; and why it appears to be blossoming in fetid *favelas* and among people living in penury. Even where it is flowering among people dogged by poverty and disease, it has a great deal to achieve in combating widespread illiteracy, inaccessibility to education, superstition, witchcraft and ancestor worship.

In short, Christianity's current dilemma is twofold. On the one hand, in the European heartland of historic Christendom people have stopped going to church on a massive scale. On the other hand, poor people elsewhere appear to be increasingly drawn to Christianity. In the first instance, the challenge for theologians is to discern why Christianity has been so resoundingly ignored. In the second, the great hurdle for theologians is to devise ways of interpreting Christian faith that do not force Africans, Asians and the inhabitants of Latin America to use the traditional theological terminology of Europe that is heavily indebted to ancient Greek philosophy. In 1900, 80 per cent of the world's Christians were located in Europe or North America. Today, more than 60 per cent live elsewhere in markedly different cultures.[5]

As untoward as it may seem, Christianity's current unsettled situation, especially in the west, can be partly explained in terms of the frequent refusal of several of its leaders both to acknowledge its manifold mistakes, and to embrace new knowledge that was entirely unavailable to Christians and others in pre-modern eras. Such a refusal makes it impossible for many people today to profess major tenets of Christian faith. All of which was seen clearly in 1941 by the German biblical scholar Rudolf Bultmann. In that year, he was confident enough to declare that the inhabitants of his age are unable to live in two different worlds:

> We cannot use electric lights and radios and, in the event of illness, avail ourselves of modern medical and clinical means and at the same time believe in the spirit and wonder world of the New Testament. And if we suppose that we can do so ourselves, we must be clear that we can present this as the attitude of the Christian faith only by making the Christian proclamation unintelligible and impossible for our contemporaries.[6]

Those who conclude that any talk of Christianity's current malaise and enfeeblement is overblown might wish to ponder a striking and quite accurate observation: there is no Christian alive today who lives in religious agreement with all other Christians, let alone with enthusiasts of alternative religions and sects.[7] After a history of about twenty centuries, Christianity has splintered into a superabundance of rival fidelities. At present, 21,000 different Christian denominations compete for members.[8] How can any one of them guarantee that it mirrors the aims and ambitions of Jesus himself? A Church that has hitherto aspired to be one, holy, catholic and apostolic is now breathtakingly atomized. Today, one can treat Churches like goods in a supermarket. An individual can choose to sample from a smorgasbord of Churches as varied as the Assyrian Church of the East, the Baptist Convention of Nicaragua, the Coptic Orthodox Church, the Evangelical Church of Greifswald, the Free Methodist Church of North America, the Pentecostal Church of God, and the Old Catholic Church of Switzerland. In such a setting, who decides who counts as a Christian, and by what criteria? Most contemporary Christians are Catholics.[9] Yet, disconcertingly, the leadership of the Catholic Church of the Roman Rite does not presently recognize several other groups of Christians as constituting legitimate Churches.[10]

The Catholic Church receives a good deal of attention in this chapter. This is so for two reasons. First, it is by far the largest of the Christian denominations, which does not, of course, imply that it is the most estimable. And second, it has a relatively long history of rejecting modern ideas, political strategies and cultural values. In this it is not alone. Strains of Protestant, Anglican, Greek, Ethiopian and Russian Churches have proved equally resistant to modern mores.

past glories and massive blunders

That Christianity is currently unsettled by significant cultural, scientific and intellectual movements unknown to the ancients is somewhat intriguing and surprising in view of its former social confidence and political power. The Christian religion's long-standing strengths are easily recognizable. It may be taken well and truly for granted that the Christian religion has been a prodigious fertilizing and civilizing force in eastern and western cultures over many centuries. The name of its hero, Jesus, could well be the most famous in recorded human history. Over nearly twenty centuries, Christianity has bequeathed to humanity a fertile reservoir of religious wisdom. The German-speaking mystical theologian Meister Eckhart (1262–1327) is a profound religious thinker. So too is his English counter-part, Margery Kempe (*c.* 1373–1430). In the past, Christianity has inspired the composition of a beguilingly beautiful repertoire of music. Gregorian chant is probably peerless as a monumental collection of monophony. The combined repertoire of English, French, German and Italian church music, ancient and modern, is unendingly arresting in terms of its dynamic rhythmic variation, fertile melodic invention, and harmonically sumptuous texture. Palestrina, Bach, Beethoven and Brahms were all Christians of one kind or another. So too were the painters Caravaggio, Raphael and Rembrandt. The names of Christians in the past who still manage to mesmerize contemporary humans are arresting to hear: Michaelangelo, Dante, Shakespeare, Copernicus, Galileo, Newton, Messaien and Martin Luther King Jr. Many of the age-old cathedrals of Christendom are bedazzlingly alluring in their architectural elegance. Moreover, few human beings alive today could claim to be more of an intellectual genius or polymath than Christian thinkers such as Augustine of Hippo, Thomas Aquinas, Duns Scotus, John Calvin, or the most impenetrable yet neatly cohering religious philosopher of the eighteenth and nineteenth centuries, Georg Wilhelm Friedrich Hegel.

Furthermore, among its major accomplishments, Christianity in the past was responsible for weaning superstitious Europeans from a reliance on magic to a belief in the capacities of reason. It succeeded in keeping higher levels of learning alive during the slaughter-baths of a barbarian past. It has stimulated brilliant philosophers such as Descartes, Kant, Pascal, Kierkegaard and Wittgenstein. Many of the world's most esteemed universities, like those of Bologna, Paris, Tübingen, Oxford, Salamanca, Cambridge, Harvard and Yale, were intention-ally founded as decidedly Christian centres of learning. Surprisingly for some, Christianity provided the intellectual environment for the birth and growth of modern empirical sciences. Those who doubt as much might care to read the scholarly writings of the medieval theologian Albert the Great. Moreover, modern Christian biblical studies in many of the world's most advanced uni-versities constitute one of the more glorious achievements of recent academic investigations. Its remarkably fine readings of abstruse texts and superbly subtle arguments have yet to be broadly explained to general publics, or assimilated by many influential Church leaders.

Despite Christianity's many praiseworthy accomplishments, it is most certainly not above reproach. Nor is it innocent of horrendous crimes and sins.
Nowadays, it is loathed as well as loved. In some quarters it has been rightly
regarded as an accomplice of rapacious colonial powers. In others, it was and is
acclaimed as the champion of economic underdogs. It is simultaneously extolled
as a haven for profoundly spiritual women, and lampooned as a quicksand of
anti-feminist sexism. Concurrently, it is derided as a persecutor of science, and
lionized as a beacon of truth. In the past, it has been a force of unbridled cruelty,
especially towards the religiously other. Indeed, it could be argued that once
Christianity received Roman imperial favour in the fourth century, 'it turned
upon other religions and unsympathetic philosophies, and even upon variations
of its own doctrines, with an ideological ferocity that was previously unknown in
the world'.[11] Many of Christianity's saints were anti-Semitic bigots. Its language
of religious vituperation has long been vile. In the name of Jesus Christ, Christian
devotees have launched crusades, slaughtered Jews, murdered Muslims, burned
women as witches, tortured those hapless enough to be convicted of heresy,
blessed battleships, and bombed abortion clinics. Nevertheless, and as insensitive
as it might now appear to say, the striking attainments of the Christian religion
are still plain for all to see.

The Christian Church in its vastly varied historical settings over nearly two
thousand years has never really been an entirely settled or carefree community.
Since its inception, it has been stymied by acrimonious internal disputes, external
criticism, occasional persecution, and uncertain direction. Latterly, though, its
problems and challenges have been compounded unendingly. Particularly during
the past three or so centuries, it has frequently found itself unnervingly confronted by rapid and far-reaching cultural, intellectual and political revolutions
around the world. Its believers, thinkers and preachers have struggled to cope
with the epochal historical transformations wrought for human beings by the
modern age.

a string of modern revolutions

In the fifteenth century Christianity encountered a revolution in geography
when Christopher Columbus discovered lands and people unknown to the Bible.
During the sixteenth and seventeenth centuries, the ancient earth-centred cosmology assumed by the Bible and medieval theology was gradually replaced
by a new heliocentric cosmology in view of the work of Nicolaus Copernicus
(1473–1543) and Galileo Galilei (1564–1642). The sixteenth and seventeenth

centuries also witnessed a religious metamorphosis in the bloodletting turmoil of the Reformation. Moreover, these centuries heralded the development of new inductive scientific methods that furnished knowledge and created technologies totally unavailable in medieval societies. In the seventeenth and eighteenth centuries, western philosophy was decidedly transformed by the evolution of critical, rationalist modes of thought. Throughout the eighteenth and nineteenth centuries Christianity witnessed a host of far-reaching and all-embracing cultural, political and industrial turnabouts and inventions. The twentieth century turned out to be a heady swirl of technological, sociological and mass-media advancements. Humans can now travel at the speed of sound and communicate at the speed of light. They can propel themselves over vast distances through water, in the air, by land or in outer space.

Do all these transmutations, considered cumulatively, represent a boon or miasma for Christianity? To repeat an earlier question, should Christianity energetically transform its doctrines and practices in the light of advanced and newly warranted knowledge? Or ought it to perpetuate itself in contemporary circumstances by rehearsing ancient insights? This book presents a cumulative case arguing that theology has changed, and must change, by allowing itself to be informed by established, irreversible findings in modern science, philosophy, democracy, analyses of religion, humanities and social sciences, modern biblical studies, historical investigations, and modern liberation movements.[12]

The number of intellectual revolutions and cultural transmutations encountered by latter-day Christianity have combined with a speedy pace of historical change. The French intellectual Jacques Attali memorably describes the effect of rapid historical transformations when he avers that

---

a chronology   Major periods and revolutions in human history of the past few millennia are as follows. The dates are arbitrary and approximate.

400–900	The Dark Ages (or early medieval period)
900–1400	The Middle Ages (or High Middle Ages)
1400–1600	Voyages of discovery; a revolution in geography
1350–1600	The Renaissance
1500–1650	The Reformation
1600s	The emergence of rationalist philosophies
1600s–1700s	The birth of modern science and the modern age
1650–1800	The Enlightenment
1800s	The age of industrialization, secularization, nationalism and colonialism
1900s	The era of global war, nuclear power and mass media
2000s	The age of transition to a polycentric globe

History is accelerating. What was beyond the grasp of imagination yesterday, except perhaps in the fertile minds of futurists and fiction writers, has already happened today. The Berlin Wall has crumbled; test-tube fertilization is routine, and a camel herder in sub-Sarahan Africa can speak on a palm-sized cellular phone to a suburban commuter in Los Angeles. Future shock is yesterday. Change is the only constant in a world of upheaval.[13]

The result of a coalescence between a broad range of intellectual and cultural alterations, on the one hand, and an accelerated pace of change, on the other, has been that traditional, institutional and orthodox Christianity is now buffeted by circumstances and ideas it has never previously encountered. As suggested above, the Christian religion does not presently enjoy a unified vision or sense of unencumbered progress. It is beset by a slew of religious and ethical controversies. Those external to it occasionally accuse it of being nothing more than a scrimmage of rival power-obsessed groups and forces. It is hamstrung by highly publicized sex scandals on the part of its supposedly holy and chaste clergy. It is bogged down in a host of intellectual impasses. It has lost its cultural hegemony in central Europe. In the capitalist and industrialized citadels of the west, it has lunged into a sociologically well-documented downward spiral of institutional detumescence. Fewer and fewer parents want their children to be initiated into the Church gathered to celebrate the memory of Jesus, the one called Christ – of whom more later. Christian church buildings in the west appear to many, it may be said, more as museums or mausoleums than as vitally functioning centres of worship. Their architecture might well be awe-inspiring. Their attractiveness, however, is very often appreciated nowadays much more by leisure-loving tourists than ardent religious devotees.

christian laments

That Christianity is currently unsettled and uncertain is not difficult to document. Its travails are amply recorded and lamented by Christian writers themselves, let alone by the debunkers of Christianity.

For instance, Christian Duquoc, a French theologian, has recently observed that an old and archaic Christianity is not responding to contemporary questions and anxieties.[14] He speaks of a contemporary allergy towards institutional religions and their existential message.[15] And he concludes that contemporary culture dooms theologians to exile since they do not share the major interests of our societies and inhabit social margins in which their obscure questions take refuge.[16]

Don Cupitt, a priest of the Church of England, shares similar concerns. He published a book in 1989 called *Radicals and the Future of the Church*. Therein he starkly concludes, 'Struggling to keep up her confidence, the church just at present clings all the more desperately to the supernatural beliefs that in the past gave her legitimacy and nourishment. But the beliefs are hopelessly vague. They have lost meaning and efficacy.' He accuses the Church of coming down 'like a ton of bricks' on anyone who dares to point out how hollow and blurred beliefs have become and he accuses the Church of being a prisoner in its own 'wilfully-maintained state of self-deception'.[17]

Don Cupitt is a prolific and loquacious author. Many of his books call for a radical root-and-branch reform of officially sanctioned Christian beliefs and patterns of worship. He wrote one of his more forceful calls for ecclesiastical reform in the same year that he published *Radicals and the Future of the Church*. His summons is contained in a collection of articles and responses devoted to England's radical theologians. Cupitt's conclusion that Christianity requires a thoroughgoing transformation in order to continue could hardly be more fervidly expressed:

> **catholicism** 'Catholicism' is used in these pages as shorthand to refer to the Catholic Church of the Roman Rite, which is occasionally designated in English-speaking countries as the Roman Catholic Church. Strictly speaking, though, there are Catholics who do not worship according to the Latin or Roman Rite. There are, for example, Byzantine-Rite Catholics in Syria, Palestine, Egypt, Jordan and Australia, and members of the Church of England who identify themselves as Anglo-Catholics. The word *Catholic* was first used by a Christian bishop, Ignatius of Antioch (*c*. 35–*c*. 107) in his *Letter to the Smyrnæans*, which teaches that wherever Jesus Christ is present so too is the catholic Church (n. 8). The term *Catholic* derives from the Greek adjective *katholikos*, which means 'universal', and from the adverbial phrase *kath' holou*, 'on the whole'. The opposite of *Catholic* is often thought to be *Protestant*, but its actual opposite is *sectarian*, which refers to a group of believers that has separated itself from the worldwide Church.[23]

> The Church is in any case still locked into a hopelessly inappropriate medieval worldview, a paranoid patriarchal rationality, and a psychologically repressive vocabulary, which are preposterously at variance with her claim to stand for human redemption. Until we put things right, the whole apparatus will increasingly do people more harm than good.[18]

Don Cupitt is emphatic in his conclusion that contemporary Christianity is alarmingly beset by difficulties: 'The Christian churches are melting away: in Europe, at least, on most of the indices of measurable decline they are currently losing almost a quarter of what's left in each decade, and a half in each generation.'[19] These comments are resonated in the work of Jan Kerkhofs:

In many countries in Europe priests and religious are almost automatically coming to be classified as being the third age. They have disappeared almost completely from schools and hospitals. There are very few parishes with more than one priest, and many thousands of parishes have to do without a resident pastor.[20]

The Flemish theologian Edward Schillebeeckx asks in an anguished fashion whether the Catholic Church has become 'a fortified temple, almost a new stronghold, from which the prophetic breath has disappeared'.[21] In 1987, Paul Collins, an Australian historian and theologian, concluded that the administration of Catholicism at its highest level has become an obstacle for Catholicism itself:

> The centralized and absolutist operation of Rome has brought modern Catholicism to a grinding halt. … The protection of papal power seems to be the constant underlying leitmotif of most papal decisions. To the outsider, the Vatican seems an extraordinarily conceited and self-absorbed institution.[22]

The last three decades witnessed a far from harmonious relationship between the curial theologians of the Vatican and other theologians dispersed around the world.[23] During that period, several Catholic theologians were punished, sacked or chastised by departments of the Vatican's administration.[24] Among those who were censured or warned were Jacques Pohier, Hans Küng, Leonardo Boff, Edward Schillebeeckx, Gustavo Gutiérrez, Charles Curran, Lavinia Byrne, Uta Ranke-Heinemann, Matthew Fox and Tissa Balasuriya.[25] This list is by no means complete. That it includes some very distinguished Christian intellectuals is a symptom of the very grave disaccord with which contemporary Catholicism is afflicted. In effect, since the end of the 1970s, the leadership of the Catholic Church has lobotomized the Church's theological mind by hounding and hindering the Church's most creative, erudite and prophetic theologians. There are, of course, many theologians, Catholic and otherwise, who wholeheartedly endorse the doctrinal remonstrances meted out by the Vatican's departments. Discord in the Catholic Church and other Churches is but one of the many side effects of Christianity's current predicament.

Quite apart from Catholic laments and squabbles, the current predicament of Christianity as such varies from country to country. There are now about 6 billion human beings populating this planet. By far the majority of them are religious.[26] While Church populations are diminishing in Europe, religious practice varies markedly from nation to kingdom. It has been observed recently that the traditionally Catholic countries of Europe are more religious than conventionally Protestant nations, but such an observation depends on what is meant by being religious.[27] It is possible to be religious without ever setting foot in a church. In England, where the state-supported Church of England enjoys the allegiance of roughly 26 million people, 'only 835,000 or so of them make it through its church doors on any given Sunday'.[28]

For British Christians, there is much to fret about regarding the viability of Christian living. The British historian Callum Brown goes so far as to speak of the death of Christian Britain:

> It took several centuries (in what historians used to call the Dark Ages) to convert Britain to Christianity, but it has taken less than forty years for the country to forsake it. For a thousand years, Christianity penetrated deeply into the lives of the people, enduring Reformation, Enlightenment and industrial revolution by adapting to each new social and cultural context that arose. Then, really quite suddenly in 1963, something very profound ruptured the character of the nation and its people, sending organised Christianity on a downward spiral to the margins of social significance. In unprecedented numbers, the British people since the 1960s have stopped going to church, have allowed their church membership to lapse, have stopped marrying in church, and have neglected to baptise their children ... a formerly religious people have entirely forsaken Christianity in a sudden plunge into a truly secular condition.[29]

Callum Brown's nomination of 1963 as an axial time in the fortunes of British Christianity is somewhat arbitrary. Even so, what he designates as the death of Christian Britain could also be interpreted as the demise of Christendom in the United Kingdom. The imperial stamp Theodosius I placed on Christianity and its government in 380 CE is currently fading in a dramatic fashion around the world. The point is well made by the contemporary theologian Douglas John Hall:

> To say that Christianity in the world at large is undergoing a major transition is to indulge in understatement. What is happening is nothing less than the winding down of a process that was inaugurated in the fourth century of the common era. To the great shift that began to occur in the character of the Christian movement under the Roman emperors Constantine and Theodosius I, there now corresponds a shift of reverse proportions. What was born in that distant century, namely, the imperial church, now comes to an end. That beginning and this ending are the two great social transitions in the course of Christianity in the world. All the alterations in between them (and of course history *is* change) are minor ones by comparison.[30]

Apart from large-scale institutional modifications, present-day Christianity is beset and enlivened by vigorous intellectual debates concerning its doctrines and ethical commitments. A number of feminist writers complain that too many women still live under the boot of patriarchy in several Christian denominations. Others bemoan that Christianity espouses an inhuman and unliveable moral code. The German theologian Uta Ranke-Heinemann concluded recently that

Catholic moral theology has lost much of its reputation in very recent times, and its elaborate antisexual edifice lies in ruins. Many a human conscience has been warped by its insane demands, with their claims to religious validity and divine authority. It has burdened people with idiotic sophistries and sought to turn them into moral acrobats instead of making them more human and philanthropic.[31]

Quite apart from Catholicism in particular, Christianity in general is also called to account for itself in view of its long-standing support for exploitative political powers. For roughly five hundred years, the Christian Church supported the European seizure of power over South America and Africa. During that time, a few brave prophetic Christians, such as the sixteenth-century friars Antón Montesino and Bartolomé de las Casas, have dared to champion the rights of the poor. In general, though, the Church to which they belonged did very little to halt the rapine advance of colonialist greed. Christianity's support for colonialism is linked to its age-old taste for imperial power:

> the Christian church and its theology consistently buttressed the expansion of empire. The majority of the church, regardless of where it stood in its conflict with modernity, blessed colonialism, neo-colonialism, extreme stratification of wealth, centuries of genocide of Amerindians, blacks, and Jews, the subordination of women, the persecution of the sexual other, and the social exclusion of the pagan. During the last five centuries the theology has glorified all of these historical projects as divine constructions of reality. The conquest and colonization of the Americas that began in 1492 is but one piece of historical evidence.[32]

Considering all of the quibbles with traditional Christianity voiced thus far, there are those who vigorously defend its integrity and history. Despite disagreements, Christians of whatever stripe, whether they be conservative or revolutionary, intellectual or unreflective, powerful or servile, Protestant or Catholic, are generally in agreement on two matters. First, collectively they affirm that Christianity is not as institutionally strong or culturally pervasive as it once was. Second, they agree that urgent action needs to be taken to keep Christian customs and beliefs alive in their diverse cultural settings. The problem is: there is no unanimity over efficacious action. For some it is preservation. For others it is innovation.

external laments

Each of the critics of officially sanctioned Christianity cited above has lived and laboured over many years as a committed Christian of one kind or another. Their observations about Christianity's current predicament are echoed in the writings of contemporary scholars who do not practise as theologians and who work externally to ecclesiastical discussions. The British sociologist Steve Bruce argues that the demise of traditional forms of religious life began with the onset of modernity and is linked to the Reformation.[33]

The French historian René Rémond charts admirably the lengthy process by which the whole of Europe was converted to Christianity. He then observes that whereas Christianity should have been a cohesive, unifying force, it actually became 'a cause of discord; Christianity divided into rival denominations, each jealously challenging the others for the honour of being the sole authentic expression of the Christian truth.'[34]

Christians normally profess belief in a benign, loving and benevolent God. Yet some Christians have recently become so overwhelmed by the scale of suffering in the past and present that they have decided not only to abandon Christianity, but to champion atheism as well. A case in point is the former Christian clergyman A.J. Mattill. Darwinian evolutionary theory convinced him that reflective people should espouse atheism in the light of pervasive suffering. In a series of heart-rending questions, he asks:

> How could a loving God have planned a cruel system in which sensitive living creatures must either eat other sensitive living creatures or be eaten themselves, thereby causing untold suffering among these creatures? Would a benevolent God have created animals to devour others when he could have designed them all as vegetarians? What kind of deity would have designed the beaks which rip sensitive flesh? What God would intend every leaf, blade of grass, and drop of water to be a battle ground in which living organisms pursue, capture, kill, and eat one another? What God would design creatures to prey upon one another and, at the same time, instil into such creatures a capacity for intense pain and suffering?[35]

Human history has undoubtedly been a tale of bloodshed and death. While previous generations were certainly aware of suffering, 'they had no sense of the millions of years of it that Darwin and his scientific progeny have uncovered, and which many of us have still not integrated fully into our benign cosmic visions'.[36]

Trying to reconcile belief in a benign Creator with human suffering has long been one of theology's most intractable difficulties. In the twentieth century, Christianity was confronted with a new human invention: thermo-nuclear bombs. Before 1945, no human generation ever possessed the technical means to destroy the human species: 'The dropping of the atomic bomb on Hiroshima on 6 August, 1945, brought humanity into a radically new historical situation.'[37] Hiroshima stands as a graphic symbol of humanity's new-found ability to obliterate whatever it cares to on this planet. Previous generations of humans tried to destroy each other, but never possessed the technologies thoroughly to do so. Pre-modern generations of humans never thought in terms of human beings being able to destroy themselves. For them, that power lay with God and God alone. Because of nuclear weaponry, humanity must now cope with a terrifying new situation which is 'a predicament not envisaged anywhere in the Bible or by subsequent Christian writers up to 1945'.[38]

Conventional Christian theology conceives of God as an omnipotent and omni-benevolent divine parent. Its language that God providentially cares for human beings seems to be misleading, if not thoroughly mistaken, for all those suppurating in human misery of the type endured in the wake of Hiroshima. After 1945, can God be glibly invoked as a providential, compassionate patron when the grinding and unrelenting torment of evil and suffering 'renders the lives of many humans a dreary, bleak, hungry, empty, drudgery, or even worse, a pain-and-sorrow-racked ordeal'?[39]

The extent to which contemporary westerners have become uninterested both in religion and in Christianity, and unmoved by many age-old theological doctrines, was recently captured in a casual way by the British *Sunday Telegraph* newspaper. Early in 2001, the *Sunday Telegraph* published the results of an opinion poll that was conducted for the British Broadcasting Corporation, which is ever interested to chart changes in social taste and allegiance. Those interviewed were asked who or what inspires or influences them. The results of the poll chime with the conclusions of Callum Brown in *The Death of Christian Britain*. According to the poll, 65 per cent of the British population at the time found Nelson Mandela inspirational; 51 per cent enthused over Richard Branson; Margaret Thatcher inspired 28 per cent of the population; 20 per cent were influenced by the Pope; 14 per cent admired the Archbishop of Canterbury; 14 per cent liked Tony Blair; 2 per cent recorded admiration for Mother Teresa. Soberingly for Christian theologians, a mere 1 per cent of the population voiced approval of Jesus Christ, who enjoyed the same level of adulation as Bill Clinton, the British royal family, Mahatma Gandhi and Winston Churchill.[40] Opinion polls are notoriously arbitrary. Yet, occasionally, they reveal entirely unexpected social preferences and fascinations.

the fiery monkish preacher

Precisely which strategy is best suited to sustain and reinvigorate Christianity remains a matter of the deepest dispute. As indicated above, while all agree that Christianity could be stronger, no agreement on how best to strengthen it has been reached. At the heart of pervasive disaccord lies the issue of what part new forms of knowledge should play in Christian life and thought. One view insists that there is no progress in knowledge, merely a sublime rehearsal of ancient insights. This view is vividly portrayed in Umberto Eco's novel *The Name of the Rose*. The novel is set in a medieval abbey. One of the abbey's oldest monks, the Venerable Jorge, is determined to prevent younger monks from gaining access to a previously lost work by Aristotle. Jorge is fearful that the work might teach the young monks to scoff at Christianity. He decides forcefully to air his views while preaching in the monastery's church. Fulminating with rage, he remands all the monks assembled that the work of their Benedictine order revolves around study and knowledge:

> Of our work, the work of our order and in particular the work of this monastery, a part – indeed, the substance – is study, and the preservation of knowledge. Preservation, I say, not search for, because the property of knowledge, as a divine thing, is that it is complete and has been defined from the beginning, in the perfection of the Word which expresses itself to itself. Preservation, I say, and not search, because it is a property of knowledge as a human thing, that it has been defined and completed over the course of the centuries, from the preaching of the prophets to the interpretation of the fathers of the church. There is no progress, no revolution of ages, in the history of knowledge, but at most a continuous and sublime recapitulation.[41]

Venerable Jorge's opinion that there is no progress in the history of knowledge is not confined to the realm of fiction. It is also espoused by several Christians today, who conclude that the knowledge required for a legitimate Christian life in current circumstances was formulated for and by human beings in a distant past. A case in point is the *Catechism of the Catholic Church*.[42] In its index of authors, not a single contemporary writer is listed, apart from the current Bishop of Rome, who ordered the *Catechism*'s publication. Its intellectual authority is thereby self-policing. For the *Catechism*, simple repetition of premodern views is coextensive with efficacious proclamation of Christian faith.

adversus modernitatem

Faced with Christianity's current predicament, numerous Christians today have decided to pit their energies against modern notions and movements. Their battle cry is *adversus modernitatem* – 'against modernity'.

Over roughly the past two hundred years, the most powerful leaders of the Catholic Church have, by and large, resolutely opposed modern ideas that enthused many people after the Enlightenment and the French Revolution.[43]

Notions peculiar to modernity were consistently denounced by a succession of relatively recent bishops of Rome. To illustrate, the French Revolutionary *Declaration of the Rights of Man and of the Citizen* (27 August 1789), defended notions of egalitarian political sovereignty, freedom of speech, of the press, and of the exercise of religion. The concept of liberty of conscience, and the idea that the state should be divorced from the Church, were also championed by the French Revolutionaries. Nevertheless, in 1832 Pope Gregory XVI declared as follows: 'From the evil-smelling spring of indifferentism flows the erroneous and absurd opinion – or rather, derangement – that freedom of conscience must be asserted and vindicated for everyone.'[44] Somewhat later, Pope Pius X wrote 'That the state must be separated from the church is a thesis absolutely false, a most pernicious error, an obvious negation of the supernatural order.'[45]

Recently, Mark Chaves has argued intriguingly and revealingly that 'Antimodernism has been a central feature of official Roman Catholic identity since the French Revolution.'[46] Spanning the past two centuries, he describes three phases of Catholic antimodernism. By studying papal publications he locates in each phase a symbolic focus that is condemned by various bishops of Rome (popes) as a pernicious spawn of modernity. He regards the first phase to have ranged from the French Revolution until the close of the nineteenth century. A variety of popes during this time sought to combat modernity. To do so, they targeted what they regarded as a perfidious idea, namely the notion of liberal democracy according to which the state must be free from control exercised by the Church. In 1832, for instance, Pope Gregory 'condemned the principles of separation of church and state implied by political liberalism'.[47] In 1864, Pope Pius IX published eighty ideas that he condemned as errors. The eightieth notion in his *Syllabus of Errors* that is denounced is the idea 'That the Roman Pontiff can and ought to reconcile and harmonize himself with progress, with liberalism, and with modern civilization.'[48] Strikingly, roughly half of the eighty ideas condemned deal with the autonomy of civil authority in relation to the Church.

By the end of the nineteenth century the Catholic Church had lost its battle to prevent modern nation-states from extracting themselves from the control of Churches. And so a second strategy of *adversus modernitatem* began around the turn of the century. This time, according to Gene Burns, the symbolic target for antimodernism tended to be intellectual as well as theological liberalism. The latter praised modern higher biblical criticism and accepted theories of biological evolution. An oft-quoted document typifying the second phase of Catholic antimodernism was decreed by Pope Pius X in 1907. It was called *Lamentabili* ('Lamentable') in Latin, and translated in English as *Syllabus Condemning the Errors of the Modernists*. It denounces many conclusions of modern biblical studies.

An intensive campaign to inoculate Catholic life from what were perceived as the corrosive dangers represented by modern philosophy was inaugurated in 1879 by Pope Leo XIII. In that year he published an encyclical called *Aeterni Patris* ('Of the Eternal Father'). Leo's strategy for protecting Catholic education from modern ideas was to command that all theology and philosophy in Catholic centres of learning was to be taught according to the mind and method of a medieval thinker – Thomas Aquinas. And so it was that *Aeterni Patris* launched a Neo-Thomist revival of medieval scholasticism in the Catholic Church of the twentieth century. This revival 'was an attempt to confront modernity, but from the very start it engaged modern thought in the interest of refuting it on the assumption that from Descartes onward, modern thought had taken an erroneous turn'.[49]

The third period of antimodernism explained by Mark Chaves is tied to the Second Vatican Council (Vatican II) and its aftermath. Considering the past two hundred years as a whole, Chaves concludes that the history of the Catholic

> **modernism and modernists**
> The word 'modernism' is ambiguous. In one sense it can merely refer to a belief in modern ideas. However, in terms of the history of the Catholic Church, 'modernism' has a more technical referent. It designates a group of Catholic scholars working around the beginning of the twentieth century. These intellectuals, labelled as modernists, attempted to incorporate into Catholic life and thought new philosophies and biblical studies that had developed in the wake of the Enlightenment. They were roundly condemned by Pope Pius X in his encyclical, *Pascendi Dominici Gregis* ('Pasturing the Lord's Flock').

Church has been marked by a consistently maintained opposition to modern movements and concepts. In his view, the only exception to that opposition was the Second Vatican Council, which assembled Catholic bishops from around the world between 1962 and 1965. Vatican II was by far the most significant event in the life of the Catholic Church in the twentieth century. Mark Chaves calls it 'the great moment of liberal success within the Catholic church'.[50] With Vatican II 'the church officially affirmed much of the modern world that it had resisted for the previous century: religious pluralism, political democracy, the separation of church and state, freedom of religious conscience, and human rights.'[51] The third wave of Catholic antimodernism was launched after the Second Vatican Council was closed: 'Contemporary Catholic antimodernism – both official and popular – is best understood as a reaction to the broad acceptance of modernity underlying the documents of Vatican II.'[52]

If liberal democracy was the first symbolic target for the Catholic strategy of *adversus modernitatem*, and biblical criticism coupled with biological evolution was the second, then the current target is women, or rather the notion that women should enjoy full gender equality in the Catholic Church.[53] Indeed, 'Opposition to gender equality is a central feature of antimodernist religious movements, now generically referred to as fundamentalist religious movements, throughout the world.'[54] The genesis of modern feminism and the issue of the ordination of women will be broached in Chapter 10.

Opposition to modern concepts and realities is not confined to Catholicism. Protestant groups of various hues frequently declare themselves as implacably opposed to theologies that accommodate modern theories. For example, the North American evangelical Protestant, J. Gresham Machen, rejected modern liberal theologies as the antithesis of Christian thought. He warned his readers in 1923 that

> the great redemptive religion which has always been known as Christianity is battling against a totally diverse type of religious belief, which is only the more destructive of the Christian faith because it makes use of traditional Christian terminology. This modern non-redemptive religion is called 'modernism' or 'liberalism'.[55]

Within Protestant circles, the British philosopher and theologian John Hick has been a prominent force for incorporating modern knowledge within theological discussions. He has been particularly concerned to point out that Christianity is not superior to other religions. Consequently, he has frequently been denounced as a heretic. Similar accusations have been levelled against the contemporary biblical scholar Gerd Lüdemann, who, though educated as a Lutheran, has challenged the credibility of orthodox Christian doctrines in his most recent publications.[56] Because of his writings he is no longer permitted by the Lutheran Church to teach its candidates for ministerial ordination in the University of Heidelberg: 'Lüdemann, originally a Lutheran, is being punished very much as the Catholic Hans Küng was punished twenty years ago – by being prevented from teaching students for the professional ministry.'[57]

Christianity's current predicament in the west is captured tellingly in a comment by Richard Holloway, the former bishop of Edinburgh: 'Most people in our culture have already decided that Christianity is a kind of consciousness that is no longer possible for them, so they have simply abandoned it'.[58]

conclusion

A great deal of what has been touched upon above now needs to be amplified in considerably more detail below. Yet overriding all, a judgement will need to be made about Venerable Jorge's adamance: 'There is no progress, no revolution of ages, in the history of knowledge, but at most a continuous and sublime recapitulation.' Are Jorge and the Book of Ecclesiastes correct to conclude 'There is nothing new under the sun'?

This much is clear: because of the demonstrable human capacity to learn, the future will be very unlike the present, just as the past differs drastically from now, and what is to come.

part II

the revolutions of modernity

3

the rise of modernity

He that will not apply new remedies must expect new evils; for time is the greatest innovator.

Francis Bacon

Christianity is a chameleon. Over time it has proved eminently adaptable to starkly diverse cultural settings. It has frequently reinterpreted, reinvented and reinvigorated itself in order to survive, occasionally in circumstances inimical to its continuance. It has been equally serviceable to twentieth-century German National Socialism and North American civil rights movements. It blossomed in medieval villages and is prominent today in contexts as varied as Oslo and San Salvador.

Despite Christianity's chameleon-like ability to adapt to disparate surroundings in the past, it remains to be seen whether it will be able to marshal sufficient resources to flourish in the future as the civilization of Christendom dissipates. The reason Christianity is no longer the religious and cultural hegemon of Europe can largely be explained in terms of the emergence of modern times, thought and mores. The purpose of this chapter is to chart the unfolding of the modern age and to consider its implications for traditional Christian theology.

the modern era

What does it mean to be modern? When did the age of modernity begin? How did it affect historic Christianity? And which catalysts sparked the formulation of specifically modern theologies that differ decidedly from all pre-modern styles of talking to and about God?

The English word 'modern' is not as immediately intelligible as it may first appear. It stems from a Latin adverb *modo*, which means 'just now' or 'at the present moment'. Hence, to speak of the modern in one sense is to denote an immediacy of time – right at the current instant. In that case, each and every generation of human beings has considered itself modern. Plato, Socrates, Jesus, Joan of Arc and Charles Darwin were all moderns of one kind or another.

On the lips of some, though, the term 'modern' simply signifies that which has progressed. For such a slant, the modern age is an epoch of inexorable human advancement. According to others, a modern person or thing is merely fashionable. The French word for fashion, *la mode*, is very close in form to *modo*. So too is the German adjective for 'fasionable', which is *modisch*. Not everyone regards being fashionable as desirable or profound. In one view, the assignation 'modern' is an insult suggesting ephemeral superficiality.

For others, anything that is modern and western merits destruction. The momentous matter of modernity, or of what is to be thought of as modern western civilization, assumed hazardous dimensions in the early stages of the twenty-first century:

> On September 11, 2001, two beautiful *modern* buildings in New York City came crashing down after two *modern* American airplanes were piloted directly into those exquisite symbols of one of the great aesthetic capitals of the world. Between the wonderful technologies that produced the World Trade Center – the Twin Towers, as they were commonly known – and the intricate advances that designed the two Boeing airplanes was the political: an ugly, excruciating politics, whose end is nothing less than the destruction and disintegration of the modern western world.[1]

Quite apart from the inherent elasticity of the word 'modern', pinpointing the beginning of what is now commonly designated as modernity or the modern era is not a straightforward affair. As the German philosopher Jürgen Habermas has authoritatively observed:

> The term 'modern' in its Latin form 'modernus' was used for the first time in the late 5th century in order to distinguish the present, which had become officially Christian, from the Roman and pagan past. With varying content, the term 'modern' again and again expresses the consciousness of an epoch that relates itself to the past of antiquity, in order to view itself as the result of a transition from the old to the new.[2]

By contrast, David Levine of the University of Toronto locates the roots of a distinctly modern world in a novel type of society that emerged after the year 1000 CE. In a fascinating study titled *At the Dawn of Modernity* he explains that the transition from an ancient time to a modern age was provoked by fundamental changes in social relations. In ancient societies social control was normally exercised by exceptionally autocratic patriarchs. In early modern times, however, a revolution in combat technology led to a dissemination of power among warrior knights: 'Feudalism developed from a military revolution. The new warfare was based on the mounted horseman's massive advantage over the foot soldier. Unorganized ground troops were smashed by the cavalry's shock force.'[3] For this perspective, feudal and early modern societies witnessed a gradual fragmentation of monarchical sovereignty and a sharing of political power between monarchs and knights. By the year 1000, France 'had been divided into fifty-five territories whose ties with the monarchy were limited, conditional, and contractual'.[4]

David Levine's placement of the dawn of modernity around the year 1000 is not a widely accepted practice among historians. Distinctly unmodern patterns of thought and styles of government exercised social domination in Europe for hundreds of years after 1000.

A different account locates the beginning of modernity around 1127. In that year, an abbot, called Suger, began to rebuild the abbey of St Denis in Paris. He supervised the development of a new architectural style that was neither classically Greek nor Romanesque. He called the new look of the abbey's basilica an *opus modernum*, or 'modern work'. What he dubbed an *opus modernum* is now called Gothic architecture.[5] The most perfect type of Gothic building ever constructed, the Sainte-Chapelle, is still standing in Paris.

A clearly contrasting version of the advent of the modern era lies with the North American historian Robert Anchor. For him, modernity, from beginning to end, encompasses the past two and a half centuries. In his book *The Enlightenment Tradition* he declares:

> The modern world-view is closely bound up with a number of significant developments, many of which link the eighteenth with the nineteenth centuries. Among them are the geographical unification of the world, ... the triumph of capitalism and modern science and their application to agriculture and industry, ... the rise of the ideas of national sovereignty and inviolable human rights, the liberal and democratic doctrines, (the rise) of socialism and communism ... These bounds are so numerous and significant that many, if not most, historians view the last two and a half centuries as forming a single historical unit.[6]

Yet another reckoning of modernity's birth comes from the philosopher Leszek Kolakowski. In his book *Modernity on Endless Trial*, he asserts that the foundation of modernity resides in science. Subsequently, it would be proper to date the emergence of modernity from the first half of the seventeenth century, when the basic rules of scientific inquiry were elaborated and codified and scientists realized – thanks mainly to Galileo and his followers – that physics was not to be conceived as a report from experience but rather as an elaboration of abstract models never to be perfectly embodied in experimental conditions.[7]

Stephen Toulmin agrees: '"Modernity" is the historical phase that begins with Galileo's and Descartes' commitment to new, rational methods of inquiry; and any suggestion that Modernity today is over or done with is suspect, being at least reactionary, and very likely irrationalist, too.'[8] Toulmin made that observation in the context of discussing Jürgen Habermas's chronology for the birth of the modern epoch. The latter does not conclude that modernity began in the fifth century, as might first appear. He merely notes that the word *modernus* was first recorded in the fifth century. He ties the birth of what is called modernity nowadays to the work of Immanuel Kant around the years 1776 or 1789. For Habermas, 'the modern era began when, inspired by the French Revolution, Immanuel Kant showed how impartial, universal moral standards can be applied to judge intentions and policies in the political realm.'[9]

Thus far, four divergent accounts of modernity's emergence have been encountered: (a) a theory of beginnings in the fifth century; (b) another around the year 1000; (c) a third located in the seventeenth century; and (d) a fourth traced to the eighteenth century. In this book, the seventeenth century will be taken as the effective entrenchment of the modern age.[10] Modernity may have been born as the Middle Ages died, yet it was not until the seventeenth century that it reached its adolescence.

And so it is that a fifth approach may well stand as by far the most instructive for attempts to comprehend the origin and unfolding of both modernity and modern theology. The Belgian philosopher Louis Dupré presciently observed in 1993 that it is only possible to understand the modern world-view by considering the collapse of medieval culture during the fourteenth and fifteenth centuries.[11]

the demise of medieval culture

Another philosopher, Albert Borgmann, has produced a particularly persuasive account of the demise of medieval culture and the gradual rise of modernity. In 1992, he published an articulate and informative study entitled *Crossing the Postmodern Divide*.[12] In the early stages of the work he describes both the general nature of medieval societies, and the processes by which they came to an end.

To begin with, in Borgmann's view medieval cultures were (a) locally bounded; (b) cosmically centred; and (c) divinely constituted. In other terms, within a medieval society people understood the purpose of their existence and their place in the world primarily in relation to a provincial community. Most medieval people did not travel extensively, but stayed from birth to death in a small village or town. By far the majority of people at the time did not live in large cities. The regions of medieval inhabitants were often exceptionally heteroglot, with inhabitants of one village experiencing embarrassing difficulties trying to decipher the dialects of an adjacent abode. Societies in the Middle Ages were cosmically centred in the sense that their members assumed that the earth stood at the hub of all cosmic reality. To say that medieval cultures were divinely constituted is simply to underscore the way their inhabitants normally believed that the hierarchical ordering among people in medieval communities had been legitimated by God.[13]

For all their artistic accomplishments, medieval cultures could be ruthlessly militaristic, barbarously vengeful, and religiously fanatical. Their inhabitants were often under-fed, ill-educated and superstitious. Even so, such cultures esteemed 'Chivalry and courtesy, community and celebration, authority and craft'.[14] They could hardly be more divergent from deracinated, hyper-individualist and ribald societies of the contemporary Occident, whose citizens are often accused of venerating unencumbered enjoyment of commodities above all else. As distinct form medieval conditions, modern circumstances appear to involve

> huge productions of wealth and decay of city centers; new knowledge and new ignorance; burgeoning pluralistic democracies and fierce new xenophobias; the memory of unspeakable holocausts and the hope of technological excellence; consumerism and multiculturalism; rich people nursing unhealed psychic wounds, the poor struggling to survive, and the earth itself in need of protection.[15]

Medieval scholars and monks, like the Venerable Jorge of *The Name of the Rose*, greatly prized ancient learning. It is precisely in relation to ancient learning that a new and far-reaching modern manner of acquiring knowledge and valuing wisdom started to emerge as the Middle Ages began to peter out.

After the European Enlightenment of the seventeenth and eighteenth centuries, many Europeans began to assume that the lot of humankind could be progressively perfected by empirical sciences and the technologies they were able to create. Such an assumption stands in sharp counterpoint to the once pervasive conviction that 'matters were better long ago in a Golden Age, and that they have gone downhill ever since then'.[16]

the debate of the ancients and the moderns

At about the time of the Renaissance, to speak in very broad terms, prominent individuals in the west began thinking in a decidedly different way; they reckoned that human beings have well and truly improved themselves and their world since the beginning of their history. In short, people like Leonardo da Vinci were enthused by the notion that indeed there is such a thing as progress in knowledge. They rejected the teaching of the Book of Ecclesiastes, for which 'There is nothing new under the sun'. In effect, 'These new thinkers contrasted the way people had thought in the past with their own way of thinking.'[17] And they called this novel style of thinking 'modern'. During the Renaissance, therefore, an intellectual conflict arose between the so-called ancients on the one hand, and the self-styled moderns on the other. The former were fervidly deferential to a past and imagined primordial golden age, while the latter were entranced by new discoveries, such as Leonardo da Vinci's plan for a parachute, which was designed in 1480.

The Florentine Renaissance was a particularly fertile breeding ground for modern designs and concepts. In Florence alone, painters, political theorists, sculptors, engineers, architects and poets were united in their enthusiasms for new, modern advancements, hitherto unavailable to ancient cultures. This remarkable fifteenth-century community included Machiavelli, Michaelangelo, Leonardo, Verrocchio, and Giuliano de Sangallo.

'Modernity', or rather *modernus*, is an ancient word. Nevertheless, used in a general sense nowadays, it normally refers to a time following the Renaissance when large numbers of human beings in the Occident espoused a growing sense of excitement about the capacities of human reason and scientific discoveries. In the latter part of the seventeenth century, enthusiasts for newly acquired knowledge were often called 'Moderns', and devotees of ancient classical learning were referred to as 'Ancients'. In the late seventeenth century, public debates between 'Ancients' and 'Moderns' came to be known as the 'Battle of the Books' in Britain, whereas in France it is remembered as the *Querelle des Anciens et des Modernes* ('The Debate of the Ancients and the Moderns'). Disputes between the two sides came to a head memorably in a session of the Académie Française meeting in Paris on 27 January 1687. During the meeting Charles Perrault (1628–1703) championed the enthusiasms of the Moderns by comparing the Age of King Louis XIV (1638–1715) to the days of Augustus (Roman emperor from 27 BCE to 14 CE). By the late seventeenth century, French was widely spoken throughout Europe, supplanting the ancient Latin language favoured by medieval scholars.[18]

the first phase of modernity's evolution

The working assumption of this book is that the current and most widespread use of the term 'modern' began in the seventeenth century. To appreciate more specifically the way the modern age came into being, it is helpful to consider its genesis in two stages. The first occurred around the late fifteenth century when the dynamism of the Middle Ages showed clear signs of being exhausted. This initial stage basically involved the demise of a medieval world-view and social system. The second stage encompassed the first efforts by religious leaders, scientists, philosophers and artists to envisage the world differently and to appropriate new knowledge in daily human existence.

As for the decline of the Middle Ages, it was quite dissimilar to the demise of ancient Greek and Roman civilization: 'Unlike the slow and convulsive decay of Greek and Roman culture, the medieval form of life, came to a swift and unambiguous end.'[19] Albert Borgmann explains this rapid deterioration by concentrating on the achievements of three men. Briefly stated, he accounts for the end of medieval civilization by concluding that 'It was shattered by the three blows that we commonly associate with Columbus, Copernicus, and Luther.'[20]

columbus   How so? It is now well over five hundred years since Cristóbal Colón, or Christopher Columbus, as he is normally known in English, arrived in the Antilles. During April of 1492, he struck a deal near Sante Fe with the King and Queen of Spain, Ferdinand and Isabella. They granted him a tenth of all treasures and merchandise that might be discovered in previously unfamiliar regions. Columbus in his diary and letters leaves 'abundant testimony to his obsession with the gold he hoped to find in the lands to which he had come'.[21]

He began his first transatlantic voyage from the southern Spanish port of Palos de la Frontera. He arrived in the Antilles, to the south-east of Florida, on 12 October 1492. Once he landed, he claimed possession of the islands by unfurling the banners of the Spanish sovereigns before the baffled eyes of the Lucay Indians. Columbus then decided to take some prisoners back to Spain with him so that they could learn, as he said, 'our speech'. Chillingly, he wrote to his sovereigns, 'with fifty men you shall have them all in subjection, and be able to do with them anything you desire'.[22] Here lies the fateful seed for the destruction of the Indies, a destruction to be discussed in Chapter 9 in the context of theologies of liberation.

Columbus's significance in the story of modernity's emergence and the genesis of modern theology lies principally in his discovery of territories and peoples that were unknown to the authors of the Bible. Before his voyages, the Bible served as an unrivalled reservoir of knowledge in western sites of learning. Medieval theologians venerated the Bible as a regnant epistemological authority and regarded the studying of its pages as the heart and soul of theology. It was regarded as an entirely trustworthy repository of true information about God, human beings, and their universe. However, the Bible is only familiar with three continents, and it tends to regard Jerusalem as the centre of the world.

A benchmark of modern thought is the intellectual posture of scepticism: self-designated authoritative pronouncements are not taken at face value upon first hearing.[23] Whether knowingly or unwittingly, Columbus's accounts of a so-called New World triggered one of the first distinctively modern sceptical attitudes towards the Bible's putative epistemological infallibility. Its reliability was open to question once it was demonstrated that its geographical knowledge was deficient. Columbus, therefore, stands as a luminous figure in a peculiarly modern revolution in geographical science. His maritime discoveries later proved to be theologically mutinous.

copernicus   Columbus, Copernicus and Luther all lived at the turning point from the fifteenth century to the sixteenth. Moreover, Copernicus and Luther were both priests. In 1543, Nicolaus Copernicus of Torún published a tract titled *De revolutionibus orbium coelestium* ('On the Revolution of the Heavenly Bodies or Spheres'). This book confirms mathematically Nicholas of Cusa's hypothesis that the earth revolves around the sun as it rotates on its axis. Cusa had speculated about an infinite universe that was determined by mathematically explained laws. Following him, Copernicus rejected the Bible's view that the earth rests at the centre of the cosmos.[24] His book of 1543 'struck at the foundations of the Aristotelian view of cosmology, and therefore at Christian theology, which had incorporated it'.[25]

Soon after Copernicus, the celebrated Galileo Galilei (1564–1642) confirmed the former's theories with a wonderful new technological invention – the telescope:

> Thus Galileo became one of the founders of modern science, which demonstrated the laws of nature and heralded the boundless investigation of nature. Two generations later Isaac Newton constructed a convincing new world system quite rationally from many fragmentary elements and became the father of classical theoretical physics.[26]

luther   If the first and second body blows to medieval civilization came from Columbus and Copernicus, the third comes from Martin Luther. Born in Eisleben in 1483, Luther was a sophisticated religious thinker. He was ordained a priest in 1507, and became a doctor of theology in 1512.[27] In the second decade of the sixteenth century he became disturbed by the practice, conducted by Catholic priests in Europe, of selling indulgences to Christian believers. Indulgences were and are declarations of a remission of punishment in a life after death. They were provided (at a price) by priests and other hierarchs. At the time of Luther, Catholics were instructed by their church leaders that the punishment for their sins in an afterlife could be reduced if they paid for an indulgence. The implication of selling indulgences is that human beings thought they could police divine punishment and mercy from a mundane vantage point. Luther thought that the notion of indulgences 'offended against the majesty of God, and undermined the awful completeness of human sin'.[28] He renounced indulgences in 1517, a date which many seize upon as the beginning of the Reformation. By 1520, 'Luther had spelled out his radical rejection of the hierarchical church and the priesthood'.[29]

On 17 April 1521, Luther found himself standing, accused, before a solemn assembly. The assembly had been convened at the imperial city of Worms and included royalty, papal envoys, nobles (so-called), and a variety of clerics. On that day he was asked to retract some of his theological writing. He pondered the ultimatum placed before him in such august company. The next day he gave his response. This is what he is reputed to have said:

> Your Imperial Majesty and Your Lordships demand a simple answer. Here it is plain and unvarnished. Unless I am convicted of error by the testimony of Scripture or clear reason, I remain convinced by the Scriptures to which I have appealed, since I put no trust in the unsupported authority of Popes or Councils because they have often erred and contradicted themselves. My conscience is taken captive by God's Word. I cannot and will not recant anything, for to act against our conscience is neither safe nor open to us.[30]

Luther thereby launched a major intellectual and religious revolt within Christianity of the west. He proposed a radically new criterion for determining authentic Christian faith. And that criterion was neither papal nor episcopal authority, but an individual's own conscience-bound interpretation of Scripture.[31] Luther represented a full-frontal challenge to those churches that relied on a clerical order of Latin-speaking religious professionals to decipher Scripture for the masses.

Steve Bruce explains the matter compendiously: 'The first and most important innovation of the Reformation was the rejection of the institution of religious professionals.'[32] In other terms, Luther and his reforming associates charged the medieval church with relying too heavily on clerical mediators who were required to undertake religious observances on behalf of a (paying) believing public.

Luther reacted sharply against such a system of religious practice that operated by paying professional religious virtuosi. He effectively called for a much greater concentration on personal piety for all believers.

Christianity, like Judaism and Islam, is a religion proffering redemption. It offers people what it regards as a superlative way of living and believing that will furnish people's blighted lives with ultimate health, prosperity, salvation or redemption. At the end of the Middle Ages, the Christianity of western Europe was Catholic. The religion of Catholicism can be defined as 'that form of Christianity which locates the saving power of God in the work and rites of an authoritative Church, descended by a reliable and continuous tradition from the time of the Apostles'.[33] Luther sounded the end of a medieval theory of salvation according to which people are saved through the ministrations of a caste of ordained deacons, presbyters, and bishops.

the second phase of modernity's evolution

Arguing over the ideas of Luther and other reformers, European countries were soon ensnared in bitter, prolonged and destructive military conflicts. The most notorious of these was the Thirty Years' War, which raged from 1618 to 1648. It is vital to ponder this conflict in any attempt to comprehend the complex way in which the modern era evolved.

In less than a generation following Columbus, Copernicus and Luther, the towering figures who torpedoed the medieval world-view and order, three other men who were alive during the Thirty Years' War began to lay the foundations of a new modern world-picture and social organization. They are now famous in the history of modern thought: René Descartes (1596–1650), Francis Bacon (1561–1626) and John Locke (1632–1704). These three are the builders of a new modern intellectual and scientific order that later became tagged as the Age of Enlightenment. They were by no means the only three. Yet focusing on them serves as a useful heuristic device for unravelling modernity's evolution, just as concentrating on Columbus, Copernicus and Luther helps to anchor attempts to chart the birth of modern times.

As for the Thirty Years' War, while it raged in Europe, both sides, Catholic and Protestant, hoped and planned to vanquish their opponents and to re-establish peace in both the Church and central Europe. However, as time wore on, it became clear that neither side was able to subdue or obliterate the other. When the war ended, with no outright victor, a real and deep intellectual and religious terror beset many Christians. A previously united European Church was now acrimoniously divided: 'Two parties were making the same claim, namely to be the true church of Jesus Christ, and neither had succeeded in winning a decisive victory over the other.'[34] In addition, 'the more it became clear that from now on there would be two Christian churches in the West, the more disruption and uncertainty grew.'[35] The war was so disruptive and debilitating that regions in what are now called north-eastern Germany – territories such as Mecklenburg and Pomerania – lost in violent conflict up to 60 per cent of their pre-war populations.[36]

The stark and intimidating problem that the Thirty Years' War posed for Christianity was this: with two rival Churches both claiming to be the authoritative arbiters of Christian faith, with two opposed groups both insisting in different ways to be the true witnesses to Jesus Christ, how could anybody be certain which group was right? The bifurcation of the western Church wrought by the Thirty Years' War spawned gnawing religious doubt and uncertainty at the centre of Europe.

descartes: doubt and certainty   As a young man, René Descartes witnessed the horrors and aftermath of the Thirty Years' War. Like many of his contemporaries, he was obsessed with a quest for certainty in human knowledge.[37] His life was driven by a deeply felt desire to establish indubitable knowledge in circumstances of endless controversy and religious contradiction. With mention of Descartes, one encounters a specifically modern challenge for theology, namely the formulation of a style of philosophy that relies on mathematics and reason, rather than on faith and revelation, to establish testable and warranted knowledge. In mathematics, Descartes found stable and progressive success, agreement and progress.[38] He noted in his seminal work, *Discourse on Method* (1637), that with regard to philosophy 'it had been cultivated for many ages by the most distinguished men, and there is not a single matter within its sphere which is not still in dispute'.[39] Descartes' principal ambition was 'to show how the world of physics, the mathematically describable world, could be reliably mapped out independently of the often vague and misleading deliverances of our sensory organs'.[40]

With Descartes, therefore, mathematics rather than the Bible began to serve as a new standard for determining incontestable knowledge. His work represents a major turning point in western thought with regard to the foundation of truth. During the Middle Ages and the Reformation, the basis for certainty for Europeans was God. People tended to argue from certainty about God to conviction about themselves. Descartes' thought shifts the origin of certitude from God to the human thinking self.[41]

Whether for good or ill, a defining idea of modernity comes from Descartes. It is the idea that people 'have the right to say what we think, to think what we want, to publish what we think, to think or publish or doubt or believe anything, without fear of censorship, excommunication, exile, or execution'.[42]

Descartes' much-discussed method for arriving at certitude is sketched in his *Discourse on Method*. The *Discourse* was his first published work. It elaborates four rules for overcoming uncertainty. These are (1) 'never to accept anything as true if I did not have a certain knowledge of its truth … and to conclude nothing more in my judgements than what presented itself to my mind so clearly and so distinctly that I had no occasion to call it into doubt'; (2) 'to divide each of the difficulties I examined into as many parts as possible'; (3) 'to direct my thoughts in an orderly manner, by beginning with the simplest and most easily known objects in order to ascend little by little, step by step, to knowledge of the most complex; and (4) 'to make enumerations so complete, and reviews so comprehensive, that I could be sure of leaving nothing out'.[43] Descartes concluded that these four principles could be employed in all fields of human enquiry. They form the basis of a distinctively modern style of critical, analytical investigation, in contrast to authority-governed approaches to intellectual research.

Descartes' much-discussed method for arriving at certainty is often referred to as the *Cogito* argument (from the Latin *cogito*, 'I think'). Having sketched the method in his *Discourse* he further elaborates it in his *Meditations on First Philosophy* (1641). Expressed in a nutshell, his method involved doubting everything until he arrived at that which is indubitable, namely the fact that he was thinking: 'I am thinking therefore I am, or I exist' (*Je pense, donc je suis*).

Descartes' *Discourse on Method* and *Meditations on First Philosophy* are two of the great inaugurating texts of the modern world. In them, he turns his back on the medieval view of the universe. They show that he had decided to doubt teachings derived solely from tradition, and conclusions drawn from sense experience. Because he could never be sure he was neither dreaming nor hallucinating, he concluded that he could only be certain of his own existence as a thoughtful being, for there can be do doubt or certainty without someone able to doubt and be certain. His method moves from the conviction of his thinking self to the construction of a new world-view informed by scientific knowledge rather than inherited traditions.[44]

In view of Descartes' life and work, it is beyond question that he was 'the chief architect of the seventeenth-century intellectual revolution which destabilized the traditional doctrines of medieval and Renaissance scholasticism, and laid down the philosophical foundations for what we think of as the "modern" scientific age'.[45]

It is worth recognizing, however, that Descartes' contributions to the emergence of a modern epoch do not rest entirely within the realm of philosophy. His work, like that of Copernicus, also contributed to the formulation of a new modern cosmology. Aristotle taught that all material is divisible into four fundamental elements: earth, water, air, and fire.[46] Descartes thought and taught otherwise. In the 1630s he composed a treatise on physics and cosmology which he called, simply, *Le Monde* ('The World'). In this work he asserted that 'the matter throughout the universe was of essentially the same type; hence there was no difference in principle between "terrestrial" and "celestial" phenomena, and the earth was merely one part of a homogeneous universe obeying uniform physical laws'.[47] The resolute rejection of the Aristotelian–Ptolemaic world-view (see Chapter 11) countenanced in medieval cultures is one of the axial features of modern thought and theology.

bacon　As indicated, Descartes was not the only luminary in the second phase of modernity's evolution. In 1620, Francis Bacon published his now famous *Novum Organum* and with it espoused a new inductive, a posteriori scientific method. He rejected a traditional medieval method of studying human nature and the world that was based squarely on the Bible. In its place, 'he called for a direct empirical analysis of natural phenomena using mathematics to quantify results'.[48] In addition, Bacon made it well known that he had no taste for an Aristotelian and medieval system of learning that was based on public disputation. In place of medieval disputation, Bacon wished to establish experiment as a foundation for ascertaining truth.[49]

Bacon thought as an empiricist. The word 'empiricist' comes from the Latin *Empiricii*, which refers to a school of physicians. It carries the notion of physicians who do not work according to theories or speculations, but who 'draw their rules of practice entirely from observation and experience – the accumulated experience of the medical profession'.[50] When Bacon refers to empiricists in his *Novum Organum*, he does not refer principally to medicine. Instead, he deploys the term to describe what is now called science:

> Those who have handled the sciences have been either Empiricists or Rationalists. Empiricists, like ants, merely collect things and use them. The Rationalists, like spiders, spin webs out of themselves. The middle way is that of the bee, which gathers its material from the flowers of the garden and field, but then transforms and digests it by a power of its own.[51]

Bacon's interest in empirical science was not a purely academic affair. He was deeply disturbed by what he regarded as pervasive human misery in the world. He viewed suffering as an intolerable reality that had to be eradicated by controlling nature. The roots of the modern technologically driven seizure of control over nature are clearly evident in Bacon's work. In 1627, he published a utopian work titled *The New Atlantis*. The major part of the book is devoted to urging his readers not to accept the miseries of their time and to persuade them that the domination of nature was urgently required.

locke   René Descartes sounded the modern theme of a mathematically assured mapping of reality. Bacon championed the modern cause of dominating nature to improve the demonstrably awful lot of hapless human beings. The English philosopher John Locke propelled the evolution of a modern age by announcing yet another major preoccupation of modern thinkers, namely the unhampered sovereignty of the individual. Locke was a fascinating man. He was born to Puritan parents in Somerset, England, in 1632. He became a Master of Arts in the University of Oxford in 1658 and then set about studying chemistry. From chemistry he moved on to study medicine and become a Bachelor of Medicine in Oxford. He was also intrigued throughout his life by moral, ecclesiastical, political and philosophical questions. He died in 1704, having spent a great deal of time during the last decade of his life writing theology. One of his most significant works is his book *The Reasonableness of Christianity* (1695). In its pages he argues that a rational person can accept Christianity as it is presented in the Bible, even while he denies the doctrine of Original Sin. His exploration of the limits of human knowledge, *An Essay Concerning Human Understanding* (1680), is one of the most distinguished works published in the history of philosophy. However, it is in his *Second Treatise of Government* (1690) that his readers encounter his defence of the sovereignty of the individual. This work is basically a celebration of the individual, of the human being's unfettered autonomy.[52]

With Locke writing in 1690, the modern era was well under way. So too was the battle between the ancient and moderns, a battle that continues unabated among Christians today.

In sum, and schematically stated, six thinkers have served in this chapter to chart the growth of the modern age. Columbus tore up the maps of the Middle Ages, so to speak. Copernicus knocked the earth from its pivotal position in the universe. Luther elevated the Bible and the believer to ultimate authority in the Church. Descartes set a course for modern thought starting with the certitude of the thinking self. Bacon called for a world bereft of suffering and devoted to the mastery of nature. And Locke championed the invigorating freedom of the individual.

rationalism and empiricism

The seventeenth-century birth of a modern sun-centred world-view inspired two distinctly modern currents of philosophical reflection. Both currents were theories of knowledge. They were concerned to determine the origin, nature and scope of human knowledge. They have come to be labelled as rationalism and empiricism. The former was inspired in part by the Jesuit mathematician Christopher Clavius (1537–1612). Clavius helped to develop modern mathematics and championed the view that mathematics is the most important instrument available to humans for discovering truth. Empiricism was greatly stimulated by the work of Galileo. This gifted astronomer did not examine the world by asking authorities for their views. He simply looked. He inspired a host of subsequent scientists to investigate the world through observation and experiment. According to rationalist thinkers, human reason is the foundational faculty by which human beings acquire knowledge. Modern rationalism thrived on the European mainland in the figures of René Descartes (1596–1650), Benedict (formerly Baruch) Spinoza (1632–1677) and Gottfried Wilhelm Leibniz (1646–1716). By contrast, modern empiricism flourished in Britain. Empiricism is a theory of knowledge according to which sense data, experiment and observation cooperate to furnish reliable knowledge. In short, modern empiricism is characterized by an experimental and inductive approach to knowledge. All knowledge is said to be acquired by induction from sense experience alone. Modern British empiricism involved John Locke (1632–1704), who was English, George Berkeley (1685–1753), an Irishman, and David Hume (1711–1776), who was Scottish.[53] All three were profoundly influenced by the English scientist-mathematician Isaac Newton (1642–1727), and his ability to describe motion in the world without deference to theology. Indeed, as Roy Porter has concluded, 'Francis Bacon was the prophet of modern science, Isaac Newton revealed the laws of the universe, and John Locke had demolished Descartes and rebuilt philosophy on the bedrock of experience.'[54]

By the time of Isaac Newton, when the seventeenth century gave way to the eighteenth, a scientific picture of the physical universe had evolved that was irreconcilable with the cosmology and chronology taught by the Bible.[55] If the Bible is wrong on what it says about the universe and people's place within it, then theologies that rely on its world-view need to be either overhauled or dumped. Much of the drama of the history of modern theology involves protracted debates about what needs to be cast aside, retained or reinvented in traditional theology.

4

the enlightenment

The LORD is my light and my salvation; whom shall I fear?

Psalm 27

A little rebellion now and then is a good thing.

Thomas Jefferson

The Enlightenment was a multifaceted movement that began in Europe during the seventeenth century and grew rapidly throughout the eighteenth. It reached its zenith around the end of the eighteenth century. It was both a distinct period of western history and a project to improve people's lives. The Enlightenment was simultaneously an intellectual earthquake in the life of Europe; a wide-ranging cultural transformation; a naked challenge to the authority of the Church; and a resolute rejection of feudal social pecking orders. It was a time of dizzying philosophical and religious debate; of striking scientific accomplishment; and of dramatic political upheaval. It generated ideas that spawned a violent revolution in England's American colonies in the 1770s, and the French Revolution that erupted in 1789. Western societies enjoy many of their current political practices and intellectual habits precisely because of the Enlightenment, and it is the influence of the Enlightenment on western societies that distinguishes them from others.

The fundamental ethos of the Enlightenment is captured in an amalgam of four wonderful words: revolution, freedom, reason and criticism. The Enlightenment was a revolution against the arbitrary exercise of authority by monarchs and the Church. It called for people to think and act freely for themselves without immature and unthinking subservience to the tutelage of priests and pastors. It championed the exercise of human reason as a superlative tool for securing knowledge, rather than appeal to divine revelation or the Bible. And it subjected every aspect of social, political and religious life to relentless criticism or analysis. Broadly speaking, its proponents would not accept any proposition or doctrine as true simply on the basis of a self-styled authoritative pronouncement. In this, the Enlightenment spurned the overarching principle of hierarchical authority that governed the Church and educational institutions throughout the Middle Ages.

The Enlightenment was Christianity's purgatory. It exposed every aspect of Christian life and thought to sceptical questioning, and enthroned the human mind, rather than dogmas or the Bible, as the ultimate judge of classical Christian theology. For over a thousand years before the Enlightenment the Church had been a dominant intellectual force in Europe. Throughout all that time the Church remained captivated by an Augustinian understanding of Christianity. The heart of that understanding was the belief that because of Adam and Eve's Fall humankind was unable to please God without extraordinary divine help. The fate of humanity was to be 'henceforth adrift in a merciless natural world over which we had little control'.[1] The beginning of the Enlightenment was simultaneously the commencement of a wide-ranging disenthralment with, and dismissal of, the Augustinian purview. Indeed, the seventeenth century was 'the first time in over a thousand years that this traditional world-view was seriously challenged'.[2]

Before the Enlightenment, the Bible was a peerless authority for theology and other academic disciplines in Christendom. Pre-modern theologians certainly produced refined rational arguments to support their beliefs, but they were much more reverential towards biblical authority than emboldened devotees of the Enlightenment. The medieval theologian Thomas Aquinas deferred to reason and revelation as dual sources for theology in his *Summa Theologiae* (*Sum of Theology*).[3] In contrast, the Prussian philosopher of the Enlightenment, Immanuel Kant, argued that theology should be practised with the use of reason alone. In 1793, he published the first modern tract devoted to the philosophy of religion. Its title announces succinctly his intellectual approach to theology and religion – *Die Religion innerhalb der Grenzen der bloßen Vernunft* (*Religion within the Limits of Reason Alone*). The phrase 'Reason Alone' could hardly be more disdainful of theologians' centuries-old custom of insisting that they can speak intelligibly about God on the basis of what they decide is God's self-revelation to human beings.

As the Enlightenment unfolded, theology entered a period of profound turmoil. The history of modern theology is very largely a protracted story of: (a) the decline of religious authority; (b) the confident questioning of past traditions; (c) the denial that aristocratic societies are divinely legitimized; (d) the cultural marginalization of classical theism; and (e) a frenetic though highly creative quest to discover new and rationally convincing ways to talk to and about God. It is also a tale of anti-intellectual fideisms, religious sentimentality, reactionary diehard dogmatisms; and imaginative attempts to defend traditional theology.

The Enlightenment was not without its limitations. The German intellectuals Theodor W. Adorno and Max Horkheimer described the Enlightenment bitingly in 1944, at the height of World War II: 'In the most general sense of progressive thought, the Enlightenment has always aimed at liberating men from fear and establishing their sovereignty. Yet the fully enlightened earth radiates disaster triumphant.'[4] Even so, during the eighteenth century, the Enlightenment proved to be a major watershed in the evolution of humankind's maturation. It undermined despotism, weakened feudalism, promoted scientific inquiry, and marshalled resistance to religious bigotry. Above all, utopian enthusiasts of the Enlightenment were motivated 'to create heaven on earth: a world without caste, class, or cruelty'.[5] Such a project, of course, has never been completed, as two global wars in the twentieth century chillingly illustrate.

Many of the Enlightenment's most ardent advocates were sophisticated Christian thinkers who were keen to recast their religious beliefs in the light of recently acquired and widely accepted knowledge around Europe. We shall encounter some of them in the pages of this book.[6] It is a common mistake to regard the eighteenth-century Enlightenment as a period of irreligion. In fact, several philosophers of the period, and their detractors, were obsessively captivated by religion. Indeed, the eighteenth century was the final occidental epoch thoroughly marked by religion. It was the twentieth century that proved to be incontestably unprecedented in human history by virtue of its widespread state-sponsored atheism and secularization. Since the Enlightenment, Christian theology has never managed to attain the cultural and academic pre-eminence it previously relished. The classical culture that it rested upon before the advent of modernity – a culture forged by Greek philosophy and medieval theology – has largely broken down. Over the past five hundred years, 'European culture gradually abandoned its preoccupation with religious and theological questions. Theology ceased to occupy the central position in Western universities and became an optional or marginal region of the intellectual landscape.'[7]

The purpose of this chapter is twofold. First, to ponder why the European Enlightenment so drastically challenged conventional Christian theology and religious customs. And second, to consider very briefly the impact the French Revolution (a political concomitant of the Enlightenment) exerted on Christianity. The chapter will concentrate principally on intellectual, cultural, and political transformations in Europe, while not wishing to give the impression that states of affairs in Europe determine ultimately what is important for Christianity to contend with or appropriate.

the enlightenment and the french revolution

The significance of the Enlightenment and the French Revolution for theological reflection today could hardly be exaggerated. As James Byrne points out, the Enlightenment was 'the first major intellectual movement to develop outside the borders of the Christian church since Christianity had become the official religion of the Empire almost a millennium and a half earlier'.[8] Once Christianity received Roman imperial favour in the fourth century, 'it turned upon other religions and unsympathetic philosophies, and even upon variations for its own doctrines, with an ideological ferocity that was previously unknown in the world'.[9] For centuries after Constantine, Christianity was able to rely on powerful monarchs to force populations to accept its world-view. The Enlightenment began to question and weaken the long-standing alliance between monarchs and the Church. It was an intellectual and cultural tidal wave that swept through Europe in the eighteenth century. Centred in Paris, it galvanized the rest of Europe and the American colonies in a quest to benefit from the capacities of human ingenuity. In all the major European languages of the eighteenth century the epoch recognized itself principally as a period of light.[10] And the source of that light was no longer religion and revelation as it had been in the Middle Ages, but reason and science.

Significant intellectual and political resources for Enlightenment thought are traceable to England and Scotland. David Hume's rejection of Christianity enthused many of his French and German philosophically inclined contemporaries. His *Dialogues Concerning Natural Religion* (1779) form one of the most articulate intellectual attacks on the viability of classical theism in the English language. Seventeenth-century English deism, articulated by Lord Herbert of Cherbury in his work *De veritate* (*On Truth*, 1642),

> **deism** is a world-view according to which God created the universe, but does not tamper with its immanent powers and movements. The English deist Anthony Collins (1676–1729) dismissed the notion that Jesus fulfilled ancient Jewish prophecies. He insisted that stories in the Bible asserting that Jesus performed miracles are entirely human, superstitious creations. Deism became increasingly popular among educated people of the seventeenth and eighteenth centuries just as the Augustinian saga of the Fall began to lose its hold over many individuals' imaginations. The eighteenth-century American political thinker Thomas Paine (1737–1809) defended deism with considerable eloquence.

also propelled the evolution of the Enlightenment with its deference to human reason and disavowal of divine revelation.

Roy Porter rightly points out that French Enlightenment *philosophes* looked to Britain as a cradle of freedom, toleration and sensible control of monarchical power. While Prussians thought that Immanuel Kant was a champion of free critical thought, in England, Ambrose Philips's magazine, titled the *Free Thinker*, had already adopted as its motto Horace's adage of *sapere aude* ('dare to be wise') in 1718, well before the term was used by Kant in 1784. Moreover, censorship was tolerated by Kant in Prussia in the late eighteenth century, whereas it had been banned in England in 1695. In short, Roy Porter mocks the idea that the Enlightenment was the creation of either French or German freethinkers. He ridicules the notion that the Enlightenment was generated by 'periwigged poseurs prattling on in Parisian salons'.[11]

As for the French Revolution, it was not simply a political skirmish in France. On the contrary, it was one of the greatest political convulsions in the entire span of recorded human history. The French Revolution began the collapse of what was at the time the most prestigious state in Europe. It enacted the crumbling of France's age-old religious structure, and 'plunged France into a generation of bitter and bloody struggles which soon engulfed much of the rest of Europe, too'.[12]

The French Revolution is a portentous historical event because of its demonstrated capacity 'to transform the stakes of political struggle throughout much of the world since 1789'.[13] Before the Revolution, Europe and its dominions were governed by absolute monarchs, with the exception of a few republics. Now there are no absolute monarchs in Europe.[14] The Revolution 'altered the political landscape of the West forever'.[15] Moreover, it represented 'probably the greatest attack on, and challenge to, the Catholic Church since the Reformation'.[16] It would be difficult to comprehend Christianity's current predicament in diverse cultures without scrutinizing a string of eighteenth-century political and intellectual revolutions that no previous generation of Christians encountered.

europe and christianity in the eighteenth century

Throughout the eighteenth century, and for a good deal of the nineteenth century as well, 'there were no central heating systems, no light bulbs, almost no indoor plumbing or clean water or toilet paper, no radios, no movies, no automobiles, no airplanes, no cheap and reliable birth control, no painkillers'.[17] In short, the gadgets and ingenious technologies so taken as marks of human progress today were entirely absent from the lives of eighteenth-century cultures, whether European, Asian or African. That is an obvious point. This is not:

> People born in 1750 had a life expectation at birth of around thirty-five years. Of one hundred children born alive, almost one half died before marrying or never married. Survivors spent most of their lives with little children underfoot so that the typical woman was usually either pregnant or nursing a child from marriage right through menopause. People born in 1750 would expect to die about twelve years before the birth of their first grandchild; we usually live twenty-five years after the birth of our last grandchild. The pre-modern life-cycle was thus compressed by the sheer weight of reproductive imperatives.[18]

Such a life cycle was decidedly altered throughout the twentieth century, but especially so in the wake of a thoroughgoing revolution in sexual mores amid western cultures over the last half-century or so.

Apart from relatively short spans of life, eighteenth-century Europeans lived in regions profoundly influenced by religious confessionalism. The word 'confessionalism' needs a little unravelling. It was not so much the general confession or profession of religious belief that marked Europe at the time. What really dominated European social life in the eighteenth century was the prominent presence of a variety of Christian denominations or confessions that were often at odds with one another. The most significant of these were Catholicism, Protestantism and Eastern Orthodoxy. Within Protestantism as such could be found a panoply of different religious sensibilities such as Lutheranism, Calvinism, Moravianism and Waldensianism.

The eighteenth century is frequently and variously described as the Age of Reason, the Age of Revolution, the Age of Enlightenment, the Age of Secularization, or even as the Age of Industrialization.[19] One could overlook all too easily, though, that the eighteenth century may also very accurately be designated the Age of Christian Confessionalism. Throughout much of the century, the lives of the great majority of Europe's inhabitants were directly organized from the cradle to the grave by one of the major Christian denominations. Indeed, 'Most Europeans of the late eighteenth century were not simply devout or generally Christian, but fierce adherents of their own particular church, whose doctrines and practices they saw as the only appropriate guide to life, the sole road to eternal salvation.'[20]

For Catholics and Protestants alike, Sundays were invariably reserved for worship in churches. In the eighteenth century, especially in its first half, worship was almost universal among Europe's population. Moreover, the daily lives of families were regularly punctuated by cycles of prayers and communal readings of the Bible. Houses that could afford to collect books would invariably contain a Bible if they were Protestant, or a tome recounting the lives of saints if they were Catholic. Crops were planted with ritual blessings and holidays were religious festivals rather than national calls to leisure.[21] The Enlightenment and the French Revolution notwithstanding, the eighteenth century in Europe was very far from being an age devoid of religious enthusiasm.

During most of the eighteenth century, education at all levels in Europe was directed by clergymen. Schools in the countryside were rare, but where they existed their primary purpose was to instil religion into the minds and hearts of young students. Children were conventionally taught catechetical doctrines, prayers, pious songs and biblical narratives.

The predominance of religious denominationalism is linked to a third major feature of ecclesiastical life in eighteenth-century Europe. Churches during that time were politically established. That is, they were protected, financed and promoted by governments that were in turn supported by armies.

Because Churches were established, they were able to regulate public life through the operation of ecclesiastical courts. Such tribunals frequently punished people rather severely for crimes and misdemeanours. Then as now, empowered churches displayed a keen interest to police sexual behaviour. Unwed mothers were customarily whipped. The patriarchal nature of Christianity at this time is particularly evident in the way women, rather than men, were stigmatised if a child was conceived in a context other than marriage.[22]

The politically established state of Christian Churches during the eighteenth century was bound to the reign of absolute monarchs.[23] In 1700, most of Europe was controlled by hereditary rulers and their aristocratic courts. More than that, some states were even ruled by prince-bishops. In 1731, for instance, the Prince-Archbishop of Salzburg was influential enough to expel Protestants from his domain. Given the unfettered rule of kings, queens, emperors and prince-bishops in the eighteenth century, one appreciates all the more the enormous shock that unhinged European principalities when Louis XVI was guillotined in 1793. Surely an assault on the king was simultaneously a rebellion against God. Such was the conclusion, at least, for many God-fearing citizens around Europe at the time.

European monarchs of the eighteenth century were widely venerated as empowered to rule by divine right. They were said to derive their authority directly from God. Their subjects ranked them second only to God.[24] Their coronation rites anointed them as God's own appointment. Monarchs could be so powerful as to be exempt from the jurisdiction of ecclesiastical tribunals – a fact that French Catholics learned to their dismay when, by royal decree, the Jesuits were expelled from France in 1765.

Derek Beales, formerly the Professor of Modern History at Cambridge University, counsels that, for the purposes of studying the eighteenth-century history of religions and culture before the French Revolution, the century needs to be divided into two periods. He nominates roughly the middle of the century as an apt point of division. With regard to the first period, he concludes that 'Until at least the 1740s the influence of Christianity and the Christian churches still pervaded the lives of Europeans, in some respects even more than in previous centuries.'[25]

That situation soon began to change: 'from about the middle of the century, while some absolute rulers became still more powerful, the Roman Catholic Church and other established churches were thrown onto the defensive intellectually, politically and culturally, as the ideas of the Enlightenment infiltrated the elites across Europe'.[26]

It is also worth registering that the first half of the eighteenth century witnessed the strengthening of the Catholic Counter-Reformation. Consequently, a fourth principal facet of eighteenth-century European life was the steady growth of Catholic opposition to Protestant Churches. By the 1760s, France could boast a total of 8000 Catholic monasteries. At the same time the territories of the Austrian monarchy housed roughly 2500 monastic foundations. The Capuchin Order of Franciscan friars grew spectacularly in numbers, from 22,000 members in 1650 to nearly 33,000 in 1750. Certainly, 'In all Catholic countries, down to the 1770s, lay men and women of all classes, in their millions, continued to join religious brotherhoods or confraternities under priestly supervision, of which the most famous were those associated with the Jesuits.'[27]

In sum, throughout much of the eighteenth century, and especially during its first half, Christian denominations thoroughly pervaded the lives of Europeans. As indicated, it was only in the latter half of the century that the influence of Christianity began to diminish demonstrably, as will be explored in more detail shortly.

A fifth cardinal characteristic of eighteenth-century European life was the baneful preponderance of warfare. From the beginning of the century to its end, Europe was wracked by a constant succession of death-dealing conflicts. To illustrate, the Great Northern War raged from 1700 to 1721, and engulfed Russia, Poland, Denmark and Saxony, pitted against Sweden and the Ottoman Empire. Between 1718 and 1720, France, Britain and Austria battled with Spain. During the Seven Years' War, from 1756 to 1763, Prussia and Britain locked horns with Austria, France, Russia, Sweden, and Saxony. These are but a few of the skirmishes that blighted the epoch. Military victories on behalf of one kingdom or another drastically transformed the map of Europe. In 1700, Poland was second only in size to Russia. In 1800, it no longer existed, having been partitioned by Prussia and Russia.

Hitherto, five prominent features of eighteenth-century European life have been adduced: (a) the relative brevity of people's lives; (b) the prevalence of Christian confessionalism; (c) the established order of Churches supported by the rule of absolute monarchs; (d) the strengthening of the Catholic Counter-Reformation; and (e) the horrors of unrelieved warfare. Here is another. For Europe, the eighteenth century was also a time of considerable population expansion and improvement in living conditions. During the century, Europe's population increased from roughly 40 to 50 million.[28] Even so, by far the majority of people lived in rural areas. Such an agriculturally based population was to change decidedly during the nineteenth century, with far-reaching consequences for Christian life and thought.

The 1700s also inaugurated a pronounced augmentation in literacy. By 1800, as many as 50 per cent of the population could read and write. Considerably improved literacy fed a flood of publishing. Novels, pamphlets, periodicals and newspapers all proliferated. In Germany alone, 500,000 publications appeared during the 1700s. During 1788, Paris had four newspapers. By the end of the following year, it enjoyed 184.[29]

The blossoming of publishing was but one dimension of a general efflorescence of cultural sophistication in the eighteenth century. Some of the most sublimely attractive music ever composed came from Europe at this time. Johann Sebastian Bach, Handel, as well as Domenico and Alessandro Scarlatti, were all composing in the early stages of the the century. Each of them produced works of profound religious eloquence and meaning. Mozart, Haydn and Beethoven dominated the latter half of the century. Indeed, Mozart completed his brilliant opera *Così fan tutte* in the very year the French Revolution ignited. His operas exultantly champion central tenets of Enlightenment thought. .

the enlightenment and christianity

Having schematically noted a few of the more outstanding facets of human existence in Europe during the eighteenth century, it is now possible to move on to a more specific pondering of the Enlightenment.

If Christian confessionalism remained regnant in Europe during the first half of the eighteenth century, such was certainly not the case by the end of the century. In 1740, Frederick the Great became King of Prussia, one of the more powerful and self-assertive territories of Europe. Frederick is significant for a consideration of the fortunes of Christianity during modernity because he did not endorse tenets of Christian faith. As king, he considerably relaxed laws of censorship in Prussia. Religious freethinkers had long been restrained and hampered by these laws. Around the same time, during the 1740s, King Louis XV of France began to challenge the Church's many exemptions from taxes. He needed all the money he could accumulate to finance his country's interminable wars. During the 1750s and 1760s, Jesuits were expelled from Portugal, France, Spain and Naples. From 1780 to 1790, Joseph II of Austria dissolved nearly half of his dominions' monasteries.

From the middle of the century onwards churches found themselves increasingly on the defensive against previously supportive monarchs. In addition, from roughly the midpoint of the century, clergy numbers fell and the population of monasteries and convents decreased, as did general respect for ecclesiastical authority. Such alterations can be convincingly explained principally, though not exclusively, with reference to the Enlightenment.

In the second half of the eighteenth century the Catholic Church and other established Christian denominations were increasingly challenged intellectually, culturally and politically as pivotal ideas of the Enlightenment were disseminated among educated groups in Europe. By the 1780s, supporters of Enlightenment ideas were turning up at a number of centres of power and influence in many European countries. They made their presence felt in academies of science and literature; as university professors; among monarchs' close counsellors and government ministers; and even in the ranks of the upper clergy.[30]

The Enlightenment was an intrepid project driven by a metaphor of light. Its governing metaphor, though, differed markedly from previous figures of speech focused on light. Before the eighteenth century, the English adjective 'enlightened' (*éclairé* in French; *verlichte* in Dutch; *aufgeklärt* in German) basically conveyed the meaning of being 'illuminated by faith'. To be enlightened was to enjoy the insights of Christian faith. This sense of 'enlightened' is still captured by the medieval motto of the University of Oxford, *Dominus Illuminatio Mea* – 'the Lord is my light'. For several centuries in the past, Jesus Christ was adulated by Christians as a light to enlighten the Gentiles. Indeed, as recently as 21 November 1964, the Second Vatican Council in Rome promulgated its *Dogmatic Constitution on the Church*, titled in Latin *Lumen Gentium*, or 'The Light of the Nations'. The first line of the constitution states, 'Christ is the light of the nations...'[31] Thousands of years earlier, the composer of Psalm 27 could chant: 'The Lord is my light and my salvation, whom shall I fear?' To this day, religious converts are still lauded as having 'seen the light'.

A change in the meaning of 'enlightenment' is clearly discernible in the eighteenth century. No one person can be given credit for coining a new metaphor of light. However, in 1704 Isaac Newton published a study of optics (*Opticks*), and revealed the multicoloured spectrum of light. Seventeenth-century advances in glass-cutting produced greatly improved telescopes. People could now study and measure the light that suffused the skies. Hence the birth of a peculiarly modern question: could an instrument of light be turned inwards into human beings to banish from their minds and hearts the darkness of ignorance spawned by customs, conventions, superstitions, dogmas and prejudices? And might it be that the new instrument to enlighten people would be human reason rather than divine revelation? Here, then, is the crux of the Enlightenment: 'In the eighteenth-century, a daring and dramatically new intellectual movement arose in western Europe. Of its many characteristics – audacity, wit, and interest in the practical and the applied – none was more important than its critical, biting edge.'[32] That edge derived its force from reason deployed as a torch to dispel the darkness of myth and fancy in people's lives.

Even before the eighteenth-century fascination with a metaphor of light, a change in the way 'enlightenment' was understood in Europe emerged during the latter half of the seventeenth century. Thereafter the word 'enlightenment' assumed the fashionable nuance of being informed by new ideas and currents of thought rather than by faith. Whereas Christ was previously regarded as the source of illumination, during the eighteenth-century Enlightenment especially the relatively novel idea emerged that ratiocination is the primary source of light, truth and knowledge for human beings. In contrast to the Middle Ages, the French philosopher Jean d'Alembert called the eighteenth century *l'âge des lumières*, 'the age of splendid illumination, of light and enlightenment. He and his fellow intellectuals, he assumed, would realize the project begun by the Renaissance: to lift the darkness that fell with the Christian triumph over the virtues of classical antiquity.'[33]

When considering what was involved in the Enlightenment, it is advisable to distinguish two major senses in which the word 'Enlightenment' is used in its more modern guise. There is a narrow and broad sense of the term. In the narrow case, the noun 'Enlightenment' refers to a mere twenty-five years of fervid intellectual activity centred in Paris. This so-called French Enlightenment encompassed the years 1750–75 and is exemplified by the production of an elephantine 28-volume encyclopedia edited by Denis Diderot and Jean d'Alembert. In French, the Encyclopedia was called *Encyclopédie: ou Dictionnaire raisonné des science, des arts, et des métiers* ('Encyclopedia: or reasoned dictionary of science, arts, and professions'). This long text was published progressively during the 1760s, and was essentially an attempt to base knowledge on critical reason rather than ecclesiastical authority. The *Encyclopédie* was designed to give people the most up-to-date knowledge of advances in science, agriculture and engineering; to instruct them on developments in philosophy, theology and political theory; and to inform them about the discoveries of new lands, peoples, cultures and foods; to enable them to have access to a source of knowledge independent from the traditional source of learning, namely, the church.[34]

This massive work was also openly dismissive of the value of religion. Its editors dedicated it to three Englishmen whom they regarded as champions of the Enlightenment. Somewhat unsurprisingly, the three individuals were Francis Bacon, John Locke and Isaac Newton. Thomas Jefferson was so stimulated by Bacon, Locke and Newton that, in 1789, he commissioned a group portrait of them to hang in his library. He wrote of them as 'the three greatest men that have ever lived, without any exception'.[35] Jefferson praised the Englishmen for having laid the foundations of superstructures that had been raised in what he called physical and moral sciences.

The *Encyclopédie* certainly captures the aim and spirit of the French Enlightenment, as is clearly indicated in d'Alembert's introduction to Volume I. In the 'Preliminary Discourse' d'Alembert enthused about the period of his time as the apex of an intellectual movement that had been hindered in recent centuries by scholasticism. He defined the spirit of his age as a commitment to comprehend everything and to take nothing for granted.[36] With regard to the French Enlightenment, one of its more famous protagonists was François-Marie Arouet de Voltaire (1694–1778), who fulminated against Christianity with a slogan he borrowed from Frederick the Great of Prussia. That slogan was simply, yet bluntly, *écrasez l'infâme* ('crush the infamous one, destroy the enemy, wipe out superstition').[37] A decade after Voltaire's death, French Revolutionaries sang of wanting to strangle the last king with the entrails of the last priest!

Leaving the French movement to one side, a wider sense in which the term 'Enlightenment' is now deployed is to designate a general intellectual climate of European thought between about 1650 and 1800. In this wider sense the Enlightenment encompassed Britain, Scotland, France, Germany and the Low Countries (which are now called Belgium and the Netherlands). The Enlightenment, understood in a broader sense, 'occasioned nothing less than the transformation of learned Western culture, with extraordinary consequences for almost all aspects of Western thought, society and culture'.[38]

While the Enlightenment is frequently taken to encompass aspects of French life and thought during the broad sweep of the eighteenth century, it is important to recall that it was an international movement. As such, it developed at different paces with distinct interests in diverse regions. When it flourished in Paris, Baroque culture was prevalent in Germany, Italy and Austria. The champions of the Enlightenment in France tended to be educated urbanites. In North America, they were principally politicians and wealthy rural landowners.[39] While French philosophers of the Enlightenment were frequently hostile to Christianity, their German-speaking counterparts occasionally tried to rejuvenate Christian theology with new philosophical systems, and in view of Newtonian physics.

Intense intellectual investigations of what the Enlightenment involved raged in the eighteenth century itself, especially in Germany. In December of 1783, a journal in Berlin, the *Berlinische Monatsschrift* (Berlin Monthly Journal), published an article by a German theologian and educational reformer. His name was Johann Friedrich Zöllner. In his article he questioned whether purely civil marriage ceremonies were really advisable and praiseworthy. He commented that 'under the name of enlightenment the hearts and minds of men are bewildered'.[40] Then, in a footnote, he asked in passing, 'What is enlightenment?'

Zöllner's question provoked some major responses. In the following year, 1784, none other than Immanuel Kant offered an article to the same journal. Kant's article was titled 'An Answer to the Question: What Is Enlightenment?' ('Beantwortung der Frage: Was ist Aufklärung?'). Here is what he said at the beginning of his text:

> Enlightenment is mankind's exit from its self-incurred immaturity. Immaturity is the inability to make use of one's own understanding without the guidance of another. Self-incurred is this inability if its causes lie not in the lack of understanding but rather in the lack of resolution and the courage to use it without the guidance of another. *Sapere aude!* Have the courage to use your own understanding! is thus the motto of the enlightenment.
>
> Laziness and cowardice are the reasons why such a great part of mankind, long after nature has set them free from the guidance of others (*naturaliter majorennes*), still gladly remain immature for life and why it is so easy for others to set themselves up as guardians.[41]

The Enlightenment was thereby a period in which human beings were emboldened to think for themselves and to exercise scepticism in face of doctrinal decrees. During the Enlightenment, reason dethroned revelation as an epistemological authority for many citizens of the modern world.

Kant's article 'What Is Enlightenment?' was remarkable not simply because of its insistence that people should

---

epistemology was a major fascination for most thinkers of the Enlightenment. The word, 'epistemology', comes from Greek and means 'a discourse, or word, about knowledge' (Greek: *episteme*, 'knowledge'; *logos*, 'word'). Epistemology conventionally involves the investigation of knowledge and is occasionally simply called 'the theory of knowledge'. As a philosophical discipline, it ponders the nature, origin, limits and scope of human knowledge.

think for themselves. Throughout history, outstanding writers and leaders have always thought for themselves. Students were taught in medieval universities to think on their feet while debating disputed questions with their masters. Kant's more notable purpose was to accuse anyone who relies on others for direction in life and thought of being lazy, immature (*Unmündigkeit*) and cowardly. Within traditional Christian circles of Kant's time, whether Catholic or Lutheran, freewheeling thinking for oneself when considering religious doctrines was not countenanced at all.

For much of the twentieth century, it was common to regard the Enlightenment in English-speaking circles as a fixed chronological period or intellectual age dominated by great thinkers like Voltaire, Montesquieu (1689–1755), Denis Diderot (1713–1784), d'Alembert (1714–1780), and Jean-Jacques Rousseau (1712–1778). Ernst Cassirer's book *The Philosophy of the Enlightenment* (1951) interpreted the Enlightenment as the exposition of ideas by pre-eminent thinkers.[42] Peter Gay followed a similar path in the 1960s. During that decade he published two noteworthy books dedicated to the Enlightenment.[43] Neither author displays a pronounced controlling interest in the political and social context of Enlightenment ideas. The intellectual canon of both writers also presents the Enlightenment as an affair of male European intellectuals, when in fact women clearly played a significant role as well. Mary Wollstonecraft, for example, published her *Vindication of the Rights of Woman* in 1792, and the Marquise du Chatelet, a companion of Voltaire, translated Newton's *Principia Mathematica* for the French public.

More recent studies of the Enlightenment, such as those by Dorinda Outram[44] and Thomas Munck,[45] stress that the Enlightenment was not so much a cluster of the ideas of famous intellectuals, but a much broader social process that affected the lives of everyone in Europe from monarchs to merchants, and priests to prostitutes. Thus understood, the Enlightenment was an unfolding process of societies coming to grips with new thinking and developing sciences.

One of the marks of eighteenth-century European life was the creation of a public sphere or forum for the free exchange of ideas. People met more frequently in coffee houses, reading clubs and Masonic lodges, to discuss the ideas they were discovering in a burgeoning publishing industry. This was the age when a new source of social authority arose, namely public opinion.[46]

Broadly speaking, enthusiasts for Enlightened thinking reversed a primacy of faith over reason and affirmed a primacy of empirical observation over divine revelation.[47] As noted in the previous chapter, Francis Bacon (1526–1626) articulated a new inductive scientific method in his *Novum Organum* of 1620. During the Enlightenment inductive thinking gained more favour in educated circles than deductive reflection proceeding from first principles.

In addition, devotees of the Enlightenment 'emphasized the natural equality and natural rights of human beings against schemes asserting the inherent superiority of one group of them, or particular charters of privilege'.[48] They also 'saw talent, work, and their products as the basis of a social hierarchy, rather than distinctions of social order based on birth or sacred rites'.[49]

The Enlightenment also bred an ethical revolt. Otherwise expressed, it urged people to gauge for themselves what is right and wrong, to take charge of their own lives, and to unshackle themselves from the numbing control of hierarchical authorities.

Alan Kors characterizes the Enlightenment as a set of developments and tendencies noticeable in Europe from the 1670s to the early 1800s. He tabulates an assortment of what he calls five 'dramatic phenomena' that mark Enlightened culture: an increasingly critical attitude towards inherited authority, especially arbitrary authority; an increasing naturalization and secularization of individuals' world-view; a broadening allegiance to the ethical criterion of utility, which is measured in terms of an augmentation of people's well-being and a diminution of human suffering; a growth of areas of life deemed subject to human reform and control; and, finally, an intensifying contempt in some quarters for religious strife coupled with a gradual promotion of the notion of toleration among the priorities of the western conscience.[50]

kant's philosophy as a major modern challenge for christian theology

Many of the enthusiasms and ambitions of the Enlightenment are typified by Immanuel Kant, who lived in the latter stages of the Enlightenment. Kant was the greatest philosopher of modernity, and hence of the Enlightenment. He is worthy of a consideration in a modern introduction to theology because, to recall Philip Clayton's sobering observations,

> Kant's *Critique of Pure Reason* confronts language about God with the greatest single challenge of its history – not because that book demonstrates the impossibility of a constitutive metaphysics once and for all (it did not), but because it brought to an end a certain innocence about the language/reality relationship. Never before had a philosopher so forcefully stated the possibility that there might be an unbridgeable cleft between the manner in which humans (necessarily) structure their world(s) and the way that the World Itself – if that phrase even makes sense any longer after Kant – really is. No thinker since Kant has been about to find counterarguments that would return us to the (relative) state of innocence thinkers enjoyed before Kant's first *Critique*.[51]

That *Critique* will be discussed below. For the moment, suffice it to register that since Kant all theologians have had to decide how to respond to his work by either accepting it, rejecting it, condemning it or modifying it.

Before Kant, it was common for theologians to attempt to prove rationally that there is a God. Thomas Aquinas famously adduced five reasons for why he believed in God.[52] Typically, such so-called proofs are of two kinds – a priori (prior to, or apart from experience) and a posteriori (stemming from experience). The former argue that God exists on the basis of a particular concept of God, independently of experience. Anselm of Canterbury's (1033–1109) assertion that God is that than which nothing greater can be thought (*aliquid quo nihil maius cogitari possit*) is part of an a priori strategy to establish that God is. A posteriori arguments are much more tied to experience. They proceed from perceived effects to supposed causes. For example, people often infer from their daily experiences of perceiving complicated patterns and structures in objects that the patterns are too intricate to be the mere by-products of pure chance, and must therefore have been created by a Divine Designer. An a priori argument can be judged true or false. It is true if its conclusion follows logically from its premises. By contrast, a posteriori arguments can only be judged probable or improbable, and not true or false. It may be likely or unlikely, highly probable or very improbable that patterns in the world are thus because of a divine design. Many pre-modern theologians, on the basis of what they regarded as proofs, were confident in declaring that human beings can know the reality of God, and speak of God, with God as the direct referent of their words. Many contemporary theologians and philosophers are similarly inclined. Kant argued otherwise. He insisted that humans do not enjoy knowledge of God and he argued that classical proofs for God's existence are not cogent. He thereby rejected dogmatic metaphysical theism. Kant was not opposed to metaphysics, but to dogmatic metaphysics. He wished to provide a more critical and secure foundation for metaphysics.[53]

metaphysics is a philosophical discipline that investigates reality. It tries to distinguish that which is real from that which is only the appearance of the real. The word 'metaphysics' comes from Greek and means 'above or beyond nature'. Traditional metaphysical questions ask whether there is a God; whether humans have souls; and whether a person's life can survive the death of his or her central nervous system. With regard to God, when humans observe their place in the world, they are not able to see God with ocular perception. It appears that there is no God. Metaphysically inclined theologians have for centuries argued that despite the appearance that there is no God, in reality God sustains all that exists.

For Kant, there is no way *to know* God. His philosophy is built on a major premiss: humans cannot know things or objects in themselves, but only their appearances. Neither things in themselves nor God falls within the scope of human knowledge. We shall return to Kant's views about knowledge presently, but first, a word would be helpful about his remarkable life. J. Deotis Roberts describes Kant as 'an ivory-tower bachelor lost in his books'.[54] Patricia Kitcher surmises that 'Kant's life, in so far as it is worth telling, was entirely a life of the mind.'[55] Such views are potentially misleading, for Kant was an urbane and gregarious man who loved regularly to entertain friends and visitors.

Kant was born on 22 April 1724, in the city of Königsberg in East Prussia. He was the sixth of nine children and the second son in a family of very modest means. His father, Johann Georg Kant, was a saddler, or leather-worker. His mother was Anna Regina Reuter. Immanuel Kant greatly admired modern Scottish philosophers – so much so that he convinced himself that some of his ancestors were Scots who had originally spelt his family name as 'Cant'. Recent historical research indicates that he was mistaken. All of his ancestors were of German provenance, even though a few of his great uncles married Scottish immigrants.[56]

Both of Kant's parents were Lutheran Pietists. Pietism began as a movement to reform the Lutheran Church in the seventeenth century. As its very name suggests, it underscored the importance of religious devotion, or piety, in a Christian's life. While Kant never entirely lost sympathy with the Pietistic faith of his boyhood, he was often highly critical of what he regarded as popular and mechanical religious observances. From his schooling and upbringing he imbibed a deep sense of human beings' capacity for evil. It remained with him throughout his life. In this, he differed from many other Enlightened thinkers who were overly optimistic about limitless human progress.

After his schooling, Kant enrolled at the Albertina University of Königsberg to study Latin literature, natural science, metaphysics, philosophy and theology. The year was 1740, and he was a boy of sixteen years of age. In exactly the same year, Frederick the Great became King of Prussia. Upon graduating Kant left the University to begin work as a private tutor. He was twenty at the time. He spent the next ten years of his life tutoring in East Prussian homes. Twice during this decade he became engaged to be married. Because he was not financially secure, both his fiancées lost patience with him and married other men. He remained a bachelor for the rest of his life. It does not follow, though, that he was a misanthropic bibliophile lost in his thoughts.

He returned to the University in 1755, and became a Master and Doctor of Philosophy. In 1770, he was installed as the University's Professor of Logic and

Metaphyics. As he became financially solvent, he was able to buy and maintain his own home on the basis of monetary investments and his professorial salary. He remained in Königsberg for the rest of his life. It has been memorably observed of him that, 'Just as Beethoven, the most revolutionary of all composers, wrote some of his most original music after he was totally deaf, so Kant, the most cosmopolitan of all philosophers, lived in an isolated province of northeastern Europe and never travelled farther than thirty miles from the place of his birth.'[57] He retired from his professorial duties in 1796, and died on 12 February 1804, at 11.00 a.m.[58] His mental capacities deteriorated in the final years of his life, and he was occasionally unable to recognize his closest friends. He was less than two months away from his eightieth birthday when he died peacefully in his bed. That such a man and such a life produced the greatest philosophical revolution of modernity makes him all the more intriguing.

That revolution can be described in terms of Kant's understanding of human knowledge. Revealingly, in the decade following Kant's accession to a chair in philosophy, he did not publish his thoughts in the form of a book. Instead, he struggled to formulate a major new understanding of knowledge. He published the fruits of his labours in May 1781, in what some would describe as the greatest single text in the entire history of western philosophy, the *Critique of Pure Reason*. This work contains a good deal of abstruse philosophical terminology invented by Kant himself. He actually wrote the *Critique* in about four months, in the sense that that is how long it took him to pen a copy by hand for his publisher. He had ruminated about what he wanted to say for many years before producing a final draft. The reason he took his time to publish the *Critique* was that he was striving to find a solution to two devastating intellectual traps which he concluded lay at the heart of the Enlightenment project. As previously suggested, the Enlightenment turned reason into its highest authority and final court of appeal, in all ethical, theological, political questions.[59]

During the Enlightenment reason was generally taken to involve two faculties or powers. In the first place, reason is a faculty of criticism. It is an ability to examine beliefs according to available evidence for them. In the second place, reason is a power of explanation. It is a capacity to comprehend events by viewing them as particular instances of general laws. The Enlightenment's general paradigm for explanation was that of a mechanism. It understood nature as a machine with laws that are quantifiable and capable of being formulated precisely in mathematical terms.[60]

Thus, reason is a power of rationally critical explanation. The word 'critical' here is crucial. Critical thinking is a style of thought that emerged very clearly with the philosophies of René Descartes and Immanuel Kant. Critical thought is not negative, but analytically reflective. Furthermore, critical thinking 'sets out to question assumptions, expose pretensions, demystify institutions and rigorously to test everything that passes for knowledge'.[61] In other terms, critical reflection is a search to establish lucid criteria for the validation of genuine knowledge.

Matters begin to thicken at this point. Reason understood as a twofold power of criticism and explanation can be taken to extremes. Indeed, by the time Kant wrote his first *Critique*, he had concluded that the Enlightenment project of critical rationalism and scientific naturalism had entered a major intellectual crisis that led the unsuspecting to fall into one of two intellectual traps. Kant saw only too well that radical criticism can lead in a straight line to radical scepticism and agnosticism.[62] Such scepticism is amply evident in the work of the philosophers George Berkeley (1685–1753) and David Hume (1711–1776). Berkeley denied that one can be certain of the existence of anything external to the human mind. Hume insisted that human beings are bereft of certain knowledge that there is a reality that corresponds to their perceptions of reality. For Hume, our beliefs about the world have no basis in reason. They are simply the result of mechanical propensities of the mind. According to him, religious belief has no rational ground whatsoever, which explains why he declared that all books of divinity should be committed to flames since they contain nothing but sophistry and illusion!

Returning to an earlier point, radical criticism can terminate all too easily in a nihilistic scepticism, or solipsistic idealism. Philosophically understood, idealism is a metaphysical theory holding that all things are constituted by mind and its ideas. If radical criticism can end in sceptical idealism, radical naturalism, or the view that nature is really a mechanism of quantifiable laws, can itself turn into in the espousal of materialism. And materialism is a world-view according to which matter with its movements and attributes is the ultimate reality of all things.

Kant wanted at all costs to overcome a fateful choice between scepticism and materialism. He hoped to support criticism while avoiding scepticism, and he intended to sustain naturalism without becoming a materialist. So he decided to use reason to examine itself. Seeing that philosophers of the early Enlightenment had understood reason in ways that slid into scepticism and materialism, Kant decided to re-examine reason and to bring reason itself before the tribunal of itself! This much is very clear from the very title of his major work, the *Critique of Pure Reason*. The overall theme of the work is the question of what knowledge humans can acquire through the use of reason alone, independently of the experiences of the senses.[63]

Three words dominate that title: 'Critique', 'Pure' and 'Reason'. By 'critique' Kant did not mean 'negative evaluation', but rather analytical inquiry. By 'pure', his own technical term, he meant a priori, or not deriving from sense experience.

By 'reason', he referred to 'conceptual elements in cognition which we bring to experience and which are not derived from it – in Kant's language, "a priori" conceptual elements'.[64] Hence, a critique of pure reason is a critical inquiry into human beings' 'capacity to know anything by employing their reason in isolation, i.e. without conjoining reason with sense experience'.[65]

All that said, it is now possible to note very well just why Kant's new philosophy is so consequential for the history of Christian thought after him. As stated previously, the *Critique of Pure Reason* confronts theology with its greatest single challenge in its very long history. How so? Before Kant's time, astronomy and cosmology had been revolutionized by Copernicus. The latter reversed a common-sense understanding of the universe, according to which the earth is the centre of all there is. Kant is seismically significant because he sparked a revolution in the way human knowledge ought be understood. In other terms, he radically challenged the common-sense view that the human mind passively receives impressions from objects external to mind.

During the Middle Ages, a particular view of human knowledge was very largely incontestable. It imagined that there is a direct correspondence between reality and people's minds – *correspondentia res et intellectus* ('a correspondence of a thing with the intellect'). Such a stance continued to dominate early modern philosophy and was espoused by Descartes and John Locke. We may call this view epistemological realism: 'if a subject S knows an object O, then the explanation for S's representing O lies ultimately in O's being the way it is'.[66]

Kant revolutionizes such an understanding of knowledge, and argues that 'The constitution of objects is … determined at the most fundamental level by the subject.'[67] He completely reverses a then standard understanding of cognition. We know reality, he instructs, not because we passively receive impressions from objects in the world, but because our minds actively determine the way objects appear to us. For Kant, the mind makes an active, 'positive contribution to the character of its perceived environment'.[68] In all previous philosophy it was assumed that in the process of knowing, the nature of an object known determines what is known about it. This assumption was not questioned before Kant. He turns it on its head and argues that in knowing, people impose on objects known some of their basic structural features. Two of the structural features that Kant instructs are imposed by our minds on objects are space and time.[69]

In 1787, Kant published a second edition of his *Critique of Pure Reason*. In its preface he says this:

> I should think that the examples of mathematics and natural science, which have become what they now are through a revolution brought about all at once, were

remarkable enough that we might reflect on the essential element in the change in
the ways of thinking that has been so advantageous to them, and at least as an experiment, imitate it insofar as their analogy with metaphysics, as rational cognition,
might permit. Up to now it has been assumed that all our cognition must conform
to the objects; but all attempts to find out something about them *a priori* through
concepts that would extend our cognition have, on this presupposition, come to
nothing. Hence let us once try whether we do not get farther with the problems of
metaphysics by assuming that the objects must conform to our cognition.... This
would be just like the first thoughts of Copernicus. [B xvi][70]

The *Critique of Pure Reason* represented something of a bombshell for Christian
theology. As a whole, the work speaks often of that which is transcendental. It
is important not to confuse Kant's word 'transcendental' with the common term
'transcendent'. The latter means 'that which lies beyond'. By transcendental,
Kant does not mean that which lies beyond all experience, but that which makes
knowledge possible. Transcendental inquiry is 'therefore enquiry into the cognitive constitution of the subject to which objects must conform'.[71] Transcendental
thought investigates conditions that make something possible. For example: eggs
are transcendental in relation to omelettes. The former are the condition of possibility for the latter.

When inquiring into what makes knowledge possible, Kant divides his *Critique*
into three major divisions, titled the Transcendental Aesthetic, the Transcendental Analytic and the Transcendental Dialectic. The first examines sensibility, pre-scientific understandings of time and space, mathematics and geometry.
The second focuses on the powers of understanding, human experience and
natural science. The third dwells on the powers of reason and God. The word
'Aesthetic' in this context come from the Greek term *aisthesis*, meaning 'sensory
perception'.

The first two sections have positive conclusions. The Aesthetic and the Analytic seek to establish that people can have knowledge of things that they can
experience. The Dialectic is more negative. It argues that humans cannot have
any kind of knowledge of anything that is not encountered in experience. Strictly
speaking, then, human beings have no knowledge of God, of angels, or of life
after death. Kant's theory of knowledge is an epistemology of limitation: it sets
clear limits on the scope of knowledge, and God does not lie within that scope.
In such a setting, severe limits are simultaneously set on theology: how can the
theologian speak tellingly of that which lies beyond his or her ken? 'Because of
revelation' would be the answer of many traditionally minded theologians. Yet
Kant dismissed appeals to revelation because they are always grounded on an
arbitrary appeal to particular historical people or events, and not on the exercise

of reason. The whole point of his *Religion within the Limits of Reason Alone* was to rid theology of what he called 'positive religion'. He uses the word 'positive' in a technical sense of 'that which is given, or laid down', from the Latin *ponere* ('to lay down'; past participle: *positus*).[72] Positive or revealed theologies are always vulnerable to robust sceptical questioning. The assertion that someone or something reveals God is invariably based on a human judgement. And human beings are fallible.

As stated above, before Kant philosophers and theologians tended to affirm a direct correspondence between the human mind or knowledge and reality. In contrast, Kant insists that humans do not know things or God at all. He concludes emphatically that a very clear distinction obtains between things in themselves, called *noumena*, and things as they appear to us in the process of cognition, called *phenomena*. The noumenal world exists independently of our perception of it, and the phenomenal world is that same world as it appears to our human consciousness. Yet innate structures of that consciousness, like the concepts of substance, causality, space and time, actively shape the way objects appear to us.

In sum, Kant's philosophy is a form of idealism called transcendental or critical idealism. It is not a form of radical scepticism like Berkeley's, because it insists that experience does provide knowledge of the appearances of things. It avoids thoroughgoing materialism by concluding that matter is not the sum total of reality. There are a priori structures of consciousness that are not furnished or produced by sensation.

Idealism has a negative and a positive meaning. Negatively, it implies that things which are taken commonly to be real are not so in fact and do not exist at all. For this view, all reality is mental or spiritual. Berkeley exemplifies such a perspective. Yet Kant is most avowedly not a metaphysical or epistemological idealist. He is clear that objects in experience can be known and that reality cannot be reduced to ideas about things. Anglophones often make the mistake that Kant represents negative idealism, which he does not. Understood positively, idealism does not reduce reality to ideas, but rather adds to a perspective of reality by concluding that what people perceive as things around them may actually have features that are higher or more ideal than their mere external features. Kant was an idealist in this sense.[73]

For many Christian theologians of the nineteenth century, Kant made Christian thought meaningful and intellectually convincing in a world shaken by post-Enlightenment scepticism. Such a view, however, fails to perceive a far darker side to Kant's legacy. In other words, it brings all reality before the judgement of human reason, including the very idea of God. Otherwise put, it regards that which is relative, reason, as though it were absolute.

kant and descartes

In the Fifth Meditation of Descartes' *Meditations on First Philosophy* an ontological argument for the existence of God is advanced. Kant was the most intimidating opponent of the argument. Descartes argued that it is impossible to think of God without also thinking that God exists. Kant's fundamental rejection of Descartes' argument is captured in a comment form the *Critique of Pure Reason*: '"Being" [i.e. existence] is obviously not a real predicate, i.e., a concept of something that could add to the concept of a thing.'[74] In other terms, saying that God exists affirms and informs nothing about God. In Kant's view, existence is not a predicate. To predicate existence of someone or something is not informative. For instance, the statement 'Bösendorfers exist' does not inform anyone about Bösendorfers. The word 'exists' says nothing about Bösendorfers. The statement will only become meaningful if additional information is provided about Bösendorfers. It so happens that they do exist because they are grand pianos manufactured in Vienna at a huge cost. They are probably the most beautiful grand pianos in the world.

Ontological arguments for the existence of God can be found in the works of Anselm, Aquinas and Descartes. Kant rejects all forms of ontological arguments as well as a posteriori arguments for the existence of God, which he concludes depend on ontological arguments.[75] Hence his legacy as a major modern challenge for traditional Christian theology.

the french revolution

Returning now to the matter of the French Revolution, it is not at all difficult to perceive how Enlightenment ideas of equal human rights and dignity would militate for social and political change in the aristocratically dominated hierarchies of Europe. It is now well over two hundred years since the French Revolution erupted. Since then, it has been subjected to close scrutiny by historians. Their work has not resulted in a generally accepted account either of what caused the revolution or of what it generally entailed.[76] During the first half of the nineteenth century, several French historians interpreted the Revolution as 'the overthrow of a "feudal" and aristocratic society by a bourgeois and capitalist one'.[77] The idea that the French Revolution was intrinsically a battle between backward Bourbon aristocrats and enlightened capitalists lasted well into the twentieth century.[78] In short, the French Revolution is variously depicted as the end of western civilization, a socio-economic war between aristocrats and peasants, a political tussle between a monarch and lesser aristocrats, an outgrowth of the Enlightenment that was driven by philosophically inclined nobles, or, more simply, an aimless long-standing riot. It may well be the case that the Revolution transpired under the influence of local and international social, political, economic and religious interests.

As a whole, the French Revolution was not confined to 1789. It unfolded in five successive stages: (1) the liberal revolution of 1789–91; (2) a Reign of Terror 1792–94; (3) the Directorial regime of 1795–99; (4) the consulate of Napoleon Bonaparte 1799–1804; and (5) the Napoleonic Empire 1804–1815.[79]

Despite widespread disagreement over how to construe the genesis and evolution of the French Revolution, at least the following can be summarized regarding its initial stages. On the eve of the French Revolution, France was an inegalitarian region with 70 per cent of the population living in rural areas and blighted by crippling taxes. At the time, French society still regarded itself as rather 'stable, changeless, and coherent by virtue of ancestral principles and age-old values: the worship of God, the power of a king, and the reign of Christian mores'.[80] The established Catholic Church was bedazzlingly wealthy. It owned roughly a tenth of all land in France. Each of its 143 bishops, without any exception, was recruited from so-called noble families.[81]

Status in France was determined by one's family lineage in relation to the royal dynasty. One could be a member of the *noblesse de l'épée* (nobility of the sword) or the *noblesse de la robe* (nobility of the robe).[82] The former were aristocrats by traditional lineage; the latter by having gained royal favour.

The lives of French peasants were blighted by abject misery as they were forced by their overlords to live in conditions of barnyard animals. Under aristocratic absolutism peasants were savagely repressed: beatings, whippings and brandings were common punishments. The death penalty was used with great abandon even for crimes such as petty theft. The countryside literally seethed with resentment and hatred.

This is what appears to have happened to spark the Revolution. On the eve of the Revolution, France's king ruled with the help of royal legal courts called *parlements* and the Estates General. The Estates General was a gathering of three different social groups, hierarchically ordered. The first Estate was constituted by the clergy, the second by the nobility, and the third by commoners. The combined Estates had not met since 1614.

By the mid-1780s, France was dogged by a major fiscal crisis of the French monarchy that resulted from military expenditure for France's involvement in the North American struggle for independence. Louis XVI needed to raise taxes. In July of 1788, he summoned the Estates General to discuss the issue of imposing taxes. The Estates met in May and June of 1789 at Versailles. It is vitally important to note that the first two Estates, the clergy and the nobles, represented about 5 per cent of the population. Yet combined, they could outvote the Third Estate, the commoners, who represented the remaining 95 per cent of the populace. Voting in the Estates General was not by head but by order or group.

The king made clear that he wanted the Estates to meet separately and by implication to vote in groups. The deputies of the Third Estate refused, saying they wanted to act in concert with the other two estates. Yet the first two Estates refused to agree. And here we stumble upon the truly revolutionary political idea that was radically to transform the face of Europe until our own day. After a stalemate of six weeks, the members of the Third Estate took a drastic step. 'They proclaimed themselves a new representative body, the National Assembly, and announced that the taxes could only be paid with the National Assembly's consent.'[83]

Suitably appalled by such a blatant challenge to his authority, the monarch dispatched soldiers to drive the rebellious deputies from their meeting hall. The deputies reassembled on the royal tennis courts and swore an oath not to disband until they had given France a new constitution.

Here one finds the onset of real social and political revolution inspired by Enlightenment ideals of equal human dignity and rights. Throughout Europe at the time, commoners were regularly conceived, as strange as it may seem, as not being part of national structures. That was reserved to nobles and clergy. The declarations of the National Assembly represented a profoundly new vision for the ordering of French society wherein there would be no stratification according to birth and privilege.[84]

The ideas of the National Assembly were eventually implemented with the assistance of violent popular uprisings. In July 1789, the king ordered regiments to take up positions in and around Versailles. The deputies of the Third Estate called on Parisians to arm themselves. Parisians, by the way, were already festering with discontent since bread prices in the capital were the highest they had been for eighty years. Tens of thousands of them scoured the city searching for weapons. Eventually they turned their attention on the fortress of the Bastille, which was a greatly loathed symbol of absolutist rule. The Bastille was a place where hapless people, arrested by royal decree, could be imprisoned indefinitely without formal charge. As is commonly known, it was stormed and seized on 14 July 1789.

Soon after, France was transformed thoroughly. On 4 August 1789, the National Assembly abolished all privileges of the clergy and nobility and annulled the Church's right to tithe. It also refused to declare Catholicism the religion of the state, and disbanded feudal systems in France.

On 27 August it adopted the *Declaration of the Rights of Man and the Citizen*. In seventeen articles the declaration championed freedom of speech, of the press, and of the exercise of religion.[85] It was a resolute rejection of a society based on a hierarchy of orders and government by monarchy. The key political principle driving the French Revolution is found in Article 3 of the Declaration: 'The source of all sovereignty resides essentially in the nation; no group, no individual, may exercise authority not emanating expressly therefrom.'[86] A great deal of international history over the past two centuries has involved continued struggle in scattered settings over precisely this principle.

On 2 November, the Assembly declared that all Church lands were at the disposal of the nation. In February 1790, religious orders were dissolved unless they were devoted to educational or charitable works. The taking of religious vows was outlawed. On 26 December 1790, all clergy were required to take an oath of loyalty to a new constitution. Half the lower clergy refused, as did most bishops. The Catholic Church was now structurally deeply divided.

One person more than anyone else lit the fuse that ignited the French Revolution. He was a French priest called Emmanuel Joseph Sieyès, who, in 1788, became Chancellor of the Cathedral Chapter of Chartres.[87] In view of political questions of the moment he wrote a striking pamphlet, which appeared in January 1789, and was titled *What is the Third Estate?* His answer to that question transformed a political crisis into a violent revolution:

> They may try in vain to shut their eyes to the revolution which time and the force of things has brought about: it is real for all of that. There was once a time when the Third Estate were serfs and the nobility was everything. Now the Third Estate is everything and nobility is only a word. But beneath this word, a new and intolerable aristocracy has slid in, and the People has every reason not to want any aristocrats.[88]

In general terms, the Revolution marked a clear trend towards secularization and de-christianization that was to affect other parts of Europe and greatly tax Christian thinkers during the nineteenth century. Secularization was impelled by an all-consequential idea that advanced the Enlightenment and the French Revolution, namely the notion that 'the human predicament could be explained without recourse to the mysteries of revealed religion'.[89] The Revolution reduced Christianity in France to its weakest state in more than a thousand years.[90] It gave birth to the modern concept of revolution itself, and emboldened people to transform their unjust social settings through reason and will.[91]

Many lament that the Enlightenment and French Revolution rendered Christian Churches poorer and less politically powerful in Europe. Being rendered thus, however, redirected Churches closer to their purpose, which was certainly not to mimic the bewigged, perfumed, manicured and languid lifestyle of Europe's powdered aristocracy.

conclusion

The Enlightenment and the French Revolution were joined in the conviction that religion is not necessary to explain the human predicament. At the heart of the western Enlightenment was an adulation of self-criticism. A high estimation of self-criticism is captured in Kant's essay and question 'What is Enlightenment?' He discovered the answer to this question 'in the human ability for reflexive thought. Reflexivity in this case provided the premise to doubt as the precondition for liberation from traditional forms, ideas and practices.'[92] The driving force of the French Revolution was the idea of unencumbered freedom. For the Revolutionaries, the age when human beings could be silenced for their beliefs, persecuted for their religions, and ruled without their consent, was dead.

Revolution, Freedom, Reason and Criticism: this quartet of words confronted Christian theology in the age of modernity with dilemmas it has yet to resolve.

5

secularity and suspicion

There is nothing stable in the world – uproar's your only music

John Keats

Life is doubt,
and faith without doubt is nothing but death.

Miguel de Unamuno

Near the end of the tumultuous nineteenth century, Christianity was condemned by Friedrich Nietzsche (1844–1900) as a petty, venomous, secretive, corrupt and vengeful perversion. His daunting diatribe was written in 1888 and first published in 1895 as *Der Antichrist (The Antichrist)*.[1] He could well have been imprisoned or executed had he lampooned the Christian Church so vociferously two hundred years earlier. His freedom to denounce state-sanctioned Churches as he pleased, without an ecclesiastical judicial reaction to straitjacket him, is one of the fruits of a modern cultural transformation commonly called secularization. This chapter undertakes three tasks. First, it explores the nature of secularization. Second, it charts the ways in which a previously tradition-bound, Church-dominated and aristocratic Europe became increasingly secular in the nineteenth century. Third, it discusses a culture of suspicion, scepticism and mistrust that arose in relation to Christianity among a cluster of prominent intellectuals in nineteenth-century Europe. In short, the chapter is dominated by the distinctively modern themes of secularity and suspicion.

Even though Europe is not the centre of the world, Christianity's public face today is inordinately represented by European values and preoccupations. After all, Lambeth Palace, the working home of the Archbishop of Canterbury, is in London. The Vatican, which directs the activities of Catholic bishops around the world, is ensconced in Rome – to state the obvious. The World Council of Churches is led from Geneva. Clearly, the centres of Christian government currently are situated in a region where the majority of Christians no longer live.

In the nineteenth century, historical and social changes, as well as intellectual movements, served to undermine any suggestion that Christianity in Europe should serve as an inspiration for human behaviour there, or in any other part of the world. Christianity's gradual slide from social prominence in the nineteenth century was particularly noteworthy in Great Britain.

Britain was the first highly industrialized and urbanized region in the world, and for most of the period of its industrialization it was a remarkably religious one. Victorian Britain illustrated that a modern, urban society can be simultaneously religious.[2] It was only in the final years of the nineteenth century and during the first half of the twentieth century that religious devotion became a more private affair rather than a focus of widespread public attention. While nineteenth-century Britain was very religious by contemporary standards, the social authority of Established Churches in the land diminished steadily as the century progressed. In the early decades of the nineteenth century, nearly the entire populations of England, Scotland and Wales were nominal Christians. Many of them were observant as well. Educated and illiterate people were generally united in regarding the Bible as devoid of error. In 1750, 90 per cent of all churchgoers belonged to the Established Churches in Britain. A hundred years later, the Established Church in Scotland accounted for only one-third of churchgoers.[3] In 1801, 'the United Kingdom of Great Britain and Ireland was a semi-confessional Protestant State.... The established Churches were fundamental to the State'.[4] In 1828, the Test and Corporation Acts (of Charles II) were repealed in England, thereby allowing Protestants who did not wish to conform to the Established Church to sit in parliament. In 1829, the Catholic Emancipation Act was passed by parliament in London, thereby signalling greater religious tolerance of denominations that differed from the Established Church, and allowing Catholics to sit in parliament.[5]

At the beginning of the nineteenth century, two major factors characterized the state of Christianity in Great Britain and most other countries of Europe. In the first place, by far the majority of the population believed the official dogmas of Christianity, even though sizeable sections of the populace did not regularly worship in churches. In the second instance, religious preoccupations and disputes were a matter of genuine public interest. Religious doctrines were hotly debated in parliament and newspapers. Such a situation is drastically divergent from the contemporary fate of Christianity in Great Britain.[6] The majority of the population appears to be fairly indifferent to Christianity and its doctrines. To grasp why such a situation currently obtains, it is advisable to consider what transpired in Europe during the course of the nineteenth century.

As previously noted, Europe was stunned by the revolutionary act of regicide when Louis XVI was beheaded in 1793. Roughly a century later, Europe was confronted with an attempt at deicide, when Nietzsche stridently trumpeted that 'God is dead.' The liberty to kill a king and rejoice at deicide (God being killed off in people's hearts and minds) are both fruits of the distinctively modern process of secularization.

secularity

The English terms 'secularization' and 'the secular' are directly related to the ancient Latin word *saeculum*. As a Latin noun, *saeculum* has a number of referents. It can refer to human life, the world, a breed or race, the present time, or the contemporary generation. However, whatever its connotation, it invariably contrasts with a cluster of Latin terms related to the English word 'sacred'. Latin has a number of equivalent words such as the adjective *sacer*, meaning 'consecrated to a deity'; the noun *sanctum*, designating a holy place; and the noun *sacrum*, denoting a sacred object, a religious observance or sanctity. In the light of which, this much seems clear: that which is secular reflects here-and-now this-worldly affairs, and is not fundamentally concerned with religion, religious belief, ecclesiastical affairs, spiritual questions, or sacred rituals. Expressed most simply, secularization is the broad cultural process by which once regnant enthusiasms for the sacred are displaced by secular preoccupations. More precisely stated, the term 'secularization' may be taken to refer to 'a complex of processes in which religion gradually came to lose its authority over other social institutions. Modern Europe, unlike its premodern past, has largely ceased to legitimize the authority of its laws, learning, and social arrangements by appeal to religious sanctions and supernatural endorsement.'[7]

In latter-day secularized countries social control is normally exercised by civil law, which punishes by imposing fines or custodial sentences on wayward citizens. Secularized societies do not condemn by threatening damnation in hellfire. They distrust a putative divine revelation as a reservoir of assured knowledge. In modern, secular cultures education is conducted on the basis of sceptical analysis rather than unreflective subservience to ecclesiastical doctrines.

Secularization can be understood in a narrow and broad sense. As for the former, before the 1870s, the word 'secularization' was generally reserved for referring either to the transfer of properties owned by churches to lay or secular ownership, or to the exodus from their orders of priests, monks, friars and nuns.[8] After then, and in a broader sense, secularization could refer to affairs of state taking precedence over religious considerations in negotiations between states and in the waging of wars. The first use of a broader sense appears to have been made by W.E. Lecky in his book of 1865, *History of the Rise and Spirit of Rationalism in Europe*. Therein he speaks of a 'secularization of the European intellect' and a 'secularization of politics'.[9] Secularization in a broad sense can also designate the process in economics and art whereby religious fascinations cede grounds to pragmatic or aesthetic interests.

As bizarre as it might seem, the nature of secularization can be illuminated with reference to rivers in Spain. The Manzanares river, which courses through the central Spanish city of Madrid, is actually an affluent of the Jarama stream, which is itself a tributary of the river Tajo. During the reign of King Philip II of Spain in the sixteenth century, his senior advisers pondered a plan to render the Tajo and the Manzanares more navigable in the hope of enhancing the economic prospects of populations geographically isolated in both rivers' environs. The advisors rejected a plan to alter the rivers' courses on the grounds that if it had been God's will for the rivers to be navigable in a different way, then they would have been rendered thus in the first place by divine initiative, just as God had once said, so they assumed, 'Let there be light.' The governors apparently thought that it would be a presumptuous infringement of the rights of divine providence were human hands to venture to improve upon what God had wisely left incomplete.[10]

The Spanish saga of proposing to render two rivers navigable illustrates admirably the difference between a medieval view of reality and later secularized construals of how human beings ought to operate in their environments. Philip II's administrators entertained a medieval world-view according to which human beings are subservient to the superior powers of God and angels, and hence patently powerless to plan for the future and to change the world because God is regarded as the all-powerful and unrivalled foundation of a static status quo. As the German sociologist Max Weber observed, a cardinal difference between primordial human religions and later world religions resides in the fact that the former were metaphysically monistic, while the later are dualistic. Primitive religion does not presuppose a bifurcation between a manifest creaturely world and an unseen divine world that controls a visible human environment. By contrast, the Abrahamic religions of Judaism, Christianity and Islam conceive of two distinct spheres of existence, the divine and the creaturely. A major facet of modern secularization is the rejection of a world-view according to which a divine realm determines the fate and fortunes of a mundane sphere.[11]

Understandably, scholars today offer diverse, though complementary, accounts of secularization's growth. The British sociologist Steve Bruce and the Flemish theologian Edward Schillebeeckx constitute a case in point. As a sociologist, Steve Bruce specializes in studying religion. He does so as an atheist. He concludes that medieval culture involved closely knit and hierarchically ordered communities that were governed directly by the doctrines and rituals of Christendom. For Bruce, 'The church of the Middle Ages baptized, christened, and confirmed children, married young adults, and buried the dead. Its calendar of services mapped onto the temporal power of the seasons. It celebrated and legitimated local life.'[12] In subsequent secularized societies, the small, cohesive, integrated, localized and religiously structured communities of the Middle Ages have 'gradually lost power and presence to large-scale industrial and commercial enterprises, to modern states coordinated through massive, impersonal bureaucracies, and to cities'.[13]

To compare once again medieval and later secularized social constellations, the former involved the Christian Church performing major social functions such as care for the sick, public education, ethical instruction of the populace, and the formulation of political policies. Modern secularization heralded a shift of social control whereby religious professionals were replaced by citizens who were trained to undertake educational and medical tasks previously exercised by priests, pastors, monks and nuns. In other terms, ministry to the infirm and education of the young passed from monks and nuns to civilly funded physicians, nurses, politicians and teachers. In his writings, Steve Bruce regularly refers to such a transfer of responsibilities as 'differentiation', by which is meant 'the fragmentation of social life as specialist roles and institutions are created to handle specific features or functions previously embodied in or carried out by one role or institution'.[14] A far-reaching consequence of differentiation is that

> the plausibility of any single overarching moral and religious system has declined, to be displaced by competing conceptions that, while they may have had much to say to privatized, individual experience, could have little connection to the performance of social roles or the operation of social systems. Religion retained subjective plausibility for some people, but lost its objective taken-for-grantedness. It was no longer a matter of necessity.[15]

In contemporary secularized societies, there is no universally accepted overarching moral law with which to regulate the behaviour of citizens. Whereas previously, societies attempted to control such behaviour 'with the all-seeing internal eye of the Godly conscience, we now try to control it with the all-seeing eye of the closed-circuit television camera'.[16]

Ironically, it must be added, the historical roots of secularization lay within Christianity itself. Indeed, causes of secularization stem both from medieval theology and from the Reformation. One of the more noteworthy theological disputes of the later Middle Ages was between Neoplatonic theologians and nominalists. The former were enthused by an unseen spiritual world. By contrast, nominalists, as their very name suggests, argued that 'the so-called spiritual realities of the Neoplatonists were no more than names (Latin: *nomen*, hence 'nominalist'), empty verbal abstractions, and that the only real entities were physical things'.[17]

Here a crucial point is encountered. Neoplatonists insisted that God, human beings and the created world all existed in a hierarchical harmony with the earth at the centre of the universe. Nominalists would not agree, and concluded that human beings simply do not know how God relates to the universe. All they know is that God created it. In other words, nominalists taught that God was unknowable and that the natural world is separate and distinct from God. The natural world could thus be studied in its own right, independently from God. With nominalists, medieval seeds for the later growth of modern secularity were sown.

One way of defining secularization is to say that it is a process by which increasingly more dimensions of human existence come to be explained by natural human reason rather than with reference to God or religion. The Reformation contributed to the growth of such a process in a rather obvious sense. Before the Reformation, the Catholic Church had already taught for centuries that the authority of Jesus Christ was passed to Peter, the first Bishop of Rome (so it was thought), and was thereafter perpetuated in the office of the papacy. Indeed, 'So long as that central assertion is not disputed, the Catholic church is relatively immune to fission and schism.'[18] The Reformation, however, led to a fragmentation of a previously more cohesive culture, and questioned the previously hegemonic authority of the bishops of Rome. Secularization grows in contexts of such social diversification and fragmentation wherein competing interpretations of reality challenge any kind of self-proclaimed authoritative account.

For Edward Schillebeeckx, secularization is a consequence of a gradual expansion of what he terms humankind's rational sphere of understanding. He differentiates between four phases in the historical unfolding of the western process of secularization. He locates the first phase, or cultural turning point, in humanity itself, especially as it existed in the twelfth and thirteenth centuries. This phase was constituted by what Schillebeeckx calls the intrusion of a horizontal element into the traditional Augustinian theology that regarded a person's relationship with God in a somewhat vertical manner.[19] He elucidates what he means by a horizontal element and a vertical manner by focusing on two examples: one dealing with ethics; the other focused on a theory of knowledge.

The ethical example concerns the attempt made by Scholastic theologians of the Middle Ages to erect a structure (natural law) between God, on the one hand, and human consciences, on the other. The basic intention of this attempt was to anchor morality in humankind itself. The epistemological illustration involves the attempts by Albert the Great and his student, Thomas Aquinas, to graft the horizontal structure of the agent intellect (*intellectus agens*) on to a medieval and Augustinian teaching according to which people enjoy knowledge because of a vertical divine illumination – that is, by a process that bypasses the mediation of a horizontal, this-worldly faculty. For Schillebeeckx, this attempt constitutes the first effort in the history of Christianity to establish the legitimacy of a principle of a rational sphere of understanding.[20]

He locates a second stage in the emergence of secularization in the last quarter of the sixteenth century. At that time Robert Bellarmine (1542–1621) formulated a theory of pure human nature (*natura pura*). According to Schillebeeckx, this theory was an interpretation of a new understanding of human nature for which the fact of being human is significant in itself (horizontalism), quite apart from any question of a post-terrestrial, supernatural destiny (verticalism).

In Schillebeeckx's schema, the Reformation constituted a third turning point in the history of secularization: 'It was particularly by its denial of the traditional conviction that it is possible to speak about God in a meaningful way within the rational sphere of understanding that the Reformation really encouraged the advance of the process of secularization that had already begun.'[21]

For the Reformers, to believe is to know. For Emmanuel Kant, to reason is to know and understand. Consequently, Schillebeeckx nominates Kant's thought as the fourth major phase in the Western process of secularization. He notes that for Kant God was a 'transcendental ideal' and not a concept arrived at from empirical data. According to Kant, 'pure reason' (*reine Vernunft*) can neither gainsay nor establish the objective reality of God. In effect, then, Kant confirmed a dichotomy between a rational sphere of understanding and religion, a division that had already taken place during the Reformation.

In Schillebeeckx's understanding, the lengthy process of secularization resulted in a functional loss for religion, churches and theology. The confidence that people had previously placed in the Church and religion has now to a large extent been transferred to a rational sphere of understanding. Hence the contemporary crisis of faith for religious believers. Within the context of an all-pervasive rational sphere of understanding, classical and traditional ways of speaking to and about God in the west have been rendered exceptionally problematical. One could even say that religion has become suspect. It is suspected of being little more than a decrepit carry-over from a superstitious past. At the very least, religion has become far more ambiguous in the minds of many after it became subject to scrutiny by modern historical, philosophical, psychological and sociological studies:

> All this undermined the traditional way of speaking of and to God. Experience too seemed to confirm the growing doubt – diseases which no prayers or miracles had been able to cure, were cured by modern drugs, fields which had remained infertile despite sprinkling with holy water, were made fertile by chemicals, and human needs were alleviated by various social provisions and economic changes in the structure of society. In view of all this, man ceased to speak of and to God in the way that had previously been taken for granted.[22]

Secular societies are those in which parents take their dangerously ill children to specialist paediatricians rather than parish priests. In cultures transformed by secularization, psychologically shattered or severely depressed individuals seek decisive help through advanced psychiatry and psychotropic drugs rather than by lighting candles in church buildings, or by confessing sins to presbyters. Secularized cultures prefer reason to religion, science to superstition, drugs to rites, entertainment to worship, sport to prayer, and leisure to supporting priests, rabbis, mullahs and yogi with money. The secular person is not a metaphysical dualist. He or she could not care less whether or not there is a higher unseen spiritual world above planet earth. What matters most for the secular citizen is money, sex and the unconstrained individual liberty to enjoy the baubles produced by the refined technologies of a world unshackled from dour pleasure-hating preachers.

comte   A major catalyst for the spread of secularization was the thought of the French philosopher and mathematician Auguste Comte (1798–1857). Compte is one of the inspirers of the modern discipline of sociology. He elaborated his ideas about social order between 1830 and 1842 with his *Cours de philosophie positive* (*Course of Positive Philosophy*). With this text Compte espoused what has come to be called a doctrine of positivism, which states that human societies can be organized and governed by positively observable facts and scientific laws. Comptean positivism is 'a belief that human behaviour is ultimately to be explained by an account of human nature, and that the ultimate grounds for moral and social action are human and not supernatural'.[23] In his *Course of Positive Philosophy* Comte divided history into three stages: the theological or Catholic; the metaphysical; and the positivistic or scientific. He argued that human understanding had improved as history transpired, and concluded that the theological phase was superseded in the late eighteenth century by a metaphysical era that was convinced of the progressive perfectibility of the human predicament, which is seen in a sophisticated state in new democratic, participatory political systems. For Compte, the French Revolution was a clash between theological and meta-physical ideologies. He championed a positivistic view of social organization that confined itself to observable facts.[24] In Britain, a host of intellectuals were won over by positivism, including George Eliot (1819–1880) and John Stuart Mill (1806–1873).

Having considered secularization and some of its historical roots in general terms, it is now expedient to consider its relation to nineteenth-century European Christianity. One needs to be well balanced when ruminating over the situation of nineteenth-century Christianity. On the one hand, Christian Churches through-out the century continued to play vital roles in social contexts, particularly in education and politics. The nineteenth-century was an era of religious action and revival. On the other hand, though, the epoch 'witnessed unprecedented pro-cesses of secularization, chiefly in urban areas and among the intelligentsia'.[25]

the nineteenth-century transformation of europe

Charting changes in the life and history of nineteenth-century Europe is a dizzy-ing endeavour. Few other periods of human history have witnessed such an extensive variety of cultural and intellectual developments. T.C.W. Blanning has recently documented some arresting observations and statistics about change in the nineteenth century. For instance, he declares that 'Europe changed more rapidly during the nineteenth century than during any prior period. Perhaps most fundamentally, its population more than doubled, from 205 million in 1800 to 414 million in 1900, not counting the 38 million who emigrated to other parts of the world in the course of the century.'[26]

If Europe's population more than doubled, then during the same span of time its economic evolution progressed to an even greater extent. According to Blan-ning, between 1830 and 1913 'the per capita Gross National Product (GNP – i.e. the total economic output for every European) increased by 120 per cent'.[27] The cotton spinning machine and steam engines were born in the eighteenth century, but throughout the nineteenth century they impelled an industrial revolution in Britain and Europe that produced 'cheaper and better clothes (mainly made of cotton), cheaper and better metals (pig iron, wrought iron, and steel) and faster travel (mainly by rail)'.[28]

In addition to a greatly expanded population and stronger economy, life in nineteenth-century Europe was radically transformed by a far-reaching transformation in the means of human communication. In 1833, Wilhelm Weber and Karl Friedrich Gauss constructed an electric telegraph at Göttingen. In 1844, Samuel Morse transmitted his first message on the Washington–Baltimore telegraph line. The invention of Morse code was a breathtaking cultural and technological achievement. Before its conception, messages needed to be transported by couriers or visible signals that could not communicate quickly over vast distances. With the invention of the telegraph and Morse code human beings could instantly address each other from vastly distant localities. Sophisticated means of communication were further enhanced in 1876 when Alexander Graham Bell invented the telephone. Communication in the nineteenth century was also improved by the widespread use of mechanized printing presses that could produce newspapers that were affordable for labourers and people with few financial resources.[29]

Complicit with a revolution in human communication during the nineteenth century was an equally impressive advancement in the mechanics of human travel. In 1879, Werner von Siemes demonstrated the workings of an electric tram in Berlin. In March of 1903, Orville and Wilbur Wright made the first successful flight in an aeroplane with a petrol engine. They flew their new machine at Kitty Hawk in North Carolina. Moving back to the beginning of the nineteenth century, in 1801 Robert Fulton built a submarine, called Nautilus, at Brest. In 1813, a steam locomotive, Puffing Billy, with smooth wheels running on smooth rails, was installed at Wylam colliery. During the following year, 1814, George Stephenson constructed the first effective steam locomotive, capable of hauling 30 tons much faster than a horse. In 1820, the first iron steamship was launched. Five years later, in 1825, Stephenson in England built the first public railway to carry steam trains. The railway became known as the Stockton to Darlington line. From these beginnings, the nineteenth century was to become the century of railways *par excellence*.

At this juncture it could be noted how very far nineteenth-century Europeans had removed themselves from the postures of Philip II's advisers and engineers. For the latter, humans are powerless to change the world because it is God's handiwork. For the former, human beings had become increasingly skilled at extensively altering their environments. By the end of the nineteenth century the citizens of Europe could travel under water, in the air and on railways. They could also communicate at the speed of sound, straddling huge expanses of territory. Such a vastly augmented ability to communicate rendered the widespread dispersal of new knowledge and scientific theories a much easier task than it had been a hundred years before.

Thus far, nineteenth-century revolutions in population growth, economics, communications and travel have all been spotlighted. For Christianity, the overriding significance of these transformations was that European societies were becoming increasingly transfixed by resolutely secular affairs. Nineteenth-century European culture was markedly more secular than in previous ages, despite the revivals of religious traditions. In the words of James Sheehan, 'what we think of as nineteenth-century culture was predominantly secular, sustained by secular values and directed towards secular ends.'[30]

Those secular interests, values and objectives are evident in still further evolutions in nineteenth-century European life apart from the ones already contemplated. A blatantly secular ambition drove nineteenth-century European colonial imperialism. By 1900, roughly one-tenth of the planet's inhabitants had seized control over most of the rest of the planet. Africa was dominated by Germany, Britain, France and Belgium. South and Southeast Asia were controlled by France, Britain, the Netherlands and Portugal. China was influenced by France, Britain and Russia. South America was governed principally by Spain and Portugal, and the Middle East and Iran were dominated by France, Britain and Russia. Colonial imperialism generated vast amounts of wealth as resources and revenues acquired in colonies were transferred to European nations. It is sobering to recall that the 'sudden influx of immense amounts of wealth into Europe during the latter part of the nineteenth century certainly fanned the feverish visions of world conquest among Europe's imperialist powers and fuelled their burgeoning weapons industries'.[31] By and large, Christian leaders blessed colonialist expansion, regarding it as a useful conduit for proselytising and missionary work. It was only well into the twentieth century that objections to colonialism became widely voiced among Christians.

Coupled with advances in the mechanics of travel and communication in the nineteenth century were sophisticated scientific discoveries. In 1800, William Herschel discovered the existence of infrared solar rays. Two years later, Thomas Wedgwood created the first photograph by copying paintings on glass. During 1819, Hans Christian Oersted discovered electromagnetism. In 1823, Charles Babbage built a calculating machine. Portentously for theology, in 1830 Charles Lyell published the first volume of his *Principles of Geography* and described the earth as vastly older than had hitherto been imagined. More famously, Charles Darwin issued his much-discussed *On the Origin of Species* in 1859. Therein he expounded a theory of biological evolution by natural selection (addressed in Chapter 11). Two years later Louis Pasteur developed a germ theory of disease. Alfred Nobel invented dynamite in 1866. In 1870, Zénobe Théophile Gramme developed the first commercially viable generator for direct current electricity. David Hughes invented the microphone in 1878. During 1894, Karl Benz built a four-wheel car. 1895 was a busy year. Wilhelm Røntgen discovered X-rays; Guglielmo Marconi invented wireless telegraphy; and Auguste and Louis Jean Lumière developed the cinematograph. The magnetic recording of sound was devised in 1899 and in 1901 instant coffee was produced.[32] With mention of cinema, recorded sound and instant coffee a world much more similar to the present one comes into view.

Nevertheless, with regard to the nineteenth-century transformation of Europe, there are a few other matters that need to be recognized apart from scientific discoveries and their technological application. Compared to the eighteenth and twentieth centuries, the nineteenth was relatively peaceful. In terms of international relations it was largely spared the devastating and unending military conflagrations that scarred eighteenth-century Europe. The two great conflicts of the nineteenth century were the Battle of Waterloo in 1815 and World War I (if indeed the nineteenth century can practically be taken to end in 1914). Amazingly, though, in the ninety-nine years between 1815 and 1914 the only significant skirmishes were conflicts over the unifications of Italy and Germany. Consequently, seven times fewer men died in proportion to the general population during the nineteenth century than during the eighteenth.[33]

While international relations were fairly calm, a number of individual countries experienced violent socio-political revolutions in the nineteenth century. For example, a revolution broke out in Paris on 27 July 1830. King Charles X abdicated the following month. On 25 August, a revolution against Dutch control arose in what is now called Belgium. During September, rulers were dethroned by popular revolts in Saxony, Hesse and Brunswick. The year 1848 heralded uprisings in Palermo, Sicily, Paris, Milan, Vienna and Berlin.[34] In the same year Karl Marx and Friedrich Engels published their *Communist Manifesto*. These uprisings were often directly inspired by the memory of the French Revolution. During the nineteenth century several nations subscribed to the pivotal political lesson of the French Revolution, which was that no government is legitimate if it does not legally involve the participation of people governed in the process of electing members of the government.

One further dimension of European life in the nineteenth century that deserves attention is the broad field of culture. In the 1800s, Europe witnessed a profound and pervasive revolution in artistic practices. During the Middle Ages and up to the eighteenth century, both Churches and aristocrats served as generous patrons to artists. Paintings of the time frequently had religious subjects, and musical composers wrote cantatas, oratorios, sacred songs and mass settings. Significantly, however, people excluded from ecclesiastical and courtly circles were often bereft of access to artistic performances and exhibitions. That situation was changed markedly in the nineteenth century when many more people were granted admission to newly constructed public concert halls and museums because they could pay. Composers began to produce more sonatas, concertos and symphonies than sacred songs. Painters turned their eyes to the world and gave birth to expressionism. Rodin captured in his sculpture the beauty and dignity of the human body.

Listening to the works of the following composers ought to be proof enough of how artistically rich the nineteenth-century evolution of cultural life in Europe was. Each of the following musicians was active in Europe at some some stage during the nineteenth century: Beethoven, Cherubini, Haydn, Rossini, Schubert, von Weber, Mendelssohn, Berlioz, Chopin, Liszt, Donizetti, Wagner, Verdi, Bruckner, Smetena, Johann Strauss, Brahms, Grieg, Mussorgsky, Bizet, Borodin, Tchaikovsky, Dvořák, Offenbach, Massenet, Rimsky-Korsakov, Richard Strauss, Debussy, Mahler and Puccini. Painters of the same time included Goya, Manet, Cézanne, Gaugin and Monet, to name but a few. Literary marvels were penned by Goethe, Pushkin, Heine, Ibsen, Flaubert, Dostoevsky, Tolstoy and Victor Hugo. Demand for literature in itself testifies to the greatly reduced level of illiteracy in northern and central Europe by the end of the nineteenth century.

Secular preoccupations in science, technology, politics, music and literature all affected Christian life and Christian thought. Throughout the nineteenth century, Protestant and Catholic theological faculties experienced a general decline in prestige and student interest. The fate of theology in this respect is a telling testimony to secularization. For example, at Protestant universities in Germany, the number of theology students declined from nearly one-third of the student body in 1830 to only 13.6 per cent in 1892. Catholic universities witnessed a proportional drop: from 11.4 per cent in 1830 to a meagre 4.8 per cent in 1892. Considering the previous cultural supremacy of theology in the Middle Ages, its ebbing prestige in modern times – both as a general form of knowledge and as a fixture in university curricula – suggests a truly momentous cultural transformation.[35]

Great Britain serves as a very clear example of secularization's transformative influence in nineteenth-century Europe.[36] It is often said that it is important for students of history to study epochs and civilizations long dead, like ancient Rome or the Middle Ages. These eras are thought to be so vividly different from this one as to be highly intriguing and positively instructive. It is often overlooked, however, that life in Great Britain a mere two centuries ago was strikingly different from current existence in the same place. In 1800, England, Scotland and Wales were societies in which by far the majority of their populations lived in rural areas and devoted their working energies to agriculture. In 1801, the population of England and Wales numbered roughly 8.9 million people. Scotland was populated by 1.6 million individuals.[37] At the beginning of the century,

Britain was ruled by a landed elite. Moreover, that class enjoyed enormous social prestige. The sons of rural barons were educated at home or were sent to great public schools to be taught to rule. Girls were normally kept at home and educated in some measure there. At the beginning of the nineteenth century, there was no compulsory elementary education directed by the state.

In addition, the universities of Oxford and Cambridge were dominated by clergy who were highly conservative in their theological outlook. Women were not able to study in either place. In the eighteenth century in Oxford there were four types of students: noble graduates, gentleman-commoners, commoners, and servitors. Each group wore an academic gown distinctive to its type at all times throughout the day. Members of each class or group were forbidden to make friends with students in any other group. Noble graduates were not required either to attend lectures or write essays. In short, Oxford throughout the eighteenth and nineteenth centuries reflected the vertical power relations of its wider social setting.[38]

In 1800, a majority of the British population was churchgoing. In the early nineteenth century, the church parish stood as the primary social and community unit of Great Britain. In a rural society, parish churches peppered the land, and a large network of clergymen serviced such parishes. The nineteenth century was the last time the parish functioned as the primary centre of social life in Britain.[39]

As for Christianity, by the end of the nineteenth century the majority of the population in Britain did not go to church, and the intellectual prestige of religion was largely broken.[40] In the year 2000, less than 8 per cent of British people attended Sunday worship in any week.[41]

the fate of secularization

If the eighteenth century ended with regicide and revolutionaries, and the nineteenth concluded with Nietzsche's proclamation of deicide, the twentieth century petered out with homicide: if Nietzsche could declare that God is dead, it is now possible to announce that Nietzsche has been killed off, or, more precisely, that his predictions of Christianity's demise have been shown to be false.

At the beginning of the twentieth century, devotees of Marx, Nietzsche, Freud and Feuerbach confidently proclaimed that religion was a thing of the past. They thought that with reason, science, technologies and machines, humankind could become its own redeemer. In so doing, it could rid the world of hunger, disease and deprivations that religion had been unable to eradicate for thousands of years.

With World War I, however, the modern machine became the machine gun, and millions of humans died before it was realized that humans and their machines do not make good Gods. And so it is that, by the beginning of the third millennium, the world is awash with religion. The world of Islam is massive and steadily growing. The entire Indian subcontinent is profoundly religious. Harvey Cox, who was an enthusiastic champion of secularization, now declares: 'the myth of secularization is dead'.[42] For Cox, humanity today is currently not witnessing the continuing secularization of Christianity, but the transformation of religion and Christianity into new forms. At present, for instance, there are roughly 400,000 Pentecostal Christians living in Sicily and expressing their faith in ways starkly divergent from traditional Catholicism in Italy.[43]

Secularization spawned a host of industrial, technological, artistic, scientific and intellectual advancements for the European mainland during the nineteenth century. Simultaneously, though, it bred what the sociologist Max Weber called disenchantment. For him, modern secularized cultures are disenchanted affairs. With the former stabilities and order of medieval culture dismissed, the inhabitants of the secular city are rendered bereft of a confident place in a divinely constituted cosmos. They become rudderless and anchorless in an ocean of conflicting views. Their critics insist they no longer 'have a sense of a higher purpose, of something worth dying for'.[44] Cultures that have become decidedly secularized generate disenchantment because their inhabitants live as soloists locked into competition with others to acquire capital. Such disenchanted people are accused by their detractors of living in self-induced exile from communal action and communication: 'The republic has become procedural, and we have become unencumbered selves. Individualism has become cancerous. We live in an age of narcissism and pursue loneliness.'[45] Or, as Alexis de Tocqueville complained in the nineteenth century, people in the democratic age tend to seek 'petits et vulgaires plaisirs', that is, petty and vulgar pleasures.[46] Yet not everyone alive today enjoys a pleasurable existence, let alone a petty or vulgar one, as Chapter 9 will lament.

One of the greatest challenges modern secularization posed for Christianity was a culture of suspicion and religious scepticism that it spawned. Several of the most eminent philosophers of the past were kindly disposed towards Christianity. Kant and Hegel, for instance, attempted to expound Christian beliefs convincingly in the wake of intense Enlightenment declarations that Christianity is an authoritarian brute; a slave master to dragooned, unreflective believers; and a blinkered carryover from an intellectually backward stage of human history. A horde of philosophers and other intellectuals after Hegel were not so kind to Christianity in particular, and religion in general. They explained the nature of religion and Christianity in entirely naturalistic ways – that is, by locating the origins of religious sensibility in human nature, rather than in an imagined supernatural realm to which human beings respond.

the masters of suspicion

In 1973, Paul Ricoeur (1913–2005), a philosopher and a Christian of the Reformed tradition, published an arresting article in New York. It was titled, 'The Critique of Religion'.[47] With this text Ricoeur argues that 'a major break occurred in the nineteenth century that has fundamentally altered the way people today read the authoritative texts of their traditions, especially the Bible'.[48] Ricoeur speaks of an interpretative revolution in the way people now regard biblical texts, and he concludes that this revolution is irreversible. He observes that the revolution is typified by a group of thinkers he calls 'the masters of suspicion'.[49] The trinity of masters he has in mind are Karl Marx, Friedrich Nietzsche and Sigmund Freud. Each of the three spoke German, and each practised a different, though interrelated profession. Marx was certainly a philosopher. He was also an economist. Nietzsche practised primarily as a philosopher, while Freud is renowned as a pioneer of psychoanalysis and psychiatry.

Cumulatively considered, these three seminal modern intellectuals constitute a powerful and negative critique of religion. Rather than encouraging people to trust their religious beliefs and traditions, they invite them to be resolutely suspicious. Hence their cognomen, 'masters of suspicion'. Philosophical scepticism is an ancient phenomenon.[50] However, the modern masters of suspicion and scepticism to be discussed here were particularly influential for a wide public; they were beneficiaries of the Enlightenment and its attendant political revolutions that eventually put an end to Christianity's punitive civil powers. They could say what they pleased, when they wanted, and in whatever medium they favoured. Their influence on subsequent generations in the west would be difficult to overestimate.

While Ricoeur spoke creatively of the masters of suspicion, he can be teased for an oversight. What Ricoeur fails to underscore in his article of 1973 is that, in order to understand the cultural impact of the three masters of suspicion, it is necessary to recognize that their very proclivity to be suspicious, rather than trusting with regard to religion, has its roots in the work of an unrivalled *Urmeister*, or archmaster, of suspicion.[51] That archmaster was yet another German-speaking philosopher, Ludwig Andreas Feuerbach (1804–1872).

In 1841, Feuerbach published a book called *Das Wesen des Christentums*, or *The Essence of Christianity*. It was translated into English by George Eliot. Her trans-

lation was published in 1854. For those committed to Christian belief, Feuerbach's
The Essence of Christianity is a book to be broached with care. It was this text that
convinced Richard Wagner, Friedrich Nietzsche, Karl Marx, Friedrich Engels,
Max Stirner and Bruno Bauer all to convert to atheism. Lest it be thought that
ideas are ineffectual, it need only be recalled that Feuerbach's book quite literally
became a factor that directly influenced the course of international history. This
is plainly so because of the impact it exerted on the lives of Marx and Engels.
When atheistic Marxism was at it prime in the middle of the twentieth century,
roughly half of the human race lived directly under its dominance.

hegel   As influential as Feuerbach proved to be, he did not live in a vacuum.
To appreciate the contours and thrust of his thought it is necessary to place him
on a broader intellectual map, so to speak. Feuerbach, the archmaster, and the
three lesser masters of suspicion, Marx, Nietzsche and Freud, all worked in the
immense shadow of Hegel. Before pondering the suspicious masters, therefore, it
is instructive to consider for a moment the life and thought of Hegel.

Georg W.F. Hegel (1770–1831) was born in Stuttgart and died in Berlin. He
studied theology in Tübingen before deciding to devote his life to philosophy.
While lecturing as a philosopher in later life, he never lost a profound interest in
theology. His most significant works are *The Phenomenology of Spirit* (sometimes
translated from German as *The Phenomenology of Mind*), the *Science of Logic*, the
Philosophy of Right (also translated as the *Philosophy of Justice*), and the *Encyclopedia
of the Philosophical Sciences*.[52] The extent to which Hegel was fascinated by religion
is evident in the lengthy series of lectures he delivered on the philosophy of
religion in the University of Berlin. Kant and Hegel produced the first modern
treatises devoted to the philosophy of religion.

Hegel was a quite different thinker from Kant. Hegel's readers are confronted
with a resolute focus on the significance of human history for all reflection, religious or otherwise. Hegel exerted an extraordinarily significant impact not only
on later philosophical reflection, but on Christian life and thought. Simply put,
Hegel drew the attention of a vast array of thinkers after him to the inescapable
significance of human history. By contrast, Kant was a highly individualistic,
subjectivist and ahistorical thinker. For Hegel, God is neither immovable nor
unchangeable. God is not a static suprahistorical being, for God is always 'dy-
namically actual and continually active in history'.[53] Hegel went so far as to say
'Without the world God is not God.'[54] Within his philosophical scheme God is
immanent in the world as a spiritual process: 'God as spirit in not external to
men and women; he is not some separate, sublime subject over and above them,

but is embodied in human history and human culture, and evolves within and through them.'[55]

In counterpoint to Kant, Hegel teaches that human thought mirrors the nature of reality, and not its own subjectivity.[56] Consequently, and philosophically stated, Hegel was an absolute idealist, rather than a subjective idealist. That is not all. Strikingly, Hegel concludes that 'the fact that objects appear to human beings in a particular way, as phenomena, is a reflection of the essential nature of those objects and of their divine intelligence rather than our own'.[57]

Clearly, then, Hegel differs from both Descartes and Kant to the extent that he was a holistic rather than a dualistic thinker. Moreover, Descartes, Kant, and Hegel's contemporary Friedrich Schleiermacher (1768–1834) underscored the significance of human reflective subjectivity in their writings. Hegel is re-markably different. He is far less enthralled by a self-contained ruminative and subjective human consciousness. He speaks of humans and their world as well as their relation to God in a far more all-encompassing way. He aspired to build a bridge, as it were, between phenomena and noumena. He argues that there is no radical bifurcation between the divine and the human, and that the divine and the human are bound together. Hence his oft-quoted conclusion in his *Phenomenology of Spirit*: 'Spirit is alone reality. It is the inner being of the world, that which essentially is, and is *per se*.'[58] In all his work, Hegel is at pains to show that God is an essence needing to manifest itself in the world and then perfect itself by perfecting the world.[59]

Hegel's concept of God is very far removed from the understanding of God espoused by Christian orthodoxy. For the latter, God is a suprahistorical, in-corporeal, personal, omnipotent, omniscient, omnibenevolent, necessary, immu-table and impassive creator of all there is.[60] God is in heaven, yet acts in the world. Atheism is always parasitic upon a particular theism. More often than not, modern atheists renounce the classical, traditional monotheistic conception of God just stated. To reject such a concept is not necessarily to aver atheism, as is clearly the case with Hegel.

Upon Hegel's death, one of his more gifted students, David Friedrich Strauss, judged that Hegel's many devotees divided into two major groups: the so-called left and right Hegelians. The three masters of suspicion, Marx, Nietzsche and Freud, together with their archmaster, Feuerbach, were all imbricated in the tradition of left, or young, Hegelians.

The dissimilarity between the two groups can be explained as follows. In essence, right-wing Hegelians used Hegel's idea that 'Spirit alone is reality' to defend both a classical notion of a radically transcendent Godhead and Prussian Lutheranism. Right-wing, or older, Hegelians included Philip Conrad Marheineke

(1780–1864) and K.F. Göschel (1784–1861).[61] Conversely, the left Hegelians tended to be metaphysical materialists rather than idealists. In other words, they did not follow Hegel by echoing his view that Spirit is ultimate reality. What they did take from Hegel was his logic and his insistence on the significance of history or historical process. Christian left Hegelians, like David Freidrich Strauss (in his youth) and Ferdinand Christian Baur, drew attention in their writings to the Hegelian notion of the historical immanence of that which is absolute. The same idea can be found in Spinoza. Atheistic left-Hegelians, like Marx and Nietzsche, 'reduced Hegel's God to the totality of human being or the historical process'.[62]

feuerbach   How they did so is clearly espied in the work of Ludwig Andreas Feuerbach. Bavaria is renowned for is fervid Christian piety. Feuerbach was born there in 1908 in the town of Landshut. He began his academic career by studying theology, like many celebrated philosophers of the eighteenth and nineteenth centuries. In 1823, he enrolled in the University of Heidelberg, where he studied under H.E.G. Paulus (1761–1851). At this stage in his life, he had already made a promise to his father not to become a disciple of Hegel.

Nonetheless, the young Feuerbach was soon to prove that he had a mind of his own. Finishing his studies in Heidelberg, he decided to move to Berlin. There he studied with the theologian Schleiermacher and the philosopher Hegel. Schleiermacher developed a theory of religion in Berlin, concluding that the essence of religion is experiential, or, more exactly, that it resides in an individual's feeling of absolute dependence on God. Feuerbach became close to Hegel, who encouraged him to pursue philosophy rather than theology. Feuerbach had grown tired of theology, so he accepted Hegel's advice and moved to the faculty of philosophy in the new University of Berlin. Unlike Hegel, though, he could not affirm that philosophy and Christianity were compatible. It would not be long before he would attack Christianity with all the venom he could muster.[63]

In 1828, Feuerbach completed a doctoral dissertation in the University of Erlangen. Shortly afterwards, in 1830, he published an acidulous assault on Christianity titled *Thoughts on Death and Immortality* (*Gedanken Über Tod Undunsterblichkeit*). He was well on the way to rejecting Christianity entirely. With this pamphlet, Feuerbach espoused a Spinozistic repudiation of a dualistic world-view. He hoped to wean his readers off a preoccupation with an unseen heavenly world and to point them in the direction of a manifest earthly world. Feuerbach explained that the purpose of his pamphlet was 'To cancel above all the old cleavage between this side and the beyond in order that humanity might concentrate on itself, its world, and its present with all its heart and soul.'[64] His pamphlet ensured that he would never enjoy an academic career in a German university.

The Essence of Christianity exerted a catalytic effect on Marx and Engels, and simultaneously rendered Feuerbach a champion of the left Hegelians. The entire work is driven relentlessly by one resilient idea. From beginning to end it is powered by the notion that the essence of Christianity resides in a psychological mechanism of projection. By projection in this context is meant 'the process by which specific impulses, wishes, aspects, of the self, or internal objects are imagined to be located in some objects external to oneself'.[65]

The Essence of Christianity is divided into two major parts. The first is entitled 'The True or Anthropological Essence of Religion'. The second is called 'The False or Theological Essence of Religion'. The first of the two parts argues that 'there is no difference between the *predicates* of the divine nature, and consequently, no distinction between the divine and human *subject*'.[66] In the second part, Feuerbach applies the argument of the first part to an examination of central Christian dogmas. Unsurprisingly, both parts are preceded by an Introduction. Within the Introduction lies a fascinating section entitled 'The Essence of Religion Considered Generally'. Here, at the outset of the book, a *fil conducteur* is put in place that serves to drive the book on and on in its unrelenting conclusions. The Introduction reveals that Feuerbach had been trained well as a theologian. It refers to a celebrated maxim of the fifth-century bishop Augustine of Hippo, according to which, 'God is nearer, more related to us, and therefore more easily known by us, than sensible, corporeal things.'[67] For fifteen hundred years, this maxim has been employed by theologians and Christian leaders to instruct people that they can enjoy an intimate rapport with God. In citing it, Feuerbach has quite a different purpose in mind. In Augustine's view, humans know God more intimately and directly than they know material things. For Feuerbach, the reason humans conclude they know God so intimately is fundamentally accounted for by the fact that their thoughts about God are nothing more than their ruminations about themselves. His central proposition is this:

> the object of any subject is nothing else than the subject's own nature taken objectively. Such as are a man's thought and dispositions, such is his God; so much worth as a man has, so much and no more has his God. Consciousness of God is self-consciousness, knowledge of God is self-knowledge. By his God thou knowest the man, and by the man his God; the two are identical.[68]

Feuerbach's point is clear: the essence of Christianity is none other than the essence of humanity itself. Theology is simply anthropology writ large. According to Feuerbach, 'Christian theology is fundamentally misguided. It is in fact completely invalid … Christianity is essentially illusory – merely a projection on a cosmic scale of processes going on within the human psyche and human society.[69] Throughout *The Essence of Christianity* Feuerbach prosecutes his message home unflaggingly. In the fifteenth of twenty-seven chapters he declares: 'The fundamental dogmas of Christianity are realised wishes of the heart; – the essence of Christianity is the essence of human feeling.'[70]

The second part of *The Essence of Christianity* contains a fascinating discussion of the concept of divine revelation (Chapter XXI). Feuerbach begins his musings by rehearsing a standard orthodox view of revelation considered in relation to reason:

> With the idea of the existence of God is connected the idea of revelation. God's attestation of his existence, the authentic testimony that God exists, is revelation. Proofs drawn from reason are merely subjective, the objective, the only true proof of the existence of God, is his revelation. God speaks to man; revelation is the word of God; he sends forth a voice which thrills the soul, and gives it the joyful certainty that God really is. The word is the gospel of life.[71]

It should be registered immediately that Feuerbach deploys classical Christian language to discuss revelation: 'God speaks to man', as he says. Feuerbach deftly observes that, to speak of God speaking, forces divine revelation to conform to human nature and physiology: 'God speaks not to brutes or angels, but to men; hence he uses human speech and human conceptions.'[72] Feuerbach engages the concept of revelation to proclaim the leitmotif of his book:

> the contents of divine revelation are of human origin, for they have proceeded not from God as God, but from God as determined by human reason, human wants, that is, directly from human reason and human wants. And so in revelation man goes out of himself, in order, by a circuitous path, to return to himself! Here we have a striking confirmation of the position that the secret of theology is nothing else than anthropology – the knowledge of God nothing else than a knowledge of man![73]

Concluding thus, Feuerbach draws attention to an acute intellectual difficulty for modern theologians. Before the Enlightenment, to speak generally, Christian theologians based their discourses on human cognitive apprehensions of the reality of God on a theory of divine revelation. Humans know Gods, so they said, because God had spoken to them. Expressed otherwise, God speaks to people; that is why they are acquainted with God.

Such an assertion is fatally vulnerable to sceptical attack. More than that, it commits the logical fallacy of *petitio principii* – that is, of assuming the truth that it seeks to establish. For a conclusion to be drawn successfully and convincingly from a premise, it must be independent of, and supportive of the premise. For example, to argue that 'all drug takers should be executed because all drug takers deserve to be executed' is not a logically convincing argument because the conclusion of the statement is basically the same as the first part of the statement and does not serve as supporting evidence that all drug takers should be executed. For an argument in favour of executing drug takers to be even remotely effective it would need to take a form like, 'Drug takers should be executed because they dangerously corrupt society.' The second part of that statement is independent of and supportive of the first part. Whether it is a probative argument is another matter.

To say that human beings know God because God has spoken to them assumes precisely what needs to be established in argument, namely that there is a God and that God speaks to human beings. To anyone declaring that God reveals the reality of God to people, a sceptic can easily rebound by asking, 'Who says so?' The answer for Feuerbach is obvious: 'Human beings say so.' Each and every assertion that a divine revelation has occurred rests on a human judgement. A particular human being decides that something or someone constitutes a divine manifestation. However, what human beings do not posses is a statement from God that God is self-revelatory. In short, the ideational content of any statement to the effect that God reveals Godself to people is purely human.

In a rhetorically provocative and intimidating fashion Feuerbach mocks those who base their assertions about knowledge of God on revelation rather than reason:

> O ye shortsighted religious philosophers of Germany, who fling at our heads the facts of the religious consciousness, to stun our reason and make us the slaves of your childish superstition, – do you not see that the facts are just as relative, as various, as subjective, as the ideas of the different religions? Were not the gods of Olympus also facts, self-attesting existences? Were not the ludicrous miracles of paganism regarded as facts? Were not angels and demons historical persons? Did they not really appear to men? Did not Balaam's ass really speak? Was not the story of Balaam's ass believed even by enlightened scholars of the last century, as the Incarnation or any other miracle?[74]

Feuerbach's pivotal chapter on divine revelation retains its full force to this day. It is fundamentally a dismissal of arguments constructed by appeal to revelation on the grounds that they are self-attesting and self-policing, and thereby nakedly authoritarian and stubbornly irrational.

In sum, by asserting that the secret of theology is anthropology, Feuerbach meant, as explained by Hans Küng, 'that in belief in God human beings as it were extract their human nature and see it as something outside themselves, separate from them. So they project their nature as an independent form as it were in heaven, call it God and worship it.[75] Feuerbach's creed announced that *Homo homini Deus est* – the human being is the human being's God.

It is precisely this creed that captivated and enthralled the three masters of suspicion, Marx, Nietzsche and Freud. Reading Feuerbach, they all concluded that he had succeeded in reducing Christian belief to nullity – it is no better to believe in God and miracles than to believe in trolls and fairies. Karl Marx, in one of his earlier writings, commented on Feuerbach in this way:

> And to you, speculative philosophers and theologians, I give you this advice: free yourselves from the concepts and prejudices of previous speculative philosophy if you wish to attain to things as they are, that is, to the truth. And there is no other way for you to truth and freedom than through the stream of fire (the *Feuerbach*). Feuerbach is the purgatory of the present time.[76]

Marx is here playing with Feuerbach's name, which literally means in German a stream (*Bach*) of fire (*Feuer*). As a name, it closely resembles the German word for purgatory, namely, *das Fegefeuer*.

Feuerbach's *The Essence of Christianity* is an epoch-making book. David Friedrich Strauss commended it by observing that 'Today, and perhaps for some time to come, the field belongs to him. His theory is the truth for this age.'[77] In the nineteenth century, 'It was Feuerbach's philosophy in which the shackles of religious authority and the Christian puritanical denial of the body seemed definitely to have been thrown off.'[78] Feuerbach's entire body of philosophical and theological reflection can be summarized in one pithy statement: God is the creation of human beings, not vice verse.

marx Karl Marx, Friedrich Nietzsche and Sigmund Freud were emboldened by Feuerbach to interpret Christianity and religion in a purely naturalistic way. Marx was born in the Rhineland town of Trier in 1818. As a boy, he was fervently religious in a Jewish family. He lost his faith while pursuing university studies. He enrolled in the University of Bonn in 1835. There he converted from theistic religiosity to neo-Hegelian philosophy. He later converted to materialism.

Marx's vast collection of writings do not contain a sustained analysis of religion. They offer, instead, a series of scattered references. His impact on modern Christian life and thought largely resides in his suggestion, following Feuerbach, that religion is illusory or ideological. He insists that religion is merely an ideology serving the interests of privileged classes. For Marx, as is often observed, religion is a narcotic, or opiate, that dulls people to the harsh reality of their lives alienated from bliss under capitalism.

nietzsche   Nietzsche lived later than Marx. The former died in 1900, whereas the latter expired in 1883. Nietzsche's collective writings offer a sweeping disparagement of Christianity. He is ardently studied in western universities to this day. He was born in the small German town of Röken on 15 October 1844. Like Feuerbach, Hegel and Marx, Nietzsche was born into a religious family. His father was a Lutheran minister. When he was only 24 years old he became a professor of classical philology in the University of Basle in Switzerland. His appointment at such a young age reveals the extent of his intellectual capacities. He taught in the university for about a decade before resigning in enfeebled health. He spent the rest of his life fairly much in solitude. The last decade of his life was marred by severe illness. In 1889, while visiting Italy, 'he collapsed on the street in a deranged mental state and suffered the first of a debilitating series of seizures and strokes'.[79]

As a *fin de siècle* philosopher, Nietzsche's main intellectual preoccupation was to debunk the guiding principles of Enlightenment modernity. In other words, he fulminated against the kind of culture in which he found himself living. He dismissed with withering critiques the ideas that science discovers certain truth, that reason furnishes wisdom, and that universal moral principles can be specified.

As a boy he was exceptionally pious. At the age of 20, however, after only one semester of studying philosophy and theology at Basel, he lost his faith. At a young age, he had already studied Feuerbach's *The Essence of Christianity*. Following Feuerbach, Nietzsche surmised that Christianity is simply an escape from reality. He opens the fifth book of his monograph *The Gay Science* by saying, 'the greatest recent event – that "God is dead"; that the belief in the Christian God has become unbelievable – is already beginning to cast its first shadow over Europe.'[80] So far as Nietzsche is concerned, Christianity is simply a vast delusional system that must be rejected. Feuerbach championed the cause of an anthropological atheism. In other terms, he argued for atheism on the basis of an understanding of human nature (anthropological atheism). Marx heralded a socio-political atheism, pointing out that religion numbs people into a stasis that prevents them from resisting their stultifying capitalist overseers. Nietzsche advances an atheism that springs from revulsion at the Christian religion (cultural atheism). He diagnoses that the culture of the late nineteenth century is intellectually and ethically bankrupt. Regarding Christianity as a pernicious antiquity, Nietzsche counselled his audience to embrace a life of the senses (see his *Human, All Too Human*) and to abandon belief in an afterlife.

In Nietzsche's works are to be found rejections of the three axial and revolutionary movements of the modern world: (a) the Enlightenment, with its enthusiasm for reason and science; (b) the French Revolution, accompanied by its defence of free and equal human beings; and (c) the Industrial Revolution, with its massively expanded means of production.

freud   With Sigmund Freud, Christian thinkers were confronted by a fourth type of atheism whose roots lay in psychology and psychiatry. Freud was born in 1856 in Moravia, now called the Czech Republic. His family moved to Vienna in 1861. He remained there until the Nazis occupied Austria. He died in London in 1939. As a young man he was educated at the Vienna Medical School. However, while still a schoolboy he actually read Feuerbach's *The Essence of Christianity*. In Vienna he studied the human mind by concentrating on physiology or, more precisely, the central nervous system of the human body. He soon learned that various obsessions, phobias and paranoia are all linked with patients' unconscious motives or memories. Moreover, he judged that such dispositions were often marked by a pronounced sexual nature going back in time.[81]

For good or ill, 'Freud's ideas established the framework for twentieth-century thinking about the mind, about human nature, about the human condition, and about the prospects of human happiness.'[82] Inspired by Feuerbach, he insisted that religion is a psychological projection; 'it is a vain attempt to fulfil our wishes'.[83] Freud shocked rationalistic disciples of the Enlightenment by contending that 'human nature by its very nature is based on vile, murderous, incestuous motives. So much for the enlightened thesis that human beings are basically good. Sexual desire is everywhere and everywhere repressed. Unhappiness was inevitable.'[84]

suspecting the masters of suspicion

For those stung by what they regard as the rebarbative critiques of Feuerbach, Marx, Nietzsche and Freud, the writings of the Swiss theologian Hans Küng can serve as an antidote. In a number of highly erudite and philosophically informed books Küng engages the ideas of the masters and finds fault with many of them while graciously commending their accomplishments. Like the work of other scholars, the writings of Feuerbach, Marx, Nietzsche and Freud are neither entirely wrong nor wholly correct.

Hans Küng was born in Sursee in Switzerland in 1928.[85] He is a prolific author who, over several decades, has written erudite disquisitions on the Church, sacraments, justification, Jesus Christ, belief and disbelief in God, the religions of the world, economics and politics, ecumenism, as well as women in the Church.

When speaking of the masters of suspicion, Küng adopts a twofold strategy. In the first place he commends them for their established insights. He insists that theology has been changed by what he regards as the permanent findings of the modern criticism of religion, 'which discovered the always possible misuse of religion for anti-human alienation (Feuerbach), for the stabilization of unjust social structures (Marx), for the moral degradation of man (Nietzsche) and for infantile regression (Freud)'.[86] In the second place Küng points out clearly that the masters of suspicion were plainly wrong in their prediction that modernity will inexorably lead to the demise of religion:

> After all the diagnoses and prognoses of Feuerbach, Marx, Nietzsche, the death
> of religion expected in late modernity has not taken place, however much the
> unenlightened childhood faith of countless individuals has (rightly) been called into
> question. Not religion, but its dying off, was the grand illusion.[87]

Küng's disquisitions about the question of God are contained in several of his works, but especially so in two of his largest books: *On Being a Christian*,[88] and *Does God Exist?* The second book contains more philosophical analysis than the first. To the question, 'Does God exist?', Küng provides a forthright answer: 'We are putting our cards on the table here. The answer will be: "Yes, God Exists." And as human beings in the twentieth century we certainly can reasonably believe in God, even in the Christian God.'[89]

In the early stages of Küng's book, *Christianity*, he sums up the question of God in modern times with a reflection on Feuerbach. He explains Feuerbach's critique of religion for his readers, and then observes that a hundred and fifty years after Feuerbach, the latter's prediction of the dissolution of religion has not taken place. Küng is wise to focus on Feuerbach's critique of religion because it generates the later critiques of Marx, Nietzsche and Freud.

According to Küng, Feuerbach's criticism of religion is fundamentally based on two principal arguments. The first is constituted by the argument of projection. The second is an argument for the extinction of religion. Küng responds to both arguments adroitly. To the first argument he responds:

> Time and again Feuerbach uses variants on the argument from individual or
> social psychology that religion is nothing but a human projection or, as Marx later
> described it pointedly in his critique of society, the 'opium of the people'. But does
> that conclusively prove that God is only a projection, that God is *only* a consolation
> conditioned by interests or only an 'infantile illusion', as Sigmund Freud was later to
> argue, along the same lines? 'Only' or 'nothing but' sentences must be treated with
> suspicion. They suggest a certainty for which there is no foundation.[90]

In short, Küng applies the method of the masters of suspicion to call their ideas into question. He invites his readers to be suspicious of the masters of suspicion. With regard to the second of Feuerbach's arguments, Küng is well aware that modern philosophers, sociologists and psychologists in Feuerbach's thrall have frequently and confidently declared that the age of religion has come to an end. Once again, Küng points out the unsteady basis of such a conclusion: 'it is an extrapolation onto the future for which ultimately no foundation can be given'.[91] Put differently, the masters of suspicion lacked a faculty to enable them to predict that religion would become extinct. In fact, quite the opposite has occurred in recent history.

where might god be?

This entire chapter has engaged with a specifically modern approach to discussing God, Christianity and religion. That approach is resolutely philosophical. All of the philosophers mentioned were German-speaking men. All were educated to an exceptionally high degree. Their conceptual sophistication and literary finesse has amused, disturbed, thrilled and challenged generations of Christians and others. However, it need not be assumed that these educated urbanites proffer the most ideal way to speak of and search for God. What if God is not where philosophers and theologians seek God? What if God is best espied in a slum rather than a university?

As for nineteenth-century secularity and suspicion, one of the greatest challenges it posed for traditional Christian theology was to question whether the Bible is infallibly informative and divinely inspired. The next chapter will grapple with that daunting question, which arose for Christianity as an aftershock of the intellectual revolutions considered in Part II of this book.

part III

aftershocks for traditional theology

6

can the bible be trusted?
modern biblical studies

The Devil can cite Scripture for his purpose.

Shakespeare

The answer to the question posed in the title of this chapter is 'No'. The discoveries of modern biblical studies reveal that the Bible cannot always be relied upon to be accurate, truthful and ethically praiseworthy in all it purports. A persistent dilemma which modern biblical scholarship poses for traditional Christian theology is that the scholarship has the potential to undermine the theology's inclination to regard the Bible's contents as divinely inspired, factually inerrant, morally prescriptive, and literally true. As the Enlightenment unfolded, so too did modern biblical studies. The former spawned the latter. The principal religious consequence of the Enlightenment for Christianity was that 'the figure of Jesus Christ and the vast system of ideas and institutions that had grown around his story as told in the Bible lost much of the political and cultural influence that had built up in Europe during the medieval period.'[1]

This chapter tells one of the more fascinating stories in the history of western civilization – the rise of modern biblical studies. Its purpose is to sketch in broad strokes the genesis of modern research on the Bible, and to consider implications for theology generated by historical investigations of the Bible, particularly during the eighteenth and nineteenth centuries. The chapter is closely related to the following one, which discusses novel ways of interpreting Jesus that emerged once higher biblical criticism reached a well-developed stage in the nineteenth century. Biblical research in the modern age is conventionally designated in two principal forms: higher and lower biblical criticism. Higher criticism probes historical questions concerning a text's place and date of composition; its authorship;

motives for its creation; and whether or not it has been edited after its original compilation. Lower criticism examines the ideas, arguments and themes of any given text, rather than details of its historical context. In both enterprises, the word 'criticism' means 'methodical and rigorous analysis'. This chapter focuses on higher biblical criticism. It is the more fundamental of the two, and determines the feasibility or otherwise of its lower cousin's conclusions.

Studies of the Bible since the Enlightenment need not be viewed as faithless attempts to sabotage Christian beliefs, or as a movement bent on torpedoing individuals' piety. Far from it. Certainly they undercut uncritical views, but they also provide foundations for building more informed understandings. The accumulated findings of modern biblical scholarship have produced a vast bank of new data about ancient Jewish cultures, the life-world of Jesus, and early Christian sympathies. Moreover, as the distinguished Catholic theologian Hans Küng points out, 'Lay people are usually unaware that the scrupulous scholarly work achieved by modern biblical criticism – which in the process has stimulated and used other disciplines (classical philology, Egyptology, Assyriology and so on) –, represented by scrupulous academic work over about 300 years, belongs among the greatest intellectual achievements of the human race.' For Küng, 'The Bible is far and away the most studied book in world literature.'[2] Such is high praise indeed. It is also entirely justified.

> **bibles**   The Bible is conventionally referred to with a capital 'B' when a collection of writings from Genesis to the Revelation of John is designated. A lower case 'b' is used to specify copies of the Bible, as in the expression 'Please hand me that stack of bibles'. The terms 'Scripture' or 'Sacred Scripture' are synonyms for the Bible in Christian circles.

Modern biblical research confronts with insuperable hurdles the view that everything stated in the Bible is both literally and historically descriptive. Historical criticism of the Bible gathered pace steadily throughout the eighteenth century, chiefly in the Protestant university faculties of Europe. Before then, as Hans Frei instructs, western Christian reading of the Bible 'was usually strongly realistic, i.e. at once literal and historical, and not only doctrinal or edifying. The words and the sentences meant what they said, and because they did so they accurately described real events and real truths that were rightly put in those terms and no others.'[3]

Consider, though, a story proposed for belief in the section of the Bible called Joshua. The first 12 chapters of Joshua have the semblance of depicting historical events after the death of Moses. They tell the tale of Joshua, a fearless warrior who is said to have known Moses, leading the Israelites to settle in

---

the bible The English word, 'Bible', derives from the Greek term *biblia* meaning 'books'. The typical Greek word for writings held sacred by ancient Jews is not *biblia* but *graphai* — that is, 'scriptures'. Both 'Bible' and 'Sacred Scriptures' refer to collections of writings venerated by Jews and Christians. There are two principal forms of the Bible: a Jewish collection of texts, and a Christian version that accepts the Jewish texts and adds others that are not contained in the Jewish Scriptures. The latter are arranged into three major groups: (a) the Torah, or Law; (b) the Prophets; and (c) the Writings. Christians usually refer to the Jewish Scriptures as the Old Testament, and to the texts unique to themselves as the New Testament. The latter contains 27 documents, including four Gospels, or proclamations of good news. Understandably, contemporary Jewish scholars often prefer to avoid the expression, 'Old Testament', so as not to give the impression that their Scriptures are obsolete. Terms such as 'the Hebrew Bible' or 'the Tanakh' are employed instead. 'Tanakh' is an acronym of the Hebrew words, *Torah* ('Law'), *Neviim* ('Prophets'), and *Ketuvim* ('Writings'). The Christian Bible alters the progression of sections in the Hebrew Bible so as to place the Prophets just before the opening of the New Testament. The impression is thereby more readily given that the Prophets led the way to Jesus. Biblical texts were composed over a span of more than a thousand years and are records of beliefs that were previously circulated in oral forms. It took Jews and Christians several centuries to agree on what to include in the Bible. A complete list of current contents can be found as early as 382 CE. An agreed list of contents is called the canon of the Bible. The Catholic Church recognizes 73 documents or books in the Bible, while Protestants normally accept 66. In the third century BCE, the Tanakh was translated into Greek — a version known as the Septuagint. The Qur'an frequently mentions and commends the Torah, Israel's major prophets, and Jesus.

Canaan, a territory the Romans later called Palestine. The aboriginal peoples of Canaan included Amorites, Hittites, Canaanites and Jebusites. The tenth chapter of Joshua describes a battle between the Israelites, commanded by Joshua, and the Amorites. The conflict takes place at the city of Gibeon. The chapter aligns the Lord God on the side of the Israelites. At one stage during the fighting, Joshua sought God's help to make the sun stand still in the sky. Extended daylight would allow more time for continued slaughter as the Israelites routed the Amorites. Consequently, so the story goes, 'The sun stopped in mid-heaven, and did not hurry to set for about a whole day' (Joshua 10:13).

Is this account of affairs credible for a contemporary reader? If not, are other biblical narratives open to doubt? The North American writer Gleason Archer adamantly defends a doctrine of biblical inerrancy as inescapably incumbent on Christians. He perceives very well that if the Bible is misleading in historical affairs and in its cosmology, then it can also be doubted in its theological conclusions.[4] Before the eighteenth century, the story of the sun's day-long stasis in the sky over Gibeon was widely accepted as veridical by Jews and Christians alike. Doubt concerning its historical reliability intensifies if it is pondered in the light of modern physics and astronomy.

The ancient Israelites appear to have thought of the sky as a dome above the earth, somewhat like the Millennium Dome in London.[5] It was quite conceivable for them to imagine that God could stop the sun in its tracks as it moved across the surface of the dome. It is now known that what appears to an observer as the sun moving overhead is actually the result of the earth revolving on its axis. Thus, for the sun to stand still, the earth would have to stop rotating. The philosopher B.R. Tilghman lucidly explains the consequences of what would happen were the earth to cease rotating:

> The circumference of the earth at the equator is only slightly less that 25,000 miles. The earth rotates once every 24 hours. This means that any object at the equator has a linear velocity of more than 1,000 miles an hour. If the earth were suddenly to stop rotating the law of inertia tells us that anything not securely tied down would continue in a straight line tangent to the surface of the earth at the original velocity of 1,000 miles an hour. If this happened there would still be bunny rabbits and toad frogs in orbit, not to mention cataclysmic disruptions of the earth's surface. The enormous inertial forces generated by such a sudden halt would have destroyed everything on the planet if not the earth itself.[6]

The point is: there are no bunny rabbits or toads orbiting in space. The fully formed earth has never been known to stop rotating. Had it ever done so, outer space would be littered with all manner of projectiles flung from the earth's surface. The story of Joshua 10 is not historically descriptive in all of its details. It is one of several biblical passages that modern biblical criticism invites readers of the Bible to regard as legendary, fanciful, mythical, or as theological proclamations.

The Enlightenment was part of a slowly evolving yet acute cultural crisis that transformed Christendom into a cluster of secular societies. The move towards a European secular culture that advanced in the eighteenth century has proved decisive and has not been reversed.[7] One of the catalysts causing many people of the eighteenth and nineteenth centuries to weaken the hold of Christianity over their lives was the gradual dissemination of the fruits of higher biblical criticism from the lecture theatres of universities to a far wider public.

Higher biblical criticism is both a richly endowed resource for modern theology and a strong challenge to Augustinian orthodoxy's pre-critical reading of the Bible. Augustine was well aware that many passages of the Bible are either cast in figurative terms or may be interpreted allegorically. When the besotted women of the Song of Solomon describes the bearing of the man of her dreams as 'like Lebanon, choice as cedars' (Song, 5:15b), we can be sure that Augustine was not tempted for a moment to imagine that the man looked like a tree of the genus *Cedrus libani*. However, Augustine did conclude that cosmic history as portrayed in the Bible, stemming from a primordial creation of the world to a cataclysmic divine judgement at the end of time, specifies what actually happened in the past and can be expected to transpire in the future. Augustine's doctrine of the Fall, like Humpty-Dumpty, if construed literally, has itself fallen from favour among many modern historically minded biblical critics. To appreciate why invites a consideration of the genesis and development of higher criticism.

The story of modern biblical studies is the tale of a loss of trust. It narrates a gradual erosion of confidence in the truth of the Bible. In 1600, most European Christians took for granted that the Bible is true and blameless. Two hundred years later, many of them were wondering which passages of the Bible could be believed, and which are deceptive or false. Moreover, for several centuries the Bible has been relied upon as a peerless fountainhead of ethical norms. Historically critical studies of its pages have alerted contemporary readers to morally repulsive features such as the encouragement it gives people to hurt, maim and slay others. The North American theologian Walter Fink draws on the work of the biblical scholar Raymund Schwager to awaken his readers to grisly biblical images of a violent Godhead. He records that,

> Raymund Schwager points out that there are six hundred passages of explicit violence in the Hebrew Bible, one thousand verses where God's own violent actions of punishment are described, a hundred passages where Yahweh expressly commands others to kill people, and several stories where God irrationally kills or tries to kill for no apparent reason (for example, Exod. 4:24–26). Violence, Schwager concludes, is easily the most often mentioned activity in the Bible.[8]

The text of Deuteronomy contains several examples of biblical bloodlust. For instance, the ensuing passage depicts Moses addressing the Israelites:

> When the LORD your God brings you into the land that you are about to enter and occupy, and he clears away many nations before you – the Hittites, the Girgashites, the Amorites, the Canaanites, the Perizzites, the Hivites, and the Jebusites, seven nations mightier and more numerous than you – and when the LORD your God gives them over to you and you defeat them, then you must utterly destroy them. Make no covenant with them and show them no mercy. (Deut. 7:1–3)

Similar scenarios can be read in Numbers 21:1–3; Deuteronomy 2:30–35; Joshua 6:17–21; and Joshua 10:28: 'Joshua took Makkedah on that day, and struck it and its king with the edge of the sword; he utterly destroyed every person in it; he left no one remaining. And he did to the king of Makkedah as he had done to the king of Jericho.' The text of Joshua informs us that every living person and animal was put to the sword in Jericho by Joshua's army: 'both men and women, young and old, oxen, sheep, and donkeys' (6:21).

A dreadful corollary of the sprees of violence ascribed to the ancient Israelites is that violence was regularly turned against the people of their tradition in subsequent historical happenings from the Crusades to the Holocaust.[9] A dire consequence of insisting that passages describing divinely planned Israelite victories in battle are literally true is that the baneful human proclivity to kill is anthropomorphically transferred on to God. Put differently, God is depicted as if God were a sword-wielding foot soldier. To deny the literal truthfulness of the passages ascribing violence to God is to speak in the wake of higher biblical criticism.

During the nineteenth century, what is now called modern historical criticism of the Bible was then called higher criticism. A historically critical method of interpreting the Bible (a) regards biblical texts as human products; (b) analyses the texts in the languages in which they were originally penned; (c) examines them within their historical contexts; (d) accepts the new scientific worldview that emerged in the seventeenth century; (e) refuses to be constrained by

> **the study of words**   In modern linguistics, *philology* involves the academic study of words, *phonology* explores the sounds of words, *morphology* examines the forms of words, *lexicology* probes the meanings of words, and *syntax* looks at the relationships between words.

ecclesiastical authorities; and (f) is informed by the findings of modern philology, phonology, morphology, lexicology, and syntax.

The Bible, by the way, is often mistakenly described as a book. In fact, it was first composed well before books were ever devised. As indicated above, the English word 'Bible' comes from the Greek term *biblia*, meaning 'books' or 'scrolls'. The original biblical texts were written on long scrolls forming a single seamless text. During the first century BCE, codices were invented. A codex is a collection of texts written on separate sheets. The modern book was devised after the codex had been used extensively in the ancient Middle East. In sum, the Bible was not originally a book in the sense of pages stitched or glued together and bound between two covers. What is now designated the Bible was composed by several authors, at different times, and in diverse places. In this it differs noticeably from the Qur'an. The Book (or Scroll) of Kings was written down as the eighth century BCE gave way to the seventh. By contrast, the Book of Chronicles was composed in the fifth or fourth century BCE.[10] Contemporary authors continue to refer to the major subdivisions of the Bible as books, but one must be on guard not to view the Bible anachronistically as if it was originally devised as a book in a modern sense. When discussing, for example, what is now called the Book of Judges, one is really referring to a text that was at first a scroll. Most of the Bible is written in Hebrew. English translations of the Bible normally translate the Hebrew word *sefer*, as book, when, more properly, it means 'text, letter, or scroll'.[11]

From beginning to end, the Bible is a miscellany of wonders: God smites the Egyptians; Moses divides the waters; Elijah ascends into heaven; Paul is entranced in a blinding vision; Jesus walks on water and is raised from death. All of the miracles, signs and wonders recorded in the Bible were recounted by people who – to state the obvious – knew nothing of Copernican astronomy or Newtonian mechanics. They lived in exactly the same world as we do, although a long time before us. They understood the world's workings in a way that readily allowed for miracles and divine interventions in daily human affairs. The emergence of modern historically critical readings of the Bible brought with it an increasing tendency for theologians and philosophers in Europe to interpret the wondrous events described in the Bible as fictive rather than factual.

the birth and growth of modern biblical studies

When considering modern biblical research, it is important not to conclude that the past three centuries were the only time the Bible was studied in sophisticated ways. Students of theology in medieval universities were very well acquainted with the Bible and with conflicting interpretations of specific passages.

There is no agreement today as to how or when higher biblical criticism originated. Nonetheless, a number of people and activities contributed to its genesis and development. In the fourteenth century ancient Greek texts began to be studied in Europe in their original language. The activity of collecting Greek manuscripts evolved into the discipline of modern textual criticism. Attention to Greek terminology created the discipline of historical philology – trying to determine the meaning of words in their original historical context. In 1516, Erasmus published the New Testament in Greek. In one sense, all modern biblical criticism derives from that publication.

Some scholars insist that higher criticism emerged from the biblical writings of Luther and Calvin in the sixteenth century. Others argue that it arose from seventeenth-century legal and humanist studies in Europe. Whatever the case, it is at least clear that stimuli for a specifically modern critical study of the Bible surfaced at different times and in a variety of localities around Europe. The Dutch lawyer and humanist Hugo Grotius (1583–1645) was a case in point. He dismissed ancient Jewish legal scriptures as archaic. Another example is represented by the Dutch philosopher Benedict Spinoza (1632–1677). He highlighted contradictions in the Old Testament and insisted that biblical texts should be studied as historical documents without regard for any putative divine inspiration. A third stimulus arose in France with the Catholic priest Richard Simon (1638–1712). He concluded that the books of the Old Testament we produced by scribal schools, and not by Moses as the Church taught.

The Protestant Reformers of the sixteenth century tended to react strongly against medieval techniques for biblical interpretation, and thereby pointed in the direction of a distinctively modern rather than a medieval method for deciphering the Bible. In starkest outline, medieval exegesis, or the process of examining a text to ascertain what its initial readers would have understood it to mean, distinguished between four senses of Scripture: (1) the historical or literal; (2) the allegorical or Christological; (3) the tropological, or moral or anthropological; and (4) the anagogical or eschatological. These four senses can be illustrated by referring to the concrete example of the city of Jerusalem. Literally understood, Jerusalem is a city in the former Roman province of Palestine. Allegorically, Jerusalem refers to the Church of the New Jerusalem. Tropologically, Jerusalem stands for the very soul of humanity. And anagogically, or eschatologically construed, Jerusalem represents a celestial, heavenly city. Crucially, while the literal sense of Scripture was certainly regarded as significant by medieval theologians, the three other senses were viewed as more essential for theology as well as religious belief and practice.

With Luther such priorities were radically reversed. Probably the single greatest contribution of Luther and his co-Reformers to biblical interpretation was his emphatic championing of the plain meaning of Scripture.[12] Luther attacked unbridled allegorizing and insisted upon the fundamental importance of the historical background of biblical works and the literal sense of texts. As he says, 'The Holy Spirit is the plainest writer and speaker in heaven and earth and therefore his words cannot have more than one, and that the very simplest sense, which we call the literal, ordinary, natural sense.'[13] John Calvin was even less in favour than Luther of allegorical construals of biblical passages: 'Compared with Martin Luther's, Calvin's approach to the Gospels reveals a striking hardening of insistence upon their literal truth. There is very little room left for any symbolic or spiritual interpretation.'[14]

Vitally, then, once Protestant exegetes began to interpret Scripture more literally, Catholic scholars were challenged to follow in kind. And so it transpired that both Protestants and Catholics downgraded the former medieval predilection for allegorical exegesis. Luther was clear that no violence should be exerted on what he called the words of God. In other terms, he taught that biblical texts should be understood in their straightforward grammatical and literal sense, unless the texts' contexts plainly forbid. Luther was convinced that all heresies arise from neglecting the so-called simple words of Scripture. The following expressions are paraphrases of biblical teachings. One can easily imagine how different Christian Churches would be today were Luther's perspective of taking seriously the plain meaning of simple words genuinely taken to heart: 'let the dead bury their dead'; 'call no man father'; 'there is neither male nor female, Greek nor Jew, slave nor master'; 'It is easier for a camel to go through the eye of a needle than for a rich man to enter the kingdom of God'; 'love your enemies and pray for those who abuse you'. The plain sense indeed!

Anyone familiar with the work of the medieval theologian Thomas Aquinas will recognize immediately that Luther, in stressing the primary importance of the literal sense was not being purely innovatory. Aquinas did the same. Nevertheless, there is a crucial difference between Luther on one side, and Aquinas on the other coupled with a majority of ancient exegetes. For the latter group, Scripture is not the only yardstick for determining the essentials of Christian faith. It is accompanied by ecclesiastical authority and tradition. Luther is an innovator in that he insists that Scripture can stand alone as a yardstick for measuring Christian faith. For Luther, the Bible is the unrivalled regulator of faith. So far as he was concerned, the Bible authenticates itself. Through it and in it God speaks to the human heart.

Luther's principle of *sola scriptura*, Scripture alone, would prove to be a major problem, if not an Achilles heel, for later modern Protestant theology. While there had been plenty of earnest and erudite study of the Bible before the advent of modernity, what distinguishes the birth of modern historical criticism in the early stages of the Enlightenment, especially in the early eighteenth century, is the rejection of the assumption that there is a direct continuity between the Bible and Christian doctrine. As Samuel Powell has noticed, during the early Enlightenment 'assumptions about revelation and inspiration and miracle and prophecy were flung aside by many as superstitious relics of an incomprehensible past'.[15] Yet without those assumptions the doctrine of the Trinity cannot be established. If the Bible is examined as a historical document like any other, rather than a cipher for God's revelation, it soon becomes clear that there is no Trinitarian doctrine in the Bible. The Bible often mentions a Father, Son and Spirit, but does not consistently or precisely explain the relations between the three. For those Protestants who jettisoned the Catholic notion of an inspired authoritative interpreting tradition in favour of the Bible alone, Christian Trinitarian doctrine became all the more difficult to establish in relation to the Bible. The doctrine of the Trinity is a product of the fourth and fifth centuries BCE. Catholics and the Orthodox can defend it because they do not rely exclusively on the Bible in their formulation of doctrines.

The sixteenth century was a crucial phase in the history of the emergence of modern biblical criticism. In Europe, from the fourth to the sixteenth centuries, philosophy and science were engaged in the service of Christianity. Scientific and philosophical wisdom enjoyed a harmonious coalescence with Christian doctrine. Most Christian thinkers of the period subscribed to the scientific and philosophical world-views of Plato and Aristotle. The profound influence of Greek thought on western culture could hardly be exaggerated. Greek thought in philosophy, literature, art and architecture set standards for the western world for over two thousand years.[16]

The harmony between Greek thought and Christian doctrine that had continued for over a thousand years was disturbed during the sixteenth and seventeenth centuries by the emergence of modern empirical science. By the seventeenth century, for the first time 'educated Europeans began to believe – not all of them, but many – that by exercising their reason alone, without appeal to religious revelation, they could penetrate to the ultimate nature of things.'[17] Faith would now have to coexist with a new type of science. The emergence of modern science fueled a transition from faith reigning alone as an authoritative source for knowledge, to faith coupled with secular reason. For Raymond Martin, the arrival of science and the transition to dual sources of authority represented 'the most momentous intellectual change in the history of Western civilization'.[18] Don Cupitt concurs and goes further: 'the huge knowledge explosion that began in the West with the Revival of Learning and the take-off of early modern science is coming to look like the single greatest event in the whole of known human history'.[19]

With both science and Christianity offering divergent interpretations of reality, sooner or later they were bound to clash. A host of names such as Copernicus, Galileo and Kepler are tied to a modern scientific movement that disabused human beings who were aware of it of the age-old belief that the earth is the universe's centre. With the modern Copernican idea that the earth revolves around the sun, it became more difficult for humans to imagine themselves as central to the cosmos. Giordano Bruno (1548–1600) went further and taught that it is meaningless to speak of a cosmic centre since the universe projects from every point to infinity. For his views, he was burnt at the stake in Rome in 1600. From his tragic death until now, a string of scientific accomplishments have unseated biblical narratives as culturally respected accounts of the origins of the world and its animals. By the beginning of the twentieth century, 'scientific challenges to Christianity had provided the basic framework for a secular alternative not only to Christianity but also to religious belief altogether'.[20]

biblical criticism and religious scepticism

The word 'criticism' comes from the Greek term *krino*, meaning 'to distinguish', 'to separate', to judge', 'to decide', or 'to choose'. During the Renaissance, several biblical manuscripts were collected and compared by Christian scholars. The comparison revealed divergent manuscripts of the same biblical narratives. Modern biblical criticism was born in the attempt to ascertain which texts were more reliable. Once the more accurate manuscripts were ascertained, it soon became apparent that they did not always provide evidence for post-biblical theological doctrines such as those concerning the Trinity. When Erasmus published his edition of the Greek New Testament, he was able to intimate that texts previously used to justify a doctrine of the Trinity are absent from the earliest recorded manuscripts of the New Testament. Such is but one illustration of how biblical criticism can evoke religious scepticism.

One of the first and greatest modern biblical critics was the Calvinist Isaac La Peyrère (1605–1665). His two most significant works were *Du Rappel des Juifs* ('Of the Reminder of the Jews') and *Prae-Adamitae* ('People before Adam'). La Peyrère was one of the first biblical commentators to decide that Moses did not write the first five scrolls of the Bible. He also insisted that human beings existed before Adam and that he and his contemporaries did not posses an accurate text of the Bible.[21] The religious scepticism typified by La Peyrère is but one instance of a much broader growth of philosophical scepticism in the seventeenth century that was emboldened by the revival of Greek Pyrrhonian scepticism in Europe during the sixteenth century. Philosophically understood, scepticism was of two kinds in the Hellenistic period – academic and Pyrrhonian (from the legendary figure Pyrrho of Elis, *c.* 360–275 BCE). The first argued that no knowledge is possible. The second held that 'there was insufficient and inadequate evidence to determine if any knowledge was possible, and hence that one ought to suspend judgements on all questions concerning knowledge.'[22] Pyrrhonian scepticism was virtually unknown in the west during the Middle Ages and was only rediscovered there in the late fifteenth century and enjoyed a highly influential revival in the course of the sixteenth and seventeenth centuries. One of its more noteworthy proponents was Spinoza.

spinoza   Benedict Spinoza brought to the study of the Bible a sophisticated knowledge of the scientific advances and philosophical debates of the seventeenth century. He was one of the first major modern thinkers to debunk the idea that the Bible is God's revelation to human beings. It is a striking irony of history that he was inspired in his labours by two religions – Judaism and Christianity. Or, rather, he was moved to argue that the Bible is a thoroughly human product because of the way the Church ill-treated his Jewish parents, and the manner in which a synagogue's leadership excoriated him when he was a young Jew.

Spinoza is a giant in the history of modern biblical criticism and an inspiration to several major western philosophers who worked in his wake. He was born in Amsterdam on 24 November 1632, during the Thirty Years' War of religion. It would be expecting far too much to imagine that an intelligent young man like Spinoza could view Christianity benignly when he knew that rival Christian groups of his day were tearing each other apart in the Thirty Years' War.

Spinoza's parents were Jewish and Portuguese. In 1492, before he was born, devout Jews were expelled from Spain. Many of them settled in Portugal. In 1497, practising Portuguese Jews were ordered to choose between converting to Catholicism, and suffering banishment from the land. Some of the Jews who remained in Spain and Portugal became Catholics under duress. Such converted Jews were publicly designated as *conversos* (converts). A good number of them publicly worshipped as Catholics while privately practising Jewish religious customs. The Spanish Inquisition set itself the task of rooting out the latter group, who were labelled *marranos* – a Spanish word for 'pigs'.

Spinoza's parents were *marranos*. They knew they could be put to death by the Inquisition were they ever discovered worshipping covertly as Jews. So they decided to abandon the Iberian peninsula for a new life in Amsterdam. Jews who fled Portugal and Spain formed the Sephardim. The Ashkenazim involved Jews of northern Europe. Sephardic Jews established a free Jewish community in the northern Netherlands from the beginnings of the seventeenth century.[23]

Most of the Jews Spinoza associated with in Amsterdam were *marranos*. He was known in their community as Baruch de Espinoza. While a boy he received a conventional Jewish education that involved studying Hebrew and Hebrew texts of the Bible, the Talmud (a collection mostly of Jewish ceremonial and civil law), Jewish philosophy, and more secular subjects such as mathematics, physics and astronomy. He eventually acquired an intimate familiarity with the entire Bible.

By the time of his early twenties, Spinoza was beset by religious doubts and attracted to what were, for his synagogue, horrendous heresies. His biblical studies led him to conclude that the Bible is replete with inconsistencies and contradictions. He conceded that the ordinances of the Torah came from human beings rather than God. In his view, it would therefore be an irrational folly to regard them as anything more than merely arbitrary and historically limited utterances. For Spinoza, God did not formulate laws in a distant past. He decided that universal and immutable laws of nature are inherent in the universe itself. Thus, according to the young Spinoza, God is an idea that can be equated with the universe itself; 'this deity was not in his view a unique and separate person existing outside the world and the nature he had created.'[24]

Spinoza was expelled from Amsterdam's synagogue with a sentence of excommunication delivered on 27 July 1616. Scholars do not agree on the exact reason for his excommunication. Whatever the motive, his co-religionists wanted to curse him.[25]

As the son of *marrano* parents, Spinoza was exposed to the passions of two different religions. Consequently, it would have been easy for him to regard them both as historically relative and perspectival. The philosopher Yirmiyahu Yovel offers the pregnant observation that 'Spinoza's break with both Judaism and Christianity was a harbinger of the modern era.'[26] He credits Spinoza with elaborating a systematic philosophy of immanence according to which there is no reality apart from historical this-worldly reality. In his own words:

> Baruch Spinoza (1632–1677) is a major figure in Western intellectual history, but his role is not always fully recognized. His philosophical revolution anticipated major trends in European modernization, including secularization, biblical criticism, the rise of natural science, the Enlightenment, and the liberal-democratic state. Above all he put forward a radically new philosophical principle that I call the philosophy of immanence. It views this-worldly reality as all there is, as the only actual being and the sole source of ethical value. God himself is identical with the totality of nature, and God's decrees are written not in the Bible but in the laws of nature and reason.[27]

Soon after he was excommunicated, Spinoza adopted Benedict as his first name. After his father died when he was 22, he earned his living working as a vendor of tropical fruits. Because he could read Latin, he was able to familiarize himself with the writings of Christian scholars in addition to his acquaintance with Hebrew literature.

Spinoza's significance for the evolution of modern biblical studies stems from his new way of viewing biblical texts that was born in his experience of suffering at the hands of religious zealots. Learning from his parents' traumas under Portuguese Catholicism, and from his own tension with the leaders of his synagogue, he became forcefully aware of the destructive forces attending human religions. He was alive to the essential intrication of religion with power. Living in Amsterdam, where the government was a theocracy heavily directed by Calvinists, he could see all too plainly that politics and theology can be intricately linked.

For Spinoza, the best way to understand the way a religion can support and control a political system is to scrutinize the Scriptures of the religion in question. Since Amsterdam's political life was dominated by Calvinism, he turned his attention to a fervid study of the Bible. The fruits of his labours appeared in 1670 with the publication of his book *Tractatus Theologico-Politicus* ('A Theological–Political Treatise'). The *Tractatus*, together with a later work, *Ethics* (1677), are Spinoza's most significant publications.

In the *Tractatus*, Spinoza defends freedom of belief, speech and thought. In short, he advances a case for a liberal democracy. In the second chapter of the book, Spinoza examines the writings of the biblical prophets. He concludes that their discourses are the fruit of a heightened imagination rather than forms of knowledge.

The *Tractatus* involves an even more daring innovation in the analysis or criticism of the Bible, which is this: Spinoza regards the Bible as a record of human history and not of God's history. He studies it like any other historical text – that is, in terms of its peculiar historical context. The upshot of his strategy is the conclusion that with the Bible, 'One is dealing not with a description of God's intervention in human affairs but one of many case histories of people employing religion for human purposes in human affairs.'[28] For J. Samuel Preus, 'The fact that we are not governed by interpreters of divine law, nor intellectually answerable to alleged divine revelations, is a major aspect of modern liberty. For this we are hugely indebted to writers of the seventeenth century, above all to the Jewish philosopher Benedict Spinoza.'[29]

Because Spinoza regarded the laws of nature as universal and immutable, he denied that divinely engineered miracles ever occur. And he dismisses the story of Joshua 10, cited in the early stages of this chapter: 'Are we, forsooth, bound to believe that Joshua the soldier was a learned astronomer?'; 'Joshua was ignorant of the true cause of the lengthened day.'[30]

Later in the *Tractatus*, Spinoza spells out his method for biblical criticism: 'The universal rule, then, in interpreting Scripture is to accept nothing as an authoritative statement which we do not perceive very clearly when we examine it in the light of its history.'[31] When Spinoza was writing this statement, both Judaism and Christianity taught that Moses wrote the Pentateuch – that is, the first five books of the Bible, including Deuteronomy. Upon examining Deuteronomy, Spinoza realized that it describes Moses' death in detail; draws attention to a thirty-day period of mourning after his death; and talks about all the prophets who came after Moses. Obviously, Moses could not possibly have written about himself in such detail following his own death. Hence Spinoza's honest conclusion: 'Such testimony cannot have been given of Moses by himself, or by any who immediately succeeded him, but it must come from someone who lived centuries afterwards, especially as the historian speaks of past times.'[32]

Spinoza was one of the first major philosophers in Europe to deny the possibility of miracles and prophecy. Not insignificantly he was born in exactly the same year as John Locke and became a fervid champion of the powers of human reason to investigate reality. He concluded that a great deal of religious faith in his day was simply a mixture of prejudices and credulities.

Spinoza's criticisms of the Bible were joined by those of the French philosopher Pierre Bayle (1647–1706), who strenuously argued that intellectuals must have complete freedom of thought and speech in intellectual contexts. He concluded that it is impossible to make rational and scientific sense out of Jewish and Christian Scriptures. He thought that reason and biblical doctrine were opposed. For instance, whereas reason teaches, for him, that nothing comes from nothing, the Bible instructs that because of God's power the world issued from nothing.

Apart from Spinoza and Bayle, yet another component of the development of modern biblical studies is represented by deists such as Edward Lord Herbert of Cherbury (1583–1648), John Toland (1670–1720) and Anthony Collins (1670–1729). Their common conviction, as deists, was that whatever can be known or affirmed in religious discourse can only be known on the basis of reason. Consequently, they denied the validity of religious statements that were based on either revelation or church teaching. They believed in God, but denied that God intervenes in the world. So they discountenanced the veracity of miracles and prophecies fulfilled.

Returning to Spinoza, it was he who posed the most serious threat to all traditional biblical interpretation preceding the seventeenth- to eighteenth-century era of critical rationalism. He declared very forcefully that Scripture should be studied for its historical interest alone, since it could, at best, merely confirm the insights that reason had already gained by means of philosophy.

Crucially, Spinoza made a distinction in biblical criticism that had not been either clearly made or systematically developed before him. He differentiated between the meaning of a biblical passage and its truth. For Spinoza, the task of the biblical interpreter is to pinpoint the meaning of a text, and not to decide upon its veracity.[33] In terms of the history of biblical studies, such a distinction is entirely modern.

The past three hundred years of historically critical musings over the Bible have all been conducted under the shadow of the great Spinoza. His method for interpreting biblical texts has lost none of its perspicacity. The method involves three steps. First, the original language of a text needs to be examined. Second, manifold themes in the Bible need to be listed, in an attempt to espy what the Bible is seeking to communicate. And third, the historical circumstances in which a biblical passage was generated need to be investigated in association with a consideration of how those passages were translated, received or canonized at later stages.[34]

Spinoza is a peculiarly modern thinker because he insists that reason must exercise control over the interpretation of Scripture, rather than authoritative religious traditions, whether Jewish or Christian. To give an example of reason controlling exegesis one need only turn to the Bible's different stories about the place whence Jesus came. According to Luke's Gospel, Jesus' parents Mary and Joseph live in Nazareth in Galilee. For Matthew's Gospel, they live in Bethlehem, in Judea. Hence, 'if we choose to grant credibility to one, it comes at a cost to the other: both cannot be true'.[35]

modern methods for biblical interpretation

Today, it is possible to differentiate at least sixteen major and interrelated interpretative approaches to the Bible. And each of these methods is tied to one or other of three major understandings of the locus of meaning. Some methods are anchored to the idea that meaning rests with the author; others proceed from the presupposition of a text-centred understanding of meaning; while a third category is tied to the belief that meaning lies with the reader. Several of the approaches are conventionally labelled with the term 'criticisim' ('disciplined analysis'), as in Form Criticism, Source Criticism and Redaction Criticism. Expressed schematically the methods can be grouped as in the box.

There is no reason why different views of the primary locus of meaning and their attendant methods need to be seen as mutually exclusive and contradictory approaches. On the contrary, fusing the three major views can furnish a much richer, integrated grasp of meaning than any one approach taken in isolation. As W. Randolf Tate observes, 'meaning results from a conversation between the world of the text and the world of the reader, a conversation informed by the world of the author.'[36]

Granting as much, it is now possible to offer brief staccato notes about each of the sixteen interpretative methods listed in the box. In starkest outline, Source Criticism was developed in the nineteenth century and may be defined as that discipline which seeks to identify the sources, especially the written sources that were relied upon when biblical texts were written. Form Criticism developed later, in Germany, shortly after the First World War. It attempts to identify biblical traditions as they were transmitted orally, before they received a final written form. Redaction Criticism studies the ways the significance of the final product of a text is altered by the inclusion of additional individual components by an editor or redactor. It also seeks to decipher the theological motives guiding a particular author's decision to include or exclude specific passages. Clearly, source, form and redaction criticisms are all concerned with texts. Even so, they remain fundamentally driven to locate meaning in terms of authorial intention because of their ambition to locate *primal* texts, reflecting the minds and life-settings of original authors, in contradistinction to the Church's later use of texts. Historical Criticism provides a basis for other types of interpretation in trying to specify the literal sense of a text, or what an author literally meant to say. It requires a knowledge of ancient languages and customs. Canonical Criticism differs from source, form and redaction criticism, in that it does not analyse passages solely in terms of their context within a particular book, but in relation to other canonical writings, indeed to the Bible as a whole. Rhetorical Criticism investigates the communicative techniques authors use to enhance the effect of their writings on readers.

Meaning with author	Source Criticism
	Form Criticism
	Redaction Criticism
	Historical Criticism
	Canonical Criticism
	Rhetorical Criticism
Meaning with text	New Criticism
	Literary Criticism
	Textual Criticism
	Formal Criticism
	Structuralism
	Social Criticism
Meaning with reader	Reader-Response Criticism
	Narrative Criticism
	(meaning also with author)
	Advocacy Criticism
	Deconstructive Criticism
	(meaning also with text)

During the 1950s, the predominance of author-centred approaches to meaning began to be displaced, or complemented, by a more pronounced concentration on the text as it now stands in its own integrity. In 1954, Warren Wimsatt and Monroe Beardsley published a now famous article titled 'The Intentional Fallacy' in which they raised the suspicion that a text is not a clear mirror of an author's mind. Their work reflects a trend in the theory of meaning that is discernible in the 1940s and 1950s, called New Criticism.[37] As an interpretative method New Criticism discountenances an author's intentions and argues that a text in itself is a sufficient basis for the location of literary meaning. Literary Criticism dates from the later twentieth century and analyses biblical texts as literary creations. It relies on insights from contemporary literary theory. Textual Criticism examines the variety of manuscripts of biblical books and compares diverse copies of the same text. There are no extant and complete original manuscripts of any of the works of the New Testament. So textual criticism has the task of working out the significance of differences between copies. Formal Criticism considers biblical passages in the light of their wider context of a complete literary work in which they appear. As a method, it is unconcerned with whether a passage describes accurately a particular political or historical state of affairs, but argues instead that its meaning is primarily decipherable in virtue of its place in a larger text. Structuralism locates meaning in the underlying patterns or structure of language, while Social Criticism scrutinizes a text as the reflection of a far larger social situation. It views a text as a window on to a wider world, so to speak.

Reader-Response Criticism as its very name suggests, is concerned with the way meaning arises when a reader reacts to a text. Narrative Criticism analyses texts in their functions as comprehensive stories. Advocacy Criticism appropriates biblical texts to challenge current religious or ecclesiastical practices. Finally, Deconstructive Criticism become prominent in the 1980s and argues that there is not fixed anchoring point from which an interpreter can ascertain an assured meaning in a text.

modern scholarship versus traditional dogma

The findings of three hundred years of modern biblical criticism have impelled some theologians to call for a radical reinterpretation or abandonment of dogmas that were once regarded as indispensable and unassailable by Christians. To illustrate this call, I shall now discuss modern biblical scholarship in relation to dogmas concerning sacraments, papal authority and the birth of Jesus Christ from a virginal mother.

Hans Küng illustrates very well a difficulty that modern biblical studies can present to theologians. As a Catholic theologian, he is fully aware that according to a binding dogmatic tradition his Church has solemnly taught that there are seven sacraments: baptism, confirmation, penance, the Eucharist, marriage, holy orders, and the anointing of the sick. Küng is also entirely cognizant that many biblical scholars deny that the Bible teaches that there are seven sacraments.

The Catholic Church today still teaches that Jesus Christ instituted the seven sacraments, and it does so in continuity with three councils of bishops meeting respectively in Lyon, 1274; Florence, 1439; and Trent, 1547.[38] In view of which, Küng and his Catholic colleagues are faced with a decision: either they ignore the conclusions of higher biblical criticism, and continue to teach that Jesus began the practice of celebrating seven sacraments, or they challenge the position of Trent and conclude that modern research tends to indicate that there is no basis in the Bible for regarding all seven rituals as sacraments. Küng follows the latter path. He accepts that baptism and the Eucharist are evident as independent sacramental actions in the Bible, but goes on to conclude that:

- There is no indication of any independent sacrament of confirmation, as can be shown precisely from Acts 8.14ff and 19:1ff.
- There is no basis for Christ's having personally instituted an anointing of the sick on the strength of James 5:14ff (even though a connection is made to Mark 6:13 and 16:17–18).
- There are no adequate references to a sacrament of 'holy orders,' serving as a condition for and investiture in the functions of church leadership (cf. 1 Tim 4:14, 5:12; and 2 Tim 1:6, 2:2).
- And least of all is there any reference to a sacrament of matrimony, much as Eph 5:21–33 speaks of the great mystery (*sacramentum* in the Vulgate), and although Jesus, according to Mark 10:2–12, forbids divorce.[39]

Another major Catholic dogma that is challenged by higher biblical criticism is the idea that the papacy stems from Jesus. *The Catechism of the Catholic Church* teaches that

The Lord Jesus endowed his community with a structure that will remain until the Kingdom is fully achieved. Before all else is the choice of the Twelve with Peter as their head. Representing the Twelve tribes of Israel, they are the foundation stones of the new Jerusalem. The Twelve and the other disciples share in Christ's mission and his power, but also in his lot. By all his actions, Christ prepares his Church.[40]

For the leaders and many believers of the Catholic Church today, the Pope, or Bishop of Rome, has inherited the mantle of authority bequeathed to him by Jesus Christ. In their view, the entire edifice of the Catholic Church, including the office of the papacy, stems from the will of Jesus Christ. It may well be the case, though, that the Catholic Church's teachings regarding its origins constitute a 'foundation myth'. That is, they may well convey a traditional wisdom, but they are not literally descriptive of the Church's actual historical genesis. For the Catholic theologian James P. Mackey, 'neither Jesus nor his earliest followers can be literally credited with the "foundation myth" currently taught by the Catholic Church.'[41]

The idea that Jesus wished to establish the Church is beset with at least four prominent difficulties generated by modern historical research. First, Jesus was a Galilean Jew and remained as such throughout his life. There are no textual sources indicating that he abandoned Jewish Temple-dominated religious customs. Second, there are several passages in the Christian Scriptures indicating that Jesus expected an imminent end to the world. If that is the case, then it is difficult to accept that he aimed to build a society to last over time for several generations. In the third place, the Christian Scriptures indicate that after Jesus' death, his disciples were exceptionally confused as to what they ought to do. As Keith Ward perceives,

> On two major, and connected, issues the apostles were totally unclear. First, they did not know whether to preach to the Gentiles or not. Second, they did not know whether they should keep Torah or not.
>
> It took Peter a threefold vision to bring him to accept that he could even speak to Gentiles, let alone preach to them.[42] The mission to the Gentiles was obviously not clearly commanded by Jesus himself, or Peter would have needed no persuasion.[43]

Fourth, and very significantly, Jesus-enthusiasts or proto-Christians were finally expelled from synagogues in Palestine in the final decades of the first century CE.[44] Before then, what are now recognizable as Christianity and rabbinic Judaism had not become clearly distinguishable and irredeemably antithetical entities.

There is no evidence that Jesus was intentionally motivated to establish a Gentile religion such as Christianity. He was a devotee of one of the several forms of Judaism prevalent in Palestine in the late Second Temple period – that is, before the year 70 CE. He may well have wished to revive or reform his version of Yahweh-faith, but in the light of modern biblical research it is taxing if not impossible to establish that he wished to abjure the religion of his ancestors.

Modern biblical analysis also qualifies confident assertions that Jesus was born of a virginal mother. For most of Christianity's history, the mother of Jesus has been venerated as a perpetual virgin. As long-standing as it may be, the dogma of the virgin birth is not only peripheral to Christian faith, it is not even specifically Christian. Ancient mythologies are replete with stories of the virginal births of Gods, pharaohs, and emperors. In the Hebrew Bible, the seventh chapter of the prophet Isaiah (eighth century BCE) contains a verse that declares: 'Look, the young women is with child and shall bear a son, and shall name him Immanuel.' In the Christian Bible, the Gospel According to Matthew quotes exactly the same verse when talking about the birth of Jesus (Matt. 1:23). In the Hebrew of Isaiah, *a young woman* is with child. Matthew translates the Hebrew term for 'young woman', *almah*, with the Greek word *parthenos*, or 'virgin'. The Septuagint also translates *almah* as *parthenos*. It may well be the case that the long tradition of venerating Jesus' mother as a perpertual virgin – that is, as a women who remained a virgin, before, during and after Jesus' birth – rests on a mistranslation of ancient terminology.[45]

fundamentalism

Nineteenth-century dismissals of dogma bred two significant Christian ripostes – a new dogma of papal infallibility among Catholics (pronounced at the first Vatican Council in 1780); and biblical fundamentalism among Protestants. Fundamentalism can be found among Catholics as well. The term 'fundamentalism' derives from an early-twentieth-century publication, *The Fundamentals*, which was written between 1910 and 1915.[46] *The Fundamentals* were a series of a dozen pamphlets produced by Protestant theologians in North America who found modern science, philosophy and biblical criticism intensely uncongenial to their faith. The publication of the pamphlets was financed by two Californian oilmen, Lyman and Milton Stewart. Between 1910 and 1915, 3 million copies of the pamphlets were sold.[47] The fundamentals involved five core doctrines: (a) that Scripture is divinely inspired and is therefore the literal, revealed word of God; (b) that Jesus Christ was literally and miraculously born of a virgin. The manner of his birth confirms his divine nature; (c) that Jesus Christ saved humanity by shedding his blood on the cross; (d) that the physical bodily resurrection of Jesus from death is assured, as is the accuracy of traditions reporting an empty tomb after Jesus' death and the appearance of Jesus to his disciples following his resurrection; and (e) that there will be a Second Coming of Jesus into the world on a Day of Judgement. None of the fundamentals can be confirmed historically or empirically.[48]

The doctrines of papal infallibility and biblical inerrancy, represented respectively by the First Vatican Council and *The Fundamentals*, are openly reactionary in the sense that they respond to new thought and historical research by seeking to inoculate religious doubt with massive doses of certainty. They are both arguments from authority. The pope and his council declare the pope to be infallible. And the fundamentalists pronounce that the Bible is without error. Declaration, however, is not demonstration. And proclamation is not apodictic elucidation.

The basic flaw of fundamentalist Christian and religious thought is its mistaken assumption that an orthodox version of Christian faith emerged among the followers of Jesus, and needs to be defended today against modern biblical critics. In fact, the first four centuries of Christianity's history were a maelstrom of controversy in which rival factions vied for the appellation 'orthodox'. The word 'orthodoxy' means 'correct teaching'. 'Heresy' means 'choice', and is used by those convinced that they teach correctly to dismiss others as choosing to deny the truth of correct teachings. For fundamentalist Catholics and Protestants, 'orthodoxy' refers to an original unified body of doctrines, dating from the time of Jesus' apostles, and shared by most Christians everywhere. In reality, as the scripture scholar Bart Ehrman elucidates, '"orthodoxy", in the sense of a unified group advocating an apostolic doctrine accepted by the majority of Christians everywhere, did not exist in the second and third centuries'.[49] For the first three or four centuries of its existence, Christianity was a motley collection of rival groups advocating a rich mixture of diverse theologies.

In 1934, Walter Bauer published a seminal book which challenged a traditional view that the first Christians constituted a unified orthodoxy from which heresies later departed. His book is called, *Orthodoxy and Heresy in Earliest Christianity*.[50] It argues that early Christianity was multifaceted, and that no one faction constituted a clear majority over and against all others. Indeed, in certain regions, beliefs that were later derided as 'heresy' were in fact the original and only type of Christianity.[51]

conclusion

Before the labours of modern archaeology, the Bible was regarded in the west as a unique book because it was thought to be both divinely inspired and much older than any other known text. Because it was invested with the status of a divinely revealed and dictated work, it was read in a strongly realistic way: its words meant and described exactly what they said. Then, on 3 December 1872, a scholar called G. Smith announced before the Society of Biblical Archaeology in London an extraordinary discovery:

> a history that was strikingly close to the biblical narrative of the Flood, even in details, but that preceded it and had obviously inspired the story in the Bible.
>   At a stroke, the Bible entered the stream of world literature and took its place in the endless chain of works issued in that entanglement of original creativity and dependency on previous sources, of fallibility and clairvoyance, which marks all advance in human thought.[52]

Given that the Bible is the most studied collection of writings in human history, it is not in the least surprising that its mistakes and inconsistencies have been clearly exposed, notably so in the age of modern biblical criticism. The net effect of the criticism has been to defang dogma. Christianity's Augustinian orthodoxy convinced many people over more than a millennium than hell awaits any person who is not saved by Jesus Christ. The orthodoxy, however, was based on the second chapter of Genesis, which imaginatively describes the rebellion of Adam and Eve. One could well fear the consequences of such a story were one convinced that it was written by Moses under the direct inspiration of God. Modern scholarship rejects Mosaic authorship and tends to the view that the story was written by an anonymous author in the tenth century BCE.

Biblical scholars have often been besmirched by fundamentalist and self-styled orthodox Christians over the past century. At least the former are to be admired for their insight and honesty in not confusing figurative professions of faith with historical events, and in not seeking to sway others with falsehoods.

7

the identity of jesus

Who could blame Jesus if he has grown
a little tired of hearing over and over
essentially the same thing about him
said, taught, proclaimed, and preached
by traditional Christianity for so many
centuries with only slight variations from
time to time?

Choan-Seng Song

Alas, we are heretics
all, and the one we subscribe to
is not love any more than the kingdom
for the sake of which we are
fools is the kingdom of heaven.

R.S. Thomas

At the heart of the Christian religion stands a Semite – Jesus from Nazareth. Jesus was not a Christian. He never heard of Christianity, and was never involved with Christianity, which formed slowly and falteringly over the four centuries after his death. Contemporary English-speaking Christians are not always aware that they talk of Jesus by extruding him from his original historical, ecological, political and religious context. Invariably, they refer to him with two anglicized Greek names, 'Jesus' and 'Christ', and thereby obscure the reality that he was a Galilean worshipper of Yahweh, the God of the Israelites. His original name was *Yeshua*, an Aramaic word meaning 'Yahweh saves'. Jesus was a Yahweh-proclaimer, not a Church-creator.

The Church that grew in his wake was excited by him and devoted to him. If one means by 'Christian' a person with faith in Jesus, then Christians were among his first followers who believed in his cause even before he was executed. If Christianity is understood as a body of people who worship a Triune God, and Jesus Christ as truly God and truly a human being, then such a group emerged during the fourth and fifth centuries, not the first.[1] The imperial Church of the fourth century and afterwards certainly worshipped Jesus. It also betrayed him. It obscured for hundreds of years the thrust of his own religious vision by identifying itself with the central content of his proclamation, the kingdom of God.[2] Historians and biblical scholars are today virtually unanimous that the pith of Jesus' preaching and teaching was the kingdom or reign of God.[3] Jesus appears to have pined for divine justice to reign in and over human injustice. The religious vision of Jesus centred on the Creator God of Israel, not the Church.[4]

We know this now, and can say it so confidently, thanks to the past two centuries of modern historical research into the life and legacy of Jesus of Galilee. Of all new questions generated by modernity for old beliefs, none is more consequential for *Christ*ian theology, than that of Jesus' identity. The governing aim of modern post-Enlightenment critical research into Christian Scriptures has been to discern his identity by carefully investigating the likely or most plausible historical circumstances in which he lived and died. The research relies on the discoveries of latter-day textual criticism of biblical texts; the archaeology of the Middle East; the geography and ecology of Jesus' local settings; and the distinctive political, economic, cultural, and religious features of his society and its wider world. The conclusions of the research are by no means always consonant with dogmatic portraits of Jesus.

In the long course of human history, few people have been more discussed than Yeshua, now habitually called Jesus in anglophone circles. Since he first attracted public attention in Galilee where he grew up, he has been a subject of keen interest, intense bickering, and profound bafflement. He continues to be a focus of fascination, not only among academics, but also within contemporary general publics. Mel Gibson's film *The Passion of the Christ* (2004) is to date the financially most lucrative R-rated/18+ film in North American cinematic history.[5]

Whether discussed in quotidian or academic registers, the question, 'Who is Jesus?', is as alive today as in any previous era. In response to the question the Christian tradition offers several answers. There has never been a single, unrivalled interpretation of Jesus in the past. It is surprising how many different views are contained in the Christian Scriptures. For the Gospel According to Mark, Jesus is portrayed as a man who gave his life as a ransom for sinful people (Mark 10:45). In Matthew's Gospel, Jesus is a champion of hungry, poor, and imprisoned people (Mt 25:31–46). According to Luke, Jesus is fundamentally a partisan liberator: he takes the side of oppressed and marginalized social underdogs (Luke 4:18–19). Of the four gospels contained in the Christian Scriptures, the fourth, John's Gospel, proved decisive in determining the contours of traditional Christian theology. For John answers the question, 'Who is Jesus?', by declaring that Jesus is the divine Logos, or Word of God, who has come from God's abode in heaven to dwell among human beings (John 1:14).[6]

The queries of who Jesus was and is, and of what he might signify for people nowadays, have been pressing preoccupations for modern theologians since the eighteenth century. As the Enlightenment gave birth to modern biblical criticism, the criticism, in turn, generated a peculiarly modern scrutiny of Jesus' identity and significance, the consequences of which will be pondered in this chapter. The distinctiveness of the modern academic study of Jesus lies in its working hypothesis that what the Bible and dogmas say about him might not accurately reflect who he was, what he did, and why he could be considered important for people today. Modern biblical investigations have revolutionized the study of Jesus. When the Bible was examined as a historical document like any other, new interpretations of him emerged that constitute a profound caesura with portrayals of him that were proclaimed by the Church for several hundred years. A major consequence of the Enlightenment was that scholars were able to investigate Jesus' identity, and debate his importance, without hindrance or persecution from the Church. Before the Enlightenment, scholars who dared question ecclesiastical teachings about him, and related doctrines, could be severely punished by civil powers policing dogmas. In seventeenth-century England and Scotland, people were still being executed for what were deemed doctrinal heresies.

Because Jesus has been the focus of curiosity and devotion for twenty centuries, it is all the more surprising that his identity is exceptionally opaque. No one even knows what he looked like. Not even his early followers could agree on how best to articulate his significance. For some he was a divine prophet like Moses, though greater than Moses; for others he was a tragic victim of exploitative political power. Over time he has been called, 'Lord', Christ', 'Messiah', 'Rabbi', 'Master', 'Son of God', 'Healer', 'Prince of Peace' and 'King'.[7] Today he is still interpreted in strikingly diverse ways. Few other names apart from his have been called upon for a broad variety of conflicting purposes. He has been invoked to bless battleships, build basilicas, launch crusades, baptize infants, murder Jews, worship God, establish universities, burn heretics, and inculpate guilt.

The single most significant consensus of twentieth-century studies of Jesus was the widespread acceptance that he was a Galilean Jew, and that he remained as much throughout his life.[8] The more one extracts him from his time, place and religious culture, the more one runs the risk of thoroughly misconstruing his identity and significance. For example, Rosemary Radford Ruether has recently drawn attention to contemporary Christians who are fond of legitimating a culture of family values they are familiar with, by averring that Jesus was a creator of families. In her book, *Christianity and the Making of the Modern Family*, Ruether cites the following passage from a North American focus group: '[Focus on the Family] attempts to "turn hearts toward home" by reasonable, biblical and empirical insights so people will be able to discover the founder of homes and creator of families – Jesus Christ.'[9] Yet if it is true that Jesus was a champion of a family-life ethos, what is to be made of a stark biblical observation like the following: 'Whoever comes to me and does not hate father and mother, wife and children, brother and sisters, yes, and even life itself, cannot be my disciple' (Luke 14:26)? In fact, Jesus as he lived 'appears quite often to have endorsed views that might be characterized as "antifamily"'.[10] In view of modern biblical research, the more Christian discourse ignores the all-determining Galilean Jewishness of Jesus' life, and the more it depicts him in a contemporary western domesticated guise, the less convincing it becomes. If Jesus was a wandering prophet who invited disciples to leave their families and follow him in his mission of announcing God the Creator's imminent intervention in the world, then it is difficult if not impossible to see how he could be construed as a creator of families.

Historically critical investigations of Jesus' identity have been under way for over two centuries. For much of that time, however, several Christian scholars have sought to specify Jesus' uniqueness by seeking to pinpoint his dissimilarity from ancient Galilean and Judean Yahweh-focused religiosities. Kant and Hegel, two of the greatest philosophers of modernity, both died in the first half of the nineteenth century, and both insisted that Jesus owed nothing to Judaism. Hegel inherited from Kant the view that Jesus was independent of Judaism.[11] Nineteenth-century Christian studies of Jesus were often tainted by an anti-Semitic cast of mind, and sought to describe what they perceived as essential differences between Jesus, on the one hand, and Galilean and Judean Semites, on the other. The enthusiasm for specifying the uniqueness of Jesus in terms of difference is clearly evident in the work of the twentieth-century biblical critic Norman Perrin. In his book *Rediscovering the Teaching of Jesus*, he concludes that 'the uniqueness of Jesus is found not in the things he shares with his contemporaries, but in the things wherein he differs from them.'[12] Two contemporary biblical scholars, Gerd Theissen and Sean Freyne, are contributing to a sea change in historical research on Jesus by advocating a criterion of historical plausibility rather than difference. A more convincing image of Jesus in their view will emerge once he is investigated by examining the likely historical, cultural and religious context in which he lived, instead of considering him over and against that context. Theissen explains his criterion in this way:

> Whereas the criterion of difference requires that it should not be possible to derive Jesus traditions from Judaism, something which can never be demonstrated strictly, the criterion of plausible historical context requires only a demonstration of positive connections between the Jesus tradition and the Jewish context, i.e., between Jesus and the land, the groups, the traditions and the mentalities of the Judaism of that time.[13]

Once Jesus is investigated carefully as a Galilean Semite wandering about in a province of the Roman Empire, and encouraging people to orientate their lives on the reign of the Creator God of Israel, a great deal of the Church's language about him can appear strangely at odds with his actual historical circumstances and religious convictions. For most of Christian history, theological discussions of Jesus' identity have been dominated by the conclusions of the Council of Chalcedon, a meeting of bishops convened in 451 CE. The bishops of Chalcedon taught that Jesus is truly God (*Deum vere*) and truly a human being (*hominem vere*).[14] Their teaching remains the core of Christian orthodoxy, but became the subject of major theological disputes over the past three hundred years. In what follows I shall (a) discuss the traditional discourse about Jesus Christ – that is, the discipline of Christology; (b) chart the modern historical process whereby some scholars became dissatisfied with the view of Chalcedon; and (c) consider some ways in which Jesus is currently being interpreted.

what is christology?

Within the discipline of Christian theology, attempts to delineate the identity and universal relevance of Jesus have normally been called Christologies. As the very word suggests, a Christology is a discourse (*logos*) about Christ. The title 'Christ' has a Greek provenance, *christos*, which translates the Hebrew term for 'Messiah' (*masiah*). A root meaning of both 'Christ' and 'Messiah' is 'God's anointed one'. A 'Christ' is someone preferred and promoted by God.

Over the centuries, Christology has been a confident intellectual discipline, conducted in universities since the Middle Ages, and in monasteries well before then. If theology is language about God, then Christology is a discourse that talks about God by referring to Jesus as God's Anointed. The point of Christology is to focus on a man, Jesus, in order to interpret him in association with God. Christology is the pivot of *Christ*ian theology. As such, it operates in a narrow and broad sense. In the former instance it seeks to shed light, first, on the historical process by which Jesus came to be called a messiah; and second, on the meaning of the title 'Christ'. In the latter case, Christology is a theory of salvation. It strives to elucidate how Jesus might help, save or redeem people living long after he did.

While Christology involves the study of a man regarded as a messiah, it so happens that there are two related, though separable, disciplines that discuss messiahs. One is primarily a Jewish undertaking called messianology. The second, Christology, has normally been the exclusive preserve of Christians, although it is important for Christians to realize that there is a substantial body of commentary on Jesus by pre-modern Islamic scholars.[15] Messianology probes Jewish expectations of divinely guided deliverance for human beings from all forms of suffering and degradation. The anticipated deliverer, or saviour, is revered as a person anointed by God. Within this orbit, a messiah could be a conqueror, king, priest or prophet, operative here and now. Before Christian thought, the concept of a messiah did not necessarily refer to a divine personage. It was more likely to connote a human being accepted by others as especially empowered by God. The Tanakh, for instance, records the anointing through popular acclamation of both Saul and David (1 Sam. 8, 10:17–27; and 2 Sam. 2:4; 5:1–3). In sum, Christology studies the same expectation as messianology – the restive and ardent hope for the immanent advent of God's liberating avenger of human cruelty. Its peculiarity, plainly, is that it names Jesus as God's beloved. It presents him as the ultimate Christ; the last and pre-eminent of all messiahs.

Historically speaking, different terms were originally used to designate the first generations of people to preach about Jesus. During the first three hundred years after his death, there was no such entity as a monolithic unified Christianity. Instead, there were several scattered groups propounding different interpretations of who Jesus was or is, and of what he accomplished. Some were called 'the Way', or the 'Followers of the Way'. Other Jesus-people or proto-Christians styled themselves as pilgrims in a New Exodus. Within about twenty years of Jesus' execution, members of the Way were situated 'in the regions now called Palestine, Syria, Cyprus, Italy, Egypt, Ethiopia, Greece, Turkey, the Balkans, and, some claimed, India'.[16] It does not follow, however, that they thereby divorced themselves from the worship of Yahweh. It took a good deal of time for Christianity to emerge clearly as a Gentile religion clearly set apart from rabbinic Judaism. The initial people who championed Jesus' cause could have been one of several rival expressions of Yahweh-faith. What they championed was Jesus' unique way of talking about Yahweh in relation to people's lives. It appears that for Jesus, the Creator-God of Israel prefers lepers, paupers, prisoners and urchins to priests, kings and merchants.

Roughly nineteen centuries ago what is now called Buddhism was expanding energetically towards central Asia and China. Its expansion was propelled by the impressively industrious Kushana empire. At exactly the same time, in other parts of the world, two additional empires made their might manifest. Nineteen centuries past, the intimidating Roman and Parthian empires controlled the vast expanse of territory that stretches from India all the way to the Atlantic Ocean. At the time – or, more exactly, around the year 125 CE – leaders of the vast Parthian and Roman empires began to notice what they regarded as a new-fangled religious devotion in their provinces. In the East of these empires, the adherents of the new religion were called 'Nazarenes'. In the West, they were labelled 'Christians'.[17]

Numerically speaking, the Christians were a tiny minority in the empires. By the year 125 CE, they amounted to approximately 100,000 persons. They were not localized in any large kind of city, ghetto or commune, but were scattered in several hundred different groups. Intriguingly, they were not coordinated by an overarching, monolithic, authoritarian or centralized institution like the Vatican. As for language, almost half of them spoke Aramaic. The rest used Greek.

What united these dispersed 100,000 Aramaic and Greek-speaking religious upstarts in the august Roman and Parthian empires was their love for the crucified criminal, Jesus from Nazareth. One hundred years after Jesus was executed, his enthusiasts were professing him as a messenger from God who was recalled after his death to a new mode of life with God. They ardently proclaimed that he would return immanently and gloriously to judge the living and the dead. They insisted that the holy texts of the Jews presaged and prefigured the words and actions of Jesus. They also proclaimed that he deserved the most ennobling of titles like 'Lord', 'Master' and 'Son of God'. His adherents in the East liked to call him a 'Prophet' or a 'Messiah'. In the West, he was often remembered as 'Christ'.

Significantly, Christology is not primarily an exercise in historical, biblical, anthropological or archaeological investigation. It is formally theological. In other words, it scrutinizes Jesus to determine his religious meaning, or relation to God. Is Jesus from God; like God; the same as God; an emissary of God; a sacrifice to God; a High Priest of God; an enthusiast for God; or a divinely inspired prophet? More disturbingly for committed contemporary Christians, Christology must respond to the sophisticated sceptical charge that Jesus was a religious revolutionary transformed and deified by the Church, which later claimed to follow him, into a disembodied Word and Ruler of the Cosmos who legitimates oppressive political establishments. Is it true that Jesus the iconoclast was changed into Christ the heavenly icon by Catholic orthodoxy? How did Jesus, the friend of layabouts and nobodies, become Christ the King who rules the world? Did not orthodoxy betray the religion *of* Jesus to perpetuate a religion *about* Jesus?

Very early in the Way's evolution, its members predicated the term *masiah*, a title mined from the Hebrew Scriptures, of a man who bore the proper name of 'Yeshua'. The proclamation 'Jesus *is* the Christ' thus came to be born. It was then contracted semantically into the apposition, 'Jesus-*the*-Christ'. From there it was compressed further into the compound name, 'Jesus Christ'.[18] It is worth noting, though, that 'Christ' is not a family name. Like the word 'Jesus', it is expressly theophoric. That is, it has an intrinsic allusion to God in its very make-up. 'Jesus' refers to salvation wrought by God. 'Christ' evokes the image of God's preferred liberator of oppressed masses.

Apart from the initial, narrow exercise of Christology, which dwells on the word 'Christ', the second and far more common practice of Christology probes the universal human question as to what might deliver people from everything that stymies them. It responds with the compound name Jesus Christ. Christology thus construed is the attempt to elaborate how Jesus, confessed by Christians as the world's Christ, is the supreme locus of God's salvation for each and every human being, alive or dead. Fusing both senses of the word 'Christology', one could define the enterprise in a nutshell: Christology is the field of intellectual inquiry that discusses the ultimate identity and universal significance of Jesus. The architectonic principle of Christology is to examine what can be known of the man Jesus so as to determine whether and to what extent he might be a cipher of God in human history. In far simpler terms, Christology dwells on the story of Jesus construed as the story of God.

Especially since the Middle Ages, theologians who have practised Christology have conventionally structured their treatises so as to pose four cardinal questions about Jesus: (a) What can be known of his life, actions, sayings, encounters, traumas, successes and debacles? (b) How is his person, or his essential identity, most accurately to be understood? (c) What did he actually achieve through his life, death, and conjectured resurrection after death? and (d) What is his abiding significance in every age including our own?

This quartet of questions has evoked a vast array of responses over the ages, and continues to stimulate rancorous interchanges in our own times. The 2000-year scrutiny of Jesus can be divided broadly into three major epochs: the first to seventh centuries; the Middle Ages; and the past three hundred or so years, loosely called modernity. The first and third eras witnessed quite fervid intellectual attempts to circumscribe Jesus' individuality. The second was one of perplexing conceptual stasis and fixity. Generally stated, when medieval theologians wrote about Jesus they did not depart boldly from definitions of him decreed by councils of bishops from the third to the eighth centuries. They were exceptionally adept at explaining the councils' declarations, while prescinding from offering new interpretations.

seven councils of bishops on jesus

1. NICAEA I (325 CE)   Convened as a response to Arius (d. 336) who held that Jesus was a creature and the foremost of all creatures. The bishops at the First Council of Nicaea taught that the Son (Jesus) is consubstantial (*homoousious*) with the Father (the Creator), and was not created by the Father.

2. CONSTANTINOPLE I (381)   Also called to counter Arianism; attended by 150 Eastern Orthodox bishops. There are no extant copies of the council's decisions.

3. EPHESUS (431)   Primarily concerned with disputes associated with Nestorius (b. after 351; d. after 451) who was accused of teaching that there are two persons in Jesus Christ, one divine and the other human (as opposed to a single person at once God and a human being). This council is remembered for its teaching that Jesus' mother is aptly called the God-bearer (*theotokos*).

4. CHALCEDON (451)   This celebrated council has been a measuring-rod for orhtodox Christian faith well into the twentieth century. Few theological theories have enjoyed such a distinguished career. Chalcedon taught that in Christ there is one person (*hypostasis/prosòpon*) and two natures (*physis* = nature), human and divine, which do not undergo *confusion, change, division,* or *separation*. This council was at pains to refute Eutyches (*c.* 378–454), who denied that there are two natures in Jesus Christ.

5. CONSTANTINOPLE II (553)   An interpretation and confirmation of Chalcedon, but with an Alexandrian slant, that is, a theology predisposed to accentuate the divine nature of Jesus proclaimed by previous councils. This council was attended mainly by Eastern bishops.

6. CONSTANTINOPLE III (680/81)   Assembled to deal with Monothelitism, the view that there is only one will in Jesus Christ, rather than a divine will and a human will. This council represents the last creative stage of early dogmatic Christological speculation until the modern era; and was rather more Antiochene than Constantinople II, that is, it was predisposed to accentuate Jesus' human nature, while not denying a divine nature.

7. NICAEA II (787)   Recapitulates and encapsulates the doctrines of the previous six councils, although within the context of a controversy over whether icons, or sacred images, should be venerated. This council permitted *iconic* expression of belief in an *incarnate* Christ.

the everlasting king

From the Second Council of Nicaea in the eighth century to the First Vatican Council in the nineteenth, no salient conciliar modifications or contradictions of dogmas about Jesus were promulgated. Once stated, the teachings of the seven Christological councils became lapidary. They were used as yardsticks to measure the perceived correctness or deviance of individuals' beliefs. Just how time-honoured these doctrines eventually became can be glimpsed in the thought of Pope Pius XII. In 1951, he decided to commemorate the 1500th anniversary of the Council of Chalcedon (451). To do so, he published a letter entitled, in Latin, *Sempiternus Rex* ('The Everlasting King'). Therewith, he reiterated the Chalcedonian doctrine that the one and the same person of Jesus has two natures: one human; the other divine. In *Sempiternus Rex*, Pius XII commemorated Chalcedon by inviting his readers to assent to two doctrines: first, the primacy of the Roman pontiff – that is, the authority of himself; and second, the doctrine of Chalcedon. In his own words:

> Let those who because of the iniquity of the times, especially in Eastern lands, are separated from the bosom and unity of the Church, follow the teaching and example of their forefathers and not hesitate to render due reverent homage to the primacy of the Roman Pontiff; and let those who are entangled in the errors of Nestorius and Eutyches penetrate to the mystery of Christ with deeper insight and accept completely the doctrine of Chalcedon.[19]

Pius XII's text does not enter into detailed discussions of what could possibly be meant by the words 'human' and 'divine', and dismisses modern attempts to reinterpret the identity of Jesus. After 1500 years, he continues the legacy of Chalcedon without any regard to a profound turmoil that beset conventional Christology in the eighteenth and nineteenth centuries.

the two great christological crises

Modern theology has been greatly taxed by a momentous debate over the identity of Jesus. The North American scholar Colin Brown alerts his readers to the consequential nature of modern scholarly discussions of Jesus:

> The Christian church has gone through many crises of faith. But two in particular overshadow all the rest, for in them the issue at stake is that which sets Christianity apart form other religions and beliefs – the identity of Jesus Christ. The first of these crises began with the appearance of Jesus and lasted into the fifth century. It went through numerous phases and had several focal points. In the fourth century,

> the Niceno-Constantinopolitan Creed met the challenge of Arianism by asserting
> the divinity of Jesus in terms of his consubstantiality with the Father. The Council
> of Chalcedon (AD 451) laid down the parameters of orthodoxy for Western Christen-
> dom which were to endure for over a millennium. ... In the mainstream of Western
> Christianity the orthodoxy of the creeds remained unchallenged until the eight-
> eenth century when fresh doubt began to be cast on the historicity of the Church's
> beliefs about Jesus, and in particular, its claims concerning his divinity. Thus began
> the second major crisis of faith concerning the identity of Jesus.[20]

Expressed otherwise, the Enlightenment was a catalyst for a far-reaching intellectual upheaval within Christianity over the nature and worth of Jesus, called
Christ. The Enlightenment involved a crucial span of a hundred years from,
roughly speaking, 1650 to 1750. As Owen Chadwick has presciently observed,
these were the really seminal years of modern intellectual history. During these
years it became evident that the Middle Ages were well and truly over. This was
the century of Newton, Spinoza, Locke, Hume, Diderot and Voltaire. Throughout
this momentous span of a century, religious thinkers were emboldened to study
'the distant origins of modern science, the beginnings of the idea of progress, the
first historical criticism of the Biblical records, the discoveries of the true nature
of other great religions and cultures of the world'.[21]

Modern biblical studies and their commentaries on Jesus have raised several
problems that theologians have been compelled to consider over the past three
centuries. The studies sparked an ardent endeavour to specify what can be
known assuredly of the identity and significance of Jesus. Modern investigators of
the Bible put its pages to the test with recently developed methods of historical
investigation and textual analysis to decide whether or not it portrays Jesus as he
was. Within the Catholic Church of the Roman Rite, governed by Pius XII and
his predecessors, the doctrinal supremacy of Chalcedon was not widely challenged
throughout the eighteenth, the nineteenth and first half of the twentieth century.
The same situation did not prevail among Protestants over the same period. The
Eastern Orthodox tradition, by the way, has no tradition of historically critical
research on Jesus in the style undertaken in western academies. Throughout the
nineteenth century, scholars in Protestant faculties of theology in Europe began
to discuss whether Chalcedon was an arbitrary, and hence dispensable, theory
couched in the categories of ancient Greek metaphysics. The Protestant debates
of the nineteenth-century German-speaking academy were ignited by a discreet,
scholarly man of the previous century: Hermann Samuel Reimarus.

reimarus　In 1778, a decade before the French Revolution, an academically
daring and religiously volatile study of Jesus by Hermann Reimarus (1694–1768)

was published postumously in Germany. 'Reimarus' is hardly a household name. Even so, like 'Spinoza', the noun 'Reimarus' demands consideration if the genesis and evolution of modern theology are to be comprehended even minimally. Hermann Reimarus is an exceptionally significant figure in the history of scholarly investigation of Jesus because he made a double distinction that is not found in Christian writings before the posthumous publication of his work. The twofold distinction he drew is this: not only does a difference obtain between what dogmas say about Jesus and the ways the Christian Scriptures depict him; there is also a divergence between what the Bible says about him and who he actually was. With Reimarus, this bipartite differentiation entered the history of theology, and the second greatest crisis of faith in Christianity's history, mentioned by Colin Brown, was effectively sparked. In the words of Albert Schweitzer, 'Before Reimarus, no one had attempted to form a historical conception of the life of Jesus. Luther had not even felt the need to gain a clear idea of the order of the recorded events.'[22]

Reimarus was a Lutheran professor of oriental languages. He spent the last forty years of his life teaching in Hamburg at the *Gymnasium Johanneum*. Between 1720 and 1721 he studied in Oxford and the Netherlands. It would be surprising, then, if he had not encountered the ideas of deists and Spinoza during those years. When alive, he was regarded by his contemporaries as a pious and devout Christian who attended church services and joined in the Christian ceremony of the Eucharist. However, because of his studies in oriental languages and his close scrutiny of ancient biblical texts, he began to harbour doubts about the historical truthfulness of many of the Bible's stories. He decided to record his misgivings in writing, so he composed a lengthy monograph titled *Apology or Treatise in Defence of the Reasonable Worship of God* (*Apologie oder Schutzschrift für die vernünftigen Verbrer Gottes*). Three copies of the manuscript are extant (two in Hamburg and one in Göttingen). They vary in length from about 1000 to 1300 pages. The entire text has never been fully translated into English. The first complete critical German edition was published in 1972, more than two hundred years after Reimarus's death.[23] Reimarus never dared to publish his text while he was alive. Parts of it were published posthumously in the 1770s by one of his admirers, Gotthold Ephraim Lessing (1729–1781).

With the permission of Reimarus's children, Lessing selected fragments for publication. He began to publish them in 1774, and by 1778 had produced seven related fragments. As a group the fragments discuss topics such as Jesus' ethical teaching, rational religion, Hebrew Scriptures, and stories about Jesus' resurrection.[24] Reimarus wanted to convince his readers that pivotal Christian doctrines do not stem from Jesus: 'Since nowadays the doctrine of the trinity of persons in

God and the doctrine of the work of salvation through Jesus as the Son of God and God-man constitute the main articles and mysteries of the Christian faith, I shall specifically demonstrate they are not to be found in Jesus' discourses.'[25]

The seventh fragment proved to be the most controversial of all. It appeared in May 1778, and was titled 'On the Intentions of Jesus and His Disciples'. The fragment asserts that there is a discontinuity between Jesus' aims and those of his followers. Reimarus' thesis was as shocking for his first audience to receive as it was simple for him to state. The central message he wished to record for any reader is that the Gospels contained in the Christian Scriptures are fraudulent. For Reimarus, Christianity was not established by Jesus, but by the deceitfulness of his disciples after his death. He hypothesized that Jesus entertained political, messianic ambition and pined for deliverance from stultifying Roman power. He concluded that Jesus' disciples viewed him as a political messiah while he was alive: 'the evangelists did not seek to conceal that they looked upon Jesus as a worldly deliverer of Israel up to the time of his death'.[26] Reimarus insisted that after Jesus' death, his intimate followers were so dispirited and crestfallen that they stole his body from a tomb and concocted a story of his resurrection so as to maintain positions of privilege. In Reimarus's view, later Christianity's doctrines that Jesus was a saviour who suffered, died and was raised from death are fraudulent products of the disciples. In other words, the Christian religion is the result of a deliberate fabrication. Jesus' aims collapsed on a cross, so the disciples set about inventing stories about him to vindicate him and themselves in the eyes of others.

> **eschatology** is a branch of systematic theology that considers the end of history and the future-directedness of human existence. 'Eschatology' comes from the Greek words *eschata* ('last' or 'ultimate things') and *logos* ('word' or 'discourse'). In traditional Christian theology, eschatology considers topics such as heaven, hell and divine judgement. With regard to Jesus, Albert Schweitzer (1875–1965) opined that Jesus was driven by a mistaken eschatological hope that God's kingdom was about to be established among people. Long after his death, the kingdom has still not been witnessed. Based at Mansfield College, Oxford, Charles Harold Dodd (1884–1973) interpreted Jesus' life in terms of realized eschatology – that is, by arguing that the kingdom had begun to be established or realized in Jesus' life and work.

This latter suggestion is entirely new in published Christian thought, although enemies of Christianity had made the same charge soon after Christianity emerged as a new historical religion. No one before Reimarus had so clearly differentiated between Jesus, as he lived in Palestine, and what the Gospels say he said and did. Reimarus was also ahead of his generation of scholars in insisting that Jesus 'was

born a Jew and intended to remain one; he [Jesus] testifies that he has not come
to abolish the law, but to fulfil it'.[27] In addition, unlike most scholars of his time,
Reimarus was aware of the significance of eschatology in Jesus' life: 'Reimarus
was the first, after eighteen centuries of misconception, again to have an inkling
of what eschatology really was.'[28]

What really shocked the first readers of Reimarus's fragments was his suggestion that Christianity is the product of a deliberate fraud on the part of Jesus'
disciples. The subsequent 200-year quest to discover who Jesus was in reality
before any overpainting by the gospels, has come to be dubbed the quest for the
historical Jesus; that is, the search for information about Jesus culled from historical sources rather than theological theories. Of the seventh fragment Albert
Schweitzer was subsequently to comment: 'To say that the fragment "The Aims
of Jesus and His Disciples" is a magnificent piece of work is barely to do it justice.
This essay is not only one of the greatest events in the history of criticism, it is
also a masterpiece of general literature.'[29]

Reimarus's seventh fragment is highly significant for the history of modern
theology for three main reasons. In the first place, the fragment introduced the
double distinction (mentioned above) into discussions of Jesus.[30] In the second
instance, Reimarus's seventh fragment is exceptional because it represents the
first fully naturalistic interpretation of Jesus ever penned. It relies entirely on
critical reason and the linguistic examination of biblical texts rather than on
dogmatic traditions. In the third place, the fragment of Reimarus is momentous
and portentous because it insists that Jesus was a Jew who remained a Jew all his
life. It is adamant that he should not be portrayed in a way that excises him from
his own religious milieu. On this point Reimarus was a full two hundred years
ahead of his time. For well over a hundred years after Reimarus, wave after wave
of books attempted to specify what can be known of Jesus through historical
research, rather than what can be preached through religious faith.

lessing It is advisable to note here that two kinds of truth have just been
delineated: truths of historical events, and truths of religious faith. During the
Enlightenment, these two types of truth were frequently referred to as accidental,
contingent historical truths, on the one hand, and necessary truths of reason,
on the other. A necessary truth is of a kind that its obverse cannot logically be
sustained. For example, it is a necessary truth of reason that bachelors are un-
married men. To assert otherwise is to advance an illogical inconsistency.

Lessing wrote eloquently of the two types of truth just mentioned. He concluded that historical truths can never serve as the legitimating basis for theological truths. Henry Chadwick has said of Lessing that he was 'the first modern

writer explicitly to emphasize that even if conclusions about historical events were more certain than they are, any religious affirmation based upon them involves a transition to another plane of discourse, that of faith'.[31]

Lessing introduced a metaphor into modern theology that has been discussed among theologians and philosophers over the past two and a quarter centuries. The metaphor in question concerns an 'ugly ditch'. Lessing's 'ugly ditch', 'if not the most frequently cited nonbiblical image within Protestant theology during the past two centuries, is certainly in the running for the dubious title'.[32] In 1777, Lessing published a remarkable essay titled 'On the Proof of the Spirit and of Power' ('Über den Beweis des Geistes und der Kraft'). In the essay, Lessing observed that, 'If no historical truth can be demonstrated, then nothing can be demonstrated by means of historical truths. That is: *accidental truths of history can never become the proof of necessary truths of reason.*' Later in the essay Lessing explains: 'That, then, is the ugly broad ditch which I cannot get across, however often and however earnestly I have tried to make the leap.'[33] Stated otherwise, if Lessing could have his way, people would be disinclined to commit themselves to religious belief on the basis of historical knowledge, such as the awareness that Jesus was a man. Knowing that Jesus was a man cannot, of itself, justify the belief, for instance, that he is the saviour of the world.

Lessing was a more penetrating thinker than Reimarus. He is also far more hermetic, aphoristic and inscrutable. His oft-quoted dicta, namely (1) that accidental historical truths can never become the evidence for necessary truths of reason; and (2) that a broad ugly ditch (*der garstige breite Graben*) separates the two kinds of truth, rehearses a distinction found in the philosophies of Gottfried Leibniz (1646–1716) and Christian Wolff (1679–1754). In Leibnizian–Wolffian terms, a distinction can clearly be made between necessary truths of reason (*notwendige Vernunftwahrheiten*) and accidental truths of history (*zufällige Geschichtswahrheiten*). However, Lessing accomplishes far more than merely rehearsing such a distinction. He also reininterprets this commonplace Enlightenment philosophical differentiation in a highly original, even anti-Enlightenment, way. Generally speaking, for devotees of the Enlightenment, human experience was of secondary importance compared with truths of reason. Many medieval thinkers would have been of a similar disposition. Lessing takes such a predisposition and turns it on its head. He does so by stressing the importance of immediate experiential evidence, which is to say that what mattered for him was not so much an antithesis between truths of reason and truths of history, but an antithesis between truths of the past and truths lived at the moment.

To realize fully what he is asserting, it is necessary to know why he called his essay, 'On the Proof of the Spirit and of Power'. This title is a phrase taken from the writings of the Greek biblical critic and theologian Origen (*c.* 185–*c.* 254 CE), whose work *Contra Celsum* echoes the biblical passage, 'in demonstration of the Spirit and power' (1 Cor. 2:4). Origen observed, as Colin Brown points out, that 'the proof of power is so called because of the astonishing miracles which have happened to confirm the teaching of Christ.'[34] Well before the Enlightenment, Christian apologists often attempted to demonstrate the truthfulness of Christianity by arguing that Jesus fulfilled ancient prophecies (the proof of the Spirit) and performed miracles (the proof of power). Lessing argued against Origen's idea that miracles constituted proof of Jesus' teaching. He concluded that miracles are no longer admissible as evidence. He effectively asserts that had he lived in the time of Jesus, and had he witnessed miracles and the fulfilment of prophecies, then he would have experienced no difficulty in believing in Jesus' teaching. He contended, though, that historical events are not binding. Information about the past always comes to contemporaries through the mediation of bygone generations, whose experiences and perceptions differ from those of later generations. In other words, Lessing judges that his contemporaries have no experience of miracles. Reports of historical information about miracles do not in themselves constitute miracles. For Lessing, history constitutes an unbridgeable ditch that separates contemporaries from the reality of Jesus; and the (necessary) truth of Christianity, or of any other religion, cannot be established by appealing to history, which by its nature is constituted by contingent truths.

Nevertheless, it is frequently overlooked in books commenting on Lessing that he was such a subtle thinker that he actually had three ugly ditches in mind, not one. In the first place, he was aware of a temporal ditch or chasm 'separating the present from religiously momentous or revelatory events of the distant past'.[35] Because of this ditch theologians and researches will never find Jesus in himself who remains lost in an irretrievable past. In the second place, Lessing observed a metaphysical ditch between historical truths and religious truths. To say that Jesus was a man is a historical and anthropological truth. To say that he is divine is not. The latter proposition belongs to the different order of religious language. Whether or not it is either meaningful or true cannot be demonstrated with historical records. Finally, Lessing was cognizant of an existential cleavage 'that potentially separates a modern-day, autonomous and secular believer from a religious message that is not only historical dubious, but probably odd and incredible as well'.[36]

Considered cumulatively, these three ditches constitute an exceptionally acute difficulty for modern Christian theology. For Lessing, no knowledge of a universal truth can be discovered in a historical particularity, such as a human being. His view would seem to strike at the heart of Christian faith, according to which in

Jesus the fullness of God can be encountered. For Christians over many centuries, in the man Jesus cohere universality and particularity; ultimacy and limitation; transcendence and immanence; supernature and nature; and divinity and humanity. Whether or not that is the case, in Lessing's terms it cannot be confirmed by reports of miracles and fulfilled prophecies.

strauss   Hermann Reimarus died a decade before his seventh fragment was published by Lessing. A new generation of biblical scholars propelled the course of modern biblical studies in his wake and in view of Lessing's pronouncements. Prominent among them was the German biblical critic David Friedrich Strauss. Strauss differed from Reimarus in one vital respect. He did not conclude that biblical portrayals of Jesus are historically and intellectually fraudulent. Instead he surmised that biblical reports about Jesus' miracles are myths. If Reimarus's thought is best encapsulated in the notion of deceit, then Strauss's work turns on the term 'myth'.

In 1835, Strauss published a lengthy book titled *The Life of Jesus Critically Examined (Das Leben Jesu kritisch bearbeitet)*. Its publication is described by Robert Morgan as 'The most dramatic theological event of a century prone to religious controversy.'[37] William Baird regards Strauss's book as a 'theological bombshell' and 'the most revolutionary religious document written since Luther's Ninety-Five Theses'.[38] Strauss's tome was a tour de force composed with a powerfully engaging rhetorical assertiveness. It exploded like a grenade in the homes of academics throughout what is now called Germany and beyond. Very quickly, it became like a Bible to a group of revolutionary intellectuals including Karl Marx, Richard Wagner and Friedrich Engels.[39]

Strauss was born in 1808, only four years after the death of Immanuel Kant, and died in 1874. He was thus a contemporary of Schleiermacher and Hegel, who both interpreted Jesus by dissociating him from the Jewish beliefs and customs of his culture. Strauss was 27 when he published *The Life of Jesus Critically Examined*. The very title of the work defers to the Enlightenment ethos of rationally controlled critique. A second, unaltered, edition was issued; and a third, altered, edition was published between 1838 and 1839. A fourth addition appeared in 1840. It was this edition that was translated into English by Mary Ann Evans, better remembered as the novelist George Eliot. Albert Schweitzer described Strauss's book in glowing terms:

> Considered as a literary work, Strauss' first Life of Jesus is one of the most perfect things in the whole range of learned literature. In over fourteen hundred pages he has not a superfluous phrase; his analysis descends to the minutest details, but he does not lose his way among them; the style is simple and picturesque, sometimes ironical, but always dignified and distinguished.[40]

The year 1835 was nothing short of a major turning point in nineteenth-century Christian life and thought. Strauss's *Life of Jesus* was met with profound shock by mainstream Protestantism. His colleagues at Tübingen decided to act. He was removed from his post. It seemed, though, that all was not lost. In 1839 the government of Zürich offered him a local professorship. The local people reacted furiously. Strauss was given a pension before he even set foot in Zürich and the government was thrown out of office.

Strauss continued to work away by himself. He published a theological study between 1840 and 1841 titled *The Doctrine of the Christian Faith*. Then he turned his back on theology and wrote instead on music, literature and politics. In 1842 he married a famous singer, Agnese Schebest. The marriage ended in 1847. He died on 8 February 1874 in his home town of Ludwigsburg after several months of suffering from an internal ulcer. The work of his youth, *The Life of Jesus Critically Examined*, had simultaneously been his life's major achievement, as well as its dramatic downfall.

Strauss's beautifully written masterpiece does not argue that Christianity arose as the result of an engineered deception on the part of Jesus' disciples. Instead it instructs that the evangelists were not historians. Rather, they were impassioned preachers. As a consequence, Strauss concluded that the Gospels are historically unreliable, not because they are based on deception, but because a good deal of their language is mythical. One of this book's first reviewers called it the most pestilential volume ever vomited from the bowels of hell.[41]

Ironically, *The Life of Jesus Critically Examined* was not an attempt to reconstruct a biography of Jesus. Instead, it proposed a new way of interpreting the Gospels. Strauss's method for analysing the New Testament is fascinating. As he examines each passage he presents three different possible interpretations. The first he calls the supernaturalistic explanation. This is simply a traditional Christian reading of the Bible, which concludes that a supernatural Godhead did indeed intervene in the historical affairs of Israel. Supernaturalists accept Gospel accounts of miracles as literally true. A second style of interpretation Strauss calls the rationalistic view. The second stance explains all events recorded in the New Testament as natural occurances. Whatever is unable to be explained rationally is to be discarded. Rationalists, unsurprisingly, are sceptical about miracles. Strauss regarded both stances as untenable. He charged Reimarus with anachronistic thinking, arguing that the disciples had no need to deceive anyone and that their new message about Jesus was the fruit of their impassioned religious imagination rather than cool, rationalistic fraud.

The Copernican revolution of Strauss's book resides in his own method of interpretation, which he contrasts with the supernaturalistic and the rationalist views and calls mythical. To all the inexplicable, supernatural stories in the New Testament, Strauss applied the term 'myth'. He defined a myth as 'a narrative relating directly or indirectly to Jesus, which may be considered not as the expression of a fact, but ... the product of an idea of his earliest followers'.[42] To be precise, Strauss identified three basic kinds of myth: historical mythi or myths are 'narratives of real events coloured by the light of antiquity, which confounded the divine and the human, the natural and the supernatural'; philosophical mythi, 'such as clothe in the garb of historical narrative a simple thought, a precept, or an idea of the time'; and poetical mythi, which are 'historical and philosophical mythi partly blended together, and partly embellished by the creations of the imagination, in which the original fact or idea is almost obscured by the veil which the fancy of the poet has woven around it'.[43]

Etymologically speaking, a myth (Greek: *mythos, mythus*) simply means a story. Strauss is historically significant for modern Christian life and thought because he introduced the concept of myth to modern investigations of Jesus' life. By arguing that several Gospel stories, especially the miracle stories, are myths, he not only suggested that they were imaginative constructions of early Christian communities; he also evacuated the stories of any kind of historical reliability. An unsettling question thereby arises: if one is not able to trust the testimony of the biblical witnesses, why should one take the Bible seriously at all? Here it is possible to see clearly why Schweitzer said that Strauss was the most truthful of theologians. Strauss followed the logic of his convictions and eventually lost his Christian faith.

Strauss applied to Christology and theology the category of 'myth' that had been developed in biblical criticism by Johann Gottfried Eichhorn (1752–1827), who was a biblical scholar, orientalist, and Professor of Philosophy in Göttingen. Even before the French Revolution, in 1779 to be precise, Eichhorn showed that the creation stories in Genesis are of the same literary genre as similar stories in ancient mythologies. Hence, why should Christians and Jews regard the creation narratives in Genesis as a revealed truth of divine revelation, and the creation story of the Roman poet Ovid as a heathen fabrication? David Leeming presses the point starkly:

> All cultures and religions have sacred stories that the common sense of people in their cultures and religions recognize as myths. The carrying off of the maiden Persephone by the god Hades is a fanciful and untrue story of someone else's religion. We call that story a myth. It is difficult to believe that the Buddha was conceived in a dream by a white elephant, so we call that story a myth as well. But of course, stories such as the parting of the Red Sea for the fleeing Hebrews, Muhammad's Night Journey, and the dead Jesus rising from the tomb are just as clearly irrational

narratives to which a Hindu or Buddhist might understandably apply the word 'myth.' All of these stories are definable as myths because they contain events that contradict both our intellectual and physical experience of reality.[44]

Strauss's ideas proved controversial 142 years after his death, when a debate about the concept of myth provoked a major theological storm in Great Britain. In 1977, SCM Press in London published a book with an arresting title – *The Myth of God Incarnate*. It was edited by John Hick, and contained ten essays by seven British scholars: Hick himself, Maurice Wiles, Dennis Nineham, Leslie Houlden, Frances Young and Don Cupitt.[45] As the very title of the book intimates, its essays collectively argue that the Christian doctrine of the incarnation is best understood as a myth. The essayists were effectively attempting to communicate to a general public major results of modern biblical criticism. A pandemonium of public outcry immediately followed the publication of *The Myth of God Incarnate*.[46] To describe the incarnation as a myth appeared to suggest that it was a widely accepted though ultimately fanciful story of the same status as tales of trolls under the bridge, the tooth fairy and Daffy Duck.

the history of the quest for the jesus of history

Once the suspicion arose in the late eighteenth century that Christian Scriptures and creeds do not necessarily portray Jesus as he actually lived in his specific historical setting, a new, peculiarly modern, endeavour to investigate him was born. That endeavour is now conventionally referred to as the quest of, or for, the historical Jesus.

Within that quest, it is possible to distinguish four different stages, which were preceded by what could be labelled as the proto-quest for the historical Jesus. While Reimarus is often described as a trailblazer and a man ahead of his time, he was actually a man writing right on cue, so to speak. In other words, his conclusions were facilitated by generations of scholars before him who began to scrutinize the Bible on a naturalistic basis. Spinoza and Richard Simon represent two such scholars. Hence, it is possible to periodize the modern quest for the historical Jesus into five stages, with one really constituting a prolegomenal phase:

1. The Proto-Quest, lasting from around 1670 to the 1770s.
2. The First Quest, spanning the work of Reimarus (1778) to Albert Schweitzer (1906).
3. The suspension of the quest or the period of no quest (1906–1953).
4. The Second Quest from 1953 to the 1970s.
5. The Third Quest, beginning in the 1980s and continuing apace today.

The proto-quest involved the development of historically critical interpretative methods for interpreting the Bible, broached in the previous chapter. Reimarus, Lessing and Strauss were giants of the first quest. However, by the beginning of the twentieth century different scholars, especially Albert Schweitzer and Martin Kähler (1835–1912), had concluded that most nineteenth-century attempts to determine what can be known historically of Jesus revealed more about the prejudices of their authors than about the Jesus of history. In 1906, Schweitzer robbed the old or first quest for the historical Jesus of its confidence with the publication of his detailed study *The Quest of the Historical Jesus: A Critical Study of Its Progress from Reimarus to Wrede (Geschichichte der Leben-Jezu-Forschung: Von Reimarus zu Wrede)*. The book surveyed the writings of the first quest and found that they unwittingly recreated Jesus in the spirit of their own times. Schweitzer was not against the use of historical methods to investigate Jesus. He simply argued that the Jesus recovered by historical research is not a post-Enlightenment middle-class rationalist philosopher, but quite an alien, remote apocalyptic figure who is unnervingly foreign to moderns. Schweitzer demonstrated that the first quest neglected the eschatological and apocalyptic features of Jesus' life, teachings and actions. Schweitzer had been led to the significance of the eschatological colouring of Jesus' world-view by Johannes Weiss (1863–1914) and his book of 1892, *Jesus' Proclamation of the Kingdom of God (Die Predight Jesus vom Reich Gottes)*. Nonetheless, because Schweitzer thought that Jesus mistakenly expected an immanent escatological consummation of history, he abandoned academic biblical scholarship and worked as a missionary doctor in Africa.

Martin Kähler helped to seal the fate of the first quest with his earlier book of 1896, *The So-Called Historical Jesus and the Historic Biblical Christ (Der sogenannte historische Jesus und der geschichtliche, biblische Christus)*. Kähler argued that it is quite impossible to drive a wedge between the Jesus of history and the Christ of faith, because the former is only known through documents written about the latter. He 'repudiated the attempt to make faith dependent on historical research'.[47]

Kähler believed that the Christ who is now preached and worshipped is the one who has influenced history. As he says,

> The real Christ, that is, the Christ who has exercised an influence in history, with whom millions have communed in childlike faith, and with whom the great witnesses of faith have been in communion – while striving, apprehending, triumphing, and proclaiming – this real Christ is the Christ who is preached. The Christ who is preached, however, is precisely the Christ of Faith.[48]

Kähler's conclusion is not unassailable because over the centuries preachers have presented Jesus to their congregations in startlingly different way, as has been clearly illustrated by Jaroslav Pelikan's book *Jesus through the Centuries* (1985). A preacher on the Christian festival of Christ the King might very well describe Jesus lyrically as a king, but it doesn't follow that Jesus really was a monarch. It is not possible that conflicting descriptions preached about Jesus all reflect his identity.

Nevertheless, the combined publications of Schweitzer and Kähler exerted an enormous influence on later Protestant theologians, and in particular on Rudolf Bultmann and Paul Tillich. Both Tillich and Bultmann separated the figure of the Jesus of history from the Christ of their faith. In 1926, to illustrate, Bultmann famously opined that, 'I do indeed think that we can know almost nothing concerning the life and personality of Jesus.'[49] The work of Bultmann is a clear indication that the net result of 'the double salvo by Schweitzer and Kähler was that for much of the first half of the twentieth century the scholarly quest for the historical Jesus was assumed to be dead.'[50]

However, the plot, as it were, does not end there. In 1953, Ernst Käsemann, one of Bultmann's former students, delivered a lecture in Germany titled 'The Problem of the Historical Jesus'.[51] Therein he argued against his mentor that, while the Gospel traditions were certainly interpreted by believing followers of Jesus, this did not mean that they were unable to preserve authentic historical memories. Bultmann's scepticism about what could be known about the historical Jesus had been too extreme. While a great deal can never be known about Jesus, Käsemann was not at all convinced that nothing historical can be known about him. He complained that an exalted Lord 'has almost entirely swallowed up the image of the earthly Lord',[52] and that there was a continuity between the preaching *of* Jesus and the early Christian preaching *about* Jesus.

During the 1950s and 1960s scholars began once again to write historical investigations of the life of Jesus. Thus was born the second quest. The first book of note to appear in this quest was Günther Bornkamm's *Jesus of Nazareth*, which was published in German in 1956.[53] Bornkamm presents his readers with a newly found confidence that Christian Scriptures preserve genuine historical portraits of Jesus: 'Quite clearly what the Gospels report concerning the message, the deeds and the history of Jesus is still distinguished by an authenticity, a freshness and a distinctiveness not in any way effaced by the Church's Easter faith.'[54] In 1959, James M. Robinson chronicled the progress of the second quest in his *A New Quest of the Historical Jesus*.[55] The trouble with many of the studies of the second quest is that they were heavily influenced by twentieth-century existentialist philosophy. As interest in existentialist thought waned in the early 1970s, so too did enthusiasm for the second quest. The second quest was also unconcerned with the distinct and varied local settings in which Jesus lived and preached.

Interestingly, the first two major studies of Jesus written by Catholics and reliant upon historical research appeared as late as 1974, for in that year Hans Küng's *On Being a Christian* and Edward Schillebeeckx's *Jesus: An Experiment in Christology* were published.[56]

In the 1980s, a new type of historical research into Jesus blossomed, which is commonly called the third quest. It is marked by four main features: (1) it evinces a pronounced interest in Jesus' Jewishness; (2) it is multidisciplinary in its method, engaging the results of archaeological and cross-cultural studies;[57] (3) it relates Jesus to the world's religions; and (4) it involves scholars who are women. Above all, the third quest exudes a quiet confidence that a good deal can be known about Jesus as he lived in Palestine. N.T. Wright typifies this confidence in his book *Jesus and the Victory of God* (1996), where he concludes: 'We can know quite a lot about Jesus; not enough to write a modern-style biography, including the colour of the subject's hair, and what he liked for breakfast, but quite a lot.'[58]

Paula Fredriksen of Boston University typifies the historical confidence of the third quest. In her book *Jesus of Nazareth, King of the Jews* she starkly observes that no reconstruction of the historical Jesus can persuade if it cannot meaningfully accommodate the following handful of indisputable facts about Jesus:

> his encounter with John the Baptizer, his popular following, his proclamation of the Kingdom of God, his crucifixion by Pilate in Jerusalem, the survival of his core followers, who took up his proclamation of the kingdom while identifying Jesus as Christ, risen from the dead, and extending the mission out from its Jewish matrix to also include Gentiles.[59]

the multiple depictions of jesus

Anyone presently reflecting on Jesus is confronted by a bewilderingly multiplex body of literature. He is currently interpreted in several usually conflicting ways. To illustrate, one finds him classified according to any of the following types: God, or more precisely, God the Son, enfleshed, embodied, or incarnate in history – construed in either a literal, mythical, or metaphorical sense; the second person of a divine Trinity; the pre-existent Logos, born before all time; the Lord of the cosmos; the Saviour of the world; a Jewish 'eschatological' (that is, end-of-the-world, final-time) Prophet, like Moses though greater than Moses;[60] a spirit-possessed healer;[61] a magician;[62] a teacher and preacher; a zealot;[63] a sapiential sage or the prophet of wisdom; a Pharisaic rabbi;[64] a Galilean charismatic; a king; a cynic;[65] a revolutionary peasant;[66] a deluded cultural misfit; a superstar;

a liberator;[67] a pedagogue of the oppressed;[68] the son of a virgin called Miriam (the Hebraic form of 'Mary'); or the offspring of Joseph.

The plurality of Jesus images in contemporary research serves as fodder for opponents of the use of historical-critical methods in Christology to declare that the profusion of titles predicated of Jesus is clear proof that modern historical inquiries are abortive attempts to discover what can only be provided by religious faith. For the opponents, one need only rehearse Chalcedon to specify the identity, singularity and excellence of Jesus. He is universally significant because he is identifiable with God. However, it is as well to recall that current attempts to characterize Jesus are not as chaotic as might first appear. Current Jesus researchers tend to fall into one of two major groups: those who regard Jesus as a prophet of apocalyptic eschatology; and those who insist that he was not an apocalyptic teacher.

> **apocalyptic eschatology**
> The English word 'apocalypse' comes from the Greek term *apocalypsis*, meaning 'revelation'. To speak of a prophet of apocalyptic eschatology is to refer to a person who proclaims that God will be revealed to human beings at the end of time and history.

Contemporary scholars who regard Jesus as a prophet of apocalyptic eschatology interpret his central message of the kingdom of God 'as a dramatic, divine intervention that would forever change the nature of human existence, when God would exercise his power to eradicate evil and extend his reign of peace and justice throughout the world'.[69] Representatives of this group include E.P. Sanders, John P. Meier, Paula Fredriksen, Edward Schillebeeckx and James Allison.[70] Those who regard Jesus as a non-apocalyptic teacher interpret his message of God's kingdom as a this-worldly call for people to shatter social boundaries and establish more egalitarian societies. Scholars of this type include John Dominic Crossan and Marcus Borg.[71] They prefer to interpret Jesus sapientially – that is, as a wise person who would not let others control his life.

from chalcedon back to galilee

It may well be the case that the two groups just mentioned are not as opposed as first appears. Jesus' life and teachings might have displayed both apocalyptic and non-apocalyptic features. There is no reason to assume that a God-obsessed apocalyptic world-view is utterly at odds with a this-worldly, ethically egalitarian and sapiental world-view.[72] In short, Jesus was a Galilean preacher of justice and a prophet of apocalyptic eschatology whose life centred on what he called God's kingdom.

A useful way of coming to grips with the historical identity of Jesus is to focus on Galilee and the way empires impinged on his life there. Jesus lived in a highly conflictual society. His people had previously suffered a baneful history of imperial subjugation. To recount that history briefly, around the year 1250 BCE, a group of non-Egyptian Semitic tribes called the *Habiru* ('foreigners') who lived in the north-east of Egypt left there and moved into Canaan. It is possible that the Habiru were later called Hebrews and that their journeys form the historical basis of the biblical narrative of the Exodus.[73] In any case, the Hebrews who established the nation of Israel endured a long history of persecution at the hands of imperial armies. An Assyrian army led by Tiglathpilesar III subjugated Galilee in 731 BCE. A Babylonian invading force conquered Jerusalem in 587–586 BCE. After Babylonian control, Persians seized and maintained power over the Israelites from 559 to 332. By 332, Alexander the Great had subsequently subdued the Israelites, only to be followed by Romans in the middle of the first century BCE. In 4 BCE, the year the Jewish King Herod died, Galilean Jews rebelled against Roman control in Galilee. General Varus, the Roman legate of Syria, dispatched legions of soldiers southwards to subdue the revolution. His army razed the city of Sepphoris, which was only an hour's walk from Nazareth. Jesus was born in a world governed by terror, and died after a short life blighted by political cruelty. Everything he said and did transpired under the shadow of imperial power in the wake of a savage history of exploitation and destitution. He remains a figure of fascination today precisely because of the way he linked a vision of a God to come with an indignation at present injustice that cries and hopes for God to come.

conclusion

To speak thus, though, is to talk about Jesus in a language far removed from dogma. The tensile difference between the two languages, historical and dogmatic, arose in the modern age. Modern theology raises a cluster of critical questions for Chalcedonian Christology. First, the method of that Christology concentrates on late rather than early documents. That is, it dwells on doctrines about Jesus formulated four hundred years after his death, instead of focusing on the Christian Scriptures that were composed during the first century on the basis of oral stories circulating among members of the Jesus movement. Second, classical Christology begins by discoursing about what cannot be known and described (God), instead of commencing with a discussion of what can be known (Jesus from Nazareth).[74] Third, the doctrine of Chalcedon lacks anchorage in Jesus' life. It ignores his life experiences and suffering, with the result that dogmatic Christologies relying on Chalcedon fixate on Jesus' death and professed resurrection to the extent of giving the impression that there was no point to his life before his execution. Finally, traditional theology has for centuries sought to interpret Jesus in abstraction from his Galilean provenance. If one wants to understand anything about an ancient Galilean Jew, it is clearly advisable to study the history, topography, ecology, economics and politics of Galilee, together with its unique religious customs.

Jesus' life unfolded under the dark shadow of imperial might, which explains the way Mark's Gospel wonderfully depicts Jesus' antidote to the poison of political imperialism: 'The time is fulfilled, and the kingdom of God has come near; repent and believe in the good news' (Mark 1:15). If this is the fulcrum of Jesus' teaching, then sadly his vision is yet to be realized. The world today is a swamp of misery, and the reign of God is not yet apparent.

8

hermeneutics:
are christian teachings unambiguous?

> Human beings are perhaps never more frightening than when they are
> convinced beyond doubt that they are right.
>
> *Laurens van der Post*

Modern biblical studies furnished a vast reservoir of new knowledge for Christian
communities and academies. They also posed a fatiguing and disquieting problem
for modern theology. Significantly, they evolved in concord with yet another
intellectual preoccupation called modern hermeneutics. No one typifies more
tragically than David Friedrich Strauss the daunting dilemma that both modern
biblical studies and hermeneutics pose for modern theology. By the time he died
in 1874, he had lost his Christian faith. As Gregory Dawes illustrates, Strauss's
work

> raised in the starkest possible terms the central question of the historical Jesus
> debate. Can the distinctive claims of the Christian tradition still be defended after
> the reliability of the documents in which they are embodied has been called into
> question? ... The authority of the Christian faith has traditionally rested on the
> reliability of the witnesses to its foundational events. Once 'the great reversal' has
> occurred, once the Bible is no longer the taken-for-granted framework of knowledge,
> what role is left for the theologian? If the Bible can no longer function as 'the
> metanarrative to end all metanarratives,' what function can it play? Strauss's final
> answer to that question was a simple one. The Bible no longer has a role to play. A
> theology that can no longer make its traditional claims is not worth attempting to
> preserve, and we must honestly face the consequences of what is effectively a loss of
> faith.[1]

It does not follow necessarily that advanced modern biblical studies lead inexorably to a dispiriting loss of religious belief. The studies might well lead

to the erosion of intellectual *naïvetés*, only to produce wiser and more accurate appreciations of the varied messages of biblical narratives.

Having considered modern biblical criticism and quests for the historical Jesus in the previous chapters, it is now possible to ponder an additional intimidating question for modern theology that is evident in the emergence of modern hermeneutics. For many Christians in the past and today, the tenets of Christian doctrine are perfectly clear to any person, dim-witted or perceptive. For others, complex interpretative skills need to be acquired in order to divine their essential meanings. The predominant purpose of this chapter is not only to explain the nature and a little of the history of hermeneutics, but also to argue that interpretative skills are required today if complex doctrines and biblical stories are adequately to be comprehended.

The issue of whether or not Christian teachings are unambiguous is not an irrelevant and intellectually airborne affair. It has serious consequences for many people's lives. Church leaders and preachers frequently interpret biblical passages and dogmas to regulate the way people live. If their interpretations are simplistic or wrong, people's well-being can be distressingly harmed. Ill-informed and false interpretations of biblical verses and dogmas can create misery for human beings struggling to cope with profound ethical quandaries. Much more will now need to be said about the nature of hermeneutics and the potential ambiguities of Christian teachings to support the assertions just made.

hermeneutics

Hermeneutics is not a household word. It could even be surmised that it is an uncommon, and resolutely off-putting, term. Rarely do friends compliment each other for being outstanding hermeneuts. Equally infrequently do they praise each other for their hermeneuses of life and love. Even so, and despite the somewhat odd resonance of the word 'hermeneutics', it would be a mistake to conclude that hermeneutics is an unimportant, arcane and epiphenomenal human activity. It would be erroneous to suppose that hermeneutics is an endeavour for the esoteric; the eclectic; the intellectually abstruse; and the bloodless, sapless, bookish types who are woefully alienated from everyone and everything that is exciting in the daily project of human living.

As strange as it may seem, hermeneutics is an indispensable part of every human being's mental make-up. Despite a widespread social and cultural unfamiliarity with the word and activities of hermeneutics, every person alive and sentient today behaves hermeneutically from morning to night. This is so because hermeneutics, explained at its simplest, is an unavoidable everyday activity of interpretation. It is a conscious, intellectual quest to discover meaning. It is driven by a single governing question: 'What does the process of interpretation involve, and can it ever uncover indubitable meaning?'

For most people's waking hours, indeed for all of their conscious and dreaming moments, they are constantly involved in the work of interpretation. That work only ceases in moments of unconsciousness, drunkenness or narcosis. Humans are doomed to think and interpret. Many turn to drugs and drink to escape the heavy burden of not being able to escape thinking, deciphering, categorizing and interpreting. When people meet, especially for the first time, they inadvertently attempt to work each other out, as it were. When people meet from remote and alien localities, trying to decipher each other becomes all the more difficult. And when people meet for the first time and make judgements about each other, on what basis could they possibly ascertain whether or not their judgements are insightful and truthful? People not only estimate each other on first encounter. They also size up objects, texts, works of art, sights and sounds, and movements that they perceive in the course of their lives. When they turn their attention to texts encountered, especially texts descendent from a distant place and time, by what means are they to console themselves that their impressions of apprehended texts are meaningful and truthful? The point here is plain and simple: human beings constantly engage in the activity of interpreting throughout their daily lives. They interpret words, texts, gestures, music, movement, mood, feelings, art, sport and sound. By their very nature, they are unable to avoid interpretation, except in states of insensibility induced by dreamless sleep or drugs.

Yet even as all people inevitably interpret, they also misinterpret. Thus it transpires that to live in a human society is to live with conflicting interpretations. Moreover, to be involved with an ecclesial society, like the Church of Jesus Christ, is to dwell in a thick fog of opposed interpretations of God and Jesus Christ. As indicated previously, Christian denominations today are riven by disputes about the meaning of Jesus' life and labours. Each denomination is not only divided within itself. It is also separated from a host of other Christian groups that offer endlessly incompatible readings of the meanings of Christian faith.

If at its simplest hermeneutics can be described as the human activity of interpretation, in a more nuanced way it could be explained as the art, theory, method and practice of interpreting language and texts so as to avoid misinterpretation and to dispel conflicting interpretations. Hermeneutics, therefore, is the methodological exploration of meaning. The rest of this chapter will attend to four matters. First, the historical provenance of the very word 'hermeneutics' will be explained. A second step will elaborate the hermeneutical problem, or

FIGURE 8.1 An anonymous replica of an original statue of the God Hermes that dates from the second century BCE, and is housed in the Museo del Prado, Madrid. It should not pass unnoticed that Hermes is depicted as a winsome young man. Such, for educated ancient Greeks, was the paradigm of the human being. This paradigm proved to be influential, and deleterious for women, in the writings of early Christian theologians.

the central dilemma that hermeneutics seeks to overcome. In the third place, a brief comment will be made on a phenomenon known as the hermeneutical circle. Finally, the modern history of hermeneutics and its relevance for modern theology will be addressed briefly.

The root of the English term 'hermeneutics' is the Greek name Hermes. In the ancient Hellenistic pantheon, Hermes was regarded as a divine emissary or messenger. His task was to convey and elucidate messages from the Gods and the High God to human beings, who would be otherwise totally bereft of a medium for understanding Godly communications. The Greek Gods, it is helpful to recall, could be playful, naughty, deceitful and lascivious. Subsequently, human beings, so it was imagined, stand in need of a helper so that they may avoid being tricked or confused by mischievous Gods. In other terms, they require the help of someone like Hermes to make sure they are not fooled by the Gods' cryptic messages. Hermes was thereby construed as an interpreter of the Gods. His name forms the root of the Greek noun *hermeneia*, meaning 'interpretation'. And the Latin equivalent of *hermeneia* is *interpretatio*, from which of course the English word 'interpretation' derives.

Since roughly the seventeenth century the term 'hermeneutics' has served to refer to 'the interpretation of texts'. It is important to note, however, that its ancient Greek usage is much more fluid. The Greek infinitive *hermeneuein*, to interpret, appears to have been deployed by the Greeks with three basic meanings: (1) 'to express aloud in words'; or 'to say or to vocalise'; (2) 'to explain', as in explaining a situation; and (3) 'to translate', as in the translation of a foreign language. Intriguingly, contemporary English carries much the same resonances. The ninth edition of *The Concise Oxford English Dictionary* defines the verb 'to interpret' in four ways: (1) to explain the meaning of foreign or abstruse words or of a dream; (2) to elucidate or bring out the meaning of a creative work; (3) to act as an interpreter, especially of foreign languages; and (4) to explain or understand behaviour in a specified manner (such as 'interpreted his gesture as mocking').[2]

To recall, the Greek verb *hermeneuein* conveys three basic meanings: to express, to explain, and to translate. English still retains these three primordial meanings. Yet even though it is possible to speak of a triplicity of meanings, it may well be possible to discern a single basic meaning underlying the three different understandings of what it means to interpret. Richard Palmer concludes that the latter is indeed the case. In his book *Hermeneutics* (1969), he observes: 'in all three cases, something foreign, strange, separated in time, space or experience is made familiar, comprehensible; something requiring representation, explanation, or translation is somehow "brought to understanding" – is "interpreted".'[3] Hermeneutics is the process by which the unfamiliar is rendered familiar.

Nowadays, philosophers and historians define hermeneutics variously. For some, hermeneutics is the interpretation of speech. For others it is the methodological exploration of meaning. For yet another group it is the interpretation of texts. Fusing these definitions together, hermeneutics is helpfully defined as the methodological exploration or interpretation of the meaning of language. Crucially, 'language' in this context does not merely refer to vocalised human sounds. Instead, language embraces several modes of human communication such as words, images, sounds, symbols, gestures and writing. All of these may properly be regarded as language. In everyday parlance people often speak of body language and sign language. Werner Jeanrond, in his book *Theological Hermeneutics*, explains language nicely when he says,

> Interpreting a text or a work of art is a linguistic activity. That means it is done through language. Here 'language' is used in the widest sense possible: a sculpture, a painting, a musical score, a ballet, a clown's act with its use of gestures – all these and other artistic expressions are realised in and through some form of language. Thus 'language' refers to more than mere verbal expressions. Therefore it is useful to distinguish between forms of verbal and non-verbal communication.[4]

Returning to a previous point, if one says that hermeneutics is the methodological exploration or interpretation of the meaning of language, it needs to be noted instantly that such a definition turns on a pivotal word, namely 'meaning'. Whereas hermeneutics, or interpretation, involves rendering familiar something that is foreign, strange or separated from us in time, the word 'meaning' is far more complex and protean. Well might one say that meaning has several meanings! To illustrate, meaning can connote intention, purpose, reference, 'to be a sign of', or simply verbal sense. It is precisely when considering meaning, when embarking on interpreting, that people land themselves in the densest thicket of hermeneutical conundrums.

the hermeneutical problem

That stated, it is now possible to proceed to the second major stage of this chapter, which is to ponder the hermeneutical problem and why it has surfaced so emphatically for religious believers and theologians today. Thus far, this chapter has simply tried to elucidate the meaning of the strange term 'hermeneutics'. Now it is time to tackle the pivotal problem with which hermeneutics consistently grapples.

It has already been noted in the consideration of the meaning of the term 'hermeneutics' undertaken above that the word basically refers to an interpretative process wherein, to quote Richard Palmer again, 'something foreign, strange, separated in time, space or experience is made familiar, comprehensible'. In other words, to interpret something is to attempt to bridge a temporal, spatial and experiential cleavage between an interpreting person and something that is alien to and chronologically separated from him or her. To speak of a hermeneutical problem is simply to acknowledge that people are severely constrained in attempting to decipher the meaning of something foreign because they cannot avoid interpreting on the bases of their own biases, knowledge, history and context, which are not at all those of the thing or person they are striving to understand. How, then, can one be sure that one can ever accurately grasp the truth and beauty of an alien object from a distant past, such as a book or musical score?

The force of the hermeneutical problem can be illustrated clearly and simply by gazing at the image in Figure 8.2. With this image the viewer is confronted with a complicated work of art. While looking at it, questions must surely multiply. Whence does it come? Who painted it? What is this image meant to communicate to its viewers? Indeed, what does this painting mean? Is its meaning obvious? Does its meaning lie in the paint? or in the mind of its creator? or in

FIGURE 8.2

an interplay between itself and a viewing subject? Perhaps it has no stable meaning at all. Why does the image depict so many skeletons? Why is its palette of colours scorched?

Its variegated subject matter appears disturbing to say the least. Consider what appears to be a tortured victim in the top right-hand corner of the painting (Figure 8.3). This sight confronts its beholder with the full force of the hermeneutical dilemma. A body dangles from a tree, held in place by a large nail under its chin. It is naked. It is desolate. Its wrists are bound high behind its back. Why has this person endured such a dreadful, solitary death (assuming the person is dead). The context of the lonely body is richly multifaceted. Is it at all possible to retrieve the intrinsic meaning of such an object from the past? If so, where is the meaning to be located, and by which means? One further question: is this image inherently religious? Religious symbols and images from the past can be exceptionally difficult to decipher.

Consider the painting by Caravaggio in Figure 8.4. This canvas is called 'St John the Baptist with a Ram'. It was completed in 1602, and is housed in the Capitoline Museum in Rome. While some interpret this image as an arresting portrayal of a young prophet, others, like Alfred Moir, describe its subject as 'a pagan little tease, uncontaminated by Christian senti-ment'.[5] The boy Baptist is embracing a ram whose snout is close to the boy's face and lips. The Baptist's thighs are splayed wantonly. What, then, is the religious meaning of this depiction of an adolescent boy? Is the painting portraying a lascivious little flirt or a holy boy? A young prophet or a bratty seducer? Could this painting be commending bestiality or inviting pederasty? For some, the beholder is offered a sublime view of a holy innocent. For others, the picture is a riot of eroticism parading as a pious painting.[6]

In the twentieth century, there were two major competing hermeneutical and philosophical approaches to the vexed question of the retrieval of meaning from the past. The first approach to resolving the hermeneutical problem is to assert that an age-old painting, like the illustrations just discussed, has meaning and truth which it will eventually reveal to its interpreters by itself. This view is typified by the German philosopher Hans-Georg Gadamer.[7] The second approach insists that it is quite impossible to glean the meaning of a past object without the help of additional information *external* to the object. This view is exemplified by the French philosopher Paul Ricoeur.

These two views of interpretation translate immediately to the field of Christian theology, which is resolutely preoccupied with the hermeneutical problem of trying to interpret texts from a long distant past. To set upon the meaning of the Book of Revelation, chapters 12 and 13, for instance, does one merely need to suppose that the text will unfold its own sense and truth, or must it be interpreted with the help of extra-biblical data and literary theories?

FIGURE 8.3

Relating those questions to the first painting mentioned above, it is opportune to ask once more, just what does it mean? Is its meaning quite clear? Have its truth and beauty manifested themselves without anyone external to the picture providing any information about it? For a disciple of Gadamer, the image will eventually reveal its essential meaning to the beholder over time. For a follower

FIGURE 8.4

of Ricoeur, though, it is not possible accurately and probingly to understand the image's point and purpose without acquiring information about its historical provenance and its creator.

Does it indeed help a process of interpreting meaning if the following information about Figure 8.2 is provided? It is called, in English, 'The Triumph of Death'. It hangs in the Museo del Prado in Madrid, not far from the statue of Hermes. It was painted by the Flemish artist Pieter Breugel 'the Elder' (1525/1530–1569). Consequently, this is a Renaissance painting. It also stems from the era of the Reformation. The directors of the Prado Museum itself interpret the painting in the following manner:

> In this work, quite complex given the number of scenes, [Breugel] wished to represent the Triumph of Death over all earthly things – as in the Danses Macabres of medieval literature. The version he gives us is that of an anguished end without the least bit of hope: even the sombre colours of the bare earth and the background fires accentuate [humankind's] uneasiness with death's arrival. Death rides in on a squalid horse, with a scythe, pushing humanity against an army of skeletons with coffin lids.[8]

All this follows in the wake of the religious strife of the Reformation. Close inspection of the painting reveals a humiliated cardinal and a mockery of the absurdity of collecting money for indulgences.

Breugel's 'Triumph of Death' serves admirably as a tool to illustrate the force of the hermeneutical problem and the quest for meaning. It also illuminates interpretative difficulties that beset Christian theology. Among Christians there are many disciples of Gadamer. For these, the Bible and doctrines of the past reveal their own meaning to any earnest inquirer. For such believers, age-old expressions of religious belief do not need complex interpretation, let alone re-interpretation.

As Christians disagree about how faith is most aptly to be interpreted or reinterpreted nowadays, the cultures surrounding the churches are, according to Don Cupitt, witnessing a massive and widespread evaporation of religious meaning.[9] As for the contemporary situation of the Catholic Church of the Roman Rite, Hans Küng is quite blunt. In his recent tome, *A Global Ethic for Global Politics and Economics*, he opines:

> millions have left the church, millions have withdrawn into themselves, and millions – particularly in the new German federal states – have not joined the church. The hierarchs responsible, sometimes confused, sometimes mendacious, prevaricate: it's not so bad. But isn't the light of Christianity slowly being quenched?[10]

In such circumstances there is evidently an urgent need for theologians to think again about how primordial Christianity can be interpreted tellingly for the benefit of contemporary human beings. There is no escaping the enormity of the dissipation of classical theological meanings nowadays. To contend that Christianity in the world at large is undergoing a few major changes is to indulge in a massive understatement.

The question is: what is to be done about classical Christian beliefs and doctrines as Christianity enters a phase of far-reaching cultural transmutation? Ought Christians to don blinkers against all types of new ideas and social configurations? Should they behave like proverbial ostriches, place their heads in sand, and pretend there is nothing wrong? Could they simply restate classical formulations of doctrine with calm confidence? Or should they wake up and realize that traditional teachings are intellectually unconvincing for most contemporary westerners?

Hans Küng, it will be recalled, chides hierarchs themselves for being responsible for a massive exodus from his Church. Some hierarchs, no doubt, would in turn accuse modish, liberal, avant-garde and dissident theologians of confusing the faithful Christians, and intellectually seducing the young away from venerable orthodoxies.

The point is: while theologians and Church leaders generally recognize a troubling crisis of faith these days, they differ widely among themselves over its causes and about what should be done to redress it. Thus it transpires that Christians align themselves with diverse priorities and strategies to keep the light of Christianity burning, to borrow Küng's phrase, and earn themselves the labels of being hermeneutical thinkers, liberal theologians, dogmatists or fundamentalists. Radicals lampoon conservatives, traditionalists vie with progressive pragmatists, while liberationists debate with papal apologists. And so, the labelling and name-calling proliferates.

the hermeneutical circle

A particularly salient feature of the human process of understanding is that it is inherently circular. Understanding occurs in a spiralling way. The twentieth-century German philosopher Martin Heidegger pointed out in his *magnum opus*, *Being and Time*, that interpretation is earthed in three things: fore-having, something known by an interpreter in advance to reading a text; fore-sight, something perceived in advance; and fore-conception, something grasped in advance. To cite his own words in English translation:

> Whenever something is interpreted as something, the interpretation will be found essentially upon fore-having, fore-sight, and fore-conception. An interpretation is never a presuppositionless apprehending of something presented to us. If, when one is engaged in a particular concrete kind of interpretation, in the sense of exact textual interpretation, one likes to appeal to what 'stands there,' then one finds that what 'stands there' in the first instance is nothing other that the obvious undiscussed assumption of the person who does the interpreting.[11]

Expressed differently, every reader of a text begins the act of reading in view of a particular perspective or predisposition that has been constructed by the reader's own personal history and cultural context. Each and every text is 'read, perceived, and interpreted within a pre-existent structure of reality. All understanding and interpretation proceed from a prior understanding or a system of making sense of reality.'[12] It view of which, it becomes clear that there is no such thing as a purely objective reading and interpretation of a text. Each reading is in some way coloured by the reader's presuppositions.[13]

To speak of a hermeneutical circle or spiral is to draw attention to the role of presuppositions in the process of interpretation: 'We always approach the act of reading a text with a particular set of pre-understandings which are then challenged or confirmed during the reading process itself.'[14] An object read, and a subject reading, mutually stimulate each other and thereby both contribute to an overall process of understanding. It is precisely because of a subject's personal presuppositions that purely objective interpretations of texts are impossible. One of the tasks of hermeneutics is to encourage readers to identity and make allowances for the predisposition they bring to a text when they read it.

the history of hermeneutics in a nutshell

Having talked about the meaning and task of hermeneutics, as well as the hermeneutical problem and circle, a few summary remarks may now be made about the history of hermeneutics.[15] In textbooks devoted to hermeneutics, it is common for accounts of the history of hermeneutics to begin with hermeneutics in the Age of Modernity. Many books begin their ruminations with an analysis of the hermeneutical theories of Friedrich Schleiermacher (1768–1834). Such an approach can readily give the impression that hermeneutic sensibilities only evolved in a sophisticated manner with the advent of philosophical modernity. In fact, hermeneutics in quite complex forms began with, and flourished among, the ancient Greeks and Romans.

Cicero and Quintilian, for instance, produced treatises devoted to interpretation, which they called *interpretatio scripti* – that is, 'the interpretation of written material pertinent to legal cases such as laws, wills, and contracts'.[16] Cicero devoted four of his works to the question of interpretation: *De inventione*, *De oratore*, *Orator* and *Topica*.

The Romans of Cicero's day were beneficiaries of Greek rhetorical tradition. Thus, when retracing the genesis of hermeneutics in the ancient world, it is advisable to chart its evolution by beginning with the Greeks of old. Homer's two great epics, the *Iliad* and the *Odyssey*, formed the background of the ancient Greek educational system. The two texts suffused both the public and the domestic lives of ancient Greeks. Hermeneutics arose historically as a need to specify the correct function and meaning of the epics in Greek culture. In later centuries and in other cultures, Greek hermeneutical thought was appropriated by Jews and Christians as they sought to decipher the meaning of epic biblical sagas.

It is important to note that ancient hermeneutics arose in the context of rhetoric – that is, the science and art of persuasion. With differing understandings of Homeric prose and public law, a hermeneutical rhetorician inherited the task of trying to persuade a wider public of the merits of a particular interpretation, over and against rival interpretations.

Be that as it may, apart from the Greeks and Romans, it is important to note the need for hermeneutics in interpreting the sacred writings of Christians. Hermeneutics, for Christians, is not a newfangled thing. Here is an intriguing vignette from the eighth chapter of the Acts of the Apostles:

> Now after Peter and John had testified and spoken the word of the Lord, they returned to Jerusalem, proclaiming the good news to many villages of the Samaritans. Then an angel of the Lord said to Philip. Get up and go towards the south to the road that goes down from Jerusalem to Gaza. ... So he got up and went. Now, there was an Ethiopian eunuch, a court official of Candace, queen of the Ethiopians, in charge of her entire treasury. He had come to Jerusalem to worship and was returning home; seated in his chariot, he was reading the prophet Isaiah. He asked, 'Do you understand what you are reading? He replied, 'How can I, unless someone guides me?' And he invited Philip to get in and sit beside him. (Acts 8:25–33)

'Do you understand what you are reading?, Philip is said to have asked. 'How can I, unless someone guides me?', comes the reply. There in a nutshell is captured the entire point and purposes of hermeneutics. Like Philip with the Ethiopian eunuch, hermeneutics seeks to guide people towards enhanced understanding.

Historically, there have been six major phases in the history of hermeneutics. The first lay in the ancient Greek and Roman readings of Homeric epics and legal documents. The second encompassed ancient Jewish and early Christian translations and clarifications of biblical texts. The third spanned the patristic and medieval eras. The fourth unfolded during the Age of Humanism and was focused on a major interpretative debate between Erasmus and Luther. The fifth began most notably in the nineteenth century with Friedrich Schleiermacher (1768–1834) and is tied to the growth of modern theological hermeneutics. The sixth and final phase has its roots in the thought of Martin Heidegger and is quite decidedly a form of philosophical hermeneutics.

In terms of the modern history of hermeneutics, Schleiermacher is significant because he saw very clearly that the process of understanding always has the potential to be mistaken. People cannot readily assume that words mean what they first think they do when they are encountered in a historical text. Misunderstandings easily arise because as time separates an interpreter from an author the meanings of words evolve and change.

Furthermore, Schleiermacher insisted that the reconstruction of an author's thought patterns rests upon the major hermeneutical principle of the hermeneutical circle. For Schleiermacher, an individual understands the meaning of a word by viewing it in relation to the entirety of a sentence, and the meaning of the sentence is dependent on the meaning of particular words. Meaning, therefore, always arises in a circular movement between part and whole.[17]

Consider, for example, the four monosyllabic words 'with', 'the', 'a', 'in'. They mean something aligned as they are, but they do not mean much. If they are related to the broader context of a sentence, they become much more intelligible and interesting, as in the case of the following sentence: 'Without hesitation, the cardinal strangled his maid with a towel in the pope's bathroom.'

In the modern period, theologians and philosophers have distinguished quite different ways of locating a text's meaning. For some, the meaning of a text or a work of art lies in the mind of an author or painter. In Schleiermacher's view, to comprehend a text is to re-experience the mental process of the text's author. He regards authorial intention as all-important in the quest for accurate understanding. Unlike Schleiermacher, Wilhelm Dilthey (1833–1911) did not focus on the mental process of an author, but insisted instead that meaning resides in the subjectivity of an interpreter. For Martin Heidegger, to understand is to be in the world. Comprehending concerns one's power to grasp one's possibility for being within the context of the world in which one lives. It is not the power, *pace* Schleiermacher, to enter into the thoughts and feelings of another person.

In short, there are basically four competing views about how people can be sure about the meaning of language. These four ways are linked to the different forms of biblical criticism that have developed over the past century. With regard to meaning, one view holds that the meaning of language resides with its author or speaker. A second theory concludes that meaning resides in a text or work of art itself. A third posture insists that meaning rests in the mind and feelings of a reader of a text. In a fourth scenario there is no such thing as a fixed, stable meaning.

In the light of all that has been said in this chapter, an unambiguous answer still needs to be given to the question, 'Are Christian doctrines unambiguous?' If they are, then modern theology can dispense with hermeneutics. If they are fraught with ambiguities and produce a multiplicity of possible meanings, then hermeneutical methods are called for in attempts to decipher them.

It can readily be illustrated that Christian teachings can be inherently ambiguous since they come to us from a bygone world that no longer exists. The necessity of acquiring hermeneutical skills to interpret doctrines can be illustrated with reference to an ancient Christian profession of faith called the Apostles' Creed. In the form it is currently professed by Christians it dates from the eighth century, but it may date in more primitive modes to as far back as the fourth century CE. The first hermeneutical skill required by a would-be interpreter of the Creed is to learn Latin, the language in which the text was originally composed. To translate the Latin is already to interpret it.

Of all the Creed's sentences, only one is historically verifiable. Namely, 'He suffered under Pontius Pilate, was crucified, died, and was buried.' The assertion that 'He was conceived by the power of the Holy Spirit' is very far from clear. So too is the sentence 'He descended to the dead.' Interpreting the other sentences is not simply an academic exercise. It is an art. Many Christian doctrines are highly ambiguous and can become more so as the period of time grows between the ages in which they were first codified. The Apostles' Creed was formulated at a vast temporal distance from contemporary human cultures. It relies on a defunct biblical cosmology that conceives of the universe in terms of heaven, earth and the underworld. How could anyone be expected to make any sense of it now without a guide, like Philip with the eunuch?

The North American biblical critic Robert Funk charges that the Apostles' Creed is forgetful of the actual life of Jesus. In his book, *Honest to Jesus*, he accuses the formulators of the Creed of giving the impression that there is nothing of consequence in Jesus' life worth considering between, on the one hand, his miraculous birth to a virgin mother and, on the other hand, his ignominious death on a Roman cross. 'The creed', says Funk, 'left a blank where Jesus should have come.'[19] Funk insists that the Jesus who is left out of the Creed, the man who lived and laboured in Galilee and Judah, would not have approved of the Creed's content, which transforms an iconoclast into an icon.[20]

> **the apostles' creed**   I believe in God the Father almighty, creator of heaven and earth. I believe in Jesus Christ, his only Son, our Lord. He was conceived by the power of the Holy Spirit and born of the Virgin Mary. He suffered under Pontius Pilate, was crucified, died, and was buried. He descended to the dead. On the third day he rose again. He ascended into heaven and is seated at the right hand of the Father. He will come again to judge the living and the dead. I believe in the Holy Spirit, the holy catholic Church, the communion of saints, the forgiveness of sins, the resurrection of the body, and the life everlasting. Amen.[18]

Funk has a point: classical Christian theology often focuses on a doctrine of incarnation while overlooking the theological significance of the entire course of Jesus' life. Yet even those traditional theologies that are anchored in a doctrine that the Logos of God became incarnate in the man Jesus cannot escape ambiguities surrounding the possible meanings of the notion of incarnation. For many centuries Christians have declared that Jesus Christ was the embodiment of God in human history. To the question 'Is the doctrine of the incarnation unambiguous?', several Christians would reply, 'Of course!' Such a straightforward response can easily be needled by a string of hermeneutical queries. When did the incarnation take place, the moment Jesus was conceived, or the instant he was born? Does the entire lifespan of Jesus constitute an incarnation? Was the movement of disciples that gathered around him part of the incarnation? If God became incarnate in time, does it follow that God is mutable?

Interpretative traps await those attempting to interpret biblical passages in addition to ecclesiastical dogmas. Consider, for instance, the passage in Matthew's Gospel where Jesus encounters Peter at Caesarea Philippi and speaks to him in the following terms: 'And I tell you, you are Peter, and on this rock I will build my church, and the gates of Hades will not prevail against it. I will give you the keys of the kingdom, and whatever you bind on earth will be bound in heaven, and whatever you loose on earth will be loosed in heaven' (Matt. 16:18–19). To this day, people tell jokes about Peter standing at the pearly gates of heaven and interrogating new arrivals with a view to deciding whether or not they may enter. Commenting on these two verses of Matthew, David Kling of the University of Miami reminds his readers that 'No other passage in the Bible has been the focus of so much controversy.'[21] Quite apart from the ancient cosmology assumed by the passage ('gates of Hades'; 'heaven'), the terminology referring to Peter binding on earth and loosing in heaven is very far from clear. These two verses have been used by the Catholic Church for several hundreds of years to argue that in promising to Peter the keys of the kingdom Jesus was thereby establishing the papacy. Thus, for many Catholics, the papacy is divinely instituted. For most Protestants it is human in origin. The papacy is currently the oldest monarchy in existence. In David Kling's view, 'the pope still remains the gravest obstacle to Christian unity'.[22] Over the past century a papal cult has been growing steadily. It has been aided by the invention of railways enabling masses of pilgrims to visit Rome; the recent custom of promoting papal jet travels around the world; and the global diffusion of televisual images of the pope, or Bishop of Rome. The contemporary geopolitical prominence of the papacy has all been built on a belief that Jesus wanted a papacy. What if he didn't? What if the story of Jesus promising keys to Peter is not a historical record, but a theological creation of the author of Matthew's Gospel? To answer this question requires a comparative hermeneutical study of passages in the Gospels of John (21: 15–17) and Mark 8:27–33, which are similar to, though different from, Matthew 16: 18–19. Of the three texts, Matthew is the only one depicting Jesus talking of 'my church'. For this and related reasons, the Catholic theologian Francis Schlüssler Fiorenza concludes, 'The Matthean text does not record an historical event at Caesarea Philippi during the earthly ministry of Jesus.'[23] For this perspective, Matthew is making a theological point about Jesus and the church, not depicting an historical event. The entire edifice of the papacy could rest on a mistake. The vignette at Caesarea Philippi, condensed in just two verses, illustrates amply the unavoidability, the ambiguities and the potential traps of hermeneutics.

The purpose of this chapter was not to describe in detail interpretative techniques that were developed by modern hermeneutical theory. A book in itself would be required to do justice to the intricacies of the techniques. In Christianity's present context of rapid and far-reaching cultural change, a primary goal of this chapter has been to illustrate that it cannot be assumed that ancient Christian beliefs and doctrines are readily intelligible to contemporary audiences. It might well be the case that Christian assemblies are dwindling in western cultures precisely because traditional Christian language is no longer either intelligible or interesting for people who are tantalized by DVDs, cinemas, computers and the Internet. Merely to repeat traditional doctrinal formulae without further ado will only serve to accelerate Christianity's slide towards social irrelevance.

part IV

**disputed questions
in the wake of modernity**

9

life in the gutter:
half-lives and have-nots

At no time has the poverty of humanity stood in such crying contradiction
to its potential wealth, at no time have all powers been so horribly fettered as
in this generation where children go hungry and the hands of the fathers are
busy turning out bombs.

Max Horkheimer

The twentieth century witnessed an unexpected mutation in the make-up of
Christianity. The transformation is yet to receive the widespread recognition it
deserves. It resides in the rapid growth of teeming masses of poor Christians in
regions far away from Europe and North America. Today, most Christians live
in Latin America, Africa and Asia, and the majority of them struggle to extrude
themselves from debilitating and dehumanizing poverty.

During the frenzy of millennial celebrations around the world during the year
2000, the momentous metamorphosis of Christianity's population was virtually
ignored in Europe, Australia and North America. To neglect the far-reaching
mutation of Christianity in the twentieth century is as ridiculous as it is to
comment on military conflicts in the same period without referring to the two
world wars, or to discuss political change in eighteenth-century France without
mentioning the French Revolution.[1]

The new world of a poor Christianity is youthful and fertile with a population that is rapidly expanding rather than stagnating and ageing. This body of
impoverished Christianity is also strongly Catholic. Indeed, Catholics presently
represent roughly half the total of Christians. In 2000, the global population of
Catholics was 1057 million out of a total of 2105 million Christians.[2] Presently,
the largest group of Anglicans are African.

At the beginning of the twenty-first century most Christians were struggling either to eke out a living or just to stay alive. Theirs is a world of half-lives, have-nots, street urchins and gutter dwellers. To speak of a half-life is rather bluntly to categorize someone who, lamentably, dies from preventable causes only halfway or far less through an anticipated lifespan. The most upsetting victims of poverty who are reduced to living half-lives suppurate in misery in Africa. In the African countries most afflicted by poverty, people can expect to live fifty years less than citizens of the world's superabundantly wealthy nations.[3]

The twentieth-century shift of Christianity's epicentre from Europe to the impoverished nations of the world is of seismic significance for modern theology. Or at least it ought to be. A great deal of what passes for modern theology and contemporary Christian discourse is blighted by a blatant parochiality: too often Christianity is equated with Europe; the Church is identified with the west; and centres of ecclesiastic power are housed in a decreasingly Christian European mainland. In 1920, the English Catholic writer Hilaire Belloc declared that 'The Church is Europe; and Europe is the Church.'[4] Today, his view is risible in the extreme. The extent to which Christianity has been transformed over the past few centuries can easily be demonstrated with a few facts. As noted previously, there are about 2 billion, or 2000 million Christians, in the world today. They constitute roughly a third of the planet's population. Of these, 480 million live in Latin America. In Africa, there are 360 million Christians, while 313 million Asians profess Christian faith. Europe is home to 560 million Christians, while 260 million can be found in North America. The situation of Christianity today differs significantly from its dispersion a hundred years ago. In 1900, there were roughly 10 million Christians in Africa. A century later, there were 360 million.[5]

The purpose of this chapter is to consider the menacing problem for theology that the abundant conglomerations of desperately poor people pose. This dreadfully daunting dilemma for modern theology has not been broached in any depth thus far in this book. Previous chapters have considered quandaries posed for relatively recent theology by scientific and political revolutions, philosophical theories, hermeneutical studies, biblical research and social secularization. The problem encountered in this chapter is quite different. It is also exceptionally distressing. It can be expressed in one phrase: dire poverty. The modern age, despite its exhilarating scientific and technological accomplishments, has not been able to arrest a steady and massive increase in the population of this planet's desperately needy peoples.

In the first half of the twentieth century, Christian theologians were not prone to writing about poverty. They were far more engaged in discoursing on Kant, modern biblical studies, ecclesiastical reform, Darwin and atheism. In the latter half of the twentieth century, the number of economically enfeebled, malnourished and starving people in the world had risen so alarmingly that a band of theologians in Latin America decided to bring the poor to the centre of theology's concerns. The work of these theologians is now called liberation theology. It has many enemies as well as practitioners. As Jesus discovered, to side with the poor can be a deadly affair. The story of the rise of liberation theology, and of subsequent resistance to its ideas, will form a major part of this chapter. While liberation theology emerged in the latter half of the twentieth century, its historical roots lie hundreds of years before then, as we shall see.

By methodological preference, liberation theologies reflect about God and God's hoped-for relation with people in the light of widespread human deprivation. The fruit of their reflections calls for a drastically revised understanding of the task and methods of theology itself. It may well turn out to be the case that liberation theologies collude to liberate theology from a long-standing, yet ultimately false and sterile understanding of what theology ought to aspire to achieve. Liberation theology is one of the more significant theological initiatives to have emerged during the twentieth century. It reflects tellingly a steadily growing theological engrossment with the plight of the poor. Pandemic poverty is most assuredly a disturbing conundrum for modern theology because theology has traditionally espoused a doctrine that God providentially cares for all human beings. Death-dealing poverty is the great gainsayer of the truthfulness of the doctrine of Divine Providence. The more poverty drives more people to despair, the less credible the doctrine becomes. Poverty is one of the most daunting of new questions posed by contemporary circumstances for old beliefs. Never before has the human population been so numerous, and never before have so many human beings struggled to stay alive because a minority of humanity is hoarding most of the planet's resources.

Before considering theologies of liberation in any detail, it is advisable to consider soberly the plight of the poor in the world of today.

the needy and the greedy

In 1950, this planet was populated by about 2.5 billion people. That number had risen to more than 6 billion by 1999.[6] In other terms, the twentieth century was an era of breathtakingly massive population growth. According to the United Nations' *Human Development Report 2003*,

> At the turn of the millennium more than 1.2 billion people were struggling to survive on less that $1 a day – and more than twice as many, 2.8 billion, on less than $2 a day. Living on $1 a day does not mean being able to afford what $1 would

buy when converted to a local currency, but the equivalent of what $1 would buy in the United States: a newspaper, a local bus ride, a bag of rice.[7]

We should note the shocking nature of these figures. Humanity has never before enjoyed such capital wealth and technological sophistication. The wealth, though, is not being distributed for the benefit of all – an age-old problem. Today, a fifth of all people (1.2 billion out of 6 billion) struggle on less than $1 a day, and nearly 50 per cent of the planet's population (2.8 billion) earn less than $2 a day.

Meanwhile, extravagantly wealthy people are simultaneously growing vastly richer: 'Between 1960 and 1995, the disparity in per capita income between the world's 20 richest and 20 poorest nations more than doubled, from 18–1 to 37–1.'[8] According to the Worldwatch Institute,

> One measure of growing disparities within wealthy nations is the widening gap between the compensation of corporate chief executive officers (CEOs) and the pay of employees. That differential grew more than fivefold during the 1990s, where it is by far the most pronounced. CEOs there made 350 times as much as the average factory worker in 2001, and sometimes were awarded lavish stock options even as layoffs were announced.[9]

Even the World Bank concedes that in the richest 20 countries of the world the average income is '37 times the average in the poorest 20 – a gap that has doubled in the past 40 years'.[10]

full lives and half-lives   In 2001, life expectancy at birth in Japan was 81.3 years. At the same time in Zambia it was 33.4. At the beginning of the twenty-first century, people in the wealthy countries of Europe, North America and Australia enjoyed lifespans that were twice as long as those of the inhabitants of Asia and the southern hemisphere. Life expectancy at birth during 2001 in Australia was 79.0 years, in Norway 78.7, in the United States of America 76.9, in the United Kingdom 77.9, in Brazil 67.8, South Africa 50.9, Cameroon 48.0, Botswana 47.4, Zambia 40, Rwanda 38.2, and in Sierra Leone 34.5.[11]

Impoverished countries not only suffer from malnutrition and starvation; they are all bedevilled by disease and unsanitary water. Very often their people are unattended by physicians. In the final decade of the twentieth century, there were 413 physicians for every 100,000 people in Norway. In Italy there were 554 physicians practising for every 100,000 citizens. In China there were 162. El Salvador endured with 107. In Chad during the same period, 3 physicians were available for every 100,000 people.[12]

Lack of income for poor people 'all too often translates into poor health, greater mortality and shorter life expectancy of the world's "have-nots". The infant mortality rate in low-income countries is 13 times the rate in high-income countries.'[13] In addition, 'Every year more than 10 million children die of preventable illnesses – 30,000 a day. More than 500,000 women a year die in pregnancy and childbirth, with such deaths 100 times more likely in Sub-Saharan Africa than in high-income OECD countries.'[14]

living with HIV or AIDS   One of the more worrying aspects of people's lives in poor countries is that they are vulnerable to infection by HIV. The United Nations observed in 2003 that around the world '42 million people are living with HIV/AIDS, 39 million of them in developing countries'.[15] The first cases of AIDS were diagnosed in the 1980s. By 1990, around 10 million people had become infected. Since then that number has more than quadrupled.[16] In 2001 in Australia, 0.07 per cent of adults between the ages of 15 and 49 were infected with HIV/AIDS. The equivalent figure for New Zealand was 0.06 per cent, for the United States 0.61 per cent, for the United Kingdom 0.10 per cent, South Africa 20.10 per cent, Swaziland 33.44 per cent, Zimbabwe 33.70 per cent, and Botswana 38.80 per cent.[17]

fabulous fortunes and dire need   Meanwhile, a well-oiled global money market is doing what it does best – feathering the nests of a small cartel of super-rich globe-trotters. According to the *United Nations Human Development 1999*, $1.5 trillion was then exchanged daily in the world's currency markets. The world's 200 richest people more than doubled their net worth to $1 trillion in the four years before 1998. The assets of the top three billionaires on this planet are more than the compared gross national product of all the least wealthy countries and their accumulated 600 million people.[18] *The United Nations Development Report 2003* records that 'The richest 5% of the world's people receive 114 times the income of the poorest 5%. The richest 1% receive as much as the poorest 57%. And the 25 richest Americans have as much income as almost 2 billion of the world's poorest people.'[19] Gotthold Lessing in the eighteenth century drew the attention of theologians to what he regarded as a great ugly ditch between necessary truths of reason and contingent truths of history. Much greater and far uglier is the contemporary chasm between the world's wealthy and starving inhabitants.

Hans Küng asks (mockingly) whether people will be made happier today by replacing 'the age old five Cs of true religion, Creed, Cult, Code, Conduct, Community' with what he calls 'the mundane five Cs of pseudo religion: Cash, Credit

Card, Car, Condominium, Country Club'.[20] For Küng, unbridled acquisitiveness and ecological despoliation has produced a world in which (by the 1990s),

- every *minute*, the nations of the world spend US$1.8 million on military armaments;
- every *hour*, 1500 children die of hunger-related causes;
- every *day*, a species becomes extinct;
- every *week* during the 1980s, more people were detained, tortured, assassinated, made refugee, or in other ways violated by repressive regimes than at any other time in history;
- every *month*, the world's economic system adds over US$0.5 billion to the catastrophically unbearable debt burden of more than $1,500 billion now resting on the shoulders of Third World peoples;
- every *year*, an area of tropical forest three-quarters the size of Korea is destroyed and lost;
- every *decade*, if present global warming trends continue, the temperature of the earth's atmosphere could rise dramatically (between 1.5 and 4.5 degrees Celsius) with a resultant rise in sea levels that would have disastrous consequences.[21]

Keith Hart concludes that current economic practices are lethal. To quote him directly:

> The economic forms we live by are themselves archaic. Indeed, capitalism could be said to be a sort of feudal economy matched to a machine revolution whose potential we barely understand. The lethal result is a polarized world society that resembles nothing so much as the old regime of eighteenth-century France, with an isolated elite controlling the destiny of powerless human masses to whose fate they are largely indifferent. Something must be done or life on this planet will soon be ruined.[22]

the poison of profit-driven people   Those unfortunate enough to be blighted by poverty are further enfeebled by the pollution generated by wealthy countries that are conspicuous for their high levels of energy consumption. One of the more dangerous by-products of patterns of consumption of profit-driven people in the well-off west is the lethal emission of carbon dioxide. Commenting on emission levels, the *Human Development Report 2002* is unsettlingly revealing. According to its statistics, during 1998 Bangladesh produced 0.1 per cent of the world total of carbon dioxide emissions. In the same year, India created 4.4 per cent; the Russian Federation made 5.9 per cent; and China belched forth 12.8 per cent. The United Kindom produced less, with a figure of 2.2 per cent. Strikingly, though, in 1998, the United States of America produced 22.5 per cent of the global total of carbon dioxide omissions.[23] Plainly, one of the wealthier corners of the globe poisons the lives of all other people on the planet, rich and poor alike.

exporting death   There is more and worse to come with regard to the behaviour of wealthy countries today. They thrive on the manufacture and export of death-dealing weapons. For example, in 2001 the United States of America exported weapons worth US$4,562 million. In the same year the United Kingdom exported $1,125 million worth of armaments. The Russian Federation exported $4,979 million, and China sold $588 million.[24]

Exported weapons have worked well. Warfare blights the lives of today's impoverished masses: 'During 1990–2001 there were 57 major armed conflicts in 45 locations.'[25] Since 1991, 'conflicts have killed as many as 3.6 million people and injured many millions more. Particularly tragic is that civilians, not soldiers, are increasingly the victims – accounting for more than 90% of deaths and injuries. Shockingly, children account for at least half of civilian casualties.'[26] The point is,

> Virtually all of the world's current armed conflicts take place in the developing world. Wars deepen the poverty and deprivation of civilian communities caught directly in the fighting, uprooted by violence, or hit by the repercussions – ruined economies, destroyed public infrastructures, and damaged public health systems.[27]

european colonial seizure of power   The massive wealth of the contemporary west was generated by two main exploitative factors: first, the modern use of technologies to dominate the planet's ecosystem and to extract its resources for financial gain; and second, the European colonial seizure of power in 1492 over what is now called Latin America. It is no accident that Hegel once quipped that the modern world began in 1492. The contemporary German theologian Jürgen Moltmann explains the economic consequences of 1492 in these terms:

> With the beginning of the modern world the Third World also came into existence, for it was in fact only the modern mass enslavement of Africans and the exploitation of America's mineral resources which provided the labour and capital for the development and advancement of the West. From the seventeenth century until well into the nineteenth, Europe's wealth was built up on the basis of a great transcontinental, triangular commerce: slaves from Africa to America; gold and silver from America to Europe, followed by sugar, cotton, coffee, tobacco and rubber; then industrial commodities and weapons to Africa; and so on.[28]

These resources, of course, financed the industrial revolution by which nations of the northern hemisphere were able to enrich themselves by using the resources of others. By 1650, 16,000 tonnes of silver and 180 tonnes of gold had been taken from South America to Europe.[29]

Is any of this relevant for theology? Should people engaged in theology and Christology worry about the exploitation of poor people? For nearly five hundred years in South America theologians and the church sided with the conquerors. As unpalatable as it may be for some, and as David Batstone and his colleagues have noted, over the past five centuries

> the Christian church and its theology consistently buttressed the expansion of empires. The majority of the church, regardless of where it stood in its conflict with modernity, blessed colonialism, neo-colonialism, extreme stratification of wealth, centuries of genocide of Amerindians, blacks, and Jews, the subordination of women, the persecution of the sexual other, and the social exclusion of the pagan. During the last five centuries theology has glorified all these historical projects as divine constructions of reality.[30]

theologies of liberation and the plight of the poor

The massive contemporary world of sick, starving, and dying people is an overwhelming preoccupation of liberation theology. If humanity's fate is to be a new constellation of winners and losers, just what might theology have to say?

Thus far in this book, discussions of modern theological problems have drawn attention to intellectuals in the northern hemisphere. During the last four decades of the twentieth century a theological revolution transpired in the southern hemisphere, beginning in Latin America. Liberation theology was initially a label given to a theological movement that emerged in Latin America during the late 1950s and throughout the 1960s. In the latter half of the twentieth century Latin American theologies began to struggle to untie theology from the interests of exploitative conquerors. Now it has become a common practice to speak of liberation theologies rather than liberation theology. In 1995, the American Jesuit Alfred Hennelly published a book titled *Liberation Theologies*, in which he distinguished nine principal varieties: Latin American; black (in the United States of America); feminist; Hispanic-American; African; Asian; first world; ecological (ecotheology); and a liberation theology of world religions.[31] What unites all nine types is twofold: first, they share a common interest in the this-worldly consequences of Christian life and thought; and second, they all advocate a partisanship with socially marginalized and exploited groups. Liberation theologies are discourses of advocacy. They are not inspired by empire, but by the historical Jesus and his predilection for the poor.

early modern origins   Contemporary theologies of liberation have remote and proximate historical roots. The former are linked to the Spanish Dominican friar, Antón Montesino, in the sixteenth century; and the second to Pope John XXIII in the twentieth century.

With regard to the more chronologically remote roots, Christopher Columbus arrived in the Antilles on 12 October 1492. Twenty years after his arrival, most of the local Taino people were dead, and other indigenous peoples of the Caribbean were either shackled in slavery or suffering military attack. In 1492, the Indian population of the Caribbean was about 5.85 million. Five hundred years later, in 1992, the population was 0.001 million Indian inhabitants.[32]

In 1510, a relatively unknown friar, Montesino, decided that he needed to speak out. Montesino arrived in Hispaniola from Spain in 1510. Once ashore, he and his companions were stung by the very high mortality rates among the slaves. The local inhabitants of Hispaniola were forced to work for their conquerors to the point of physical exhaustion and death. They were also highly susceptible to European diseases. Montesino and his companion friars were so distressed that so many slaves had perished in a mere two decades that they decided to compose an impassioned sermon to be delivered in front of the island's new and belligerent governor, Admiral Diego Colón, the son of Cristóbal Colón (Christopher Columbus). The friars collectively wrote a sermon and signed their names to the text. They then chose Montesino to deliver it in their name. They fixed a day for his preaching: the Fourth Sunday of Advent (just before Christmas), 1510. Moreover, they selected a biblical passage to anchor the sermon. It was John the Baptist's cry as recorded in the Gospel of John, 'I am the voice of one crying out in the wilderness, "Make straight the way of the Lord", as the prophet Isaiah said' (John 1:23). The Dominican Order of friars, of which Montesino and his colleagues were members, was founded by a Castilian Spaniard, called Dominic, in the second decade of the thirteenth century. It is officially known as the Order of Preachers (*Ordo Praedicatorum*). Preaching was and is the preaching friars' primary work. In Montesino, their mandate and mission has not found a better incarnation.

Once they had signed their collective sermon, the friars of Hispaniola invited the governor and all the island's senior military commanders to attend their little church. In front of the conquerors of the island, Montesino began his sermon, the contents of which were preserved by Bartolomé de las Casas. Facing the powerful, Montesino fulminates:

> You are all in mortal sin! You live in it and you die in it! Why? Because of the cruelty and tyranny you use with these innocent people. Tell me, with what right, with what justice, do you hold these Indians in such cruel and horrible servitude?

On what authority have you waged such detestable wars on these people, in their mild, peaceful lands, where you have consumed such infinitudes of them, wreaking upon them this death and unheard-of havoc? How is it that you hold them so crushed and exhausted, giving them nothing to eat, nor any treatment for their diseases, which you cause them to be infected with through the surfeit of their toils, so that they 'die on you' [as you say] – you mean, you kill them – mining gold for you day after day? And what care do you take that anyone catechize them, so that they may come to know their God and Creator, be baptized, hear Mass, observe Sundays and Holy Days? Are they not human beings? Have they no rational souls? Are you not obliged to love them as you love yourselves? Do you not understand this? Do you not grasp this? How is it that you sleep so soundly, so lethargically? Know for a certainty that in the state in which you are you can no more be saved than Moors or Turks who have not, nor wish to have, the faith of Jesus Christ.[33]

Las Casas owned slaves at the time of Montesino's sermon. He was so moved and humbled by Montesino's defence of the poor that he eventually joined the Dominicans and devoted the rest of his life to defending subjugated peoples, in the Caribbean and in Mexico. In 1542 he published a short book whose very title captures his life-long preoccupation: *A Short Account of the Destruction of the Indies* (*Brevísima relación de la destrucción de las Indias*).

Montesino's preaching caused such outrage that the Spanish king, Ferdinand V, ordered the friars of Hispaniola to stop preaching against the conquerors. The friars refused and redoubled their efforts. They are the forerunners of contemporary liberation theologians in Latin America five centuries later.[34] The significance of their work would be difficult to exaggerate. They effectively restored to Christianity its ancient prophetic function of being a religion of and for the oppressed, rather than a religious legitimation of monarchies.[35]

twentieth-century roots Although prophetic Christianity was implanted by prophetic Dominican and Franciscan friars in Latin America, it was not long before Christian leaders throughout the region aligned themselves with Spanish and Portuguese invaders. For most of the region's modern history, Christianity lost its function of defending oppressed peoples.[36]

For much of the history of modern theology poverty was not normally an explicit theological theme. After the Reformation, theologians were much more likely to debate the Bible's authority, the papacy and the sacraments. After the Enlightenment, theologians became preoccupied with new critical philosophies and revolutions in science. Throughout all this time individual Christians certainly worked to alleviate poverty, but theologians rarely wrote tomes devoted to human salvation considered in the context of material poverty. Salvation nearly always meant salvation from sin, not poverty.

In the twentieth century, Pope John XXIII (1881–1963) effectively inspired the rebirth of Latin American liberation theology, the distinctiveness of which lies in its insistence that salvation is not an other-worldly matter, but is intrinsically linked to material well-being, poverty, violence and injustice. John XIII died in 1963 after a brief papacy. He was elected as Bishop of Rome in October 1958. In 1962 he made a radio broadcast in Latin to speak about the Second Vatican Council that was about to begin. He surprised his listeners by declaring that the Church should not just be a Church for the poor, but a Church of the poor. We should note his name very well: John XXIII. His predecessor John XXII (*c.* 1244–1334) condemned the idea that Jesus was poor, a dispute reflected in Umberto Eco's novel *The Name of the Rose*. After John XXII's condemnation, poverty and the plight of the poor were largely absent from the official theology of the Catholic Church until the late nineteenth century. Pope John XXIII placed poverty once more very clearly before the minds and hearts of theologians and ecclesiastical leaders.

The Second Vatican Council confirmed John XXIII's worries about the poor. Its *Pastoral Constitution on the Church in the Modern World* (*Gaudium et Spes*) was promulgated on 7 December 1965. Its opening lines declare: 'The joys and hopes, the grief and anguish of the people of our time, *especially of those who are poor or afflicted*, are the joys and hopes, the grief and anguish of the followers of Christ as well.'[37]

Vatican II finished its deliberations in 1965. Three years later, in 1968, a conference of Latin American bishops, called CELAM, was held at Medellín in Colombia. These bishops tried to apply John XXIII's preoccupation with the poor to the desperately impoverished situation of Latin America. Liberation theologies began to emerge clearly in the wake of this Latin American meeting of bishops.

The bishops of Medellín enjoyed the benefit of the advice of someone who has become one of the greatest contemporary theologians – Gustavo Gutiérrez. The bishops coined a catchword for their concerns – 'the preferential option for the poor'. On a continent that has witnessed a centuries-long alliance between the Church and conquerors, the bishops taught that Christians, as an urgent priority, need to reflect about God and Christ with a new method that begins with a practical engagement to redress poverty.

Gutiérrez took over into his own theology the bishops' catchphrase. His subsequent body of writings, considered collectively, constitute a massive articulation of the essence of Christianity in terms of a preferential option for the poor. In 1971 he published a book titled *A Theology of Liberation*. Therein he describes the method of liberation theology as a critical reflection on Christian praxis in the light of the Bible.[38] His description turns on three major terms: critical reflection, praxis and the Bible. 'Praxis' is a neologism in English. It is an Ancient Greek word that designates a particular kind of action. It refers not to an unreflective, mindless activity like turning on a light switch, but to an action that is simultaneously guided by a theory. Praxis is a word used by Aristotle in contrast to *theoria* (theory) and *poiesis* (the production of goods). In its initial Greek context praxis 'refers to almost any kind of activity which a free man might like to perform; in particular, all kinds of business and political activity. Only activities involving bodily labour seem to be excluded from its meaning, and also to some extent merely intellectual activities such as thinking and reflecting.'[39] So praxis is neither pure reason nor pure action, but an action informed by a theory.

In the nineteenth century Karl Marx developed a philosophy of praxis arguing that knowledge arises principally through action. His point is simple and correct. Were I to seek knowledge about Canada I could look in books or I could travel through its regions. I can be sure that the action of travelling through the country would give me a richer form of knowledge that reading about Canada in an encyclopedia.

Both Gutiérrez in particular, and liberation theologians in general, are often criticized for using the concept of praxis in theology. They are charged with importing a Marxist term into theology. In 1984, the Vatican's Sacred Congregation for the Doctrine of the Faith published a document that is critical of the use of Marxist ideas in liberation theology.[40] It is vital to note, however, that praxis is a biblical concept, not simply a Marxist one. The Greek title of the Acts of the Apostles is actually the Praxes of the Apostles (*ΠΡΑΞΕΙΣ ΑΠΟΣΤΟΛΩΝ*). The concept of praxis stands right at the heart of Christian Scripture. In Gutiérrez's theology, praxis refers to the preferential opting for the poor that is inspired by the theory, so to speak, of the Gospel of Jesus' message of the reign of God rather than the reign of corporate chief executive officers. Gutiérrez and other liberation theologians are inspired primarily by Marx's Eleventh Thesis on Feuerbach rather than his notion of violent class struggle. The thesis asserts that 'The philosophers have only *interpreted* the world in various ways; the point is to *change* it.'[41] The inspiration of this aphorism in Gutiérrez's work is evident in his book *A Theology of Liberation*. Therein he cites a passage by Schillebeeckx that was published in the year before his own book appeared: 'It is evident that thought is also necessary for action. But the Church has for centuries devoted its attention to formulating truths and meanwhile did almost nothing to better the world. In other words, the Church focused on orthodoxy and left orthopraxis in the hands of nonmembers and nonbelievers.'[42]

Theologians who practise theology with the aim of striving to free, unshackle or liberate economically, politically and spiritually downtrodden people may be called liberation theologians. However, they may be labelled as such, not because they work to establish social justice, but because they speak of God *in* connection with poverty, injustice, and the relief or liberation of suffering. They do not talk about God by discussing Kant's *Critique of Pure Reason*! Prominent liberation theologians include the Peruvian theologian Gustavo Gutiérrez; the three Brazilians Leonardo and Clodovis Boff, and Hugo Assman; the Argentianian José Míguez Bonino; Juan Luis Segundo of Uruguay; the Mexican José Miranda; Jon Sobrino of San Salvador; and, from Sri Lanka, Aloysius Pieris and Tissa Balasuriya.

The distinctiveness of liberation theologies can be glimpsed initially by comparing them with a quite different, centuries-long understanding of the nature of theology. Broadly speaking, for much of western theological history, theology has been conceived as a *fides quaerens intellectum*, a faith seeking (theoretical) understanding; or a *fides quaerens intellectum historicum*, a faith groping for a historical comprehension, or an understanding of itself in history. To the question, 'How does one learn to speak of God', theologians in modern western universities have long replied along the following lines: 'Study Hebrew, Greek, and Latin; contemplate the Bible in reverential solitude; read books; labour in libraries; listen to professors; obey tutors; write essays; avoid pubs and disreputable people; and strive to pass examinations. That's the best route to discovering God.'

The essential point to retain here is that theology has frequently been conceived as a primarily theoretical, intellectual, somewhat bookish quest to attain an understanding of God. In stark contrast, liberation theology is not primarily a *fides quaerens intellectum*, but a *fides quaerens liberationem* – that is, a faith in search of practical liberation for the underdogs of human history. It is a God-talk that swells from the ugly underbelly of human societies at present. It is not respectable. It not glamorous, and it's not university-based. It is a theology for and by the so-called losers of the world: the nuisances, nobodies, scum and dregs of our planet. Liberation theology springs from sites of suffering. It seeks to link God-talk to a recognition that 'evil and suffering are rife, that they pervade the lives of a great proportion of humanity, and that their grinding and unrelenting torment renders the lives of many humans a dreary, bleak, hungry, empty, drudgery, or even worse, a pain- and sorrow-racked ordeal.'[43] In sum, liberation theology is a theology articulated on behalf of all those who are actually and aggressively stigmatized in our world. As Gustavo Gutiérrez proclaims in his book *The Power of the Poor in History*, 'The question of God in Latin America will not be how to speak in a world come of age, but rather how to proclaim God as Father in a world that is inhumane. What can it mean to tell a nonperson that he or she is God's child?'[44]

ten features of liberation theology

Contemporary liberation theology has at least ten principal features that can be presented briefly as follows.

First, and this is an obvious point, liberation theology is like any other theology. That is, its overriding aim is to speak of God. As Gustavo Gutiérrez points out, with liberation theology, 'God and God's love are, ultimately, its only theme.'[45]

Second, if God is the cardinal *theme* of liberation theology, *the poor* are the pre-eminent source, or *locus theologicus*, for speaking of God. Consequently, liberation theology effectively has two superintending focuses: God and the poor. The first is its ultimate preoccupation, while the second constitutes its principal means for addressing God. Liberation theologians customarily speak of a preferential option for the poor. They insist that in institutions of political and economic oppression around the world, the Church should defend the poor as an urgent and fundamental duty.

Third, this preference for the poor is inspired primarily by the Bible, and not by Marxist theory or practice. Liberation theologians defer with tireless regularity to the prophets and the Gospels in order to underscore a constant biblical motif – God's predilection for the downtrodden that is mirrored and Jesus' dealings with people.

Fourth, liberation theology ties political and economic liberation to human salvation. It concludes that salvation is not merely a matter of a person fretting in a self-absorbed mode about his or her spiritual well-being or sinful state. Rather the question is who or what saves people from all that stymies human communities in their entirety and in their wider world. Bluntly put: it's no use telling individuals that God loves them and saves them when they are starving to death!

Fifth, liberation theologies regularly defer to the Exodus story of the Bible as a paradigm for illustrating that individual salvation is linked to social transformation. If God liberated the Hebrews from bondage in Egypt, then God is clearly concerned with politically oppressive and exploitative regimes.

Sixth, liberation theologians tend to counter the common conclusion that Jesus was apolitical, and argue instead that he was killed by political powers strictly because of his life and work that were resolutely political in the sense that they were diametrically antithetical to death-dealing, subjugating political powers. Jesus may not have been politically insurrectionist, but he was executed by a Roman prefect who was not in the habit of killing theologians and philosophers.

Seventh, an exceptionally significant feature of liberation theologies is that, methodologically and epistemologically speaking, they emphasize the priority of praxis over theory. In other terms, they aver that correct belief (orthodoxy) can only stem from correct action (orthopraxis). In this they are entirely correct. It is possible for people effortlessly to quote the Bible or defend orthodox doctrines while at the same time turning their backs on refugees and strangers. Action, not words, is revelatory of a person's identity.

Eighth, most liberation theologians have been influenced in some way or other by Karl Marx, even though their primary textual inspiration is the Bible. Their interest in Marx, however, does not lie in his views on religion or atheistic materialism, but in his sociological analysis and philosophical emphasis on praxis. Marx's eleven *Theses on Feuerbach* are all concerned with praxis. Liberation theologians have taken Marx's Eleventh Thesis to heart and have concluded that, previously, theologians have merely interpreted the world, whereas the point is to transform it.

Ninth, liberation theologies insist that social structures or institutions, like money-markets, world banks or strong governments, can be no less violent and destructive in their operations than the actual use of harmful physical force.

Finally, liberation theology, especially in its Latin American guise, involves the formation of basic ecclesiastical communities (BECs). Beginning in the late 1950s, small groups were gathered in Latin America wherein poor people met regularly for prayer, worship, communal mediation, Bible readings, and discussions of the participants' religious and social lives. In this way, poor people themselves became a new breed of theologian. Hence, liberation theology has a new addressee, the poor person, rather than the sceptical post-Enlightenment European citizen, and a new practitioner – the economic underdog rather than the priestly academic!

Considered together, these ten characteristics present a stark and telling exception to a great deal of classical, purely speculative theology. Gustavo Gutiérrez captures that exceptional challenge in two memorable texts. In his book *The Power of the Poor in History*, he forcefully states: 'What is to be done away with is the intellectualizing of the intellectual who has no ties with the life and struggle of the poor – the theology of the theologian who reflects upon the faith precisely from the point of view of those whom the Father has hidden his revelation: the 'Learned and clever' (Matt. 11:25).[46] Gutiérrez writes in his book *On Job* of 'the wasted energy of intellectuals who get excited but do not actually do anything: they are incapable of taking a step forward, because the impulse that makes them string arguments together is purely verbal.'[47]

Liberation theologies, it seems clear, call for action on behalf of those who are having their noses ground into the dust, and their veins bled dry. All of which led Gutiérrez to define the method of liberation theology as critical reflection on praxis in the light of the Bible. For such as theology, theory or contemplation is not insignificant at all. It simply follows as a second step after an ethical engagement for the poor. As Christopher Rowland explains: 'The commitment to, and solidarity with, the poor and vulnerable are the necessary environment for stimulating the intellectual activity which enables liberation theology to begin. The key thing is that one first of all does liberation theology rather than learns about it. Or, to put it another way, one can only learn about it by embarking on it.'[48] It is precisely the engagement that will generate an understanding of God, it is argued, that conforms with the visions of God adumbrated in the ancient scriptures of Jews, who were, let's face it, continually having their faces ground into the dust by imperial homicidal overlords!

the vatican's displeasure with liberation theology

Over the past four decades, liberation theology has emerged, grown, faltered, and changed. It varies from country to country. It has been chastised for neglecting the plight of poor women and for employing outdated tools of economic analysis. However, its most significant opponent has emerged clearly over the past twenty or so years. That opponent is the Vatican – or, rather, senior prelates within Vatican City.

Two stories clearly demonstrate that the Vatican is bent on straitjacketing liberation theology. Both revolve around two distinguished Latin American archbishops. The first concerns Oscar Romero, whom many regard as a martyr. His statue graces the edifice of Westminster Abbey's entrance. It should not pass unnoticed that he has been so venerated by a major centre of worship of the Church of England, and not by the Church in Rome.

In 1980, Oscar Romero was serving as the Archbishop of San Salvador in El Salvador. In 1979, he excommunicated the president of El Salvador on a charge of failing to stop the murder of priests and nuns who were devoted to working with poor people. By 1979, Romero had become deeply unpopular with the military government of the president. He had also become a figure of suspicion in Rome. During 1979, the Holy See, the centre of power in the Vatican, petitioned Georgetown University in Washington not to confer an honorary degree on Romero, who was to be fêted, in part, for his championing of the rights of poor people. Timothy Healy, the president of the university, refused and travelled to San Salvador to bestow the degree.

Here is where the plot thickens. In the following year, around 20 March 1980, three senior cardinals decided to move against Romero. Each cardinal worked as a prefect for one of the sixteen bureaucratic departments of the Vatican, which are called Congregations. The three involved were Silvio Oddi, the Cardinal Prefect of the congregation for Clergy; Franjo Seper, Prefect of the Congregation for the Doctrine of the Faith; and Sebastiano Baggio, Prefect of the Congregation for Bishops. These three recommended to Pope John Paul II that he reassign Archbishop Romero elsewhere. They were apparently worried that Oscar Romero's 'preferential for the poor' and his incessant criticism of his military government were threatening to divide the Church of El Salvador. The information regarding the intentions of the three cardinals is based on an interview conducted with Cardinal Oddi. Cardinals Seper and Baggio are now dead, so cannot account for themselves. Cardinal Oddi, however, seems clear that the decision to move Oscar Romero was based on the Vatican's disapproval of the Latin American Church's involvement in politics.[49] Cardinals Oddi, Seper and Baggio need not have worried. Before their decision to remove Oscar Romero could be carried out, he was assassinated while presiding at Mass in the Cathedral of El Salvador on 24 March 1980.[50]

A second story illustrating the Vatican's continuing opposition to liberation theology concerns Dom Hélder Câmara Pessoa. From 1964 to 1985, he was the Archbishop of Olinda and Recife in northeastern Brazil. The year he was installed as archbishop, a military dictatorship took over Brazil. Hélder Câmara immediately objected publicly. He denounced the army's repression of citizens. The government did not dare to assassinate him because he had already earned an international reputation as a champion of human rights. The military leaders devised an alternative strategy. One of their sympathizers was emboldened to murder an assistant to the archbishop. A 27-year-old priest, Antônio Henrique, was one of the archbishop's closest and more energetic helpers. In May of 1969, he was kidnapped, tortured and murdered: 'His body, naked and mangled, was found two days later in the meridian of a highway that surrounds Recife.'[51] Around ten thousand people attended his funeral, though the local press virtually ignored it.

The city of Recife lies right next to the sea. So it has a large port. In fact, it has operated as a major port for four hundred years. Throughout those years it has been ravaged by poverty. In the 1950s, up to 70 per cent of its population was illiterate. However, between 1959 and 1964, Church-sponsored schools were established to improve literacy. The poor could hardly arrive at their own understanding of the Bible if they could never read it for themselves, a point well recognized by the magisterial Protestant Reformers four centuries earlier.

As Archbishop of Olinda and Recife, Hélder Câmara directed his priests to organize community groups, analyse social and economic structures, and establish more schools for literacy. In a major gesture of solidarity with the poor, he moved out of the archbishop's palace to live in a small flat. He thus became seriously vulnerable to violent attack. His house was eventually strafed by machine guns, but he escaped injury. In the seminaries of his region, the archbishop insisted that students for the priesthood live among very-low-income families and in slum neighbourhoods. He believed that 'neither God nor the church could be understood only through classroom study, but must be complemented through work with those dearest to God – the poor'.[52]

Hélder Câmara's work reversed a long-standing and traditional alliance between the Catholic Church in Brazil and political governments. In 1968, he denounced his government once again and was consequently forbidden to speak publicly. He insisted, though, that he needed to be able to reach his people through commenting publicly on the Bible. So, from 1969, he was allowed to broadcast a weekly radio programme.

Hélder Câmara stood down as Archbishop of Olinda and Recife. As a replacement, the Vatican installed an implacable opponent of liberation theology. In 1990, his opposition to liberation theology became plain for all to see. Here, then, is a second story illustrating contemporary official opposition to theologies of liberation. In the north-western corner of Recife is a low-income neighbourhood called the Hill of the Immaculate Conception. The Hill was the seat of a national shrine in honour of Mary, the mother of Jesus. In other words, it was a Brazilian national symbol of Catholic religiosity. Since 1978, the local community had been led by a priest, Reginaldo Veloso, a devoted practitioner of liberation theology. He encouraged the neighbourhood's various BECs to view Mary not so much as the pious mother of Jesus, but as a very poor person living in material conditions like her son's and their own. On 19 October 1990, the Hill was stormed by military police. The new archbishop, Dom José Cardoso, had arranged for the police to be sent in. And why? To cut locks off the local church doors and to install a new parish priest who would not encourage liberation theology.[53]

conclusion

Liberation theology may sound revolutionary and new-fangled. In fact it is a return to ancient practices when theology was not practised as a discipline of the academy. Academic theology, as I say, has long neglected the sufferings of poor people. It has often colluded in the expansion of imperial powers. Liberation theologians are leading the way nowadays in liberating theology itself from its long-standing forgetfulness of the poor.

As humanity progresses into the twenty-first century, major tectonic movements are under way in Christianity as its numerical heartlands shift from the northern hemisphere to the regions of the South. Christianity is already well on the way to becoming, numerically speaking, both a non-European religion and the religion of the poor people of this planet. In such a context, to speak of a preferential option for the poor is not to trumpet a platitude, a political agenda, or a strategy for the Church. Fundamentally the preferential option for the poor 'is a statement about the identity and purpose of God'[54] and the essence of Christianity. What defines the God proclaimed by the Bible is not the possession of admirable attributes, 'but a commitment to justice for the poor and the marginalized'.[55] By speaking of God's preference for the poor, liberation theologians have taken the age-old Christian imperative to care for the poor from the realm of ethics to the realm of theology proper. All of which is captured in the Latin hymnic phrase: *ubi caritas et amor, ibi Deus est*, 'Where there is charity and love, there too is God.' That is all liberation theology is trying to say.

IO

no girls allowed:
christianity and feminist theology

Frailty, thy name is woman.
Shakespeare

Feminism is a form of advocacy. It argues that the male and female sexes are equal, and on that basis insists that females should enjoy the same human rights as males. Women have always formed a major part of the Church and have contributed to its religious life throughout twenty centuries. For most of that time, though, they were not always able to enjoy the same rights as men. There has never been a female pope – despite the legend of Pope Joan.[1] In many Christian denominations today women are not permitted to preach. In such a setting, feminism signals inescapable anxiety for Christianity and its traditional theology. It can be derided, dismissed and joked about, but feminism remains a profoundly destabilizing new question for old beliefs, especially the belief that only men should rule the Church, teach its devotees and preach to its believers. Christian orthodoxy easily gives the impression that it celebrates and perpetuates a man's world. It speaks of God as if God were male. It worships a Father Creator who sent a son into the world. The son is exalted as one who set about calling an inner circle of twelve men with the purpose of establishing a Church to be governed by men. Traditional Christian theology is overwhelmingly the product of men's pens. The exclusion of women from leadership in the Church, and from the Church's academies, was only exposed and challenged on a wide-ranging scale with the evolution of feminist theologies in the latter half of the twentieth century.

For most of Christendom's history, women and girls were not educated to the same degree as men and boys. Pre-modern Christian theologians normally assumed that females are anthropologically and biologically inferior to males.

On the basis of their assumption, women were denied full gender equality in the Church, and in wider societies, for the larger part of Christianity's existence. They were relegated to a lowly status in the Church partly because in pre-modern eras the Church always found itself implanted in, and serving the interests of, much larger male-dominated and women-disparaging civil societies. From the fourth century until the eighteenth, Christianity was encased in Christendom. It assumed the body of a civilization governed by men, reflective of the interests of men, and expressive of the violence of men. Of all the new questions generated for old beliefs by modern theology, one of the most pressing stems from the rise of feminism in the nineteenth and twentieth centuries. Liberation theologies emerged in the twentieth century to give theological voice to previously voiceless impoverished people around the globe. Feminist theologians also opt to redress the voicelessness and victimization of marginalized people, although in their case with regard to women, poor or otherwise.

The University of Oxford is a revealing illustration of how women have been treated and mistreated by pre-modern Christian and western traditions. Advanced learning has been carried out in different forms in Oxford over the past nine hundred years. Like many other ancient universities, Oxford was established in large part for the training of clergymen.[2] Many of its original houses of residence were founded by religious orders of celibate men such as the Benedictines, Cistercians, Franciscans and Dominicans. In view of Oxford's very long history, it is really quite shocking and thought-provoking (for contemporary sensibilities) that before 1920 women could not become members of the University. It was not until after World War II, in 1948, that the first woman was appointed to a full professorship in Oxford. That is not very long ago at all. Clearly, for the majority of the University's life women were resolutely excluded from its academic life.[3] How is such a situation best explained? Is it because women are inherently stupid? Could it be because their primary business is to cook for husbands and nurture babies, rather than read books? Might it be the case that women were excluded for so long because they are, by nature, mindless flirts who would only distract men from the serious business of academic research? Another explanation for the long-standing exclusion of women from Oxford can be made in terms of traditional Christian theology. Before the twentieth century, Oxford was a microcosm of a macroscopic European Christian culture. The theology of that culture was thoroughly coloured by Ancient Greek and Middle Eastern understandings of human nature that regarded women as intrinsically inferior to men.

Feminism is an invention, as it were, of the nineteenth century. Theological feminism is a creation of the twentieth century. The first person to use the word 'feminism' was the French campaigner for women's political rights Hubertine

Auclert. She coined the term in 1882.[4] It may seem surprising that a woman would have to campaign for political rights for women in France a full century after the French Revolution. It needs to be borne in mind, however, that the French Revolutionaries had no intention of allowing women, Jews or homosexuals to participate in democratic processes of government. Liberty, equality and fraternity were all for men who were sufficiently well off to pay taxes.

While Hubertine Auclert coined the term 'feminism' in the late nineteenth century, voices crying out for women to be regarded as equal to men in human dignity can be detected much earlier. One need only recall a little-known woman living six hundred years ago in France. Her name was Christine de Pizan (1365–1430). As the daughter of an Italian astrologer, she came to France to participate in the court of King Charles V and Queen Jeanne de Bourbon. In 1405, she published a book titled *The Book of the City of Ladies*, which makes the following arresting observation: 'There is not the slightest doubt that women belong to the people of God and the human race as much as

> **common terms in feminist discourse**   *Feminism*: the belief that the sexes are fundamentally equal and the advocacy of women's rights and privileges where and when they are denied. *Sexism*: the belief that one sex is superior to another and the practical discrimination against one sex on the basis of a belief in superiority. Men and women can both be sexist in their thought and behaviour. *Patriarchy*: a system of organizing human societies in such a way that men, normally elderly men, govern younger men, women and children. *Androcentrism*: the belief that the male human being is the paradigm of the human species. Whereas patriarchy is a form of social structuring, androcentricism is a way of thinking. Both men and women can be androcentric in their understanding of humanity. *Misogyny*: the hatred of women. *Gynophobia*: the irrational fear of women.

men and are not another species or dissimilar race.'[5] As amazing as it may seem now, standard educated opinion in the west before the late eighteenth century held that women formed a separate and inferior species to men.[6] De Pizan was well aware that depriving women of education easily created the impression that they were inferior to men. She set about arguing adroitly that women were of the same human rank as men. She was, of course, something of a voice crying in the wilderness, whose ideas only became more widely acknowledged in the nineteenth century with the advent of modern feminism. The Christian culture in which Christine de Pizan lived had been profoundly influenced in its attitude to women by a long line of distinguished male Christian theologians and Church leaders. To understand the force of her plea, it is advisable to consider the views of some of these male ecclesiastics.

the christian tradition on women and men

Here is a quotation from one of them: 'The body of a man is as superior to that of a woman as the soul is to the body.' A double disparagement is advanced with this text: first, that a woman's body is inferior to a man's; and second, that the human body is inferior to a soul, whatever that might be. The male author of these thoughts turns out to be one of the towering, most oft-quoted, and frequently studied authorities in the entire history of Christian theology. He was the principal theological influence on Thomas Aquinas, one of the greatest geniuses of theological history. He also spent fifteen years of his life cohabiting with a woman. So, even while loving and lusting after her for several years, this theologically authoritative author was still able to insist that 'The body of a man is as superior to that of a woman as the soul is to the body.'

The person who penned these words was Augustine of Hippo (354–430). He wrote them in his treatise *Contra Mendacium* (*Against Lying*: 7–10).[7] Augustine's views concerning the superior status of men in relation to women are by no means either unusual or atypical. For most of Christian history women have been treated like doormats. The magisterial theologians of Christian history have, by and large, spoken of women in disparaging, insulting and demeaning terms. Augustine was convinced that only men are fully created in the image of God. Consequently, he concluded that the subordination of women to men is intrinsic to God's own design for the world.[8]

Augustine, like anyone else in the past, was a product of his time and place – in his case the fourth and fifth centuries in Africa. He was born in Thagaste in what is now called Algeria. When he was young he was educated in Latin literature and rhetoric. He also knew some Greek. In the Latin culture of his youth, boys and men, rather than girls and women, were educated according to the classical writings of ancient Greek philosophers and Roman lawyers. By contemporary western standards, the views of bygone Greeks and Romans about women are quite disturbing. Nonetheless, their views passed into Christian theology, where they have remained to this day. As I say, feminism spells considerable trouble for traditional Christian theology.

A good way to discern how and why modern theological feminism emerged is soberly to take stock of the way women have been described and treated, not only in the Christian past, but in the pre-modern history of humanity. When talking about men, women, boys and girls in the past, it is important to be wary of the ever-present danger of lapsing into historical anachronism – that is, of surmising that peoples long dead and far distant thought and acted like people today. The inhabitants of the contemporary west speak endlessly of sexuality.

Ancient peoples did not. The very word 'sexuality' was coined around the year 1800.

Furthermore, contemporary westerners tend to think in dichotomous terms in matters sexual. They frequently speak of heterosexual or homosexual, gay or straight, individuals. Such bifurcations were unknown in ancient cultures. To clarify, it is now well known and amply studied that bygone Roman and Athenian cultures did not draw a sharp distinction between heterosexuality and homosexuality. The very words are modern creations. In Athens, part of an educated adolescent boy's training into adulthood 'entailed a hierarchical sexual and tutorial relationship with an older man, who most likely was married and may have had other sexual partners as well'.[9] Augustine's view that the male body is more estimable than the body of a woman merely perpetuates the older Roman and Athenian notion that only the male is a perfect human being.

Plato and Aristotle were the two most significant philosophers of Athens, and their influence on Christian theology is incalculable. Both were suspicious of the 'distracting power of sexual passion', 'warning that it distracted men from reason and the search for knowledge'.[10] What is important to register about these two philosophers is that, first, they were not interested overly in the sexual lives of women; and, second, they espoused the view that the paradigm of the human being is a male. Indeed, they taught that males were conceived during sexual encounters that were optimum. Females were conceived when the weather was hotter.[11]

The influence of Plato and Aristotle on later Christian thinkers would be difficult to exaggerate. According to Aquinas, for instance,

> Only as regards nature in the individual is the female something defective and manqué. For the active power in the seed of the male tends to produce something like itself, perfect in masculinity; but the procreation of the female is the result either of the debility of the active power, of some unsuitability of material, or of some change effected by external influences, like the south wind for example, which is damp, as we are told by Aristotle.[12]

In addition to Plato and Aristotle, the Bible also exerted a strong influence over Augustine, Aquinas and other major thinkers of the Christian tradition in their understandings of the status of women in relation to men. From the biblical text of Leviticus and from Athenian philosophers, early Christian writers imbibed an exceptionally unbalanced view of male–female relations that is not peculiar to the Christian Church, but merely reflective of the way women were treated in the ancient world of Rome, Athens and around the Middle East. To illustrate, Leviticus 12 teaches that God spoke to Moses telling him to speak to the people of Israel in the following terms:

If a woman conceives and bears a male child, she shall be ceremonially unclean for seven days; as at the time of her menstruation, she shall be unclean. On the eighth day the flesh of his foreskin shall be circumcised. Her time of blood purification shall be thirty-three days; she shall not touch any holy thing, or come into the sanctuary, until the days of her purification are completed. If she bears a female child, she shall be unclean for two weeks, as in her menstruation; her time of blood purification shall be sixty-six days (Lev. 12:2b–5).

This text passed directly into Christianity and served to justify the exclusion of women from sacred places. The fourth century CE Synod of Laodicea taught: 'Women are not allowed to approach the altar.'[13]

In ancient Latin-speaking territories, menstruation was often treated with disgust. Of menstrual blood, the Roman writer Pliny the Elder could declare:

Contact with the monthly flux of women turns new wine sour, makes crops wither, kills grafts, dries seeds in gardens, causes the fruit of trees to fall off, dims the bright surface of mirrors, dulls the edge of steel and the gleam of ivory, kills bees, rusts iron and bronze, and causes a horrible smell to fill the air. Dogs who taste the blood become mad, and their bite becomes poisonous as in rabies. The Dead Sea, thick with salt, cannot be drawn asunder except by a thread soaked in the poisonous fluid of the menstrual blood. A thread from an infected dress is sufficient. Linen, touched by the woman while boiling and washing it in water, turns black. So magical is the power of women during their monthly periods that they say that hailstorms and whirlwinds are driven away if menstrual fluid is exposed to the flashes of lightning.[14]

A resolute pagan bias against women, coupled with a blood taboo, entered deeply into later Christian thought. For example, the Christian biblical scholar Jerome (*c.* 345–420) could comment: 'For our salvation the Son of God became the Son of Man. Nine months he awaited his birth in the womb, undergoing the most revolting conditions there, to come forth covered with blood.'[15] The way early Christian writers imitated the Greeks in relegating women to an inferior position is evident in the thought of Clement of Alexandria (*c.* 150–215). In his work *Paidagogos* (III.50.1), Clement addresses the topic of appropriate sports for men and women. He concludes that

Men should either engage in wrestling stripped or play ball. … Even women should be permitted some form of physical exercise, not on the wrestling-mat or running track, but in spinning and weaving, and if need arise, supervising the cooking. Moreover, they are to fetch whatever we need from the larder with their own hand.[16]

Somewhat later, John Chrysostom (347–407) merely sighs when he thinks of women: 'The whole sex is frail and frivolous', he says in his *Homily* 9 on 1 Tim. 2:15, which also states: 'Yet she will be saved through childbearing.'

One reason why Christian thinkers for centuries thought of women as inherently deficient lies in the area of human physiology and biology (a word coined in 1802). K.E. von Baer discovered the function of the ovum in 1827. Before then, it was not widely realized that females contribute just as much as males to the process of forming new human beings. As Uta Ranke-Heinemann points out, 'According to Aristotle male activity and female passivity extended to the generative act: men "beget" or "engender" offspring while women merely "receive" or "conceive".'[17] Aristotle went so far as to call a woman an *arren peperomenon*, that is, 'a mutilated male'.[18] Aquinas, in his *Summa Contra Gentiles*, surmises that women possess less physical and spiritual strength than men, and that men have more consummate intelligence and greater virtue (III.123). In his *Summa Theologiae* he instructs that women should not witness wills because of their defective intelligence (II/II.q. 70.a. 3). In speaking thus, Aquinas is simply deferring to ancient pagan Roman law, according to which: (1) women are to be excluded from all civil and public responsibility; (2) women may not function as witnesses; (3) women may not act as guardians for other people; and (4) women may not launch court cases.[19]

In sum, for several hundred years Christian thinkers of pre-modern epochs were definitively influenced in their attitude to women by biological ignorance, biblical prejudices and pagan Roman law. On the nature and status of women, three of the greatest geniuses of western civilization, Aristotle, Augustine and Aquinas, were lamentably wrong. Nevertheless, their combined theological authority is so great that to this day several Christian denominations will not allow women to preach or assume roles of ecclesiastical leadership.

Greek, Roman, Patristic and medieval prejudices against women were carried forth well into the Reformation. Martin Luther, a well-trained Augustinian in his earlier life, declared in his 1519 sermon on marriage that 'A woman is created to be a companionable helpmate to the man in everything, particularly to bear children.'[20] In his *Lectures on Genesis* he instructs: 'Even as the sun is more excellent than the moon, so the woman, although she is a most beautiful work of God, nevertheless was not the equal of the male in glory and prestige.'[21] John Knox, in his *First Blast of the Trumpet against the Monstrous Regiment of Women* (1558) decries female political leadership as unnatural. For John Calvin, too, in his *Commentaries on the Book of Genesis*, women are engaged in an unequal relationship with men.

In western history, however, biases against women were not confined to ecclesiastics. One of the great intellectual leaders of the French Enlightenment, Jean-Jacques Rousseau (1712–1778), was perfectly alarming with his views on girls and women. In 1762, he published one of the most widely read books in eighteenth-century continental Europe. The book was called *Émile* and deals with the taxing topic of how best to educate children. As Barbara Caine and Glenda Sluga have pointed out, 'The popularity of Rousseau's text undoubtedly owed much to the way in which it laid out a child-centred approach to education in which the child's curiosity was the main driving force, while its physical and mental development determined the educational programme.'[22]

Nevertheless, Rousseau makes abundantly clear that education should be sex-specific. Émile in the book is a boy and by far the greater proportion of the text is devoted to his education. A final chapter is devoted to his friend Sophie. Throughout the book Rousseau explained how the development of reason and judgement needed to be stimulated in a boy: 'Émile would learn to endure hardship, to explore the natural world, to develop physical strength and control, to exercise his own judgement and independence and to live according to his own values and beliefs.'[23] And Sophie? For Rousseau her education must be exactly the opposite. In his view, she could be tied to a chair and forced to play with dolls. While Émile's freedom was to be encouraged, she could be tethered and taught to be submissive.

the historical emergence of feminism and theological feminism

Bluntly stated, until the late eighteenth century women were systematically besmirched in the west in both Church and society. Feminism is a distinctively modern development that seeks to redress the relegation of women to inferior ranks in relation to men. It took over a century for feminism to emerge clearly as a major new question for old beliefs. Its historical unfolding will be sketched below, following a brief consideration of the words 'feminism' and 'sexism'.

The North American theologian Anne Clifford defines feminism as 'a social vision, rooted in women's experience of sexually based discrimination and oppression, a movement seeking the liberation of women from all forms of sexism, and an academic method of analysis being used in virtually every discipline'.[24] Joann Wolski Conn defines feminism in slightly different terms as 'both a coordinated set of ideas and a practical plan of action, rooted in women's critical awareness of how a culture controlled in meaning and action by men, for their own advantage, oppresses women and dehumanises men'.[25] Crucial to Clifford's understanding of feminism is liberation from sexism. She explains sexism as

> The erroneous belief, conviction, or attitude that one sex, female or male, is superior to the other by the very nature of reality. Although it is possible for either females or males to be treated as inferior, historically, women have been more negatively affected by sexism than men.[26]

The Christian Church and its traditional theology are scarred by sexism. It has been the laudable achievement of twentieth-century feminist theologians to heighten awareness of the debilitating consequences that sexism still exerts within Christianity. Their voices echo champions of feminist causes in the eighteenth and nineteenth centuries. Scholars currently writing on feminism conventionally distinguish three principal phases or waves in the emergence of modern feminism. The first took place during the nineteenth century. A second wave transpired during the 1960s and 1970s in Europe and North America. It was during this phase that *theological* feminism emerged. The first phase of feminism was not concerned with theology as such, but with securing political and social rights for women. A third wave of feminism began in the 1980s, and is distinguishable by its concern for the large variety of women's experiences and difficulties in all regions of the globe; not just in Europe or North America. With regard to the first phase, Rita M. Goss declares in her recent book, *Feminism and Religion*:

> For the most part, overtly religious issues were not central to the nineteenth-century women's movement. Most nineteenth-century feminists wished neither to blame religion for women's position nor to advocate a changed position for women in the church. They simply wanted to gain certain basic rights for women without taking on religion as either ally or foe.[27]

The nineteenth-century movement to secure women's rights stemmed directly from the antislavery activities of women in North America. The first women publicly to denounce slavery in the United States of America were two sisters, Angelica and Sarah Grimké, who belonged to a slaveowning family in the South. From 1836 onwards they spoke out strongly and articulately against slavery. Their local churches reacted furiously and denounced the sisters as unwomanly and unchristian. Deeply offended by such insults, the sisters produced pamphlets that began to deal directly with women's rights. These two proto-feminists began to compare the oppression of slaves with the social and religious repression of women. Sarah Grimké wrote that 'God made no distinction between men and women as moral beings. ... To me it is perfectly clear that whatever it is morally right for a man to do, it is morally right for women to do.'[28]

Angelica Grimké eventually married the abolitionist leader Theodore Weld. Thereafter the two sisters retired from public life. Their cause, though, was taken up by a Quaker minister in Philadelphia. Her name was Lucretia Mott. For forty years Lucretia attacked what she called 'do nothing' Christianity – that is, a Christianity that did nothing to abolish slavery. In 1840 she travelled to London with Elizabeth Cady Stanton to attend the World Anti-Slavery Convention. Both women were denied seats as delegates on the Convention floor.

They responded by organizing the first Women's Rights Convention in Seneca Falls, New York. It was held in 1848. 'The Declaration of Sentiments and Resolution', written by Mott and Stanton and adopted by the Convention, was modelled on the American Declaration of Independence, but included women where that famous document had excluded them. Thus, it begins by stating that 'all men and women are created equal; that they are endowed by their creator with certain inalienable rights.'[29]

The daringness and forthrightness of the Grimké sisters is plain for all to see in a wonderful letter they wrote to Queen Victoria of Great Britain on 26 October 1837. What is striking about their letter is its complete lack of obsequiousness. They addressed the queen as their sister and equal:

Dear Sister

Accustomed as thou art to receive the homage of an admiring nation, we know not how thou wilt be prepared to receive a communication from two women who dare not approach thee with the language of adulation. We feel that as moral and immortal beings we all stand on the same platform of *Human Rights* and therefore that we have the same duties and the same responsibilities.[30]

When the nineteenth century gave way to the twentieth, women had already begun to win the right to vote. Thereafter, however, feminist consciousness began to wane, especially in the wake of two traumatic global wars. Indeed, feminist concerns were effectively silenced by the rise of fascism. Added to that, 'From the Depression through the 1950s the vision of equality, justice and peace that inspired the nineteenth-century Christian feminists' movements was largely forgotten. The 1960s saw a reawakening of the struggle for racial justice, followed by the anti-war movement.'[31] During the 1950s a few lonely voices drew attention to the forgetfulness of significant contributions women have made to human development. One such voice was Simone de Beauvoir, who captured the problem of sexism and feminism brilliantly with the title of her book *Le deuxième sexe* (*The Second Sex*), which was published in French in 1949 and in English in 1953.

Twentieth-century feminists initially had no idea that women in the nineteenth century had already articulated coherent feminist theories. Their theories, however, were systematically excluded from standard history books, and had to be rediscovered by recent research. With the advent of the 1960s, feminism was reborn in its second wave. In the late 1950s and throughout the 1960s, women began to pursue advanced studies in theology in Western Europe and North America. Their education produced a new band of theology professors. Two of the first were Mary Daly and Rosemary Radford Ruether.

Mary Daly was launched on her career as a feminist academic because of the sexism of the Catholic Church. In the early 1950s, as a Catholic, she could not gain entry to a Catholic theology faculty in the United States. As a consequence she applied to study in the University of Fribourg, because as a Swiss state university it could not exclude women. While she was studying in Fribourg she decided to visit Rome during the Second Vatican Council (1962–65). The visit changed her life dramatically. Obtaining a pass from a journalist she entered St Peter's Basilica in Rome one day during a session of the Second Vatican council. There she saw over two thousand bishops and cardinals all dressed up in their finery. Here is how she describes what she saw in her subsequent book, *The Church and the Second Sex* (1968):

> Every day during that month-long visit in Rome was fascinating, but one day in particular was important. I borrowed a journalist's identification card and went into St Peter's for one of the major sessions. Sitting in a section reserved for the press, I saw in the distance multitudes of cardinals and bishops – old men in crimson dresses. In another section of the basilica were the 'auditors': a group which included a few Catholic women, mostly nuns in long black dresses with heads veiled. The contrast between the arrogant bearing and colorful attire of the 'princes of the church' and the humble self-deprecating manner and somber clothing of the very few women was appalling.[32]

Mary Daly returned to Fribourg and completed a doctorate in philosophy and a doctorate in theology. She then returned to the United States and taught until recently at Boston College. In 1971, she led a major revolution in feminist thought and theology. In that year she was invited to be the first women ever to preach in Harvard University's famous memorial church. For her to be invited was initially regarded as a significant success for women. However, at the end of the sermon, Daly indicated that her patience with Christianity had come to a decided end. She finished her preaching by describing the women's movement as 'an Exodus community'. Those words uttered, she began to walk out of the church and invited her listeners to follow her. Hundreds of women and several men did.[33] Her invitation still stands. In third-wave feminism since the 1980s, feminists have divided between those who wish to reform patriarchal Christianity, and those who think that Christianity is irredeemably sexist and oppressive.

Feminist theologians who continue to work within a Christian tradition include Rosemary Radford Ruether, Elisabeth Schüssler Fiorenza, Elizabeth Johnson and Mary Grey. In a powerful essay of 1983, Fiorenza alerted a generation of theologians, men as well as women, to the systematic historical exclusion of women from Christianity's public collective memory. Her programmatic essay was titled *In Memory of Her: A Feminist Reconstruction of Christian Origins*. She begins her book by drawing attention to the passion account in Mark's Gospel: that is, the section of the Gospel dealing with Jesus' suffering and death in the last week of his life. Three figures are prominent in the account: Judas, Peter and an unnamed woman. Judas betrays Jesus and Peter denies him, yet the woman anoints his feet. In response to her actions, Jesus pronounces in Mark, 'And truly I say to you, wherever the gospel is preached in the whole world, what she has done will be told in memory of her' (Mark 14:9). Hence the title of Fiorenza's book, *In Memory of Her.* The point that Fiorenza makes with reference to the anonymous women is this:

> the woman's prophetic sign-action did not become a part of the gospel knowledge of Christians. Even her name is lost to us. Wherever the gospel is proclaimed and the eucharist celebrated another story is told: the story of the apostle who betrayed Jesus. The name of the betrayer is remembered, but the name of the faithful disciple is forgotten because she was a woman.[34]

As Christianity developed and spread, it assumed many of the customs of its surrounding patriarchal Roman and Greek cultures, and the original contribution of women in the movement gathered around Jesus were lost from sight.

Because of that loss, other feminist theologians conclude that Christianity is irredeemably sexist or that its Christologies are mythological. Daphne Hampson and Mary Daly are examples of such theologians. Mary Daly's early writings are exceptionally deferential to the theological tradition initiated by Thomas Aquinas. In her doctoral dissertation in theology she wrote in resolutely traditional categories, like the following: 'In the present life infused supernatural wisdom and the acquired wisdom of theology remain distinct, although their ultimate finality – the Beatific Vision – is the same.'[35] The Beatific Vision, the sight of God a saved person can expect in heaven, is a fundamental theme in Aquinas' theology. Mary Daly published her thoughts on the Beatific Vision in 1965, the last year of the Second Vatican Council. Two decades later, Daly was writing like this:

> A contemporary graphic example of the male as great mother is pope John Paul Two ('he loves you'), the granite-jawed, white-robed superstar who has charmed millions of TV viewers and live audiences as well, particularly since his 1979 debut as visiting Queen of Heaven descending upon continent after continent in a special airplane. Championing many of the values of the vacuous eighties, such as imprisonment in the family, fetal rights, and discreet christian gynocide, this pope could be nominated Male Mother of the Decade.[36]

Such prose is meant to shock. Catherine Keller assesses Daly's work in the the following terms:

> If the creative rage inscribing Daly's work mars the image of serene timelessness connoted by the 'classical', nonetheless the conceptual density, the linguistic originality, and the sheer prophetic impact of her writing will place her among the great religious authors of Western civilization – truly, from her perspective, a case of dubious honor.[37]

The merit of Mary Daly's publications is a disputed question. What is sure is that her career as a feminist academic was sparked by her visit to a male-dominated session of the Second Vatican Council in 1965 while she was a doctoral student of the French Dominican dogmatician, J.-H. Nicolas.

if god is male, then the male is god

Feminist theology challenges a long-standing Christian custom of speaking about God with nouns and pronouns that are exclusively masculine in gender. A good example of this custom is the opening paragraph of the *Catechism of the Catholic Church*. In the following quotation of the Catechism's first paragraph, emphasis has been added to every masculine resonance. The paragraph bears the title of 'The Life of *Man* – to Know and Love God', and continues thus:

> God, infinitely perfect and blessed in *himself*, in a plan of sheer goodness freely created *man* to make *him* share in *his* own blessed life. For this reason, at every time and in every place, God draws close to *man*. He calls *man* to seek *him*, to know *him*, to love *him* with all *his* strength. *He* calls together all *men*, scattered and divided by sin, into the unity of *his* family, the Church. To accomplish this, when the fullness of time had come, God sent *his Son* as Redeemer and Saviour. In *his Son* and through *him*, he invites *men* to become, in the Holy Spirit, *his* adopted children and thus heirs to *his* blessed life.[38]

This text is a riot of sexist language. When listening to it one thinks immediately of Mary Daly in her book *Beyond God the Father* (1973) when she says, 'if God is male, then the male is God.'[39] Her comment is the most celebrated observation in contemporary feminist theology.

The point is that language works. It communicates to people specific impressions. If children are exposed to God-language that is exclusively male-gendered, that language will effectively function to connote and denote masculinity in God.[40] If one speaks of God as a man, then one must be aware that one is not talking about God. Gendered pronouns of any kind are best avoided when speaking of God so as not to give the impression that God is a person. There are those who become irritated by the suggestion that feminism causes untoward difficulties for classical theologies that speak of God in terms of 'He' and 'Him'. Avoiding such pronouns, however, is not a question of appeasing feminists. It is a matter of idolatry. To insist that masculine gendered pronouns must be used when referring to God is to regard as absolute something (a word) which is arbitrary. Idolatry, by definition, is the recognition as absolute of that which is finite. Words are always arbitrary. Theological words are always perilously arbitrary.

the ordination of women

The question of whether or not women should be ordained deacons, presbyters (priests) or bishops has sharply focused the issue of women's relation to Christianity. That this question sharply focuses the status of women within Christianity is ironical. To be ordained is to enter a hierarchy. By definition, hierarchy is a form of government exercised by priests over lay people. It is not a democratic form of government. Many feminists have complained vociferously that hierarchic rule in the church is a betrayal of the Gospel of Jesus Christ. Several other feminists campaign to have women admitted to the ranks of hierarchs.

Certain Protestant denominations ordained women over a century ago. The Church of England began the practice in the early 1990s. The Orthodox Churches and the Catholic Church refuse to do so. At present, Catholic theologians are forbidden to discuss the issue. If they write about it in public they risk censure and dismissal. During the debate on the ordination of women conducted by the Synod of the Church of England on 11 November 1992, Stephen Sykes, the Bishop of Ely, correctly informed the synod that there was more agreement among Catholic theologians that women can legitimately be ordained than there was among Anglican theologians at the same time.[41] The synod was a model of charity in dealing with opposed viewpoints. In 2005, the synod voted to remove any legal obstacles to the consecration of women as bishops: not the beginning of the end, but the end of the beginning.

Authoritarian dampening of discussion before an issue has been studied attentively can very easily breed either fideism or irrationalism among believers. It can also spawn discursive shallowness in Churches' public discourse. If theologians are unable to create a language that stands assuredly before the strictest canons of intelligibility and truthfulness that are relied upon by major disciplines in today's universities, then theology becomes denominationally ghettoized and loses a public hearing.

During the past decade, Catholics have been prevented by the Holy See from debating women and priesthood. Discussion has been unilaterally foreclosed. Since the Holy See made clear ten years ago that Catholics may not promote women to public priesthood, it is exceptionally striking that Catholic theologians around the world have fallen silent, with only a few notable and sometimes embattled exceptions. What does their collective muteness mean? Eric Borgman, speaking only of Dutch Catholic theologians, argues that their silence indicates a blindness to theology's role and function in modern culture.[42] What he says of Dutch Catholics can easily be applied to a more international scene. The worldwide silence of Catholic theologians is a disservice to other Catholics who long to have the possibility of women confirmed in officially sanctioned ministries publicly aired, and who are sometimes deeply troubled by a cacophony of conflicting arguments. Whether theologians agree or disagree on the question, some of them could at least devote time to talking and writing about it openly.

Towards the end of the twentieth century Pope John Paul II and Cardinal Joseph Ratzinger stated solemnly that Catholics do not believe that women could ever be priests. It is not clear how they know what Catholics really believe because they have not been asked.

some official arguments[43]

Debates over the ordination of women really only surfaced prominently among Catholics in the 1970s. In 1975, Pope Paul VI penned a letter, 'Response to the Letter of His Grace the Most Reverend Dr F.D. Coggan, Archbishop of Canterbury, concerning the Ordination of Women to the Priesthood'.[44] It deployed a line of argument that has hardened in subsequent texts from the Vatican on the same issue. The argument runs along the following lines: Jesus was a sovereignly free man who did not conform to misogynist cultural customs of his day. Women were quite important for him. Even so, he did not choose any women to join his elite group of twelve apostles. Instead, he exclusively selected men. These male apostles formed the foundation of a new Church he wished to erect over and against Judaism. Hence, it follows that in order to be faithful to the Lord Christ Jesus one must not fly in the face of his wishes by inviting women today to assume the functions of priests.

After Pope Paul's letter to Archbishop Coggan, (Latin Rite) Catholic theologians debated its contents. As a result, the Pope directed the Vatican's Congregation for the Doctrine of the Faith (CDF) to explain further Catholicism's views on presbyteral women. The explanation was published the next year as *Inter Insigniores* ('Among the More Distinguished').[45] John Paul II enunciated a similar line of argument in 1988 with his apostolic letter, *Mulieris Dignitatem* ('On the Dignity of Women').[46]

Even so, academic theologians persisted in worrying about priesthood and women. Their concerns elicited even more episcopal clarifications. On 22 May, 1994, John Paul II proclaimed an apostolic letter, *Ordinatio Sacerdotalis* ('On Priestly Ordination'). There he argued that presbyteral ordination must be reserved for men alone. He solemnly declared that his Church is absolutely devoid of any authority whatsoever to confer priestly ordination on women. Portentously, he stated that his judgement in this matter is to be held definitively by believers.

Once again, intellectual misgivings continued to needle Catholic scholars. Thus it transpired that an even blunter statement was prepared by the Vatican. It landed like a bombshell in our public and theological worlds as one of the strangest texts the Vatican ever produced last century. It was called *Responsio ad Propositum Dubium* ('Response to a Doubt that has been Proposed'), and was published by the CDF on 11 December 1995.[47] This text confirmed the thrust of the cluster of recent papal arguments that stretch back to 1975. Stupifyingly, it decreed that the teaching against the ordination of women is part of the deposit of faith, and that it has been infallibly proposed *ab ordinario et universali magisterio* – that is, by the ordinary and universal *magisterium*.

---

the use and abuse of magisterium The modish Catholic code-word *Magisterium* is ubiquitous nowadays in Vaticanic prose. It was, of course, mentioned by Saint Augustine in his Sermon 23. In its ancient usage, however, it simply meant the function of a teacher, called a *magister* ('master') in Latin. From the Middle Ages to the dawn of modernity, the term *magisterium* applied mainly to theological masters in universities. Today the word is used in an entirely different sense. Indeed, the notion of *magisterium*, employed as a theological category to legitimate bishops' teachings, is a historical novelty. It was not used before the nineteenth century as a word in technical theological nomenclature.[48] It came into its own as late as 1950 with Pius XII's encyclical *Humani Generis* ('The Human Race'). Moreover, one need only read the work of Cardinal Yves Congar for a sobering semantic clarification of *magisterium*, which is neither a biblical nor an apostolic expression.[49] Consequently, and in the light of historical data, it appears a duty of a theologian to challenge those who perpetually invoke a latterly concocted mystique of 'Big-M-*Magisterium*' in order to impress with authority, by pointing out that their invocation is based on a recent and questionable abstraction. Which is not at all to say that authoritative episcopal teachings lack an ancient pedigree or are always misplaced. When bishops speak truthfully with attested information, they also pronounce authoritatively. So, too, do theologians.[50]

The *Responsio* presents Catholics with an intimidating self-styled *binding state-ment* in a *non-binding document*. Otherwise stated, even according to Catholic doc-trine, the CDF does not enjoy the capacity of infallibility. So Catholics were left speechless before a document of the CDF that presumes to speak of an infallible tenet of faith without even conforming to the legal requirements of the current Catholic *Code of Canon Law*, which clearly lays down the criteria that must be met before any doctrine can be styled as 'infallible'.

Once again, whether Catholics around the world actually profess the belief that women priests are inimical to Catholic faith is another matter. For present purposes, it is important simply to realize that John Paul II and the CDF asserted plainly and politically that Catholic faith today does not allow for the possibility of women priests.

an illuminating clarification from the bible

The heart and soul of traditional Christian thinking is the study of the Sacred Page, or the analysis of biblical texts. A most distinctive feature of modern biblical studies is that they have been liberated from the interpretative control of Churches. Before the dawn of the modern era, one challenged ecclesiastical interpretations of the Bible at one's peril. Before the tolerations of modernity, the stake and gallows were always possibilities for exegetical recalcitrants. Once Church and state became unhinged, it eventually became possible for academics in universities of the state to examine canonical texts without fear of punishment from Churches.

The result is extremely revealing, especially regarding the complicated ques-tion of women's Christian ministry. The CDF stands firm against the ordination of women on the grounds that Jesus of Nazareth selected twelve men, called apostles, or more particularly the Twelve Apostles, to perpetuate in history the Church he wished to establish. The New Testament clearly indicates that there were several other apostles apart from the Twelve. On the night before Jesus was tortured and slaughtered, he is said to have initiated both the sanctified priesthood of the Apostles, and the sacrament of the Eucharist. Once appointed, so this argument runs, the Apostles ordained others, who in turn installed men to act as priests, bishops and deacons in the Church that professed Jesus as Christ. Because Jesus exclusively chose men to belong to the Twelve, the CDF now asserts that, from his own choice to current circumstances, the Catholic Church has faithfully transmitted his priorities throughout twenty centuries of subsequent history. One is therefore not at liberty arrogantly or treacherously to betray the mind of Christ.

Such is the official story of a major Church. But what about the findings of ecclesiastically independent faculties of contemporary universities? With them a remarkably different discourse is encountered (although it must be conceded that academics do not agree on the subject of the ordination of women). What follows are a few of its major conclusions. One of the most historically attested characteristics of Jesus was that he was most certainly not a priest. In the culture of his time, he was what could called a Jewish layman of Roman prefectorial Palestine. It is unlikely he had any intention of founding a Church, because he was already a member of a great Church – that is, the Jewish People of God.[51] According to their own self-understanding, they were chosen because they were oppressed. When Jesus selected twelve men as his primordial followers or Apostles, his motives could well have been determined by two cardinal factors: (a) to establish them as telling symbols of the ancient Twelve Patriarchs of Israel (see the Book of Genesis); and (b) to express a hope that the scattered Twelve Tribes of Israel would one day be restored to their former unity.[52]

Note well this word 'Patriarch'. Quite a few Christians are perplexed today by the prospect that women were among Jesus' most prominent followers, yet none of them was chosen by him to belong to the Twelve. Why not? Could their absence from the Twelve, and their subsequent exclusion from the priesthood, be explained on straightforward socio-cultural grounds? Because ancient Mediterranean societies were patriarchal, according to one view it would have been inconceivable for Jesus to have chosen women as leaders or priests.

Such an explanation is ultimately unconvincing because there are several biblical warrants for concluding that Jesus was not a patriarchal paternalist. Women were hardly excluded from his ambit. Paul's Letter to the Romans even names Junia as an apostle, though not one of the Twelve.[53] So why did women not count among the Twelve?

The reason is evident, though frequently overlooked. It is a question of Jewish symbolism. Just as the number eleven is highly significant for cricketers, the figure twelve is religiously charged for Jews like Jesus. He chose a dozen men as the twelve pillars of his group to activate quite a precise Jewish symbolic reference which can easily be lost on those who do not think and feel as Jews. In other words, Jesus' inner band of a dozen men symbolically refers to the Twelve Patriarchs of Israel and to Israel's separated Twelve Tribes that are named after the *sons* of Jacob and that were scattered by the ancient Assyrians.

The selection of men alone to designate the Patriarchs and Tribes is thus perfectly understandable. Were a composer to write an opera about the legend of King Arthur and *his* Knights of the Round Table, the characters of the knights would feature prominently. None of them would be cast as a woman or a soprano for the simple fact that women were never knights. Similarly, a woman could hardly be listed among the Twelve because none of the Patriarchs, or the sons of Jacob, was a woman! Whether they might be designated as apostles like Junia, or ordained as priests in a church looking to the future, is entirely another matter. To be sure, that the collection of twelve primary Apostles figures prominently in accounts of Christian origins cannot credibly be used to exclude women from liturgically confirmed leadership in churches. The Twelve do not legitimate a new Church or cultic priesthood, but refer to an ancient Semitic family. There is no textual evidence whatsoever in the Christian Scriptures *demonstrating* a direct link between the work of the Twelve and the threefold ministry that evolved later in Christian history, namely the service of the episcopate, presbyterate and diaconate. As I say, the symbolism of the Twelve primarily refers to the past, and points to the future in the sense of expressing a hope in the eventual restoration of a cohesive group of twelve Jewish tribes. The twelvefold future-hope alludes to a confederation of Semites; not to a college of bishops.

It is totally inadmissible *on the level of the Christian Scriptures* to argue decisively against the ordination of women on the basis of either the will of Christ or his choice of the Twelve.[54] Indeed, there are only two recorded statements attributed to Jesus in the Bible that explain his choice of the Twelve, and both of them refer to the Twelve Tribes of Israel (Matt. 19:28; and Luke 22:30). Jesus did not ordain anyone. He was not a priest, and instituted neither men nor women as priests.

conclusion

The challenge and opportunity that feminism poses for theology is not difficult to explain. Before modern times, theology was very largely articulated on the basis of the experiences of male, normally celibate, theologians. Lists of great theologians of the past refer unrelievedly to men like John, Paul, Origen, Augustine, Aquinas, Luther and Calvin. Theologians who were women, such as Catherine of Siena and Teresa of Ávila, are remembered mainly for the mystical treatises that they wrote as nuns enclosed in monasteries. The twentieth century will be recalled for many things, but in terms of the history of theology it will be recalled as the era during which highly educated women, married and celibate, published theological treatises on a large scale. If women's experiences are fundamentally different from men's, then female experiences now present the enterprise of theology with a vast new reservoir of resources that only women know and experience directly.

11

god, quarks and quasars: modern science and christian thought

We have grasped the mystery of the atom
and rejected the Sermon on the Mount.

Omar Bradley

If ignorance of nature gave birth to the Gods,
knowledge of nature is destined to destroy them.

Paul-Henri, Baron d'Holbach

Science and theology cohabited happily in the west from Christianity's early stages until the Renaissance. They still do in many respects, but the rise of modern science during and after the sixteenth century jarred with major Christian doctrines, especially those describing the structure of the universe. A succession of ground-breaking scientific discoveries in the modern age have generated a chain of new questions for old beliefs. The purpose of this chapter is to discuss generally some of these questions.

Roughly speaking, Christianity's scientific outlook before the advent of modernity was based on the physics and biology of Aristotle (384–322 BCE); the astronomy of Ptolemy (mid-second century CE); the mechanics and mathematics of Archimedes (*c.* 287–212 BCE); and the cosmogony of the Bible.

The word 'science' simply means 'knowledge', from the Latin *scientia*. During the Middle Ages, theology was often regarded as the queen of the sciences. With the growth of modern western civilization, theology was toppled from its perch as the sovereign science. The history of modernity's birth is also the story of the blossoming of a new scientific understanding of the world. The sixteenth century has been described as a time in which 'everybody believed in the supernatural; everybody believed, more or less, in magic or the possibilities of magic;

everybody believed, to a greater or less extent, in the stars.'[1] That might be an exaggeration, but westerners today are generally less credulous with regard to the magical and the supernatural than their sixteenth-century ancestors were. Over the past five centuries, the western understanding of the world has been weaned from Aristotelian science and the world-picture of the Bible by four major intellectual movements: (i) the scientific revolution of the sixteenth and seventeenth centuries; (ii) modern biology and Charles Darwin's theory of evolution by natural selection; (iii) higher biblical criticism; and (iv) twentieth-century physics and mechanics.

Understood in a modern sense, science is a type of knowledge generated by practical observation and repeated experimentation. It is 'a branch of knowledge conducted on objective principles involving the systematized observation of and experiment with phenomena, especially concerned with the material and functions of the physical universe,'[2] As Hans Küng instructs,

> The revolution of modernity was primarily an intellectual revolution. As the English politician and philosopher Francis Bacon proclaimed at a very early stage, knowledge is power. And in fact science proved to be the first great power of rising modernity. What Bacon proclaimed, but still hardly provided any empirical or scientific basis for, was initiated methodologically by Galileo, Descartes and Pascal, who were followed by Spinoza, Leibniz and Locke, Newton, Huygens and Boyle. They all laid the foundations for the new sense of the superiority of reason, which promised a quasi-mathematical certainty.[3]

When considering the rise of modern science it is important not to conclude, first, that all scientists of the last five centuries agreed with each other in their research; and, second, that all scientists were opposed to religion in general and Christianity in particular. Some of the giants in the development of modern science, like Locke, Descartes, and Newton, were exceptionally religious individuals. Moreover, to take the case of Darwin alone, at the time he advanced his biological theories, scientists and theologians both agreed and disagreed with him. Modern science is not a homogeneous, unified and strife-free phenomenon.

aristotle's cosmology

The chief consequence for theology of modern science is that the latter does not require or lead to the former. By contrast, Aristotle's cosmology was closely related to what later theologians would call God and what Aristotle himself called the Unmoved Mover. The Greek word *kosmos* means 'order', whereas *logos* refers to 'a reasoned account'. Cosmology, therefore, involves theories, analyses and accounts of the phenomena of the universe. The first documented use of the word *kosmos* in the sense of a 'world order' comes from Anaximenes.[4]

cosmology/cosmogony/ cosmography Discourses, old and new, which strive to account for the way the observable universe is constituted are conventionally called *cosmologies*. By contrast, theories concerning the particular time when the universe came into being are referred to as *cosmogonies*. Significantly for theology, Christian doctrines that speak of creation are often mistakenly regarded nowadays as cosmological theories. Strictly speaking, though, the Christian doctrine of creation is not a type of scientific cosmology. Fundamentally, it is a teaching about God and God's possible relation to all things. *Cosmography*, by contrast, is a scientific charting of the general features of the universe.

Aristotle and his teacher Plato both concluded that the cosmos is 'a unique world consisting of a spherical earth surrounded by a spherical heaven with nothing outside it'.[5] His world is everlasting – that is, without a beginning or end. He explains in his work *De Caelo* (*On Heaven*) that below the moon there are four elements – earth, water, air and fire – and everything changes. From the moon to the outer circumference of the cosmos there is no change except for motion in place.[6] As Aristotle explains in Book VIII of his *Physics*, all motions in the world require an external power that initiates movement but is itself unmoved. Hence, a first Unmoved Mover is the power causing all cosmic motion. For Aristotle, physics and cosmology lead to theology because the ultimate cause of motion in the world is external

to the world and can be identified with God. Aristotle makes the move from physics and cosmology to metaphysics and theology in his *Metaphysics* Λ.[7] Medieval theologians accepted his cosmology, even though they insisted that the world had a beginning because the Bible says so. During the Enlightenment, the understanding of power that dominated ancient and medieval cosmologies was gradually torpedoed by a notion that cosmic power does not derive from beyond the world, but can be viewed as immanent in the world and coinciding with the very nature of bodilyness.[8]

from ancient and medieval to modern world-views

Medieval theology was largely based on the cosmology of Aristotle as modified by the Egyptian astronomer, Claudius Ptolemy (second century CE). Modern theology was born once theologians began to write on the basis of a quite new scientific picture of the cosmos.

SPHERE OF THE FIXED STARS
SPHERE OF SATURN
SPHERE OF JUPITER
SPHERE OF MARS
SPHERE OF THE SUN
SPHERE OF VENUS
SPHERE OF MERCURY
SPHERE OF THE MOON
EARTH

FIGURE 11.1   The Ptolemaic picture of the universe with earth at the centre

David Laird Dungan of the University of Tennessee, Knoxville, follows Louis Dupré, in placing the beginning of modernity at the end of the Middle Ages. For Dungan, a modern world-view originated in the late fourteenth century with the breakdown of a medieval intellectual and cultural synthesis. He opines that modern ideas and goals reached their fulfilment in the world empires built by European nation-states during the nineteenth century. And he shackles the death of the modern world-view with the world wars of 1914–18 and 1939–45.[9]

In Christian theology, from its embryonic formulations right up until the High Middle Ages, the Aristotelian–Ptolemaic cosmology (see Figure 11.1) was complemented by the world-view of the Bible. In general, biblical authors assumed a vision of the world that was essentially Mesopotamian. In ancient Mesopotamian cultures the universe involved four basic components: 'sky, atmosphere, earth, and the watery realm beneath the earth'.[10] Significantly, the universe was thought to be ordered hierarchically according to a tripartite schema: heaven, earth and a netherworld. Exactly the same schema is found in ancient Babylonian literature, according to which a three-tiered cosmos is arranged pyramidally thus:

Heaven – The realm of the Gods and celestial bodies

Earth – The realm of humans and nature

Netherworld – The realm of Gods and the dead[11]

The ancient world-view of the Graeco-Roman age (see Figure 11.2) is well described by the North American biblical scholar, Robert Funk. In his book, *Honest to Jesus*, he discusses the way images presently connected with Jesus among a general population tend to be linked to an ancient picture of the universe. He explains:

> That worldview was made up of a three-tiered cosmos: an earth in the shape of a pancake, flat with arching heavens overhead and fiery regions below. The mountains at the edge of the earth functioned as pillars to hold up the skies, and beyond those mountains lay utter darkness, on one side, and perhaps the Elysian Fields, on the other.[12]

For biblical cosmology, activities in heaven generated physical consequences on earth and earthly events were mirrored in heaven: 'If war begins on earth, then there must be, at the same time, war in heaven between the angels of the nations in the heavenly council.'[13] As Walter Fink has insightfully noted, 'Not only the Bible, but also the Greeks, Romans, Egyptians, Babylonians, Indians and Chinese – indeed most people in the ancient world – shared this worldview, and it is still held by large numbers of people today. It just happened to be the view

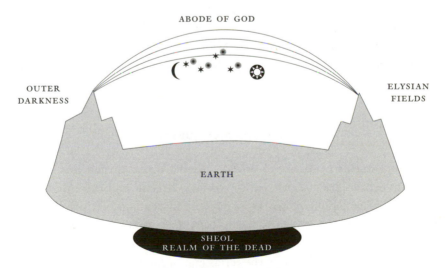

FIGURE 11.2   A picture of the cosmos of the Graeco-Roman age

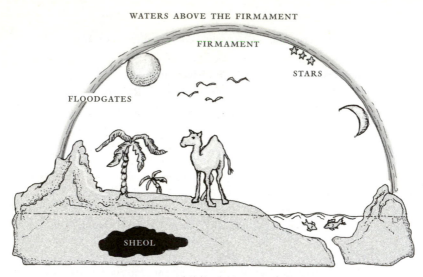

FIGURE II.3   A biblical picture of the cosmos

current when the Bible was written.'[14] Victor Matthews and Don Benjamin sketch
a biblical conception of the cosmos that is similar to Robert Funk's illustration
of an ancient Graeco-Roman world-view (see Figure II.3).[15]

There is not a single comment about God and human beings in the entire
Bible that does not presuppose that the universe is static, hierarchically ordered
and centred on the earth. The world-view of Aristotle, modified by Ptolemy,
and echoed throughout the Bible, persisted unrivalled among untold numbers
of human beings right up until the Renaissance (see Figure II.4). The resolute
rejection of this world-view is one of the axial features of modern thought and
theology.

quarks and quasars

The four elements of Aristotle's world – earth, water, air and fire – no longer
suffice to explain planet earth and the cosmos. Arisotle and the Enlightenment's
philosophes knew nothing of quarks or quasars. Even a hundred years ago, people
did not talk in terms of quarks and quasars. It was only with the evolution of
twentieth-century astronomy and astrophysics that the two terms entered the
English language. As strange as the terms may seem, it is easier to come to grips
with what they signify than the referent of the word 'God'. It is possible to say

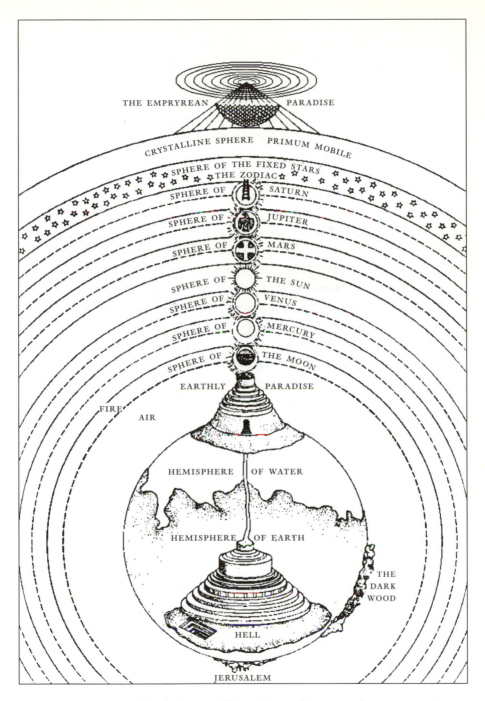

FIGURE 11.4   Medieval picture of the universe from Dante's *Divine Comedy*

more about quarks and quasars than God, because the former are constituents of the universe, whereas God is not in the world. Because God is not a person or observable thing, human beings are severely hampered if not entirely incompetent in their attempts to speak meaningfully and truthfully about God. Theology can never be more that an inconclusive stuttering.

In contrast to Aristotelian science, contemporary physicists conclude that all matter currently known to human beings is made up of particles from two principal particle families: quarks and leptons. Quarks can be differentiated in six varieties, which relate to one another in groups of three pairs. Similarly, leptons constitute a family of six elementary particles that include the electron, muon and tau particles, together with their associated neutrinos. Quasars, on the other hand, are highly energetic cores of active galaxies. An active galaxy, in turn, emits a vast amount of energy from its central region, known as its nucleus.

What is the point, though, of talking about leptons, quarks, quasars and active galaxies in a modern introduction to theology? The answer is quite straightforward. Modern science, with its resolutely unbiblical and non-dogmatic terminology, provides an intellectually convincing explanation for the way things are that is not in any way dependent on the Bible. Its account of the workings of the world has for many people today supplanted the explanatory powers of the Bible and Christian doctrine. As indicated, the world-views of the Bible and of classical Christian doctrine are informed by pre-modern understandings of the nature of the physical universe. It is the daunting task of contemporary theologians to formulate a new theological world-view that takes account of a vast bank of new scientific data about the structure of the cosmos and the place of human beings in it.

an inescapable god

Because of the rise of modern science, it has become much more difficult for many people now to conceive of God's relation to the world they hear described by contemporary scientists. A vast difference between ancient and current ways of talking about humans in relation to God can be illustrated with reference to Psalm 139 of the Tanakh. Psalm 139 is one of the finest, most evocative pieces of religious prose ever composed. It is a rhetorically rhapsodic and beguiling text. The psalmist addresses God in intimate terms:

> O LORD, you have searched me and you know me.
> You know when I sit down and when I rise up;
> You discern my thoughts from far away.

You search out my path and my lying down,
and are acquainted with all my ways.
Even before a word is on my tongue,
O LORD, you know it completely.
You hem me in, behind and before,
and lay your hand upon me.
Such knowledge is too wonderful for me;
it is so high that I cannot attain it.
Where can I go from your spirit?
Or where can I flee from your presence?
If I ascend to heaven you are there;
if I make my bed in Sheol, you are there... (vv. 1–8)

It is important to register the notion of Sheol in the psalm. The psalm clearly evinces an ancient, pre-scientific (in a modern sense) world-picture. It is impossible to escape the presence of God: 'Where can I go from your spirit?'; or 'Where can I flee from your presence?' These questions and all of the 150 psalms in the Bible were composed thousands of years ago in the Near East. Their deference to God and the inescapability of God contrast vividly with Robert Naeye's book *Through the Eyes of Hubble*:

Five billion years ago, long before the earth and Sun were born, a star exploded. This wasn't just any star, it was a supergiant star hundreds of times larger than the Sun. For a few days, the flash of the explosion nearly equalled the combined light of all the Galaxy's 200 billion stars. The cataclysm spewed gaseous debris in all directions at speeds thousands of times faster than a bullet. A shock wave of energy ripped through the surrounding space, plowing up gas and dust as a snow-plow piles up snow. The blast and radiation wreaked devastation, destroying or sterilizing any hapless planets that lay in their path.

But out of this appalling destruction were planted the seeds of new life. The gradually weakening shock wave eventually rammed into a tenuous cloud of cold gas, causing it to start contracting under the force of gravity. Tens of millions of years later, this cloud formed a newborn star. And 4.6 billion years after that, on one of the small chunks of debris left over from the formation of the star, intelligent beings emerged who could ask questions about their origin. If this scenario is correct, our planet, our Sun, our solar system, everyone we know, everyone we love, everything we ever cared about – all of these things owe their existence to a stellar cataclysm that occurred some five billion years ago.[16]

A striking feature of the passage just cited is that it makes no reference to God whatsoever. On the contrary, it instructs that everything people know, love and care about stems from a supergiant star. This means that life comes from stars, or more precisely, from the light emitted by stars. As the contemporary physicist Lee Smolin asserts, 'light is the ultimate source of life. Without the light coming from the sun, there would be no life here on earth. Light is not only our medium of contact with the world; in a very real sense, it is the basis of our existence.'[17]

If light is the source of life, what is the source of light? The word 'God' has traditionally been linked to that question, for, as observed in Chapter 1, the Latin expression for 'God', *Deus*, is related to the word for day, *dies*. That God is the source of life, however, is a postulate of theology, and not an undisputed conclusion of modern sciences.

The Godless account of the life's origins offered by the astronomer Robert Naeye could not be more alien to the God-obsessed confidence of Psalm 139. The psalmist sings that God is unavoidable with a disposition that contrasts vividly with the experiences of many present-day westerners, who complain either that they cannot sense God anywhere, or that they do not want to be pestered by religious people.

The contemporary western nonchalance about God and increasing lack of interest in theology are linked to the way modern science has shattered many people's belief in the world-view of the Bible. In the early stages of the nineteenth century, most people living in Great Britain believed that the earth was roughly 6000 years old. They followed, of course, the now infamous calculations of the seventeenth-century Archbishop of Armagh, James Ussher. According to Ussher, the world was created by God on 23 October 4004 BCE. He calculated this date from the age the Bible records for Adam's descendants.[18] He taught that Noah's flood occurred in December 2349 BCE.

During the nineteenth century, however, the general public's belief that the world is only 6000 years old was steadily eroded thanks, in part, to the pioneering work of the geologist Charles Lyell. From 1831 to 1833, Lyell was Professor of Geology at King's College, London. Between 1830 and 1833 he published a three-volume work titled *Principles of Geography, being an Attempt to Explain the Former Changes of the Earth's Surface by Reference to Causes now in Operation.* These books were based on thirty years of Lyell's work as a barrister-turned-geologist. During three decades he examined fossils in strata of the earth and soon came to realize that this planet is vastly older that 6000 years. It is now known that the earth and its solar system were formed some 5 to 6 billion years ago. Lyell made an important contribution to specifying the history of earth by identifying the Pliocene, Miocene and Eocene eras of the Tertiary period (about 50 million to 5 million years ago).[19] Such a vast duration of time cannot be reconciled with the Bible's chronology of earth's history. Lyell's work relied upon the findings of the new distinctively modern discipline of geology that emerged in the late eighteenth century with stratigraphy (the study of rock layers) and palaeontology (the study of fossils in rocks).

The dating of the earth posited by geologists in the nineteenth century constitutes a most pressing problem for those biblical and dogmatic theologies that presuppose a universe of a much younger age, and a world that is hierarchically structured with a heaven above, and an underworld within the terrestrial world. For the Bible, human beings were created in the first days of creation. Their progeny can be listed in successive generations until the birth of Abraham. Yet the timescale from Adam and Eve to Abraham is nowhere near as vast as the scale of 4.4 million years that it took for the first hominid ancestors of human beings to develop into *Homo sapiens* some 40,000 years ago.

god-talk and world-views

Clearly, one of the greatest challenges for modern theology stems from newly acquired scientific knowledge about the constitution and age of the universe. It may well be the case that God is dead in many people's hearts nowadays because God is still designated and discussed by several theologians and church leaders on the basis of a world-view espoused by pre-modern religious believers and discarded by contemporary westerners.

Gordon Kaufman has devoted his professorial career to clarifying the way each and every theology is parasitic upon a particular world-view. Until his retirement, Kaufman (b. 1925) was the Edward Mallinckrodt, Jr, Professor of Divinity in Harvard University's Divinity School. In a series of books he explains very well the way classical understandings of God have become problematical, if not meaningless, for many of the inhabitants of the contemporary west. He does so with reference to imaginative and integrative symbolic world-views.

The pivot of Kaufman's case is the notion that all human beings create images of the universe in which they live. All human beings have lived in exactly the same world-space, but the ways in which they intellectually chart the layout of their common shared world has differed markedly over time. Moreover, each of the world's religions, ancient and new, maps its own universe: 'Each in its own way locates where we humans are, where we come from, where we are going. Each deals with the perils of the journey, the pain, suffering, and death, the disparities of rich and poor, of injustice and war.'[20]

The point is, all human beings function in their daily lives with a particular understanding of what the world is, of what it means to be human, and of what is ultimately important. These three concepts – the world, humanity and ultimacy

– are the constitutive elements from which world-views are imaginatively created. Inhabiting the same world, humans envision it differently depending on their diverse mental impressions of the cosmos, humanity and absoluteness. This is a crucial point: each and every theology that has ever been produced is based on a particular world-view that encompasses the three conceptual symbols of the world, humanity and ultimacy. For western theists, God is the name for that which is unconstrained or ultimate. Language about God is inescapably linked to a particular cosmology and anthropology because people can only talk about God in relation to themselves in a particular place and time.

Gordon Kaufman knows the philosophy of Kant very well. The former learned from the latter that the very concepts of 'the human' and 'the world' logically cannot be conceived independently of each other. For Kant, human thought would be impossible without a concept of the world:

> For if the mind had no such notion, it could not hold all the ideas and experiences and things and events, with which it must deal, together in a way that would enable us effectively to focus attention on them and relate them to one another, to reflect on them and think them and gain some understanding of them in their relations to one another.[21]

Without a notion of the world, cosmos or universe, individuals would simply not be able to act, since to act is to be able to place oneself within a structure, in relation to other elements within the structure. According to Kaufman, all theologians presuppose a concept of the human, a notion of the world, and a symbol of God. 'All we can know or experience or can imagine', he says,

> can be given a place within this threefold categorical scheme; and what we ordinarily call 'faith in God' is simply human life lived within the terms it prescribes: all experiencing and reflecting, all imagining and thinking, all deciding and acting take place within this threefold pattern.[22]

The English word 'God' is a western concept. Its origins lie in ancient Middle Eastern polytheism. The conception of the world now held by most educated modern people in the west is quite different from that found in the Bible and in the ancient Middle East.[23] Hence the pressing need nowadays for theologians to engage with contemporary astronomy, astrophysics, cosmology and biology. In 1983, the physicist Paul Davies published an intriguing book titled *God and the New Physics*. In his view, 'although science cannot and does not resolve all religious issues it does have deep implications and significance for our thinking about them.'[24] Moreover, for Davies, 'The new physics has overturned so many common sense notions of space, time, and matter that no serious religious thinker can ignore it.'[25] Davies underscores very well the significance of modern science for modern theology. Paul Brockelman, Professor of Religious Studies and Philosophy at the University of New Hampshire, is of the opinion that contemporary physics has spawned for the first time in over three hundred years a real dialogue between scientists and theologians. As he observes in his book *Cosmology and Creation*, the dialogue is surely unparalleled and revolutionary.[26] The upshot of the dialogue is that theologians are increasingly challenged to rethink the classical notion of a God who is outside or above a three-story world of heaven, earth and hell. So far as Joseph Campbell is concerned, 'the old notion of a once-upon-a-time First Cause has given way to something more like an immanent ground of being, transcendent of conceptualization, which is in a continuous act of creation now'.[27]

Modern geology, astronomy and astrophysics have revealed that the world is not a three-layered structure with earth at the centre with an age of 6000 years. Our universe is anywhere between 12 and 15 billion years old; and the earth was formed 5 to 6 billion years ago. In addition the observable universe contains 100 billion galaxies; and each galaxy contains 100 billion stars. The task of completely revising language about God in the light of such a cosmology has barely begun. What is now clear is that pre-modern theologies are based on world-views that are, in terms of science, defunct. If the cosmologies and anthropologies undergirding theologies are false, then so too are the theologies themselves.

medieval and newtonian world-views Ian Barbour, until his recent retirement, was Professor of Physics as well as Professor of Religion, as well as Professor of Science, Technology, and Society, in Carleton College, Minnesota. In 1998, he published a laudable book called, *Religion and Science*. Therewith he illustrates amply the difference between pre-modern and explicitly modern scientific and theological world-views. He characterizes the medieval view of nature or of the world as a combination of Greek and biblical ideas that can be explained in terms of six features. In the first place, the world was seen as a fixed order. While there was change within it, its basic structures were regarded as immutable. Second, it was purposeful or teleological. Every creature reflected a divine plan or purpose. Third, the world was substantive in that its components were either material or mental substances. Fourth, the cosmos was hierarchically arranged with lower entities serving higher ones. God was above men, men above women, women above animals, and animals above plants. This, obviously, is a highly anthropocentric view. All that exists must serve the purposes of humanity. Fifth, the world is dualistically constituted with contrasting souls and bodies, spirits and materials, perfect eternal forms and imperfect embodiment in a material world. Sixth and finally, the medieval view regards the cosmos as a kingdom, an ordered society existing under a sovereign Lord.[28]

Such a view of the world, as is well known, was gradually altered or challenged in the light of the work of Copernicus, Galileo and Isaac Newton. In the seventeenth century, Newton formulated a law of gravity and three laws of motion describing the dynamical behaviour of objects. The Newtonian world-view contrasts with the medieval cosmology in that it recognizes that the components of reality change, or are rearranged to a greater extent than had been previously imagined. The second feature of the Newtonian world-picture was that the world is regarded in a determinist way. That is, all events in the world are determined by mechanical causes rather than by divine purpose or action. Third, it was an atomistic view according to which atoms rather than substances are the basic constitutive parts of reality. Fourth, the world was not hierarchical but reductionistic. That is, it reduces, so to speak, an explanation of events from speaking of God's actions, to explaining all events with reference to physical laws at the lowest levels of reality. Fifth, it too was a dualistic world-view in which Newton accepted Descartes's dualism between mind and body. Finally, the entire Newtonian perspective can be encapsulated in the image of a machine rather than a kingdom. The world operates according to its own internal mechanical laws.[29]

Both medieval and Newtonian-enthused theologians often conceived of God as transcendent or external to nature. The psalmist, to recall, says to God: 'You discern my thoughts from far away.' The world-view of the psalm was carried over into medieval cosmology. Although God is present everywhere for the psalmist, God is also said to be remote. However, were the psalmist to ascend to heaven, God would be found there. And were the psalmist to descend into Sheol, there too God could be experienced.

For Newtonians, God is absent from the operations of the world. Newtonian mechanics led many people in the eighteenth century to espouse deism, the view that God created the world but, after the act of creation, refrains from controlling the events of the world.

scientific world-view   In contrast to both medieval and Newtonian world-views, Ian Barbour delineates the world-view generated by twentieth-century science once again in terms of six major features. First, nature is not regarded as a fixed order, but as inherently evolutionary and emergent. Second, in place of fixed determined laws of nature, change combines with law in the operations of the world. Third, nature is regarded as relational and interdependent: all things are interconnected with all other things. Fourth, holistic concepts and systems complement attention to separate components of particular systems. Fifth, there is a hierarchy within each organism rather than a hierarchy of value among beings as in the medieval world-view. Finally, the primary image of the world is no longer a kingdom or machine, but a community. The world is a community of historically interdependent beings.[30]

During the nineteenth and twentieth centuries two great revolutions spawned an entirely new understanding of human beings and their universe. The first was a revolution in biology and was incarnate in the life and work of Charles Darwin. The second was a revolution in physics, astronomy and mechanics, which is frequently discussed in relation to a so-called big bang theory of cosmic origins and dimensions.

darwinian evolutionary biology   Turning to the first, in 1995 Daniel C. Dennett, published a book called *Darwin's Dangerous Idea*. In the early stages of the book he makes a riveting observation:

> Let me lay my cards on the table. If I were to give an award for the single best idea anyone has ever had, I'd give it to Darwin, ahead of Newton and Einstein and everyone else. In a single stroke, the idea of evolution by natural selection unifies the realm of life, meaning, and purpose with the realm of space and time, cause and effect, mechanism and physical law. But it is not just a wonderful idea. It is a dangerous idea.[31]

What is this idea that is deemed dangerous? Why is it dangerous? For whom is it dangerous? To begin with, Darwin published what Dennet calls his dangerous idea in 1859 with the publication of what some regard as the greatest book of the nineteenth century, *On the Origin of Species by Means of Natural Selection*. Therein Darwin elaborates a theory of evolution of living species that accounts for design in living beings that does not speak of God or theology at all. Before Darwin – and Richard Dawkins agrees on this – the best explanation for the ordered and adaptive features of living organisms seemed to be that of divine intelligent design. Contrapuntally, Darwin's theory of the evolution of living species involves five fundamental principles, which are very well explained by J. Wentzel van Hussteen in his wonderful little book *Duet or Duel? Theology and Science in a Postmodern World*:

(i)   At any stage in the history of a species of a species, there will always be variation among different members of the species (the principle of variation).

(ii) At any stage in the history of a species, more members are born than can survive to reproduce (the principle of the struggle for existence).

(iii) At any stage in the history of a species, some of the variation among members of the species is variation with respect to properties that effect the ability to survive and reproduce: some members of a species therefore have characteristics that can help them survive and reproduce (the principle of variation in fitness).

(iv) Heritability is the norm, and most properties of an organism or member of a species are inherited by its descendents (the principle of inheritance).

(v) Typically the history of a species will show the modification of that species in the direction of those characteristics which help their bearers to survive and reproduce; and these characteristics are then likely to become more prevalent in successive generations of the species (the principle of natural selection).[32]

Darwin was not the first person to speak of biological evolution. Robert Chambers had done so in 1844. However, Darwin's views were buttressed by years devoted to collecting specimens of species while he was sailing on *The Beagle*.

For whom, though, is Darwin's idea of evolution by natural selection dangerous, or subversive, or unsettling? In effect, it may be regarded as dangerous for religious believers because it wrecks any hope that the universe is there for a reason. The idea is dangerous if evolutionary science has shattered 'every pious illusion that life and existence were planned from all eternity'.[33]

John Haught argues in his book *God after Darwin* that Darwin evinced two dangerous ideas, not one. In the first place, the evolution of species by natural selection suggests that differences between species occur randomly, not because of a purpose or plan. In the second instance, Darwin's thought is unsettling for Christian orthodoxy in its conclusion that humans were not created apart from animals, but evolved from other animals over millions of years.

To appreciate the shock many felt in Britain upon the publication and public discussion of *On the Origin of Species*, it is necessary to recall that before the mid-nineteenth century, by far the majority of British people believed that the world was roughly 6000 years old. Before Darwin, most Christians assumed that humans were created apart from animals and above animals. After all, in the first chapter of Genesis God creates all living creatures before creating humankind separately in God's own image. For traditional theology, human beings mirror the image of God. The universal Christian orthodoxy of the early nineteenth century was that each species had been separately created, and that a particular species could not develop out of another.

The impact of Darwin's ideas on the general public is well documented by Owen Chadwick:

More educated Englishmen doubted the truth of the Christian religion in 1885 than thirty years before. And in 1885 many persons, whether they doubted or affirmed, blamed 'science' alone for this change in opinion. Some of them talked as though 'science' alone was responsible. And among those who blamed science, some fastened upon the name of Charles Darwin as a symbol, or centre, or intellectual force, of an entire development of the sciences as they came to bear upon the truth of religion.[34]

After Darwin, a new term was coined in England – unbelief. The Religious Census of 1851 had already discovered that a large proportion of British people were indifferent to religion. That indifference appears to have been exacerbated by the legacy of Darwin. Indeed, as Chadwick concludes,

> The Christian Church taught what was not true. It taught the world to be 6,000 years old, a universal flood, and stories in the Old Testament like the speaking ass or the swallowing of Jonah by a whale which ordinary men (once they were asked to consider the question of truth or falsehood) instantly put into the category of legends. ... The churches taught something that could no longer be believed, and therefore all the other teaching of the churches fell into question.[35]

The consequences of Darwin's work are very far from being appropriated by officially sanctioned Christian doctrines. For example, the current *Catechism of the Catholic Church* solemnly teaches that the biblical story of Adam and Eve, or rather the third chapter of the Book of Genesis, 'affirms a primeval event, a deed that took place at the beginning of the history'.[36] This teaching is solemnly declared. It is also false. Chapter 3 of Genesis is a myth. It does not provide any reliable information about the historical genesis of a human species. What it does say about human origins is false. To regard it as factually true is to violate its literary form as a myth. The point of the Genesis stories of creation is to affirm that the God of the Israelites is the creator of the world, not the God Marduk, or any other God. After speaking of a primeval event that took place at the beginning of history, the Catechism concludes that death is a consequence of the disobedience of Adam and Eve. With a primordial couple called Adam and Eve, the Catechism instructs that *'Death makes its entrance into human history'*.[37] This teaching is decidedly odd. Death could not possibly have made its entrance into human history with a primordial set of first parents because hominid species had suffered and died for thousands of years before *Homo sapiens* emerged. Suffering, decay and death were experienced by dinosaurs, let alone by human beings:

> There has been death since the origin of life on earth; it is part of the process of living. Plants and animals have known death since life evolved on this earth more than three billion years ago. In anthropogenetic terms these are our 'ancestors'. Only through the descent of our life from their life did 'death enter into human history', not from the disobedience of the 'first human beings'.[38]

What is intellectually arresting if not religiously breathtaking about Darwinian biology and contemporary cosmology is their combined suggestion that all reality is regarded as interrelated and evolutionary. All that exists, everything there is, living and inanimate, has changed over time and is related to everything else that exists.

big bang cosmology   Strikingly, the new regnant (though not the exclusive) cosmology that emerged in the twentieth century, and is now called big bang theory, postulates that everything in the universe stems from a singularity. In 1927, the Belgian priest and astronomer, Georges Lemaître, formulated a cosmology that is now called big bang theory. The term 'big bang' was coined in the 1940s by the British astronomer Fred Hoyle. He intended it as a term of derision for a theory he thought was as elegant 'as a party girl jumping out of a cake'.[39] The term, however, was both to survive and to stick.

John Gribbin summarizes big bang theory in these terms: 'An overwhelming weight of evidence has convinced most astronomers that the universe came into being at a definite moment some fifteen billion years ago, in the form of a superhot, superdense fireball of energetic radiation.'[40]

So, according to big bang cosmology, our universe stems from an initiating event. Yet the very word 'bang' suggests an explosion. Even so, the expansion of the universe from an initiating singularity

> is not so much an explosion from an initial and initiating 'bang' out into empty space as it is an expansion of space and time itself, like (as one scientist has put it) raisin bread dough before it is baked rising and taking the raisins with it. In other words, space and time are not static vessels in which the universe is expanding, as Newton envisaged them, but rather are the expanding dimensions of the universe itself.[41]

Paul Brockelman helpfully summarizes the findings of modern geology, astronomy, biology and physics in a six-stage schema of what he calls 'Creation Timeline' (see box).

conclusion

The details of the new cosmology sketched by Paul Brockelman's creation timeline illustrate wonderfully how enormously fertile modern science has been. However, it is not the constitutive details of his sketch that primarily interest the theologian today. Many of the details could well be corrected in the future. Others are disputed among scientists themselves. The Christian theology of creation is quite compatible with a number of cosmologies for the simple reason that it is not a scientific cosmology or biology, but a discourse about God. What attracts the theologian is the idea that everything and everyone is related to, and

INITIAL STAGE (15 billion years ago)

0 seconds	Infinite singularity
10^{-43} seconds (temp: 10^{32}K)	Gravitational force separates
10^{-35} secs (temp: 10^{28}K)	Strong nuclear force separates
10^{-10} secs (temp: 10^{15}K)	Weak nuclear and electromagnetic forces separate
1–3 minutes	Matter emerges in particles along with helium and hydrogen

FORMATION OF GALAXIES

300,000 years after (2000K)	Hydrogen and helium form lumpy clouds
1–5 billion years after	Around 50 billion galaxies form

FORMATION OF THE SOLAR SYSTEM AND EARTH (5–6 billion years ago)

9–10 billion years after	A sun (Tiamat) in the Orion arm of the Milky Way explodes as a supernova spewing forth heavy elements such as carbon, oxygen, and nitrogen
10 billion years after	Sun, earth and solar system form

THE EMERGENCE OF LIFE

11–12 billion years after	First microscopic forms of life
3–4 billion years ago	DNA, photosynthesis, and sexual regeneration
700 million years ago	Familiar multicellular creatures emerge in the sea
550 million years ago	First shellfish appear. The Cambrian explosion of new forms of marine life, including first vertebrates, which lead to myriad life forms (fish, plants, animals, mammals) which are familiar today
400 million years ago	Life emerges from the sea
235 million years ago	Dinosaurs appear
216 million years ago	First mammals appear
210 million years ago	Breakup of Pangaea and formation of continents
90 million years ago	Flowering plants predominate

THE EMERGENCE OF HUMAN LIFE

4.4 million years ago	First hominid ancestor of both humans and apes and chimpanzees
2.8 million years ago	First humans: *Homo habilis*
2.4–1.0 million years ago	Humans spread around the world: *Homo erectus*
200–300,000 years ago	Archaic *Homo sapiens*

THE DEVELOPMENT OF HUMAN CULTURAL AND SPIRITUAL WISDOM

40,000 years ago	First cultural remains of modern *Homo sapiens*
35,000 years ago	Neanderthals die out
12,000 years ago	Neolithic culture
3500 years ago	Classical cultures
450 years ago (1543)	Copernicus and modern culture
Now (15 billion years later)	Science sees the whole in the new technology[42]

derives from, a singularity. Carbon atoms in human bodies all stem from distant, exploded stars. And those stars all emerged in the wake of the big bang. Reality, therefore, 'is an inclusive narrative of an evolutionary process in which all the parts are linked and ultimately derived from a singular one.'[43]

If such a view is accepted, how is God to be conceived in relation to the cosmos? If reality is evolutionary, dynamic, emergent, and interrelated, how does God relate to all that is non-Godly? Indeed, how is God to be reconceived on the basis of new scientific knowledge that no previous generation has ever enjoyed?

These questions can be addressed in association with one of the greatest of all scientific discoveries, which occurred in 1929. In that year, the North American astronomer Edwin Hubble measured the distance of the Andromeda galaxy and other galaxies using the Cepheid technique. Because of his discovery of redshift in light from galaxies beyond the Local Group, he inferred that the universe is expanding, and thereby removed the need for Einstein's cosmological constant in its original form.[44] Before Hubble, no human being could confirm so convincingly that our universe is not static, but expanding. From the initial Singularity until now, cosmic history has been a vast creative dynamism that has produced human beings dealing with nanotechnology and quantum computation. Gordon Kaufman describes the creative dynamism pushing cosmic evolution as Serendipitous Creativity, a concept he concludes can be identified with God.[45] God is the unexpectedly surprising creative dynamism within the universe impelling the evolutionary progression from separating gravitational forces to Edwin Hubble. Such a concept is neither traditional nor orthodox, but it stands as a clear attempt to construct a concept of God that is informed by contemporary science. Kaufman's understanding of God as cosmic Serendipitous Creativity is no better and no worse than any other. God has never been described well or depicted properly because God is not a knowable thing in the universe. Whatever theologians state about God is muttered against the profound silence of a much deeper and inescapable nescience.

12

modern encounters
between major religions

> We have just enough religion to make us hate,
> but not enough to make us love one another.
>
> *Jonathan Swift*

A common complaint laid against religions by atheists is that religions produce violence. A brief consideration of history seems amply to justify the truth of the charge. Current sites of violence around the world often appear to have religious belief at their core. Religions produce doctrines about people and their world and require their devotees to adhere passionately and faithfully to the world-view painted by doctrines. Each religion, though, sketches a different world-view. All of the religious understandings of the world cannot be equally true. One, some or all must be false or misleading in what they assert. Zoroastrianism (founded in the sixth century BCE) teaches that there are two rival powers in the cosmos – a spirit of goodness and a power of evil. Christianity denies such a dualism and insists that nothing rivals the power of God. When one religious tradition slights the beliefs of another, the potential for violent conflict easily arises. In the past, Christianity has frequently related to other religions by treating them in the same way that early Christians were treated by some of the Roman emperors – with violent persecution. For as long as Christendom enjoyed a cultural hegemony in the west, it was easily able to ignore, deny or imperil other religions. Violence perpetrated against other religions was often unwittingly legitimated by the Church's theologians. Cyprian of Carthage (d. 258), for instance, coined the adage *extra ecclesiam nulla salus*, 'there is no salvation outside the Church' (Epistles 73:21). Inspired by such a theology, zealous Inquisitors later interrogated and punished people who refused to become Christians as an urgent matter of having to save the souls of those who were not baptized. Cyprian's maxim was still defended by Christians in the first half of the twentieth century. Confidence in upholding it began to wane in the latter half of the twentieth century, largely because of the phenomenon of globalization.

Expressed at its simplest, globalization is an international process by which the economies and cultures of the globe have become steadily more interconnected through satellites, television, air travel and computers. Wayne Ellwood aptly defines globalization thus:

> Globalization is a new word which describes an old process: the integration of the global economy that began in earnest with the launch of the European colonial era five centuries ago. But the process has accelerated over the past quarter century with the explosion of computer technology, the dismantling of trade barriers and the expanding political and economic power of multinational corporations.[1]

The technologies driving globalization and quickening its pace have been a major catalyst for enabling the world's manifold religious traditions to become increasingly aware of each other. The purpose of this chapter is to consider religious pluralism in a globalized world, and, more specifically, Christianity's relations with other religious traditions. The term 'religious pluralism' now designates a fact of reality: the world is home to a vast variety of religious world-views and ways of living. Two questions dominate what follows. Is Christianity inherently superior to all other religions? Can anyone be saved outside the Christian Church?

Such queries are far from purely academic and inconsequential. The urgency of the questions just posed, and of considering religious pluralism in a globalized era, are captured well by Hans Küng in his book *Judaism*. At the beginning of that monograph he declares memorably, 'No peace among the nations without peace among the religions. No peace among the religions without dialogue between the religions. No dialogue between the religions without investigation of the foundations of the religions.'[2]

religious pluralism

Working out how religious traditions should relate to each other is quite a daunting task. An excellent introduction is provided by Harold Coward, director of the Centre for Studies in Religion and Society at the University of Victoria (Canada). For Coward,

> Religious experience has been defined as the quest for ultimate reality. In pursuing this quest, religions often seem to have an inherent drive to claims of uniqueness

and universality. Many religions exhibit an inner tendency to claim to be the true religion, to offer the true revelation as the true way of salvation or release. It appears to be self-contradictory for such a religion to accept any expression of ultimate reality other than its own. Yet one of the things that characterizes today's world is religious pluralism. The world has always had religious plurality. But in the past two decades the breaking of cultural, racial, linguistic and geographical boundaries has been on a scale that the world has not previously seen. For the first time in recorded history we seem to be rapidly becoming a true global community. Today the West is no longer closed within itself. It can no longer regard itself as being the historical and cultural centre of the world and as having a religion that is the sole valid way of worship. The same is true for the East. Today everyone is the next-door neighbour and spiritual neighbour of everyone else.[3]

In 1995, the English philosopher and theologian John Hick (b. 1922) published a smallish book titled *The Rainbow of Faiths: Critical Dialogues on Religious Pluralism*. As with the case of Harold Coward's book, the beginning of Hick's essay presents the following sobering ideas:

> At the end of the twentieth century Christianity is in deep crisis. The theological structure developed by the Western church has come to seem hollow and irrelevant to the majority of Westerners, and seems foreign and alien, as an extension of Western cultural hegemony, to many Christians in Africa, India, China, and the East generally.[4]

That stated, Hick observes that there are several aspects to the recent profound crisis that Christianity has endured. Nevertheless, he announces that his new book is concentrated on only one of the features of the crisis, namely 'the widespread realization that Christianity is only one among several great world religions'.[5] He goes on to speak of religious pluralism in these terms:

> Judaism, Islam, Hinduism, Buddhism now appear to many as different but, judging by their fruits in human life, equally authentic responses to God, the Divine, the Ultimate, the Real. This (often implicit rather than explicit) acceptance of religious pluralism carries with it a need to rethink the dogmas that imply Christianity's religious superiority not only for those of us who have been formed by it but for the entire human race. When this is done, an intellectually honest and realistic Christian faith may yet be able to speak to a deep religious concern that exists as strongly as ever among a Western population that has long since ceased to be captivated by traditional institutional religion.[6]

John Hick speaks eloquently of a recent ready acceptance of religious pluralism by many people today. However, can that acceptance be reconciled with Christianity's time-honoured, traditional and orthodox self-understanding? Can Christianity regard itself as just one among several equally authentic and truthful religions? Or might it be the case that Christianity is manifestly superior to all other religions in terms of the truthfulness of its beliefs and the superlativeness of its way of living in the world?

The status of Christianity in relation to other religions constitutes still another major problem for modern theology, largely because of the recently augmented awareness of the world's vastly varied religions. The question of Christianity's significance in relation to other religions is as ancient as Christianity itself. However, over the past half a century, this question has emerged not simply as a major issue, but as one of the most urgent dilemmas with which Christian theology now needs to grapple.

John Hick is clear that 'Christianity is only one among several world religions.'[7] In his earlier book, *The Metaphor of God Incarnate*, he lucidly raises the problem that the plurality of world religions inevitably poses for modern theology:

> The traditional understanding of Jesus of Nazareth is that he was God incarnate, who became a man to die for the sins of the world and who founded the church to proclaim this. If he was indeed God incarnate, Christianity is the only religion founded by God in person, and must as such be uniquely superior to all other religions.[8]

Hick is far from convinced that 'Christianity is the only religion founded by God in person, and must as such be superior to all other religions.' In the twentieth century, no Christian theologian was more path-breaking in dealing with the issue of religious pluralism than John Hick. He concludes that all religions share a common core – an interest in the Ultimately Real. His view differs starkly from the Christian tradition.

religious exclusivism and pluralism

Christianity's own tradition has endowed it with a peerless rank among other religions. The Gospel According to John records Jesus as saying of himself, 'I am the way, and the truth, and the life. No one comes to the Father except through me. If you know me you will know my Father also. From now on you do know him and have seen him' (John 14: 6–7). The key idea in this passage is that no one approaches God except through Jesus. The same kind of restrictive path to God is evident in a sermon attributed to Peter in the Acts of the Apostles: 'There is salvation in no one else, for there is no other name under heaven given among mortals by which we must be saved (Acts 4:12). The axial notions of this text are 'no one else' and 'no other name'. For this perspective, salvation (from sin) is not possible without Jesus.

The idea of 'no other name' has become central to the theological publications of Paul Knitter, another contemporary theologian absorbed by theological dilemmas generated by current religious pluralism. Knitter is a North American theologian who has published two especially noteworthy disquisitions on Christianity and other religions. Their titles are *No Other Name? A Critical Survey of Christian Attitudes toward the World Religions* (1985), and *Jesus and the Other Names: Global Mission and Global Responsibility* (1996). Both titles resonate with the terminology of Acts 4:12. Knitter's strategy for dealing with the problem posed for Christian self-understanding by religious pluralism is to challenge the idea that truth must be understood in either/or terms or as a scientific matter of cause-and-effect relations. For Knitter, seeking truth involves not a quest for certainty, but an ever-increasing understanding. In Knitter's view, truth must now be regarded as relational: 'what is true will reveal itself mainly by its ability to relate these other expressions of truth and to grow through these relationships'.[9] Knitter readily accepts that Christianity is not exclusively true in relation to other religions.

Returning, though, to what has been said in the past about Christianity's relation to other ways of seeking divinely wrought salvation, John 14 and Acts 4 are two particularly prominent texts that appear to insist that Christianity is the only valid path both to God and to a saved, redeemed or fully healthy human state. There is, however, another and far more chilling text from the Christian canon of Sacred Scripture that has been used frequently to justify the violent oppression of Jews in the course of history after Jesus was crucified. The text is found in the Gospel According to Matthew:

> So when Pilate saw that he could do nothing, but rather that a riot was beginning, he took some water and washed his hands before the crowd saying, 'I am innocent of this man's blood; see to it yourselves'. Then the people as a whole answered, 'His blood be on us and on our children!' So he released Barabbas for them; and after flogging Jesus, he handed him over to be crucified. (Matt. 27:24–6)

Commenting on this passage, the distinguished Catholic exegete Raymond Brown concluded that 'one cannot ignore its tragic history in inflaming Christian hatred'.[10] In a footnote he quotes, presumably with approval, a description of the passage calling it 'one of those phrases which have been responsible for oceans of human blood and a ceaseless stream of misery and desolation'.[11] It is one thing to regard Judaism as secondary to Christianity; and quite another to kill Jews as murderers of Christ. The question of religious pluralism, in other terms, is not at all an innocuous speculative game.

Yet another illustration of an exceptionally influential exclusivist Christian teaching is expressed by a council of bishops in Florence–Ferrara (1442), which met more than a millennium after Cyprian of Carthage spoke of no salvation being obtainable outside the Church. The bishops of the council taught dogmatically that

> The holy church of Rome firmly believes, confesses and proclaims that no one – not just the heathen but also the Jews, heretics and schismatics – outside the Catholic church can have a part in eternal life, but that they will go to the hell fire, 'that is prepared for the devil and his angels' (Matt. 25:41) unless they allow themselves to be received into the church before their life's end.[12]

Few Catholic teachings are clearer: all heathens, Protestants, Anglicans, Jews, Buddhists, Muslims, Hindus, heretics and schismatics are doomed to the un-ending torments of the fires of hell if they die before being received into the Catholic Church. The teaching of the Council of Florence–Ferrara has been Catholic dogma for over five centuries and has never been flatly contradicted by another council. The Second Vatican Council came close in the twentieth century with an ambiguous teaching that anyone who sincerely seeks God can be saved: 'Those who, through no fault of their own, do not know the Gospel of Christ or his church, but nevertheless seek God with a sincere heart, and, moved by grace, try in their actions to do his will as they know it through the dictates of their conscience – these too may attain eternal salvation.'[13] The bishops of Vatican II did not specify explicitly what seeking God 'with a sincere heart' entails. Is God's will obeyed by feeding the hungry, or by going to church? In addition, the council does not consider explicitly the salvific prospects of people involved with religions that are not theistic.

Most of the bishops of Florence–Ferrara and Vatican II lacked intimate familiarity with the doctrines of religions apart from Christianity. An increased awareness of the religiously other has been greatly aided in the modern era by technologies of communication. On the significance of these, Anthony Giddens concludes 'in the mid-nineteenth century, a Massachusetts portrait painter, Samuel Morse, transmitted the first message, "What hath God wrought?", by electric telegraph. In so doing, he initiated a new phase in world history. Yet the advent of satellite communication marks every bit as dramatic a break with the past.'[14]

Giddens's point is obvious. Instantaneous electronic communication was unknown to anyone before, roughly, 1850. Its invention has radically transformed the ways in which human beings now deal with each other. Instantaneous electronic or satellite communication is but one factor in the process of globalization, which is partly a burgeoning awareness that all localities on the planet are interconnected with all other localities.

There are at least ten recent historical developments that have colluded in drawing people's attention to the inescapable fact that this earth is populated by a plethora of religious customs and beliefs. The first development is globalization, which has brought religious traditions into much closer contact than at any previous stage of human history. The second was the First World War, which was launched by a Christian German emperor and waged between nominally Christian nations. The blood-letting of the war seriously questioned the extent to which the nations waging it were actually Christian. A third development is represented by the advent of widespread travel by jets catapulting travellers from one corner of the globe to another in relatively brief spans of time and bringing them into actual contact with previously unencountered religious aliens. Fourth, large-scale transmigrations of peoples from east to west and from north to south have brought religiously different people face to face. Fifth, the invention of television readily gives people images of alien cultures and unfamiliar religious practices. Television sets can be housed in huts in the Amazon jungle or on atolls of the Pacific Ocean. Amazonians can watch and listen to the Archbishop of Canterbury preach. And the Archbishop of Canterbury can watch voodoo practitioners in Latin America cutting the throats of chickens. Nearly-naked village dwellers in the mountains of Papua New Guinea can watch splendidly attired cardinals celebrate Mass in Rome's St Peter's Basilica, while the cardinals can view Baptists singing their hearts out in Alabama. A sixth development mirrors the fifth: satellite and Internet connections. In the seventh place, the demise of colonialism has enabled previously styled colonials to migrate and inhabit the former bases of colonial power. Indian Hindus can now play cricket in Manchester; Pakistani Muslims can drive taxis in Toulouse; Sikhs can run businesses in Birmingham; and Shintoists can open nightclubs in Berlin. The establishment of the State of Israel in 1948 constitutes an eighth major historical catalyst for the growing awareness of religious diversity. In the new state Jews could establish centres of higher learning without fear of persecution. In ninth place, the formation of faculties of religious studies over the past twenty or thirty years has produced a new breed of scholars who are able to investigate the phenomenon of religion without being controlled by the Church. Tenth and finally, postmodern philosophies, according to which there is no truth or absolute value, challenge the notion that a religion can define absolute truth absolutely.

All of these ten factors placed religious pluralism squarely on the agenda of Christian theologians in the latter half of the twentieth century. Religious pluralism is a major conundrum for contemporary theology because it presents Christianity with a full frontal challenge to abandon its centuries-long tradition of insisting that Christianity is exclusively true and manifestly superior to all other religions.

john hick on axial time

John Harwood Hick has responded to the challenge in a creative way. He was born in Scarborough, England, in 1922. As a boy he attended Bootham School in York. As a child he was taken to his local Anglican church services, which he later described as 'a matter of infinite boredom'.[15] After his schooling he enrolled in the University of Hull to study law. At Hull he became beguiled by the Inter-Varsity Fellowship and underwent a religious conversion to Evangelical Christianity. He was later to regard his newfound religious enthusiasm as a fundamentalist expression of Christianity.

Leaving Hull, Hick studied philosophy in Edinburgh and Oxford. In 1953, he became a minister in the Presbyterian Church and began to work at a church in Belford in Northumberland. He stayed there for three years before moving to North America where he was appointed as Professor of Philosophy at Princeton Theological Seminary in New Jersey. Trouble was looming for him. In 1961 and 1962 he was formally accused of heresy by members of the Presbyterian Church on a charge that he did not believe in the Virgin Birth. No punishment, though, was meted out to him.[16]

In 1967, he began teaching in the University of Birmingham. His experiences in Birmingham were to prove decisive for his subsequent reflections on religious pluralism. After teaching there he moved to California to teach at the Claremont Graduate School. During the 1990s he moved back to Birmingham, to reside as a Fellow of the Institute for Advanced Research in Arts and Social Sciences at the University of Birmingham.

Birmingham is alive with prominent communities of Muslims, Sikhs, Hindus and Jews. Encountering them on a daily basis prompted Hick to explore the nature of the world's major religions. His direct encounters with devotees of religions other than his own, coupled with intensive study of the world's religions and regular worldwide travels, provided him with the material to write a major study of religion, which he published in 1989: *An Interpretation of Religion: Human Responses to the Transcendent*. His more recent thought can be scrutinized in his book *The Fifth Dimension: An Exploration of the Spiritual Realm* (1999).

The basic difficulty that engages John Hick's thought on religion is as follows. As a new century presently unfolds, the world has in a certain sense become smaller. With new means of transportation and communication people can visit each other quickly, and speak with each over vast distances in an instant. Because of television, anyone can be more familiar with the face and life of Nelson Mandela than with the face and life of a next-door neighbour. So the world is a web of inter-connected localities, and has grown smaller in the sense that far-flung people and places are now brought visually and electronically into the homes of anyone who wishes to turn on a television. This very process of globalization augmented people's *visual* familiarity with the religious other. Who in the west had heard of the Taliban twenty years ago? In some ways westerners have become less provincial and more cosmopolitan in their awareness of the religiously alien. The problem arising for reflection on religion, a problem engaged by John Hick, is that many religious traditions still claim exclusive authority for their beliefs and teachings. Conventionally, Christianity has been one such tradition. For centuries it has put to the sword anyone refusing to convert to the Gospel of Jesus Christ.

John Hick rejects the traditional exclusivist understanding of Christianity's status in relation to other religions. In his book *An Interpretation of Religion* he espouses a theory of religious pluralism that is developed in several of his other books, most notably in *God and the Universe of Faiths* (1973), *God Has Many Names* (1980) and *The Rainbow of Faiths* (1995).

Religious pluralism can be defined negatively and positively. Negatively speaking, religious pluralism 'is the denial that any one religious tradition has a monopoly on salvific truth. Positively, it is the affirmation that the great religions of the world represent, under the guise of different cultural expressions, essentially the same religious truth about salvation.'[17] Religious pluralism, positively defined, is reliant on two major assumptions. First, that what people do and believe with their lives is normally determined by where they were born. A person born in Thailand is more likely to become a Buddhist than a Methodist. In other terms, anyone's involvement with any religion can be regarded as accidental and dependent on place of birth. Second, religious pluralism positively defined assumes, more controversially, that

> at the center of the world's great religions is found a common or universal core. Those who believe this usually (even predictably) identify this core of authentic religion as an experience with a universal, transcendent reality and a consequent cultivation of selflessness. According to the pluralist hypothesis, this is what all great religions are really about.[18]

To understand John Hick's interpretation of the religions of the world and the way they relate to each other, it is necessary to consider the concept of an axial age. The German philosopher Karl Jaspers speaks of an axial age in his book *The Origin and Goal of History* (1953). John Hick elaborates Jaspers' views at length in *An Interpretation of Religion* and *The Fifth Dimension*. The basic idea involved in speaking of an axial age is to pinpoint a turning point in human history when religions of salvation and liberation began to differentiate themselves from archaic or pre-axial religions. According to Hick, around the middle of the first millennium BCE ... in a band of time stretching from about 800 to 200 BCE, remarkable individuals appeared across the world, standing out from their societies and proclaiming momentous new insights. In China there were Confucius, Mencius, and Lao-Tzu (or the anonymous writers of the *Tao Te Ching*) and Mo-Tzu. In India there were Gautama, the Buddha; Mahavira, the founder of the Jain tradition; the writings of the Upanishads and later of the *Bhagavad Gita*. In Persia there was Zoroaster. In Palestine there were the great Hebrew prophets – Amos, Hosea, Jeremiah, the Isaiahs, Ezekiel. In Greece there were Pythagoras, Socrates, Plato, Aristotle.[19]

As Hick notes, 'This immensely significant hinge of human thought has come to be known as the axial age. If we see Christianity as presupposing Judaism, and Islam as presupposing both Judaism and Christianity, all the present major world religions trace their roots to this axial period.'[20]

The crucial difference between pre-axial and axial traditions is that people of pre-axial ages were prone to accept their world as dominated by fate or as given and unchangeable. The axial age is thought to have heralded a widespread sense of the incompleteness of human existence and a craving for betterment, salvation and liberation.

In other terms, axial religions realized that the world is awry and that human beings are responsible for improving their lot. The key flaw in human nature for pre-axial religions – according to this theory – is self-centredness. The remedy for ego-centredness is a radical transformation to a reality-centred life. This, says Hick, is what all the great world religions are really about at their core. All axial religions express, in diverse ways: '(1) the recognition of a transcultural and transcendent Reality and source of all things; and (2) the need to identify oneself with this reality, to become transparent to it, to be inspired and uplifted by it, and thereby to attain a degree of selfless or genuine saintliness.'[21]

As stated previously, religious pluralism is an ancient challenge for quite diverse religious traditions. With John Hick, however, the question of religious pluralism was brought to the fore in contemporary theology in an increasingly globalized human setting. Indeed, one might well speak of John Hick's Copernican revolution in theology. He urges his readers to renounce both religious exclusivism and triumphalism. He invites them to regard diverse religions as manifold manifestations of a common core, namely the Ultimately Real.

Now, as surprising as it may seem, Hick's way of talking about religions as different perceptions of the one and the same Ultimate Reality is actually inspired by two perspicacious Christian thinkers, Thomas Aquinas and Immanuel Kant. As John Hick explains in his articulate treatise *The Rainbow of Faiths*, his entire approach to religions assumes the now very widespread view that what is perceived is always partly constructed by the perceiver. Our concepts enter into the formation of our aware-ness. The basic epistemological principle was enunciated long ago by Thomas Aquinas when he wrote that 'Things known are in the knower according to the mode of the knower'.[22] Now the mode of the religious knower is differently formed within the different traditions. Hence the different awareness of the Real around which these traditions have developed. In modern times it was Immanuel Kant who has argued most influentially that perception is not a passive registering of what is there but is always an active process of selecting, grouping, relating, extrapolating, and endowing with meaning by means of our human concepts.[23]

Moreover, Kant, as is well known, distinguished between a noumenal world – that is, the world as it exists unperceived by people – and a phenomenal world, which is the world of appearances perceived by human beings. Humans do not know the Real in itself, but only as it appears to them. Different people will inevitably perceive it diversely. Hence the plurality of religions, yesterday and today.

It is important to register at this stage that not all religions affirm belief in God. If John Hick is to be believed, there are two basic religious categories: (1) the deity (the Real as personal); and (2) the absolute (the Real as non-personal). Whether people perceive the Real as either personal or impersonal will depend on their cultural setting. Nevertheless, it is the same Real, or Reality, so this theory avers, to which they all refer.

so-called anonymous christians

Thus far, this chapter has focused mainly on religious imperialism or exclusivism, typified by the Council of Florence–Ferrara, and religious pluralism, exemplified by John Hick.

A much discussed alternative view of how Christianity should understand itself in relation to other religions – neither exclusivist, nor imperialist nor plural-istic – was published by the German theologian Karl Rahner. His multi-volume *Theological Investigations* contain an essay entitled 'Christianity and Non-Christian Religions',[24] in which he tabulates four theses concerning religions. First, 'Chris-tianity understands itself as the absolute religion, intended for all men, which cannot recognize any other religion beside itself as of equal right.'[25] Second, a non-Christian religion can be recognized as a lawful religion because it con-tains 'supernatural elements arising out of the grace which is given to men as a gratuitous gift on account of Christ'.[26] Third, Christianity 'does not simply confront the member of an extra-Christian religion as a mere non-Christian but as someone who can and must already be regarded in this or that respect as an anonymous Christian'.[27] Fourth and finally, the Church will regard itself today not so much as 'the exclusive community of those who have a claim to salvation but rather as the historically tangible vanguard and the historically and socially constituted explicit expression of what the Christian hopes is present as a hidden reality even outside the visible Church'.[28]

Rahner explains each of his four theses in detail. A strength of his view is that he recognizes clearly the uniqueness of Christianity. He realizes well that religions are each distinct in their content of faith and, as such, each demands a total commitment: 'A theology cannot be at once Christian–Muslim–Hindu or whatever; it needs to be either one or the other.'[29] However, his theory of anonymous Christianity could strike others as condescending and paternalistic towards religions apart from Christianity. It would not please a hater of football to be told that he or she is really an anonymous lover of football. Similarly, a decrier of Christianity needs to be free to deny the legitimacy of Christianity and to have nothing to do with it. Rahner has still not entirely severed his link with the legacy of Cyprian of Carthage: *extra ecclesiam nulla salus*. In the light of which, Edward Schillebeeckx offers a much more enlightening maxim: *extra mundum nulla salus* ('Outside the world there is no salvation'). For Schillebeeckx, the question of salvation is a driving force of history and is not confined to religions. Thus, 'salvation from God comes about first of all in the secular reality of history and not primarily in the consciousness of believers who are aware of it'.[30]

conclusion

Each of the three main (by no means only) stances with regard to religious diversity discussed in this chapter is open to criticism. The first view, religious chauvisism, imperialism or exclusivism, denies the worth of different religions, insists that Christianity is solely true, and that religious pluralism is a regrettable situation that must be overcome. Its principal flaw is to presume to delineate how and what God might do to save people from all that bedevils them. John Hick's proposal that religions are but distinct interpretations of that which is ultimately real could appear to overlook the vast differences and mutual contra-dictions between religions. Religions that flatly contradict each other are difficult to reconcile as being ultimately focused on the same reality. Rahner's thesis of anonymous Christianity denies people the freedom to renounce Christianity.

Religious diversity need not be regarded as a lamentable situation that ought to be overcome by preaching and missionary work. On the contrary, it is only to be expected and welcomed as a fact of reality: while God, Yahweh, Allah, Adonai, the Real, or that which is Ultimate remain obscure to human beings, no single religious tradition could ever hope to capture in history the plenitude, or full richness, of the absolute. The word 'religion' most probably comes from the Latin *religare*, 'to bind together'. Whether, by religion, people bind themselves together as a community, or seek collectively to encounter or attach themselves to a transcendent reality, the different religions of the globe are at base distinct interpretations of diverse human experiences and journeys.

conclusion

theology's paramount task

Because one loves nobody, one imagines one loves God.

Charles Péguy (1873–1914)

The heart is the highest court and as a person matures, all matters must eventually be brought before it. Unless – as is so often the case with us humans – the heart has been replaced with attachment to dogma.

Gabrielle Lord

New conditions breed new questions, which, for theologians, demand new forms of thinking and communicating. Such has been the working assumption of this book. Human beings have always been questioning animals. While some of their queries are flippant and fleeting, others abide, generation after generation, wherever humans are found. Why is there a universe? What is the point of living? Is there anything or anyone worth loving, hoping for, believing in, or journeying towards as ultimately estimable? Why is life for so many such a cruel, loveless, lonely and harrowing ordeal?

Christianity has responded to all of these questions in a rich variety of ways, but its most famous and long-standing account of the point and purpose of both human existence and cosmic destiny has been the three-act Augustinian drama of the Fall of Adam and Eve; Reconciliation between God and humanity achieved through Christ's divinely willed death on a Cross; and God's apocalyptic Judgement of humanity at the culmination of human history. Fall–Cross–Judgement is thus the archetypal Christian story of humanity's relation to God. The three-act drama can be compressed even further into two words, illustrated in neon lights on the front cover of this book: 'Jesus Saves'. As Christianity begins its twenty-first century, its Augustinian paradigm of theology has met the fate of the Berlin Wall. As often noted in these pages, Christianity no longer serves as the cultural cement of western societies as it once did during the heyday of Christendom in Europe. By and large, Europeans have stopped worshipping in churches on any regular basis. And they have stopped worshipping on a massive scale. Their abandonment of traditional Christianity is probably irreversible. The principal reason they stay at home is that they are educated enough to realize that the world and its inhabitants can no longer be described in terms unaware of the findings of modern science. In such a setting, the uniqueness of modern theology springs from the ways its practitioners respond to a complex chain of historical and intellectual revolutions since the fifteenth century that collectively unseated Christianity's former social prominence. The chapters of this book have touched upon early-modern and modern intellectual revolutions in geography, astronomy, scientific method, critical philosophy, biblical studies, historical Jesus research, biology, physics and hermeneutics. They have pondered the intellectual revolutions in concert with social and political transformations represented by the Enlightenment, the French Revolution, secularization, a gaping and growing wealth–poverty divide, feminism, and religious diversity. Other revolutions could be examined, such as the sexual revolution of the last forty years in the west and the emergence of what many call the postmodern condition in the latter half of the twentieth century. They are worthy of book-length investigations in their own right. All of the movements just mentioned and the ideas generating them have produced the present world order, or rather disorder, of over 6 billion human beings, choking to death in a pollution of their own making, waging wars within societies blighted by AIDS, and divided between a superabundantly wealthy few living on islands of luxury surrounded by oceans of massive human misery.

From beginning to end, this book has been driven by a single question, posed in the first sentence of its second chapter. Is there such a thing as progress in knowledge? Obviously so, or assuredly not? More specifically, should conventional Christianity radically modify its doctrines and practices in the light of advanced knowledge only generated in modern times? Or ought it perpetuate itself in contemporary settings by recapitulating ancient wisdoms? My answer to the book's impelling question – as might have been guessed! – is that Christianity and its traditional theology need far-reaching revision. This is not the view of a good many Christian leaders and thinkers, who conclude that modernity is the enemy, not the helper, of Christianity in its ongoing task of self-expression and public self-justification in changing historical circumstances. They continue to talk about God and human attempts to encounter God by ignoring or slighting forms of knowledge newly discovered in the modern age. They are confident they can sustain and proclaim Christian beliefs by faithfully rehearsing ancient Christian doctrines about God and Jesus considered in relation to people.

To recall, for the Venerable Jorge in Umberto Eco's novel *The Name of the Rose*, 'There is no progress, no revolution of ages, in the history of knowledge, but at most a continuous and sublime recapitulation.'[1] His contemporary descendants are legion. They are also fatefully mistaken. The trouble with unswerving repetition of orthodox doctrines is that the doctrines were formulated on the basis of a defunct cosmology and anthropology stemming principally from the towering figures of Aristotle and his teacher, Plato. In a poignant paradox, the very strategy of the simple repetition of ancient creeds, coupled with a distain for all things modern, turns out, with regard to a viable Christian faith, to be an unintended act of sabotage. Repetition is not demonstration; faithful proclamation is not co-extensive with convincing argumentation. Rant, bluster and bombast are neither fine-spun analyses nor well-documented accounts. Rehearsing ancient thought in isolation from new knowledge torpedoes any chance of articulating meaningfully and truthfully a Christian theological vision because, unlike Augustine, Aquinas, Dante, Luther and Calvin, people now know that there is no hell in the bowels of the earth, and no heaven above a canopy of stars. The fact that the Augustinian theological paradigm is not as popular as it was five hundred years ago does not in itself establish that it is unconvincing. Modern knowledge does. Bultmann was right:

> We cannot use electric lights and radios and, in the event of illness, avail ourselves of modern medical and clinical means and at the same time believe in the spirit and wonder world of the New Testament. And if we suppose that we can do so ourselves, we must be clear that we can present this as the attitude of the Christian faith only by making the Christian proclamation unintelligible and impossible for our contemporaries.[2]

People can now know (if they bother to study the matter) that Moses did not write the first five books of the Bible; that the story of Adam and Eve ought not be read as literally descriptive; that apostles who knew Jesus did not write the Gospels; that Jesus did not commission a papal court; that Jesus did not formulate the doctrine of the Trinity; that the world is not 6000 years old; and that men are not humanly better than women. To repeat: human beings today are party to the information that they inhabit a planet in a galaxy of 100 billion stars within an expanding universe of 100 billion galaxies. They are aware that animal species can change into other species and that human beings, genetically speaking, have cabbages for cousins.

A century ago, the leadership of the Catholic Church turned many of its most innovative theologians into psychologically shattered stamp-collecting zombies. The theologians were vilified as 'modernists' and sacked from their tertiary teaching posts. Having spent their lives devoted to scholarship, they were left to uproot weeds from their gardens and play chess. Worse fates could be devised! Their crime was to attempt to reconcile traditional Christian thought with the spirit of the Enlightenment, modern science – especially the biology of Darwin – and historical-critical readings of the Bible. A hundred years later, the leaders of the same Church are engaged in the same activity – killing off creative thought that diverges from the tripartite Augustinian theological paradigm of Fall–Atonement–Judgement. Catholicism began the twentieth-first century in the same way that it entered the twentieth – governed by an autocratic papacy pronouncing a rigid dogmatism involving a galloping Mariology.[3] When the College of Cardinals in Rome elected Joseph Ratzinger as Pope Benedict XVI during 2005, they wilfully continued the legacy of Pope John Paul II. The cardinals also trumpeted to the world that they intend to lead the Catholic Church by not modernizing, by not listening, but not discussing, by not learning from contemporary sciences, and by not reforming. The Catholic Church is now locked into a dire state of intellectual stasis.

The Church of England has a different problem: it is still caught in the trammels of political establishment. The prime minister of its supreme governor, the British sovereign, chooses its bishops after a process of consultation. In such a setting it can be difficult for the Church's preachers and teachers to proclaim what is remembered of the religious vision of Jesus if it conflicts with the policies of the government of the day.

Returning to the governors of the contemporary Catholic Church, they are not alone in their resolute doctrinal anti-modernism. Protestant evangelical fundamentalism, virulently alive a century after its birth, sprang into action as a reactive anti-modern strategy. Papal dogmatism and Protestant fundamentalism are bedfellows, and are thereby guilty of the same offence. They both regard as absolute (dogmas and the Bible) that which is human, finite and perspectival. Dogmas enshrine human concepts of God, not divine doctrines of the divine. The Bible was not written in heaven, but in a dusty corner of the earth. Every syllable of every word its scrolls contain was penned by a human being in the ancient Middle East, where men fought each other endlessly, and arrogantly dominated women, as they described God in terms more applicable to themselves than God. Dogmas and the Bible are by no means devoid of wisdom, but their wisdom is human and limited rather than absolute and universal. They are corrigible and incomplete, not set in stone. Humans have no sure way of demonstrating that anything they ever say of God represents God in the least.

In the early stages of the twenty-first century, the clear strategy for perpetuating Christianity adopted by mainline North American Protestant Churches, the Catholic Church, and Orthodox Churches is to respond to the myriad new questions hurled at old beliefs by new knowledge unearthed over the past three centuries and more by either championing the Bible as the Word of God (in the case of Protestants), or by defending pre-modern dogmas (in the instance of the Catholic and Orthodox Churches). Both strategies – championing and defending – are energetically advanced yet ultimately futile. They are proposed and ardently defended through fear of change, fear of having traditional authorities challenged, and fear of allowing recently discovered knowledge to confirm that some old beliefs are baseless and profitless.

It is a striking irony of recent times that the inability of Church leaders to criticize their biblical and dogmatic certitudes has done more to cause masses of well-intentioned people to abandon Christianity than they could ever have imagined. The official defenders of Christian faith turn out to be its unwitting gravediggers. Nevertheless, in a book styled as *A Modern Introduction to Theology*, it is more important to address theology's currently most daunting challenge than to accuse leaders of Churches of failure. Theology's most intimidating challenge today is to talk about God in a new way that takes into account the current predicament of humanity. The way needs to be new because the predicament is. The contemporary setting of humanity is without historical precedent. At worst, the predicament involves a death-dealing conflict between humans and their life-sustaining environment. On a smaller scale, it encompasses a series of dire conflicts within and between the planet's human population, which has never before been so large and endangered. Relations between human beings today involve

> permanent, nerve-fraying conflict: blacks against whites; straights against gays; gays against priests; priests against abortionists; blacks against Jews; Orthodox Jews against reformers; Jews against Arabs; Arabs against Jews; sun people against ice people; citizens against immigrants; Latinos against Koreans; people who work against those who don't; urban folk against suburban and rural dwellers; bad guys against everyone, cops against bad guys, lawyers against cops.[4]

Well might one ask, though, 'What's new?' Human beings have always been at loggerheads or each other's throats. Why does contemporary inter-human conflict stand as the biggest challenge for modern theology? It doesn't. Of all the conflictual polarities just mentioned, there is more and worse to come. Theology's most daunting challenge today does not stem from inter-human conflict, but from a human conflict with the ecosystem of the planet. The conflict is well explained by the Muslim scholar Ziauddin Sardar:

> The greatest event of the 20th century, outstripping even its horrors – two world wars, mass, mechanised slaughter, the imminence of Armageddon, holocaust and ethnic cleansing – was the invention of the mass market for consumer goods; the

apotheosis of the Industrial Revolution. Desiring the accoutrements of a lavish lifestyle is probably a primordial urge, but only in the 20th century did it become a practical proposition for large parts of a whole society.[5]

The point is that contemporary consumerism is calamitous for humans and their habitat. Sardar continues:

> The economic disparities of our world are grosser now than ever before in history. Never, since the day the original *homo sapiens* first stood on two legs, have so few consumed and controlled so much. The richest 20 per cent of the world's people, that's us and our like, now consume 86 per cent of all goods and services, 45 per cent of all the meat and fish, 58 per cent of all the energy, 84 per cent of all the paper and 87 per cent of all the vehicles.[6]

Some 70 per cent of the planet's people never ever use a telephone, let alone a computer. The United States of America is home to 272.9 million people – 3 per cent of the world's total population. This 3 per cent consumes over half of all the goods and services of the planet and produces roughly 25 per cent of global pollution. This country has 30,000 tonnes of chemical weapons, spends $8 billion per year on cosmetics, houses the world's largest stockpiles of smallpox and anthrax, and boasts a massive military machine.[7]

The binge of consumer nest-feathering around the world during the nineteenth and twentieth centuries has come at a dreadful cost. It has now become clear that human beings have attained the power to destroy the very conditions that make their lives possible. The dropping of an atomic bomb on Hiroshima on 6 August 1945 ushered human beings into a new predicament and phase of their history 'not envisaged anywhere in the Bible or by subsequent Christians up to 1945'.[8] Never before had humans possessed the technology to obliterate themselves.

Reporting in the year 1999, the United Nations Environment Programme observed that in the late 1990s,

> annual emissions of carbon dioxide were almost four times higher than the 1950 level and atmospheric concentrations of carbon dioxide had reached their highest level in 160 000 years. According to the intergovernmental panel on Climate Change, 'the balance of evidence suggest that there is a discernible human influence on global climate'.[9]

In other words, human beings are presently wilfully poisoning their own atmosphere and living in a polluted fog they have produced through profligacy. Even so, nothing will stop them buying cars and travelling in jets. In addition to atmospheric pollution and climate change,

> With the massive expansion in the availability and use of chemicals throughout the world, exposure to pesticides, heavy metals, small particulates and other substances

poses an increasing threat to the health of humans and their environment. Pesticide use causes 3.5 to 5 million acute poisonings a year. Worldwide, 400 million tonnes of hazardous waste are generated each year.[10]

This planet's water reservoirs are so dirty that 6000 children die of diarrhoea *every day* because they have no access to clean water. That is twice the number of deaths recorded in the Twin Towers collapse on 11 September 2001. And it occurs every day – without comment, let alone outcry.

All this represents theology's most daunting challenge today. Why? Because the contemporary human onslaught on the very physical conditions that enable biotic organisms to survive calls into question the age-old tendency of Christian theology to speak of God – or Jesus – as a saviour. The orthodox Christian understanding of God conceives of God andromorphically on the model of a human agent. God is said to act intentionally in the world. According to this view, as Gordon Kaufman explains, God is envisioned as 'a kind of cosmic person who had created the world, who cared for his creation (I use male pronouns deliberately here, in articulating the traditional understanding of God), who loved humankind and hence entered into human history itself to bring salvation to humans'.[11]

Such an understanding of God as an agent who acts to save humans fails to address, let alone provide a solution to, the worst problem of human existence today, which is the human-propelled despoliation of the earth's ecosystem, otherwise called the ecological crisis:

> Humanity, as we are beginning to understand, is deeply situated within the evolutionary-ecological processes on planet Earth.... In this context, it is becoming increasingly difficult to imagine God as one who might, or even can, directly transform and make right what we are so rapidly destroying.[12]

Human beings have trapped themselves in a mess they have only become aware of over the past three decades. The destruction of the ecosystem is an issue that never taxed Schleiermacher, Calvin, Scotus, Origen, Aristotle, or Plato. The critical issue now facing theologians and all other human beings

> is not a matter of finding a way to live with or overcome despair, meaninglessness, guilt, or human suffering generally – all largely problems of human *subjectivity*. Rather, it is a matter of the *objective* conditions that make human life possible: we are destroying them, and it is we who must find a way to set them right.[13]

Theology's most daunting hurdle today is to formulate a language about God that does not expect God to rectify what humans are so systematically destroying. Only a wide-eyed utopian would fail to see at the beginning of the twenty-first century that human history is not manifestly a history of salvation. Visible indices indicate that it could be history of perdition. Human history *could* be a history of salvation, but human beings have wilfully chosen a path to perdition. They cannot now expect God to save them from a predicament they have freely created for themselves. They ought to accept responsibility for what they have done; and they ought to accept the life-threatening consequences of what they are doing. For the moment, however, our counterfeit god is Greed. Our religion is Consumption. And our fate is extinction. It is a duplicitous act to expect or ask God to save humanity from disaster while, at the same time, wilfully creating the disaster. In sum, theology's paramount task is to devise ways of speaking about God that are not overly human-centred, blind to their much larger planetary and cosmic setting, and prone to depict God as an interfering agent who will repair the life-threatening damage people daily inflict on their biosphere.

As for Christianity, its most irksome current challenge in a religiously rivalrous world is to realize that it is not absolute and eternal. Theologically speaking, only God is absolute. To believe in God is refreshingly to relativize all finite things. No person is ever ultimate. Churches, doctrines and beliefs are all provisional and mortal. Belief in God is radically subversive of all human discourses and dispositions that set upon finite realities as if they were absolute and unconstrained. All religions, Christianity included, are secondary, not primary to people's lives and physical well-being. Christianity is a human construct. It is one path on which millions follow in search of God, happiness, hope and peace. It is not the only way.

Furthermore, one of the more glaring reasons Christianity is widely ignored in the west now is that it is too little related to Jesus. Most Christians in the west today are property owners. Jesus was not. Most Lutheran, Presbyterian, Methodist, Anglican and Baptists preachers, pastors and priests who insist that they are disciples of Jesus are married. There is no evidence Jesus ever was. The Catholic Church is still governed by a feudal, medieval hierarchical system that celebrates resistance to change and distaste for novelty. Its contemporary governance has nothing to do with Jesus. Most current Christians do not expect human history to come to an end tomorrow. Jesus very probably did. Many countries presently populated mainly by Christians, such as Germany, France, the United Kingdom and the United States of America, all produce vast terrifying arsenals of deadly weapons. Jesus was executed as a victim of a similarly lethal power.

conclusion

In speaking so much in this book of modern problems for modern theology, and of new questions for old beliefs, my aim was not uncritically and modishly to praise all things novel, and to slight as crass and ignorant all things ancient. My primary purpose was much simpler: to argue and illustrate that genuine progress in knowledge has generated challenges for contemporary theologians that pre-modern theologians never met. The latter cannot by faulted for not surmounting hurdles they never encountered, while the former cannot by slighted for seeking new styles for talking about the One called God in the recent history of *Homo sapiens*.

As for human beings' enduring questions as to whether or not there is a God; of what God is like; whether humans will blow themselves up; and whether Jesus will gloriously come again into the world to judge the living and the dead, to save humanity from perdition, and to establish in plenitude the kingdom of God, only one reality will answer them – the future.

notes

one

1. David Ford, *Theology: A Very Short Introduction* (Oxford and New York: Oxford University Press, 1999), p. 3; and Keith Ward, *Religion and Creation* (Oxford: Clarendon Press, 1996), p. 3.

2. Consult the *Oxford Dictionary of English Etymology*, ed. C.T. Onions (Oxford: Clarendon Press, 1996), p. 404.

3. See Régis Debray, *God: An Itinerary* (London and New York: Verso, 2004), p. 17.

4. See Francis Schlüssler Fiorenza and Gordon D. Kaufman, 'God', in Mark C. Taylor, ed., *Critical Terms for Religious Studies* (Chicago and London: University of Chicago Press, 1998), pp. 136–59; esp. pp. 140–42.

5. For a philosophical discussion of divine attributes consult Joshua Hoffman and Gary S. Rosenkrantz, *The Divine Attributes* (Oxford: Blackwell, 2002), esp. pp. 9–11.

6. On this matter consult David B. Burrell, *Freedom and Creation in Three Traditions* (Notre Dame, IN: Notre Dame University Press, 1993), pp. 3–4.

7. See Gareth Jones, ed., *The Blackwell Companion to Modern Theology* (Oxford: Blackwell, 2004).

8. See Arnold Hermann, *To Think Like God: Pythagoras and Parmenides, The Origins of Philosophy* (Las Vegas, NV: Parmenides, 2004).

9. Cicero, *The Nature of the Gods*, trans. P.G. Walsh (Oxford: Clarendon Press, 1997; originally written in the latter stages of the first century BCE).

10. See Debray, *God: An Itinerary*, p. 16.

11. See David Leeming, *Jealous Gods and Chosen People: The Mythology of the Middle East* (Oxford and New York: Oxford University Press, 2004), pp. 37–40.

12. See Mark S. Smith, *The Early History of God: Yahweh and the Other Deities in Ancient Israel* (San Francisco: Harper & Row, 1990), p. xix.

13. See George Hart, *Ancient Egyptian Gods and Goddesses* (London: British Museum Press, 2001).

14. Plato, *Republic*, Book II, 379A, trans. Robin Waterfield (Oxford: Oxford University Press, 1993), p. 73.

15. For the original Greek of Plato's dialogue see *Plato: The Republic*, Loeb Classical Library, 2 vols (London: William Heinemann; and Cambridge, MA: Harvard University Press, 1953), vol. I, p. 182.

16. Leeming, *Jealous Gods and Chosen People*, p. 9.

17. See Albert Borgmann, *Holding On to Reality: The Nature of Information at the Turn of the Century* (Chicago and London: University of Chicago Press, 2000), pp. 42–4; Denise Schmandt-Besserat, *Before Writing* (Austin, TX: University of Texas Press, 1992), vol. I, p. 1; and David Diringer, *The Alphabet: A Key to the History of Mankind*, 3rd edn (London: Hutchinson, 1968), vol. I, pp. 17–112.

18. Richard Dawkins, *Unweaving the Rainbow* (London: Penguin Books, 1999), pp. 12–13.

19. See Richard Southwood, *The Story of Life* (Oxford: Oxford University Press, 2003), pp. 229–230.

20. See Karl Barth, *Church Dogmatics*, I.1: *The Doctrine of God*, 2nd edn (Edinburgh: T & T Clark, 1995), p. 295.

21. For a succinct history of such councils see Norman P. Tanner, *The Councils of the Church: A Short History* (New York: Crossroad Publishing, 2001).

22. See Wolfhart Pannenberg, *Systematic Theology*, 2 vols (Grand Rapids, MI: Eerdmans, 1991), I, p. 18, where he discusses Buddeus.

23. Consult Paul Tillich, *Systematic Theology*, 3 vols (Chicago: University of Chicago Press, 1951–57).

24. David F. Ford, 'Introduction to Modern Christian Theology', in David F. Ford, ed., *The Modern Theologians: An Introduction to Christian Theology in the Twentieth Century*, 2nd edn (Oxford: Blackwell, 1997), pp. 1–20; p. 2. Consult also, Hans W. Frei, *Types of Christian Theology* (New Haven and London: Yale University Press, 1992).

25. Charles Flowers, *Instability Rules: The Ten Most Amazing Ideas of Modern Science* (New York: John Wiley, 2002), p. 8.

26. On the modern distinction between reality and appearance, see Richard Francks, *Modern Philosophy: The Seventeenth and Eighteenth Centuries* (London and New York: Routledge, 2003), pp. 3–8.

27. For an introduction to ancient and modern understandings of the Trinity consult David Coffey, *Deus Trinitas: The Doctrine of the Triune God* (New York and Oxford: Oxford University Press, 1999); and David S. Cunningham, *These Three Are One: The Practice of Trinitarian Theology* (Oxford: Blackwell, 1998).

28. John Hick, *The Metaphor of God Incarnate* (London: SCM Press, 1993), p. 9.

29. Tanner, *The Councils of the Church*, p. 21.

30. Translation by Norman Tanner, ed., *Decrees of the Ecumenical Councils* (London: Sheed & Ward; Washington: Georgetown University Press, 1990), p. 24.

31. See Terence Dickinson, *From the Big Bang to Planet X* (Ontario: Camden House, 1993), p. 17.

32. See Martin Rees, *Just Six Numbers: The Deep Forces that Shape the Universe* (London: Phoenix, 2002), p. 7.

33. John Gribbin, *Science: A History 1543–2001* (London: Allen Lane/Penguin, 2002), p. xvii.

34. Julian Young, *The Death of God and the Meaning of Life* (London: Routledge, 2003), p. 21.

35. Ibid., p. 1.

36. Ibid., pp. 1–2.

two

1. Such is the view, at least, of Don Cupitt in his book *Reforming Christianity* (Santa Rosa, CA: Polebridge Press, 2001), p. 1.

2. Mark S. Smith, *The Origins of Biblical Monotheism: Israel's Polytheistic Background and the Ugaritic Texts* (Oxford: Oxford University Press, 2001), p. 3.

3. See Don Cupitt, *After God: The Future of Religion* (London: Weidenfeld & Nicolson, 1997), pp. vii–xv; esp. p. vii.

4. *The Concise Oxford Dictionary of Current English*, 9th edn, ed. Della Thompson (Oxford: Clarendon Press, 1995), p. 1076.

5. See Lamin Sanneh and Joel A. Carpenter, eds, *The Changing Face of Christianity: Africa, the West, and the World* (Oxford and New York: Oxford University Press, 2005).

6. Rudolf Bultmann, 'New Testament and Mythology: The Problem of Demythologizing the New Testament Proclamation', in *New Testament and Mythology and Other Basic Writings*, ed. Schubert M. Ogden (Philadelphia, PA: Fortress Press, 1989 [1941]), pp. 1–43; pp. 4–5.

7. For an account and comparison of the vast array of contemporary Christian denominations, see Ted A. Campbell, *Christian Confessions: A Historical Introduction* (Louisville, KY: Westminster John Knox Press, 1996).

8. Consult Pat Fisher, *Religion in the Twenty-first Century* (London: Routledge, 1999), p. 59.

9. Ibid., p. 65.

10. Congregation for the Doctrine of the Faith, *Dominus Iesus: On the Unicity and Salvific Universality of Jesus Christ and the Church* (London: Catholic Truth Society, Publishers to the Holy See, 2000), p. 22: 'the ecclesial communities which have not preserved the valid Episcopate and the genuine and integral substance of the Eucharistic mystery, are not Churches in the proper sense; however, those who are baptized in these communities are, by Baptism, incorporated

in Christ and thus are in a certain communion, albeit imperfect, with the Church.'

11. J.C.A. Gaskin, ed., *Varieties of Unbelief: From Epicurus to Sartre* (New York: Macmillan, 1989), p. 9.

12. See Hans Küng, *Theology for the Third Millennium: An Ecumenical View* (New York: Doubleday, 1988), pp. 162–3.

13. Jacques Attali, *Millennium: Winners and Losers in the Coming World Order* (New York: Time Books, 1991), p. 3.

14. Christian Duquoc, *Christianisme: Mémoir pour l'avenir* (Paris: Éditions du Cerf, 2000), p. 9. Translations of Duquoc's original French are my own.

15. Christian Duquoc, *L'unique Christ: La symphonie différée* (Paris: Éditions du Cerf, 2002), p. 8.

16. Christian Duquoc, *La théologie en exil: Le défi de sa survie dans la culture contemporaine* (Paris: Bayard, 2002), p. 7.

17. Don Cupitt, *Radicals and the Future of the Church* (London: SCM Press, 1989), pp. 29–30.

18. Don Cupitt, 'Responses', in David L. Edwards, *Tradition and Truth: The Challenge of England's Radical Theologians 1962–1989* (London: Hodder & Stoughton, 1989), pp. 282–6; p. 285.

19. Don Cupitt, *Reforming Christianity*, p. 1.

20. Jan Kerkhofs, 'The Shortage of Priests in Europe', in Jan Kerkhofs, ed., *Europe without Priests?* (London: SCM Press, 1995), pp. 1–40; p. 1.

21. Edward Schillebeeckx, *For the Sake of the Gospel* (London: SCM Press, 1989), p. 41.

22. Paul Collins, *Papal Power: A Proposal for Change in Catholicism's Third Millennium* (London: Fount, 1997), p. x.

23. See Richard McBrien, *Catholicism*, 3rd edn (London: Geoffrey Chapman, 1994), p. 3.

24. See Paul Collins, ed., *From Inquisition to Freedom* (London and New York: Continuum, 2001); and Hans Küng and Leonard Swidler, eds, *The Church in Anguish: Has the Vatican Betrayed Vatican II?* (San Francisco: Harper & Row, 1987).

25. For accounts of the troubles of the theologians mentioned here, consult Paul Collins, ed., *From Inquisition to Freedom* (London: Continuum, 2002); Ted Schoof, ed., *The Schillebeeckx Case* (New York/Ramsey: Paulist Press, 1984); and Küng and Swidler, eds, *The Church in Anguish*.

26. For statistics, consult Ian S. Markham, ed., *A World Religions Reader* (Oxford: Blackwell, 1997), pp. 356–7.

27. See Grace Davie, *Religion in Modern Europe: A Memory Mutates* (Oxford: Oxford University Press, 2000), p. 11.

28. Stephen Bates, *A Church at War: Anglicans and Homosexuality* (London and New York: I.B. Tauris, 2004), p. 7.

29. Callum G. Brown, *The Death of Christian Britain* (London and New York: Routledge, 2001), p. 1.

30. Douglas John Hall, *The End of Christendom and the Future of Christianity* (Valley Forge, PA: Trinity Press International, 1997), p. 1.

31. Uta Ranke-Heinemann, *Eunuchs for Heaven: The Catholic Church and Sexuality* (London: André Deutsch, 1990), p. 302.

32. David Batstone, Eduardo Mendieta, Lois Ann Lorentzen and Dwight N. Hopkins, eds, *Liberation Theologies, Postmodernity, and the Americas* (London and New York: Routledge, 1997), p. 13.

33. See Steve Bruce, *Religion in the Modern World: From Cathedrals to Cults* (Oxford: Oxford University Press, 1996), chs 2 and 3; and *God is Dead: Secularization in the West* (Oxford: Blackwell, 2002), esp. ch. 1.

34. René Rémond, *Religion and Society in Modern Europe* (Oxford: Blackwell, 1999), p. 19.

35. A.J. Mattill, Jr, *The Seven Mighty Blows to Traditional Beliefs* (Gordo, AL: Flatwoods Press, 1995), p. 32.

36. John F. Haught, *God After Darwin: A Theology of Evolution* (Boulder, CO, and Oxford: Westview Press, 2000), p. 20.

37. Gordon D. Kaufman, *Theology for a Nuclear Age* (Manchester: Manchester University Press, 1985), p. 16.

38. Ibid.

39. Yeager Hudson, *The Philosophy of Religion* (Mountain View, CA: Mayfield, 1991), p. 119.

40. *Sunday Telegraph*, 13 January 2002, p. 11.

41. Umberto Eco, *The Name of the Rose* (London: Vintage, 1998), p. 399.

42. *Catechism of the Catholic Church*, rev. edn (London: Geoffrey Chapman, 1999). The first edition of this Catechism appeared in French in 1992.

43. Consult Anthony Mioni, ed., *The Popes against Modern Errors: 16 Papal Documents* (Rockford, IL: Tan Books, 1999).

44. Quoted in Eugene C. Bianchi and Rosemary Radford Ruether, eds, *A Democratic Catholic Church: The Reconstruction of Roman Catholicism* (New York: Crossroad, 1992), p. 45. This comment is contained in Gregory XVI, encyclical, *Mirari Vos*, published in 1832 to condemn religious indifferentism and the idea that people may exercise freedom of conscience in choosing a religion.

45. Pius X, *Vehementer Nos*, quoted in Maureen Fiedler and Linda Rabben, eds, *Rome Has Spoken: A Guide to Forgotten Papal Statements and How They Changed through the Centuries* (New York: Crossroad, 1998), p. 49.

46. Mark Chaves, *Ordaining Women: Culture and Conflict in Religious Organizations* (Cambridge, MA and London: Harvard University Press, 1997), p. 120.

47. Gene Burns, *The Frontiers of Catholicism: The Politics of Ideology in a Liberal World* (Berkeley: University of California Press, 1992), p. 27.

48. Cited in ibid., p. 27.

49. William Hill, 'A Theology in Transition', in Mary Catherine Hilkert and Robert J. Schreiter, eds, *The Praxis of the Reign of God: An Introduction to the Theology of Edward Schillebeeckx*, 2nd edn (New York: Fordham University Press, 2002), pp. 1–18; p. 9.

50. Chaves, *Ordaining Women*, p. 123.

51. Ibid., p. 124.

52. Ibid.

53. See ibid., pp. 124–9.

54. Ibid., pp. 128–9.

55. J. Gresham Machen, *Christianity and Liberalism* (Grand Rapids, MI: Eerdmans, 1997 [1923]), p. 2.

56. See, for example, Gerd Lüdemann, *Jesus after 2000 Years* (London: SCM Press, 2000); and *The Great Deception: And What Jesus Really Said and Did* (London: SCM Press, 1998).

57. Don Cupitt, *Emptiness and Brightness* (Santa Rosa, CA: Polebridge Press, 2001), p. 17n.

58. Richard Holloway, *Doubts and Loves: What is Left of Christianity* (Edinburgh: Canongate, 2001), pp. 14–15.

three

1. Hugh J. Silverman, 'Introduction: Jean-François Lyotard – Between Politics and Aesthetics', in *Lyotard: Philosophy, Politics, and the Sublime*, ed. Hugh J. Silverman (New York and London: Routledge, 2002), pp. 1–19; p. 1.

2. Jürgen Habermas, 'Modernity – An Incomplete Project', in Hal Foster, ed., *Postmodern Culture* (London: Pluto Press, 1985), pp. 3–15; pp. 3–4.

3. David Levine, *At the Dawn of Modernity: Biology, Culture, and Material Life in Europe after the Year 1000* (Berkeley, Los Angeles and London: University of California Press, 2001), p. 18.

4. Ibid., p. 25.

5. See Richard Appignanesi and Chris Garratt, *Introducing Postmodernism* (Cambridge: Icon Books, 1995), p. 6.

6. Robert Anchor, *The Enlightenment Tradition* (Berkeley: University of California Press, 1967), p. 3.

7. Leszek Kolakowski, *Modernity on Endless Trial* (Chicago and London: University of Chicago Press, 1997), p. 7.

8. Stephen Toulmin, *Cosmopolis: The Hidden Agenda of Modernity* (Chicago: University of Chicago Press, 1990), pp. 8–9.

9. Ibid., p. 8.

10. In agreement with J. Deotis Roberts, *A Philosophical Introduction to Theology* (London: SCM Press and Philadelphia: Trinity Press International, 1991), p. 122.

11. See Louis Dupré, *Passage to Modernity: An Essay in the Hermeneutics of Nature and Culture* (New Haven, CT: Yale University Press, 1993), pp. 1–12.

12. Albert Borgmann, *Crossing the Postmodern Divide* (Chicago and London: University of Chicago Press, 1992).

13. Ibid., p. 5.

14. Ibid., p. 21.

15. Gordon W. Lathrop, *Holy Things: A Liturgical Theology* (Minneapolis, MN: Fortress Press, 1998), p. 1.

16. A.K.M. Adam, *What is Postmodern Biblical Criticism?* (Minneapolis, MN: Fortress Press, 1995), p. 2.

17. Ibid.

18. See Wolfgang Wutzler, 'Ancients and Moderns', in Alan Charles Kors, ed., *Encyclopedia of the Enlightenment*, 4 vols (Oxford and New York: Oxford University Press, 2003), I, pp. 55–57; p. 56.

19. Borgmann, *Crossing the Postmodern Divide*, p. 7.

20. Ibid., p. 21.

21. Gustavo Gutiérrez, *Las Casas: In Search of the Poor Jesus Christ* (Maryknoll, NY: Orbis

Books, 1995), p. 23.

22. This quotation and additional details of Columbus's arrival in the Antilles are taken from Gutiérrez, *Las Casas*, p. 23.

23. See Philip Clayton, *The Problem of God in Modern Thought* (Grand Rapids, MI: Eerdmans, 2000), pp. 1–18.

24. See David Laird Dungun, *A History of the Synoptic Problem: The Canon, the Text, the Composition, and the Interpretation of the Gospels* (New York: Doubleday, 1999), p. 150.

25. George Smoot and Keay Davidson, *Wrinkles in Time: The Imprint of Creation* (London: Little, Brown, 1993), p. 3.

26. Hans Küng, *The Catholic Church: A Short History*, (London: Weidenfeld & Nicolson, 2001), p. 153.

27. Chris Cook and Philip Broadhead, *The Longman Handbook of Early Modern Europe 1453–1763* (Harlow: Longman, 2001), p. 159.

28. Diarmaid MacCulloch, 'The Reformation 1500–1650', in Richard Harries and Henry Mayr-Harting, eds, *Christianity: Two Thousand Years* (Oxford: Oxford University Press, 2001), pp. 132–61; p. 143.

29. Seán F. Hughes, 'Diversity and Orthodoxy: The 16th Century', in Adrian Hastings, Alistair Mason and Hugh Pyper, eds, *Christian Thought: A Brief History* (Oxford: Oxford University Press, 2002), pp. 88–107; p. 90.

30. Quoted in Dungan, *A History of the Synoptic Problem*, p. 157. Georg Rörer, the first editor of Luther's works, added two short sentences to this passage: 'On this I take my stand. I can do no other.' Diarmaid MacCulloch describes these sentences as 'the most memorable thing Luther never said'. See his book, *Reformation: Europe's House Divided, 1490–1700* (London: Allen Lane, 2003), p. 131.

31. See Martin Luther, 'Von der Freiheit eines Christenmenschen', in Karin Bornkamm and Gerhard Ebeling, eds, *Ausgewählte Schriften*, 6 vols (Frankfurt: Insel, 1982), vol. 1, pp. 238–63.

32. Steve Bruce, *Religion in the Modern World: From Cathedrals to Cults* (Oxford: Oxford University Press, 1996), p. 14.

33. Euan Cameron, 'The Power of the Word: Renaissance and Reformation', in Euan Cameron, ed., *Early Modern Europe: An Oxford History* (Oxford: Oxford University Press, 1999), pp. 63–101; p. 81.

34. Klaus Scholder, *The Birth of Modern Critical Theology* (London: SCM Press, 1990), p. 11.

35. Ibid.

36. Ronald G. Asch, *The Thirty Years' War: The Holy Roman Empire and Europe, 1618–48* (London: Macmillan, 1997), pp. 185–6.

37. See Georges Dicker, *Descartes: An Analytical and Historical Introduction* (Oxford: Oxford University Press, 1993), p. 13.

38. For Descartes' estimation of mathematics, consult Janet Broughton, *Descartes' Method of Doubt* (Princeton and Oxford: Princeton University Press, 2002), p. 8.

39. René Descartes, 'A Discourse on Method', in *The Rationalists*, trans. John Veitch and others (New York: Doubleday, 1960), pp. 39–96; p. 44.

40. John Cottingham, 'René Descartes (1596–1650)', in Ted Honderich, ed., *The Philosophers: Introducing Great Western Thinkers* (Oxford: Oxford University Press, 1999), pp. 59–65; p. 60.

41. See Küng, *The Catholic Church*, p. 154.

42. John D. Caputo, *On Religion* (London and New York: Routledge, 2001), p. 62.

43. These four principles are summarized in James Byrne, *Glory, Jest and Riddle: Religious Thought in the Enlightenment* (London: SCM Press, 1996), p. 56. The original text is contained in J.D. Cottingham, R. Stoothoff, and D. Murdoch, eds, *The Philosophical Writings of Descartes* (Cambridge: Cambridge University Press, 1985), vol. I, p. 120.

44. On the epochal significance of Descartes' philosophy, see Andrew Bowie, *Introduction to German Philosophy: From Kant to Habermas* (Cambridge: Polity , 2004), p. 5.

45. Ibid., p. 59.

46. Lisa Rosner, ed., *The Hutchinson Chronology of Science* (Oxford: Helicon, 2002), p. 19.

47. Cottingham, 'René Descartes (1596–1650)', pp. 59–60.

48. Dungan, *A History of the Synoptic Problem*, p. 151.

49. See Stephen Gaukroger, *Francis Bacon and the Transformation of Early-Modern Philosophy* (Cambridge: Cambridge University Press, 2001), p. 10.

50. Bas C. van Fraassen, *The Empirical Stance* (New Haven and London: Yale University Press, 2002), p. 32.

51. Francis Bacon, *Novum Organum*, trans. and ed. Peter Urbach and John Gibson (Chicago

and La Salle, IL: Open Court, 1994), Book
1, Aphorism 95, p. 105.

52. On Bacon and Locke, see Borgmann, *Crossing the Postmodern Divide*, pp. 23–25..

53. Roberts, *A Philosophical Introduction to Theology*, p. 124.

54. See Roy Porter, *Enlightenment: Britain and the Creation of the Modern World* (London: Allen Lane/Penguin, 2000), p. 6.

55. See Peter Addinall, *Philosophy and Biblical Interpretation: A Study in Nineteenth-Century Conflict* (Cambridge: Cambridge University Press, 1991), p. 8.

four

1. L.W.B. Brockliss, *Calvet's Web: Enlightenment and the Republic of Letters in Eighteenth-Century France* (Oxford: Oxford University Press, 2002), p. 1.

2. Laurence W.B. Brockliss, 'The Age of Curiosity', in Joseph Bergin, ed., *The Seventeenth Century, The Short Oxford History of Europe* (Oxford: Oxford University Press, 2001), 143–84; p. 152.

3. Thomas Aquinas, *Summa theologiae*, Ia. I. 8.

4. Theodor W. Adorno and Max Horkheimer, *Dialectic of Enlightenment*, trans. John Cumming (London and New York: Verso, 1997 [1944]), p. 3.

5. Richard Rorty, 'The Continuity between the Enlightenment and "Postmodernism"', in Keith Michael Baker and Peter Hanns Reill, eds, *What's Left of the Enlightenment: A Postmodern Question* (Stanford, CA: Standford University Press, 2001), pp. 19–36; p. 19.

6. Vincent A. McCarthy offers a profound discussion of philosophical attempts to render Christian faith intellectually convincing in the wake of the Enlightenment. See his *Quest for a Philosophical Jesus: Christianity and Philosophy in Rousseau, Kant, Hegel, and Schelling* (Macon, GA: Mercer University Press, 1986).

7. Michael H. McCarthy, *The Crisis of Philosophy* (Albany, NY: State University of New York Press, 1990), p. xii.

8. James Byrne, *Glory, Jest and Riddle: Religious Thought in the Enlightenment* (London: SCM Press, 1996), p. 32.

9. J.C.A. Gaskin, ed., *Varieties of Unbelief: From Epicurus to Sartre* (New York: Macmillan, 1989), p. 9.

10. For a lively introduction to the Enlightenment, see Lloyd Spencer and Andrzej Krauze, *Introducing the Enlightenment* (Duxford: Icon Books, 2000), esp. p. 3.

11. Roy Porter, *Enlightenment: Britain and the Creation of the Modern World* (London: Allen Lane/Penguin, 2000), p. 4.

12. Dust jacket of H.T. Mason and W. Boyle, *The Impact of the French Revolution* (Gloucester: Sutton, 1989).

13. Harles Breunig and Matthew Levinger, *The Revolutionary Era 1789–1850*, 3rd edn (New York and London: W.W. Norton, 2002), p. 1.

14. The expression 'absolute monarch' needs to be used with caution because it can give the false impression that such a ruler could be politically unconstrained in any way. In reality, powerful kings and queens of the French past often needed to cooperate and negotiate very prudently with aristocrats of their courts. See T.C.W Blanning, *The Culture of Power and the Power of Culture: Old Regime Europe 1660–1789* (Oxford: Oxford University Press, 2002); Paul Kléber Monod, *The Power of Kings: Monarchy and Religion in Europe, 1589–1715* (New Haven and London: Yale University Press, 1999); E.N. Williams, *The Ancien Régime in Europe: Government and Society in the Major States 1648–1789* (London: Pimlico, 1999 [1970]).

15. Margaret C. Jacob, *The Enlightenment: A Brief History with Documents* (Boston and New York: Bedford/St Martins, 2001), p. 3.

16. W. Doyle, 'The Principles of the French Revolution', in Mason and Doyle, *The Impact of the French Revolution*, pp. 1–10; p. 2.

17. David Levine, *At the Dawn of Modernity: Biology, Culture, and Material Life in Europe after the Year 1000* (Berkeley: University of California Press, 2001), p. 7.

18. Ibid., p. 8.

19. See Derek Beales, 'Religion and Culture', in T.C.W. Blanning, ed., *The Eighteenth Century* (Oxford: Oxford University Press, 2000), pp. 131–77; p. 131.

20. Jonathan Sperber, *Revolutionary Europe 1780–1850* (Harlow: Longman, 2000), p. 29.

21. Ibid., with variations.

22. Ibid.

23. Consult, in particular, Paul Kléber Monod, *The Power of Kings: Monarchy and Religion in*

Europe, 1589–1715 (New Haven and London: Yale University Press, 1999); Williams, *The Ancien Régime in Europe.*

24. See Daniel Roche, *France in the Enlightenment* (Cambridge, MA, and London: Harvard University Press, 2000), p. 356.
25. Beales, 'Religion and Culture', p. 132.
26. Ibid.
27. Ibid., p. 137. See p. 138 as well for the figures just cited.
28. T.C.W. Blanning, 'Introduction: The Beneficiaries and Casualties of Expansion', in T.C.W. Blanning, ed., *The Eighteenth Century* (Oxford: Oxford University Press, 2000), pp. 1–10; p. 1.
29. See Breunig and Levinger, *The Revolutionary Era 1789–1850*, p. 6.
30. Sperber, *Revolutionary Europe 1780–1850*, p. 35.
31. Austin Flannery, ed., *Vatican Council II: Constitutions, Decrees, Declarations* (Northport, NY: Costello, 1996), p. 1.
32. Jacob, *The Enlightenment*, p. 1.
33. Isaac Kramnik, ed., 'Introduction', in *The Portable Enlightenment Reader* (New York: Penguin, 1995), pp. ix–xxiii; p. ix.
34. James Byrne, *Glory, Jest and Riddle: Religious Thought in the Enlightenment* (London: SCM Press, 1996), p. 1.
35. *The Portable Thomas Jefferson*, ed. Merrill D. Peterson (Harmondsworth: Penguin, 1977), pp. 435–6.
36. See Byrne, *Glory, Jest and Riddle*, pp. 136–7.
37. Ibid., p. 2.
38. Alan Charles Kors, 'Preface', in Alan Charles Kors, ed., *Encyclopedia of the Enlightenment*, 4 vols (Oxford: Oxford University Press, 2003), vol. I, pp. xvii–xxii; p. xvii.
39. See Louis Dupré, *The Enlightenment and the Intellectual Foundations of Modern Culture* (New Haven and London: Yale University Press, 2004), p. 5; and Ernst Cassirer, *An Essay on Man* (New Haven: Yale University Press, 1944), p. 222.
40. Quoted in James Schmidt, ed., *What Is Enlightenment? Eighteenth-Century Answers and Twentieth-Century Questions* (Berkeley: University of California Press, 1996), p. 2.
41. Ibid., p. 58.
42. Ernst Cassirer, *The Philosophy of the Enlightenment* (Princeton, NJ: Princeton University Press, 1951.).
43. Peter Gay, *The Enlightenment, An Interpre-*

tation: The Rise of Modern Paganism (New York and London: W.W. Norton, 1966); and *The Enlightenment, An Interpretation: The Science of Freedom* (New York and London: W.W. Norton, 1969).

44. Dorinda Outram, *The Enlightenment* (Cambridge: Cambridge University Press, 1999).
45. Thomas Munck, *The Enlightenment: A Comparative Social History 1721–1794* (London: Edward Arnold, 2000).
46. Blanning, 'Introduction', p. 4.
47. Sperber, *Revolutionary Europe 1780–1850*, p. 34.
48. Ibid.
49. Ibid.
50. For Alan Kors' own formulation of these phenomena see his preface to the *Encyclopedia of the Enlightenment*, cited p. xvii n37.
51. Philip Clayton, *The Problem of God in Modern Thought* (Grand Rapids, MI, and Cambridge: Eerdmans, 2000), p. 263; emphasis added.
52. Thomas Aquinas, *Summa theologiae*, I, q. 2, art. 3.
53. George di Giovanni, *Freedom and Religion in Kant and His Immediate Successors* (Cambridge: Cambridge University Press, 2005), p. 32.
54. J. Deotis Roberts, *A Philosophical Introduction to Theology* (London: SCM Press, 1991), p. 130.
55. Patricia Kitcher, 'Immanuel Kant', in Steven M. Emmanuel, ed., *The Blackwell Guide to the Modern Philosophers: From Descartes to Nietzsche* (Oxford: Blackwell, 2001), 223–58; p. 223.
56. For an excellent account of Kant's life, and the details of his ancestry, see Allen W. Wood, *Kant* (Oxford: Blackwell, 2005), ch. 1, esp. pp. 3–4.
57. Ibid., pp. 8–9.
58. Manfred Kuehn, *Kant* (Cambridge: Cambridge University Press, 2001), p. 422.
59. Consult Frederick Beiser, 'The Enlightenment and Idealism', in *The Cambridge Companion to German Idealism*, ed. Karl Ameriks (Cambridge: Cambridge University Press, 2000), pp. 18–36; p. 18.
60. See ibid., p. 19.
61. Don Cupitt, *The Sea of Faith: Christianity in Change* (London: British Broadcasting Corporation, 1985), p. 251.
62. See Beiser, 'The Enlightenment and Idealism', p. 20.

63. Anthony Savile, *Kant's Critique of Pure Reason: An Orientation to Its Central Theme* (Oxford: Blackwell, 2005), p. 1.

64. Sebastian Gardner, *Kant and the 'Critique of Pure Reason'* (London and New York: Routledge, 2000), p. 23.

65. Ibid.

66. Ibid., p. 40.

67. Gardner, *Kant and the 'Critique of Pure Reason'*, p. 40.

68. John Hick, *An Interpretation of Religion: Human Responses to the Transcendent* (London: Macmillan, 1989), p. 240.

69. Georges Dicker, *Kant's Theory of Knowledge: An Analytical Introduction* (Oxford and New York: Oxford University Press, 2004), p. 32. For Kant's own statements regarding space and time see his *Critique of Pure Reason, Cambridge Edition of the Works of Immanuel Kant*, trans. and ed. Paul Guyer and Allen W. Wood (Cambridge: Cambridge University Press, 2000), A33/B49, p. 163; and A39/B56–A42/B59, pp. 166–8.

70. Ibid., p. 110.

71. Gardner, *Kant and the 'Critique of Pure Reason'*, p. 46.

72. See Garrett Green, *Theology, Hermeneutics, and Imagination: The Crisis of Interpretation at the End of Modernity* (Cambridge: Cambridge University Press, 2000), pp. 26–30.

73. See Karl Ameriks, 'Introduction: Interpreting German Idealism', in Karl Ameriks, ed., *The Cambridge Companion to German Idealism* (Cambridge: Cambridge University Press, 2000), pp. 1–17; pp. 8–9; and Frederick C. Beiser, *German Idealism: The Struggle against Subjectivism, 1781–1801* (Cambridge, MA, and London: Harvard University Press, 2002), esp. pp. 351–2 (on 'absolute idealism').

74. Immanuel Kant, *Critique of Pure Reason*, p. 567, A596/B624.

75. Ibid., p. 563, A591/B619.

76. On the causes of the French Revolution, see William Doyle, *Origins of the French Revolution* (New York: Oxford University Press, 1999). For an insightful survey of diverse interpretations of the Revolution consult Baily Stone, *Reinterpreting the French Revolution: A Global-Historical Perspective* (Cambridge: Cambridge University Press, 2002), pp. 1–10.

77. Norman Hampson, 'The Origins of the French Revolution: The Long and the Short of It', in David Williams, ed., *1789: The Long and the Short of It* (Sheffield: Sheffield Academic Press, 1991), pp. 15–32; p. 15.

78. Such a view, for instance, is championed by Georges Lefebvre, *The Coming of the French Revolution* (Princeton, NJ: Princeton University Press, 1947).

79. Lynn Hunt, 'French Revolution: Overview', in Kors, ed., *Encyclopedia of the Enlightenment*, vol. 2, 80–84; pp. 80–81.

80. Daniel Roche, *France in the Enlightenment* (Cambridge, MA, and London: Harvard University Press, 2000), p. 6.

81. Murray Bookchin, *The Third Revolution: Popular Movements in the Revolutionary Era*, vol. 1 (London: Cassell, 1996). p. 253.

82. Ibid., p. 252.

83. Sperber, *Revolutionary Europe 1780–1850*, p. 65.

84. Ibid.

85. Ibid., p. 69.

86. Reproduced in Kramnick, ed., *The Portable Enlightenment Reader*, p. 467.

87. My attention was drawn to the significance of Sieyès by John Dunn, *Setting the People Free: The Story of Democracy* (London: Atlantic Books, 2005), pp. 102–111. Consult, too, Jean-Denis Bredin, *Sieyès: La clé de la Révolution française* (Paris: Éditions du Fallois, 1988).

88. Emmanuel Sieyès, translated in Michael Sonenscher's edition of Sieyès' *Political Writings* (Indianapolis, IN: Hackett, 2003), p. 147. For the French original, see Marcel Dorigny, ed., *Œuvres de Sieyès* (Paris: Éditions d'Histoire Sociale, 1989), vol. 1, 'Tiers état', p. 98.

89. Norman Hampson, 'The Enlightenment', in Euan Cameron, ed., *Early Modern Europe: An Oxford History* (Oxford: Oxford University Press, 1999), pp. 265–97; p. 289.

90. See Adrian Hastings, ed., *Modern Catholicism* (London and New York: SPCK and Oxford University Press, 1991), p. 1.

91. See Roy Porter, 'The 1790s: "Visions of Unsullied Bliss"', in Asa Briggs and Daniel Snowman, eds, *Fins de Siècle: How Centuries End 1400–2000* (New Haven and London: Yale University Press, 1996), pp. 125–55; p. 125.

92. Raymond L.M. Lee and Susan E. Ackerman, *The Challenge of Religion after Modernity: Beyond Disenchantment* (Aldershot: Ashgate, 2002), p. 1.

five

1. Friedrich Nietzsche, *Twilight of the Gods and The Antichrist* (London: Penguin, 1990), pp. 198 and 199.
2. See James Obelkovich, 'Religion', in F.M.L. Thompson, ed., *The Cambridge Social History of Britain 1750–1950*, vol. 3: *Social Agencies and Institutions* (Cambridge: Cambridge University Press, 1996), pp. 311–56.
3. See David Hempton, *Religion and Political Culture in Britain and Ireland: From the Glorious Revolution to the Decline of Empire* (Cambridge: Cambridge University Press, 1996), p. 2.
4. Stewart J. Brown, *The National Churches of England, Ireland, and Scotland 1801–1846* (Oxford: Oxford University Press, 2001), p. 1.
5. See Chris Cook, *The Longman Companion to Britain in the Nineteenth Century* (London and New York: Longman, 1999), p. 168.
6. See Philip Toynbee, *Part of a Journey: An Autobiographical Journal 1977–1979* (London: Collins, 1981), pp. 291–2.
7. Thomas Albert Howard, *Religion and the Rise of Historicism: W.M.L. de Wette, Jacob Burckhardt, and the Theological Origins of Nineteenth-Century Historical Consciousness* (Cambridge: Cambridge University Press, 2000), p. 17.
8. See Hugh McLeod, *Secularisation in Western Europe, 1848–1914* (London: Macmillan, 2000), p. 1.
9. W.E. Lecky, *History of the Rise and Spirit of Rationalism in Europe*, 2 vols (New York: D. Appleton, 1879 [1865]), vol. II, pp. 99–100.
10. This story is recounted in Michael Landmann, *Problematik: Nichtwissen und Wissenverlangen im philosophischen Bewußtsein* (Göttingen: Vandenhoek & Ruprecht, 1949), p. 55 n13.
11. See Max Weber, *Sociology of Religion* (London: Methuen, 1965 [1922]); and John Ellis and Jon Simons, 'Max Weber (1864–1920)', in Jon Simons, ed., *From Kant to Lévi-Strauss: The Background to Contemporary Critical Theory* (Edinburgh: Edinburgh Press, 2002), pp. 81–96; p. 84.
12. Steve Bruce, *Choice and Religion: A Critique of Rational Choice* (Oxford: Oxford University Press, 1999), p. 11.
13. Ibid.
14. Ibid., p. 8. See too, Steve Bruce, *Religion in the Modern World: From Cathedrals to Cults* (Oxford: Oxford University Press, 1996), pp. 39–43.
15. Ibid., p. 12.
16. Ibid.
17. David Laird Dungan, *A History of the Synoptic Problem* (New York: Doubleday, 1999), p. 149.
18. Bruce, *Choice and Religion*, p. 10.
19. See Edward Schillebeeckx, *God the Future of Man* (London and Sydney: Sheed & Ward, 1986 [1969]), pp. 56–7.
20. Ibid., pp. 57–8.
21. Ibid., p. 59.
22. Ibid., pp. 61–2.
23. Simon Dentith, *Society and Cultural Forms in Nineteenth-Century England* (London: Macmillan, 1998), p. 43.
24. For a succinct account of secularization and Compte's Positivism consult Nicholas Atkin and Frank Tallett, *Priests, Prelates, and People: A History of European Catholicism since 1750* (London and New York: I.B. Tauris, 2003), pp. 167–88, esp. pp. 168–9.
25. Howard, *Religion and the Rise of Historicism*, p. 17.
26. T.C.W. Blanning, 'Introduction: The End of the Old Regime', in T.C.W. Blanning ed., *The Nineteenth Century* (Oxford: Oxford University Press, 2000), p. 1.
27. Ibid.
28. Niall Ferguson, 'The European Economy, 1815–1914', in Blanning, ed., *The Nineteenth Century*, pp. 78–125; p. 90.
29. For the discoveries mentioned in this and the following paragraph consult H.E.L. Mellersh, R.L. Story, Neville Williams, and Philip Waller, *Chronology of World History: 10,000 BC–AD 1994*, compact edn (Oxford: Helicon, 1995), pp. 242–92.
30. James J. Sheehan, 'Culture', in Blanning, ed., *The Nineteenth Century*, pp. 126–57; p. 130.
31. Dungan, *A History of the Synoptic Problem*, pp. 167–8.
32. See Mellersh et al., *Chronology of World History*, pp. 246–90; and Lisa Rosner, ed., *The Hutchinson Chronology of Science: From the Astronomers of Stonehenge to the Cloning of the Gene* (Oxford: Helicon, 2002).
33. Blanning, 'Introduction: The End of the Old Regime', p. 2. Consult, too, John A. Lynn, 'International Rivalry and Warfare', in

T.C.W. Blanning, ed., *The Eighteenth Century* (Oxford: Oxford University Press, 2000), pp. 178–217.

34. See Jonathan Sperber, *Revolutionary Europe 1780–1850* (Harlow: Longman, 2000), ch. 8; and Robert Gildea, *Barricades and Borders: Europe 1800–1914*, 2nd edn (Oxford: Oxford University Press, 1996), ch. 4.

35. Howard, *Religion and the Rise of Historicism*, p. 18.

36. See Simon Dentith, *Society and Cultural Forms in Nineteenth-Century England*, chs 1–4.

37. Chris Cook, *Britain in the Nineteenth Century*, p. 111.

38. See Graham Midgley, *University Life in Eighteenth-Century Oxford* (New Haven and London: Yale University Press, 1996), ch. 1, esp. pp. 12–15.

39. Colin Matthew, 'Introduction: The United Kingdom and the Victorian Century, 1815–1901', in Colin Matthew, ed., *The Nineteenth Century*, Short Oxford History of the British Isles (Oxford: Oxford University Press, 2000), pp. 1–38; p. 11.

40. Dentith, *Society and Cultural Forms in Nineteenth-Century England*, p. 30.

41. Callum G. Brown, *The Death of Christian Britain* (London and New York: Routledge, 2001), p. 3.

42. Harvey Cox, 'The Myth of the Twentieth Century: The Rise and Fall of "Secularization"', in Gregory Baum, ed., *The Twentieth Century: A Theological Overview* (Maryknoll, NY: Orbis Books, 1999), pp. 135–43; p. 143.

43. Cox, 'The Myth of the Twentieth Century', p. 137.

44. Charles Taylor, *The Ethics of Authenticity* (Cambridge, MA, and London: Harvard University Press, 1991), p. 4.

45. A. Borgman, *Crossing the Postmodern Divide* (Chicago and London: University of Chicago Press, 1992), p. 3.

46. Alexis de Tocqueville, *De la Démocratie en Amérique*, 2 vols (Paris: Garnier–Flammarion, 1981), vol. II, p. 385.

47. Paul Ricoeur, 'The Critique of Religion', *Union Seminary Quarterly Review* 28 (1973), 205–12; p. 205.

48. Garrett Green, *Theology, Hermeneutics, and Imagination: The Crisis of Interpretation at the End of Modernity* (Cambridge: Cambridge University Press, 2000), p. 11.

49. Ricoeur, 'The Critique of Religion', p. 205.

50. See Richard Popkin, *The History of Scepticism: From Savonarola to Bayle* (Oxford and New York: Oxford University Press, 2003), esp. ch. 2, which deals with the revival of Greek scepticism in the sixteenth century.

51. See Green, *Theology, Hermeneutics, and Imagination*, pp. 11–19.

52. Georg Wilhelm Friedrich Hegel, *Phenomenology of Spirit* (Oxford: Oxford University Press, 1977 [1807]); *Science of Logic* (London: Allen & Unwin, 1969 [1812–16]); *Philosophy of Right* (Cambridge: Cambridge University Press, 1991 [1821]); and *Encyclopedia of the Philosophical Sciences* [1830], 3 vols (Oxford: Oxford University Press): vol. I: *Logic* (1975); vol. II: *Philosophy of Nature* (1970); and vol. III: *Philosophy of Mind* (1971).

53. Hans Küng, *Does God Exist? An Answer for Today* (New York: Crossroad, 1999 [1988]), p. 188.

54. Georg W.F. Hegel, *Werke in zwanzig Bänden. Werkausgabe*, ed. Eva Moldenhauer and Kerl Michel (Frankfurt: Suhrkamp Verlag, 1970), vol. XVI, p. 192. For a succinct account of Hegel's understanding of God, see Frederick Beiser, *Hegel* (London and New York: Routledge, 2005), pp. 142–6.

55. *Hegel's Preface to the 'Phenomenology of Spirit': Georg Wilhelm Friedrich Hegel*, trans. and running commentary by Yirmiyahu Yovel (Princeton and Oxford: Princeton University Press, 2005), p. 17.

56. Peter C. Hodgson, *Hegel and Christian Theology: A Reading of the Lectures on the Philosophy of Religion* (Oxford: Oxford University Press, 2005), p. 7.

57. Paul Guyer, 'Absolute Idealism and the Rejection of Kantian Dualism', in Karl Ameriks, ed., *The Cambridge Companion to German Idealism* (Cambridge: Cambridge University Press, 2000), pp. 37–56; p. 37.

58. Hegel, *Phenomenology of Spirit*, p. 86.

59. Peter Singer, 'Georg Wilhelm Friedrich Hegel 1770–1831', in Diané Collinson, ed., *Fifty Major Philosophers* (London and New York: Routledge, 1987), pp. 96–9; p. 98.

60. See Joshua Hoffman and Gary Rosenkranz, *The Divine Attributes* (Oxford: Blackwell, 2002); and Richard Swinburne, *The Christian God* (Oxford: Clarendon Press, 1998).

61. Steve Wilkens and Alan G. Padget, *Christianity and Western Thought: A History of Philosophers, Ideas & Movements*, vol. 2: *Faith & Reason in the 19th Century* (Downers Grove,

IL: InterVarsity Press, 2000), p. 88.

62. Ibid., p. 92.

63. For details of Feuerbach's life see Wilkens and Padget, *Christianity and Western Thought*, pp. 114–26.

64. Cited in Frederick Gregory, *Scientific Materialism in Nineteenth-Century Germany* (Dordrecht: D. Reidel, 1977), p. 16.

65. Paul Avis, *Faith in the Fires of Criticism: Christianity in Modern Thought* (London: Darton, Longman & Todd, 1995), p. 4.

66. Ludwig Feuerbach, *The Essence of Christianity*, trans. George Eliot (Amherst, NY: Prometheus Books, 1989 [1841]), p. 12.

67. Augustine, *De Genesi ad litteram*, l. v. c. 16, in Feuerbach, *The Essence of Christianity*, p. 12.

68. Feuerbach, *The Essence of Christianity*, p. 12.

69. Avis, *Faith in the Fires of Criticism*, p. 2.

70. Feuerbach, *The Essence of Christianity*, p. 140.

71. Ibid., p. 204.

72. Ibid., p. 206.

73. Ibid., p. 207.

74. Ibid., p. 205.

75. Hans Küng, *Christianity: Its Essence and History* (London: SCM Press, 1994), p. 12.

76. Karl Marx, in D. McLellan, ed., *Karl Marx: Early Texts* (Oxford: Basil Blackwell, 1972), p. 25.

77. Quoted in Eugene Kamenka, *The Philosophy of Ludwig Feuerbach* (London: Routledge & Kegan Paul, 1970), p. 15.

78. J.W. Burrow, *The Crisis of Reason: European Thought, 1848–1914* (New Haven and London: Yale University Press, 2000), p. 7.

79. Robert C. Solomon and Kathleen M. Higgins, *What Nietzsche Said* (New York: Schocken Books, 2000), p. xvii.

80. Friedrich Nietzsche, *The Gay Science* (Cambridge: Cambridge University Press, 2001 [1887]), p, 199.

81. See Jim Hopkins, 'Freud and the Science of the Mind', in Simon Glendinning, ed., *The Edinburgh Encyclopedia of Continental Philosophy* (Edinburgh: Edinburgh University Press, 1999), pp. 377–89; pp. 377–8.

82. Solomon and Higgins, *What Nietzsche Said*, p. 254.

83. Wilkens and Padgett, *Christianity and Western Thought*, p. 352.

84. Solomon and Higgins, *What Nietzsche Said*, p. 254.

85. For details of Küng's life, see Robert Nowell, *A Passion for Truth: Hans Küng, A Biography* (London: Collins, 1981).

86. Hans Küng, *Theology for the Third Millennium: An Ecumenical View* (New York: Doubleday, 1988), p. 163.

87. Ibid., p. 7.

88. Hans Küng, *On Being a Christian* (New York: Image Books/Doubleday, 1984 [1974]).

89. Küng, *Does God Exist?*, p. xxiii.

90. Küng, *Christianity*, p. 13.

91. Ibid., p. 14.

six

1. John Kent, 'Enlightenment', in Leslie Houlden, ed., *Jesus in History, Thought, and Culture: An Encyclopedia*, 2 vols (Santa Barbara, CA, and Oxford: ABC-CLIO, 2003), vol. I, pp. 245–9; p. 245.

2. Hans Küng, *Judaism: The Religious Situation of Our Time* (London: SCM Press, 1992), p. 24.

3. Hans W. Frei, *The Eclipse of Biblical Narrative: A Study in Eighteenth and Nineteenth Century Hermeneutics* (New Haven and London: Yale University Press, 1974), p. 1.

4. Consult Gleason L. Archer, *Encyclopedia of Biblical Difficulties* (Grand Rapids, MI: Zondervan, 1982), esp. pp. 20ff.

5. Consult J. Edward Wright, *The Early History of Heaven* (New York and Oxford: Oxford University Press, 2000), ch. 3, esp. p. 92.

6. B.R. Tilghman, *An Introduction to the Philosophy of Religion* (Oxford: Blackwell, 1994), p. 108.

7. See Kent, 'Enlightenment', p. 245.

8. Walter Wink, *The Powers That Be: Theology for a New Millennium* (New York: Galilee Doubleday, 1998), pp. 84–5.

9. See Gerd Lüdemann, *The Unholy in Scripture: The Dark Side of the Bible* (Louisville, KY: Westminster John Knox Press, 1997), p. 74.

10. See William M. Schniedewind, *How the Bible Became a Book: The Textualization of Ancient Israel* (Cambridge: Cambridge University Press, 2004), pp. 3–5 and 17–20.

11. Ibid., p. 4.

12. Consult Moisés Silva, 'Clear or Obscure?', in Moisés Silva, gen. ed., *Foundations of Contemporary Interpretation* (Leicester: Apollos, 1997), pp. 62–74; p. 62.

13. Martin Luther, in *Works of Martin Luther* (Philadelphia, PA: Holman, 1930), vol. 3, p. 350.

14. David Laird Dungan, *A History of the Synoptic*

Problem: The Canon, the Text, the Composition, and the Interpretation of the Gospels (New York: Doubleday, 1999), p. 185.

15. Samuel M. Powell, *The Trinity in German Thought* (Cambridge: Cambridge University Press, 2001), p. 63.

16. See Louis Crompton, *Homosexuality and Civilization* (Cambridge, MA, and London: Belknap/Harvard University Press, 2003), p. 1.

17. Raymond Martin, *The Elusive Messiah: A Philosophical Overview of the Quest of the Historical Jesus* (Boulder, CO, and Oxford: Westview, 1999), p. 3.

18. Ibid., pp. 3–4.

19. Don Cupitt, *Emptiness and Brightness* (Santa Rosa, CA: Polebridge Press, 2001), pp. 7–8.

20. Martin, *The Elusive Messiah*, p. 6.

21. See Richard Popkin, *The History of Scepticism: From Savonarola to Bayle* (Oxford and New York: Oxford University Press, 2003), p. 221.

22. Ibid., p. xvii.

23. See Richard H. Popkin, *Spinoza* (Oxford: Oneworld, 2004), p. 6.

24. Yirmiyahu Yovel, *Spinoza and Other Heretics: The Marrano of Reason* (Princeton, NJ: Princeton University Press, 1989), p. 5.

25. See Popkin, *Spinoza*, ch. 3.

26. Yovel, *Spinoza and Other Heretics*, p. 13.

27. Ibid., p. ix.

28. Popkin, *Spinoza*, p. 59.

29. J. Samuel Preus, *Spinoza and the Irrelevance of Biblical Authority* (Cambridge: Cambridge University Press, 2001), p. 1.

30. Benedict de Spinoza, *A Theologico-Political Treatise, and A Political Treatise*, trans. R.H.M. Elwes (New York: Dover Publications, 1951), pp. 33, 34.

31. Ibid., p. 101.

32. Ibid., p. 124.

33. For an excellent and more detailed account of Spinoza's way of interpreting the Bible, see Gregory W. Dawes, *The Historical Jesus Question: The Challenge of History to Religious Authority* (Louisville, London and Leiden: Westminster John Knox Press, 2001), ch. 1.

34. See ibid., pp. 40–41.

35. Paula Fredriksen, *Jesus of Nazareth: King of the Jews: A Jewish Life and the Emergence of Christianity* (London: Macmillan, 2000), p. 23.

36. W. Randolph Tate, *Biblical Interpretation: An Integrated Approach*, rev. edn (Peabody, MA: Hendrickson, 1997), p. xxiv.

37. The trend takes its name form John Ransom's book, *The New Criticism* (Norfolk, CN: New Directions, 1941/1968).

38. *Catechism of the Catholic Church*, Part Two, Section Two: 'Christ instituted the sacraments of the new law. There are seven: Baptism, Confirmation (or Chrismation), the Eucharist, Penance, the Anointing of the Sick, Holy Orders and Matrimony', p. 276. Sacraments are defined by this *Catechism* as 'perceptible signs (words and actions) accessible to human nature. By the action of Christ and the power of the Holy Spirit they make present efficaciously the grace that they signify' (p. 249).

39. Hans Küng, *Theology for the New Millennium: An Ecumenical View* (New York: Doubleday, 1988), p. 88. With regard to the abbreviations for biblical books contained in this quotation, most editions of the Bible contain a list that explains the texts to which the abbreviations refer.

40. *Catechism of the Catholic Church*, p. 176, no. 765.

41. James P. Mackey, *Modern Theology: A Sense of Direction* (Oxford: Oxford University Press, 1987), p. 133.

42. Acts 10: 9–16.

43. Keith Ward, *Religion and Community* (Oxford: Clarendon Press, 2000), pp. 138–9.

44. See Hans Küng (on the 'cursing of heretics' in Jabneh), *Judaism* (London: SCM Press, 1992), p. 359.

45. Consult Edwin D. Freed, *The Stories of Jesus' Birth: A Critical Introduction* (Sheffield: Sheffield Academic Press, 2001), esp. pp. 48–9; and Gerd Lüdemann, *Virgin Birth? The Real Story of Mary and Her Son Jesus* (London: SCM Press, 1998), esp. pp. 70–71.

46. A.C. Dixon and R.H. Torrey, eds, *The Fundamentals* (Chicago: Testimony Publishing, 1910–1915).

47. David S. Katz, *God's Last Words: Reading the English Bible from the Reformation to Fundamentalism* (New Haven and London: Yale University Press, 2004), p. 312.

48. For a spirited critique of the fundamentals, see John Shelby Spong, *A New Christianity for a New World: Why Traditional Faith is Dying and How a New Faith is Being Born* (New York: HarperSanFrancisco, 2001), pp. 1–20.

49. Bart D. Ehrman, *The Orthodox Corruption of Scripture: The Effect of Early Christological Controversies on the Text of the New Testament* (New York and Oxford: Oxford University Press, 1993), p. 7.

50. Walter Bauer, *Rechtgläubigkeit und Ketzerei im ältesten Christendum* (Tübingen: J.C.B. Mohr/Paul Siebeck, 1934); translated as a second English edition by Robert Craft et al., eds, *Orthodoxy and Heresy in Earliest Christianity* (Philadelphia: Fortress, 1971).

51. Ibid.

52. Jean Bottero, *The Birth of God: The Bible and the Historian*, trans. Kees W. Bolle (University Park, PA: Pennsylvania State University Press, 2000), pp. 3–4. The discovered history comprised the eleventh and last tablet of the *Epic of Gilgamesh*, which itself draws on an earlier work, *The Poem of the Supersage*, which dates from about the seventeenth century BCE.

seven

1. For informative discussions of the complex issue of the historical formation of Christianity, see Daniel Boyarin, *Border Lines: The Partition of Judaeo-Christianity* (Philadelphia: University of Pennsylvania Press, 2004); Paula Fredriksen, 'The Birth of Christianity and the Origins of Christian Anti-Semitism', in Paula Fredriksen and Adelle Reinhartz, eds, *Jesus, Judaism and Christian Anti-Semitism: Reading the New Testament after the Holocaust* (Louisville and London: Westminster John Knox Press, 2002), pp. 8–30; John Dominic Crossan, *The Birth of Christianity: Discovering What Happened in the Years Immediately after the Execution of Jesus* (New York: HarperSanFrancisco, 1998); William Horbury, *Jews and Christians in Contact and Controversy* (Edinburgh: T & T Clark, 1998); R.P.C. Hanson, *The Search for the Christian Doctrine of God: The Arian Controversy, 318–381 A.D.* (Edinburgh: T & T Clark, 1988); and Richard A. Norris, ed. and trans., *The Christological Controversy* (Philadelphia: Fortress Press, 1980).

2. Thus the *Catechism of the Catholic Church*: 'The Church is ultimately *one, holy, catholic and apostolic* in her deepest and ultimate identity, because it is in her that "the kingdom of heaven", the "reign of God", already exists, and will be fulfilled at the end of time' (no. 865, p. 201).

3. See Geza Vermes, *The Authentic Gospel of Jesus* (London: Penguin, 2004), pp. 405–10; and Bruce Chilton, *Pure Kingdom: Jesus' Vision of God* (Grand Rapids, MI: Eerdmans, and London: SPCK, 1996).

4. For an excellent discussion of Jesus and Jewish understandings of God and creation, see Sean Freyne, *Jesus, a Jewish Galilean: A New Reading of the Jesus-Story* (London and New York: T & T Clark International, 2004).

5. See Kathleen E. Corley and Robert L. Webb, eds, *Jesus and Mel Gibson's 'The Passion of the Christ': The Film, the Gospels and the Claims of History* (London and New York: Continuum, 2004), p. 1.

6. See Tatha Wiley, ed., *Thinking of Christ: Proclamation, Explanation, Meaning* (New York and London: Continuum, 2003), p. 13; and Paula Fredriksen, *From Jesus to Christ: The Origins of the New Testament Images of Jesus* (New Haven and London: Yale University Press, 1988).

7. Consult Jaroslav Pelikan, *Jesus Through the Centuries: His Place in the History of Culture* (New Haven and London: Yale University Press, 1985).

8. Geza Vermes was a trailblazer with respect to reminding contemporary scholars that Jesus was undeniably a Jew. He presents his case in a quadruplet of books published between 1973 and 2003: *Jesus the Jew* (London: Collins, 1973); *Jesus and the World of Judaism* (London: SCM Press, 1983); *The Religion of Jesus the Jew* (London: SCM Press, 1993); and *Jesus in His Jewish Context* (London: SCM Press, 2003).

9. 'Focus on the Family'; cited in Rosemary Radford Reuther, *Christianity and the Making of the Modern Family* (London: SCM Press, 2001), p. 3.

10. Ibid.

11. For Hegel's attitude to Jews, see Yirmiyahu Yovel, *Dark Riddle: Hegel, Nietzsche, and the Jews* (Cambridge: Polity Press, 1998).

12. Norman Perrin, *Rediscovering the Teaching of Jesus* (London: SCM Press, 1967), p. 39.

13. Gerd Theissen and Annette Merz, *The Historical Jesus: A Comprehensive Guide*, trans. John Bowden (London: SCM Press, 1998), pp. 117–18. For a more detail explanation of the criterion of historical plausibility, see Gerd Theissen and Dagmar Winter, *The Quest for the Plausible Jesus: The Question of*

Criteria (Louisville and London: Westminster John Knox Press, 2002), pp. 201–12. Consult, too, Stanley E. Porter, *The Criteria for Authenticity in Historical-Jesus Research: Previous Discussions and New Proposals* (Sheffield: Sheffield Academic Press, 2000), pp. 113–23; and Freyne, *Jesus, a Jewish Galilean*, pp. 8–12.

14. For the original Greek of Chalcedon's teaching, see *Decrees of the Ecumenical Councils*, ed. Norman P. Tanner (London: Sheed & Ward, and Washington, DC: Georgetown University Press, 1990), vol. I, pp. 86–7.

15. See Tarif Khalidi, ed. and trans., *The Muslim Jesus: Sayings and Stories in Islamic Literature* (Cambridge, MA, and London: Harvard University Press, 2003).

16. Walter H. Wagner, *After the Apostles: Christianity in the Second Century* (Minneapolis, MN: Fortress, 1994), p. 5.

17. This and the following two paragraphs are broadly based on the work of Étienne Trocmé, *The Childhood of Christianity* (London: SCM Press, 1997), p. vii.

18. For these distinctions I am indebted to Raymond E. Brown, *An Introduction to New Testament Christology* (London: Geoffrey Chapman, 1994), pp. 3ff.

19. Pius XII, *'Sempiternus Rex': On the Fifteenth Centenary of the Council of Chalcedon* (Rome: Typis Polyglottis Vaticanis, 1951), p. 4.

20. Colin Brown, *Jesus in European Protestant Thought 1778–1860* (Durham, NC: Labyrinth Press, 1985), p. xv.

21. Owen Chadwick, *The Secularization of the European Mind in the 19th Century* (Cambridge: Cambridge University Press, 2000 [1975]), p. 5.

22. Albert Schweitzer, *The Quest of the Historical Jesus* (London: SCM Press, 2000 [1906]), p. 14.

23. Hermann Samuel Reimarus, *Apologie oder Schutzschrift für die vernünftigen Verehrer Gottes*, 2 vols, *Im Auftrag der Joachim Jungius Gessellschaft der Wissenschaften Hamburg herausgegeben von Gerhard Alexander* (Frankfurt: Suhrkamp Verlag, 1972).

24. For a fuller account of the seven fragments see Brown, *Jesus in European Protestant Thought*, pp. 2–6.

25. Hermann Samuel Reimarus, *Reimarus: Fragments*, ed. Charles H. Talbert and trans. Ralph S. Fraser (Philadelphia: Fortress Press, 1970), p. 76.

26. Ibid., p. 136.

27. Ibid., pp. 71–2; brackets added.

28. Schweitzer, *The Quest of the Historical Jesus*, p. 23.

29. Ibid., pp. 15–16.

30. Writing in 1984, the French theologian Christian Duquoc posited a different double distinction in Christology. He speaks of a difference between the historical Jesus and Christ, and a difference between Christ and God. See his book, *Messianisme de Jésus et Discretion de Dieu: Essai sur la limite de la christologie* (Geneva: Labor et Fides, 1984), p. 9.

31. Henry Chadwick, 'Lessing, Gotthold Ephraim', *Encyclopedia of Philosophy*, ed. Paul Edwards, 8 vols (London and New York: Macmillan, 1967), vol. IV, pp. 9–14; p. 12.

32. Gordon E. Michalson, *Lessing's 'Ugly Ditch': A Study of Theology and History* (University Park, PA, and London: Pennsylvania State University Press, 1985), p. 1.

33. For the two quotations in this paragraph see Gotthold Lessing, 'On the Proof of the Spirit and of Power', in *Lessing's Theological Writings*, trans. Henry Chadwick (Stanford, CA: Stanford University Press, 1956), pp. 51–6; p. 53.

34. Brown, *Jesus in European Protestant Thought*, p. 18.

35. Michalson, *Lessing's 'Ugly Ditch'*, p. 8.

36. Ibid.

37. Robert Morgan with John Barton, *Biblical Interpretation* (Oxford: Oxford University Press, 1998), p. 44.

38. William Baird, *History of New Testament Research*, 2 vols (Minneapolis, MN: Fortress Press, 1992), I, p. 246.

39. Van A. Harvey, *Feuerbach and the Interpretation of Religion* (Cambridge: Cambridge University Press, 1997), p. 25.

40. Schweitzer, *The Quest of the Historical Jesus*, p. 74.

41. See Marcus J. Borg, *Jesus in Contemporary Scholarship* (Valley Forge, PA: Trinity Press International, 1994), p. 186.

42. David Friedrich Strauss, *The Life of Jesus Critically Examined*, trans. George Eliot (Ramsey, NJ: Sigler Press, 1994), p. 86.

43. Ibid., p. 53.

44. David Leeming, *Myth: A Biography of Belief* (Oxford and New York: Oxford University Press, 2002), pp. 8–9.

45. John Hick, ed., *The Myth of God Incarnate*

(London: SCM Press, 1977).

46. Consult Michael Goulder, ed., *Incarnation and Myth: The Debate Continued* (London: SCM Press, 1979); Robert G. Crawford, *The Saga of God Incarnate* (Pretoria: University of South Africa, 1985); and T.V. Morris, *The Logic of God Incarnate* (Ithaca, NY: Cornell University Press, 1986.

47. Ben Witherington III, *The Jesus Quest: The Third Search for the Jew of Nazareth* (Carlisle: Paternoster Press, 1995), p. 10.

48. Martin Kähler, *The So-Called Historical Jesus and the Historic, Biblical Christ*, trans. Carl Braaten (Philadelphia, PA: Fortress Press, 1964 [1896]), pp. 66–7.

49. Rudolf Bultmann, *Jesus and the Word*, trans. Louise Pettibone Smith and Ermine Huntress Lantero (New York: Charles Schribner's Sons, 1958), p. 8.

50. Witherington, *The Jesus Quest*, p. 11.

51. Ernst Käsemann, 'The Problem of the Historical Jesus', (1953), reprinted in Ernst Käsemann, *Essays on New Testament Themes* (London: SCM Press, 1964), pp. 15–47.

52. Ibid., p. 46.

53. Günther Bornkamm, *Jesus of Nazareth* (New York: Harper, 1960).

54. Ibid., p. 24.

55. James A. Robinson, *A New Quest for the Historical Jesus* (Naperville, IL: A.R. Allenson, 1959).

56. Originally published as Hans Küng, *Christ Sein* (Munich: Piper Verlag, 1974), and Edward Schillebeeckx, *Jezus, het verhaal van een levende* (Bloemendaal: Uitgeverij H. Nelissen, 1974).

57. Reliance on the discoveries of contemporary archaeology of Galilee and the Near East is an unmistakable feature of the third quest. Consult Jonathan L. Reed, *Archaeology and the Galilean Jesus: A Re-Examination of the Evidence* (Harrisburg, PA: Trinity Press International, 2000); Marianne Sawicki, *Crossing Galilee: Architectures of Contact in the Occupied Land of Jesus* (Harrisburg, PA: Trinity Press International, 2000); Carsten Peter Theide, *The Cosmopolitan World of Jesus: New Light from Archaeology* (London: SPCK, 2004); and John J. Rousseau and Rami Arav, *Jesus and His World: An Archaeological and Cultural Dictionary* (London: SCM Press, 1986).

58. N.T. Wright, *Jesus and the Victory of God* (London: SPCK, 1996), p. 123.

59. Fredriksen, *Jesus of Nazareth, King of the Jews*, p. 268.

60. Thus Edward Schillebeeckx, *Jesus: An Experiment in Christology* (New York: Crossroad, 1981); and E.P. Sanders, *The Historical Figure of Jesus* (London: Penguin, 1993).

61. As in Steven L. Davies, *Jesus the Healer: Possession, Trance, and the Origins of Christianity* (London: SCM, 1995).

62. Morton Smith, *Jesus the Magician* (San Francisco: Harper & Row, 1978).

63. S.G.F. Brandon, *Jesus and the Zealots* (Manchester: Manchester University Press, 1967).

64. Harvey Falk, *Jesus the Pharisee* (New York: Paulist Press, 1985).

65. For a review of this notion see Hans Dieter Betz, 'Jesus and the Cynics: Survey and Analysis of a Hypothesis', *Journal of Religion*, 74/4 (October 1994), pp. 453–75.

66. Thus, John Dominic Crossan's quartet: *The Historical Jesus: The Life of a Mediterranean Jewish Peasant* (San Francisco: Harper, 1991); *Jesus: A Revolutionary Biography* (San Francisco: Harper, 1994); *The Essential Jesus: What Jesus Really Taught* (San Francisco: Harper, 1994); and *Who Killed Jesus? Exposing the Roots of Anti-Semitism in the Gospel Story of the Death of Jesus* (San Francisco: Harper, 1995).

67. According to Leonardo Boff, *Jesus Christ Liberator: A Critical Christology of Our Time* (London: SPCK, 1978); and Sebastian Moore, *Jesus the Liberator of Desire* (New York: Crossroad, 1989).

68. William R. Herzogg, *Parables as Subversive Speech: Jesus as Pedagogue of the Oppressed* (Louisville, KY: Westminster/John Knox Press, 1994).

69. Fredriksen, *Jesus of Nazareth, King of the Jews*, p. 273.

70. Consult E.P. Sanders, *Jesus and Judaism* (London: SCM Press, 1985), and *The Historical Figure of Jesus* (London: Penguin, 1993); John P. Meier, *A Marginal Jew: Rethinking the Historical Jesus*, 3 vols, The Anchor Bible Reference Library (New York and London: Doubleday, 1991, 1993, 2001); Paula Fredriksen, *From Jesus to Christ*, and *Jesus of Nazareth, King of the Jews*; and Dale C. Allison, *Jesus of Nazareth: Millenarian Prophet* (Minneapolis: Fortress Press, 1998).

71. See John Dominic Crossan, *Jesus: A Revolutionary Biography* (New York: HarperSanFrancisco, 1994); and Marcus J. Borg,

Jesus at 2000 (Boulder, CO: Westview Press 1997).

72. See Freyne, *Jesus, a Jewish Galilean*, pp. 136–7.

73. See David Leeming, *Jealous Gods and Chosen People*, p. 17.

74. See Wiley, *Thinking of Christ*, p. 18.

eight

1. Gregory W. Dawes, *The Historical Jesus Question: The Challenge of History to Religious Authority* (Louisville, KY: Westminster John Knox Press, 2001), p. 354.

2. Della Thompson, ed., *The Concise Oxford Dictionary of Current English* (Oxford: Oxford University Press, 1995), p. 713.

3. Richard Palmer, *Hermeneutics: Interpretation Theory in Schleiermacher, Dilthey, Heidegger, and Gadamer* (Evanston: Northwestern University Press, 1969), p. 14.

4. Werner Jeanrond, *Theological Hermeneutics: Development and Significance* (London: SCM Press, 1994), pp. 7–8.

5. Alfred Moir, *Caravaggio*, (New York: Harry N. Abram's, 1982), p. 92.

6. For a more detailed discussion of possible interpretations of this painting, see Leon Bersoni and Ulysse Dutoit, *Caravaggio's Secrets* (Cambridge, MA, and London: MIT Press, 1998), pp. 79–83.

7. Consult Hans-Georg Gadamer, *Philosophical Hermeneutics* (Berkeley and Los Angeles: University of California Press, 1977).

8. *Museo del Prado Guide* (Madrid: Aldeasa, 1994), p. 8; brackets added

9. Don Cupitt, *After God*, p. vii.

10. Hans Küng, *A Global Ethic for Global Politics and Economics* (London: SCM Press, 1997), p. 152.

11. Martin Heidegger, *Being and Time* (New York: Harper & Row, 1962), pp. 191–2.

12. W. Randolf Tate, *Biblical Interpretation: An Integrated Approach*, 2nd edn (Peabody, MA: Hendrikson, 1997), p. 187.

13. Hans-Georg Gadamer elucidates the hermeneutical circle in *Truth and Method*, 2nd edn (London: Sheed & Ward, 1989), pp. 265–71.

14. Jeanrond, *Theological Hermeneutics*, p. 6.

15. For an excellent overview of the history of hermeneutics consult Anthony C. Thiselton, *New Horizons in Hermeneutics: The Theory and Practice of Transforming Biblical*

Reading (London: HarperCollins, 1992), pp. 142–203.

16. Kathy Eden, *Hermeneutics and the Rhetorical Tradition: Chapters in the Ancient Legacy and Its Humanist Reception* (New Haven and London: Yale University Press, 1997), p. 7.

17. See Friedrich Schleiermacher, *Hermeneutics and Criticism* (Cambridge: Cambridge University Press, 1998), p. 24.

18. Quoted in the *Catechism of the Catholic Church*, pp. 47–8.

19. Robert W. Funk, *Honest to Jesus: Jesus for a New Millennium* (New York: HarperSanFrancisco, 1996), p. 303.

20. Ibid., p. 300.

21. David, W. Kling, *The Bible in History: How the Texts Have Shaped the Times* (Oxford and New York: Oxford University Press, 2004), p. 47.

22. Ibid., p. 46.

23. Francis Schüssler Fiorenza, *Foundational Theology: Jesus and the Church* (New York: Crossroad, 1984), p. 90.

nine

1. See Philip Jenkins, *The Next Christendom: The Coming of Global Christianity* (Oxford: Oxford University Press, 2002), p. 1.

2. At least according to David B. Barrett, George T. Kurian, and Todd M. Johnson, eds, *World Christian Encyclopedia*, 2nd edn (New York: Oxford University Press, 2001), p. 4.

3. See Ted Honderich, *After the Terror* (Edinburgh: Edinburgh University Press, 2002), p. 18.

4. Hilaire Belloc, *Europe and the Faith* (New York: Paulist, 1920), p. ix.

5. Consult Jenkins, *The Next Christendom*, pp. 1–3.

6. *World Bank Atlas 2000* (Washington, DC: World Bank, 2000), p. 18.

7. UNDP, *Human Development Report 2003* (New York and Oxford: Oxford University Press, 2003; published for the United Nations Development Programme), pp. 40–41.

8. Worldwatch Institute, *Vital Signs: The Trends that Are Shaping Our Future, 2003–2004* (London: Earthscan, 2003), p. 18.

9. Ibid., p. 18.

10. *World Development Report 2000/2001: Attacking Poverty* (Oxford: Oxford University Press, 1999; published for the World Bank), p. 3.

11. *Human Development Report 2003*, pp. 237–8.
12. *World Bank Atlas 2000*, pp. 166–9.
13. Worldwatch Institute, *Vital Signs*, p. 19.
14. *Human Development Report 2003*, p. 8.
15. Ibid.
16. Ibid., p. 41.
17. Ibid., pp. 258–60.
18. *Human Development Report 1999* (New York and Oxford: Oxford University Press, 1999; published for the United Nations Development Programme), pp. 1 and 3.
19. *Human Development Report 2003*, p. 39.
20. Hans Küng, *A Global Ethic for Global Politics and Economics* (London: SCM Press, 1997), p. 274.
21. Hans Küng, *Global Responsibility: In Search of a New World Ethic* (London: SCM Press, 1991), p. 2.
22. Keith Hart, *Money in an Unequal World* (New York and London: Textere, 2001), p. 3.
23. *Human Development Report 2002* (New York and Oxford: Oxford University Press, 2002; published for the United Nations Development Programme) pp. 212–15.
24. Ibid., pp. 216–17.
25. Ibid., p. 45.
26. Ibid.
27. Worldwatch Institute, *Vital Signs*, p. 20.
28. Jürgen Moltmann, *God for a Secular Society: The Public Relevance of Theology* (London: SCM Press, 1999), p. 13.
29. See Chris Brazier, *The No-Nonsense Guide to World History* (London: Verso, 2003), p.66.
30. David Batstone, Eduardo Mendieta, Lois Ann Lorentzen and Dwight N. Hopkins, eds, *Liberation Theologies, Postmodernity, and the Americas* (London and New York: Routledge, 1997), p. 13.
31. See Alfred T. Hennelly, *Liberation Theologies: The Global Pursuit of Justice* (Mystic, CT: Twenty-Third Publications, 1997), p. 5.
32. Wayne Ellwood, *No-Nonsense Guide to Globalization* (London: Verso, 2001).
33. Quoted in Gustavo Gutiérrez, *Las Casas: In Search of the Poor Jesus Christ*, trans. Robert R. Barr (Maryknoll, NY: Orbis Books, 1993), p. 29.
34. For a detailed discussion of the friars of Hispaniola, see Gutiérrez, *Las Casas*, pp. 27–44.
35. Ibid., p. 44.
36. On the history of the Church in Latin America over the past five centuries consult

Alfred Hennelly, *Theology for a Liberating Church: The New Praxis of Freedom* (Washington, DC: Georgetown University Press, 1989), pp. 26–8. Hennelly draws on the work of the Argentinian historian Henrique Dussell.
37. *Vatican II: Constitutions, Decrees, Declarations*, ed. Austin Flannery (Northport, NY: Costello; and Dublin: Dominican Publications, 1996), p. 163; emphasis added.
38. See Gustavo Gutiérrez, *A Theology of Liberation*, trans. Caridad Inda and John Eagleson, 2nd edn (Maryknoll, NY: Orbis Books, 1988 [1971]), pp. xxix and 11.
39. Nicholas Lobkowicz, *Theory and Practice: History of a Concept from Aristotle to Marx* (New York and London: University Press of America, 1967), p. 9.
40. Sacred Congregation for the Doctrine of the Faith, *Instruction on Certain Aspects of the Theology of Praxis [Libertatis Nuntius]* (London: Catholic Truth Society, 1984), pp. 17–22.
41. Karl Marx, 'Theses on Feuerbach' (1845), in John E. Toews, *The Communist Manifesto by Karl Marx and Frederick Engels with Related Documents* (Boston and New York: Bedford/ St. Martin's Press, 1999), p. 139.
42. Edward Schillebeeckx, 'La teología', in *Los catôicos holandeses* (Bilbao: Desclée de Brouwer, 1970), cited in Gutiérrez, *A Theology of Liberation*, pp. 8 and 181 n35.
43. This rhetorically powerful description of suffering is by the philosopher Yeager Hudson, who discusses evil and suffering, though not in the context of considering liberation theology. His account of evil is contained in *The Philosophy of Religion* (London and Toronto: Mayfield, 1991), p. 119.
44. Gustavo Gutiérrez, *The Power of the Poor in History* (London: SCM Press, 1986), p. 57.
45. Gustavo Gutiérrez, 'The Tack and Content of Liberation Theology', trans. Judith Condor, in Christopher Rowland, ed., *The Cambridge Companion to Liberation Theology* (Cambridge: Cambridge University Press, 1999), pp. 19–38; p. 19.
46. Gutiérrez, *The Power of the Poor in History*, p. 103.
47. Gustavo Gutiérrez, *On Job: God-Talk and the Suffering of the Innocent*, trans. Matthew J. O'Connell (Maryknoll, NY: Orbis Books, 1987), p. 29.
48. Christopher Rowland, 'Introduction: The Theology of Liberation', in Rowland,

ed., *The Cambridge Companion to Liberation Theology*, pp. 1–16; p. 4.

49. Consult Jonathan Kwitney's biography of John Paul II, *Man of the Century* (New York: Henry Holt , 1997), p. 353. Kwitney asserts that Oddi offered this information during an interview.

50. See John L. Allen Jr, *Cardinal Ratzinger: The Vatican's Enforcer of Faith* (New York and London: Continuum, 2000), p. 150; and Jon Sobrino, *Witness to the Kingdom: The Martyrs of El Salvador and the Crucified Peoples* (Maryknoll, NY: Orbis Books, 2003), ch. 1.

51. Robin Nagle, *Claiming the Virgin: The Broken Promise of Liberation Theology in Brazil* (New York and London: Routledge, 1997), p. 3.

52. Ibid., p. 13.

53. Ibid., pp. 13–14.

54. David N. Field, 'On (Re)centering the Margins: A Euro-African Perspective on the Option for the Poor', in Joerg Rieger, ed., *Opting for the Margins: Postmodernity and Liberation in Christian Theology* (Oxford and New York: Oxford University Press, 2003), pp. 45–69; p. 51.

55. Field, 'On (Re)centering the Margins', p. 51.

ten

1. Alain Boureau, *The Myth of Pope Joan* (Chicago and London: University of Chicago Press, 2001).

2. Keith Ward, 'Why Theology Should Be Taught at Secular Universities', *Discourse* 4/1 (Autumn 2004–5), pp. 22–37; p. 22.

3. For the history of women in Oxford consult Brian Harrison, ed., *The History of the University of Oxford*, Volume VIII: *Twentieth Century* (Oxford: Oxford University Press, 1994), ch. 13.

4. Bonnie S. Anderson and Judith P. Zinsser, *A History of Their Own: Women in Europe from Prehistory to the Present*, vol. 2 (New York: Harper & Row, 1988), p. 492 n1.

5. Christine de Pizan, *The Book of the City of Ladies*, trans. Earl Jeffrey Richards (New York: Persea Books, 1982 [1405]), p. 187.

6. See Anne M. Clifford, *Introducing Feminist Theology* (Maryknoll, NY: Orbis Books, 2001), p. 39, n. 2. For a discussion of de Pizan's work, see pp. 9–11.

7. Quoted in John Boswell, *Christianity, Social Tolerance and Homosexuality: Gay People in Western Europe from the Beginning of the Christian Era to the Fourteenth Century* (Chicago: University of Chicago Press, 1981), p. 157.

8. See Marry E. Wiesner-Hanks, *Christianity and Sexuality in the Early Modern World* (London and New York: Routledge, 2000), p. 31.

9. Ibid., p. 27.

10. Ibid., p. 25.

11. Ibid.

12. Thomas Aquinas, *Summa Theologiae*, ed. Thomas Gilby, trans. Edmund Hill (Blackfriars edn, London: Eyre & Spottiswoode, 1964), vol. XIII, Ia, q. 92, art. 1.

13. Cited in Maureen Fiedler and Linda Rabben, eds, *Rome Has Spoken: A Guide to Forgotten Papal Statements, and How They Have Changed Through the Centuries* (New York: Crossroad, 1998), p. 115.

14. Pliny the Elder, *Natural History*, Book 28, ch. 23, 78–79; quoted in John Wijngaards, *The Ordination of Women in the Catholic Church: Unmasking a Cuckoo's Egg Tradition* (London: Darton, Longman & Todd, 2001), p. 54.

15. Jerome, Letter 22, *To Eustochium*, §37; Quoted in Wijngaards, *The Ordination of Women in the Catholic Church*, p. 54.

16. Clement of Alexandria, *Paidagogas* III, 50.1.

17. Uta Ranke-Heinemann, *Eunuchs for Heaven: The Catholic Church and Sexuality* (London: André Deutsch, 1990), p. 164.

18. Aristotle, *De animalium generatione*, 2, 3.

19. Wijngaards, *The Ordination of Women in the Catholic Church*, p. 53.

20. Martin Luther, 'Sermon on the Estate of Marriage', in *Luther's Works*, ed. J. Atkinson (Philadelphia: Fortress Press, 1966), vol. XLIV, p. 8. In addition, consult Rosemary R. Ruether, *Introducing Redemption in Christian Feminism* (Sheffield: Sheffield Academic Press, 1998).

21. Martin Luther, 'Lectures on Genesis', in *Luther's Works*, vol. I, pp. 68–9.

22. Barbara Caine and Glenda Sluga, *Gendering European History* (London and New York: Leicester University Press, 2000), p. 11.

23. Ibid.

24. Clifford, *Introducing Feminist Theology*, pp. 16–17.

25. Joann Wolski Conn, 'New Vitality: The Challenge from Feminist Theology',

America, 165 (5 October 1991), p. 217.

26. Clifford, *Introducing Feminist Theology*, p. 272.

27. Rita M. Goss, *Feminism and Religion* (Boston: Beacon Press, 1996), p. 36.

28. Cited in Eleanor Flexner, *Century of Struggle: The Women's Rights Movement in the United States*, rev. edn (Cambridge, MA: Belknap/Harvard University Press, 1975), pp. 45–8.

29. Cited in Goss, *Feminism and Religion*, p. 37.

30. In Gerda Lerner, *The Feminist Thought of Sarah Grimké* (Oxford and New York: Oxford University Press, 1998), p. 50.

31. See Ruether, *Introducing Redemption*, p. 60.

32. Mary Daly, *The Church and the Second Sex*, 2nd edn (Boston: Beacon Press, 1985), p. 10.

33. This event is recounted in Catherine Keller, 'Mary Daly', in Donald W. Musser and Joseph L. Price, eds, *A New Handbook of Christian Theologians* (Nashville, TN: Abingdon Press, 1996), pp. 127–34; p. 129).

34. Elisabeth Schüssler Fiorenza, *In Memory of Her: A Feminist Theological Reconstruction of Christian Origins*, 2nd edn (London: SCM Press, 1994 [1983]), p. xliii.

35. Mary F. Daly, *The Problem of Speculative Theology* (Washington, DC: Thomist Press, 1965), p. 40.

36. Mary Daly, *Pure Lust: Elemental Feminist Philosophy* (New York: HarperSanFrancisco, 1984), pp. 82–3.

37. Keller, 'Mary Daly', p. 127.

38. *Catechism of the Catholic Church*, rev. edn (London: Geoffrey Chapman, 1999), p. 7.

39. Mary Daly, *Beyond God the Father*, 2nd edn (Boston: Beacon Press, 1985 [1973]), p. 19.

40. See Gail Ramshaw, *God beyond Gender: Feminist Christian God-Language* (Minneapolis, MN: Fortress Press, 1995), esp. p. 27.

41. See *The Ordination of Women of Women to the Priesthood: The Synod Debate, 11 November 1992* (London: Church House Publishing, 1993), p. 37.

42. Erik Borgman, 'De kerk als schijnbaar fundament: Over het zwijgen van de theologie, en het doorbreken daarvan', *Tijdschrift voor Theologie* 35 (1995), pp. 358–72; pp. 358–9.

43. For an enlightening account of recent episcopal teachings see, Lavinia Byrne, *Woman at the Altar: The Ordination of Women in the Roman Catholic Church* (London: Mowbray, 1994).

44. *Acta Apostolicae Sedis (AAS)* 68 (1976), p. 599.

45. See *AAS*, 69 (1977), pp. 98–116.

46. See *AAS*, 80 (1988), p. 1715.

47. *AAS*, 87 (1995), p. 1114.

48. At least according to Edmund Hill who, in his researches, has not found a technical-theological use of *magisterium* before 1835. See discussion in his *Ministry and Authority in the Catholic Church* (London: Geoffrey Chapman, 1988), pp. 75–88, esp. pp. 1 and 77, to which I am indebted.

49. See Yves Congar, 'Pour une histoire sémantique du terme "magisterium"', *Revue des sciences philosophiques et théologiques* 60 (1976), pp. 85–98.

50. In this context, see especially Jacques M. Gres-Gayer, 'The Magisterium of the Faculty of Theology of Paris in the Seventeenth Century', *Theological Studies* 53/3 (1992), pp. 424–50; p. 424.

51. See John P. Meier, 'Reflections on Jesus-of-History Research Today', in James H. Charlesworth (ed.), *Jesus' Jewishness: Exploring the Place of Jesus within Early Judaism* (New York: Crossroad, 1991), pp. 84–107; p. 90.

52. With regard to Jesus, the Twelve, and Jewish apocalyptic eschatological theologies focused on the restoration of Israel's lost cohesiveness; see E.P. Sanders, 'The Life of Jesus', in Hershel Shanks (ed.), *Christianity and Rabbinic Judaism: A Parallel History of Their Origins and Early Development* (London: SPCK, 1993), pp. 41–83; pp. 52 and 57; and *The Historical Figure of Jesus* (London: Penguin, 1993), pp. 184–8; Paula Fredricksen, *From Jesus to Christ: The Origins of the New Testament Images of Jesus* (New Haven and London: Yale University Press, 1988), pp. 81–3 and 102; and Marcus J. Borg, *Jesus in Contemporary Scholarship* (Valley Forge, PA: Trinity Press International, 1994), ch. 1.

53. Although some scholars interpret the name Junia as masculine, it is more commonly understood as feminine. The Church Fathers Origen, John Chrysostom and Jerome all regarded Junia as a woman.

54. For a fuller explanation of this point consult Peter Schmidt, 'Ministries in the New Testament and the Early Church', in Jan Kerkhofs (ed.), *Europe Without Priests?* (London: SCM Press, 1995), pp. 41–88; p. 60.

eleven

1. A.L. Rowse, *The Elizabethan Renaissance* (London: Macmillan, 1972), p. 227.
2. *The Concise Oxford Dictionary of Current English*, 9th edn (Oxford: Clarendon Press, 1995), p. 1236.
3. Hans Küng, *The Catholic Church: A Short History* (London: Weidenfeld & Nicolson, 2001), p. 153.
4. M.R. Wright, *Cosmology in Antiquity* (Routledge: London and New York, 1995), p. 4.
5. Daniel Graham, 'Introduction', in J.L. Ackrill and Lindsay Judson, eds, *Aristotle, Physics, Book VIII* (Oxford: Clarendon Press, 1999), pp. ix–xvii; p. xii.
6. Ibid., p. xii.
7. Ibid., pp. xiv–xv.
8. See Louis Dupré, *The Enlightenment and the Intellectual Foundations of Modern Culture* (New Haven, CT and London: Yale University Press, 2004), p. 18.
9. David Laird Dungan, *A History of the Synoptic Problem: The Canon, the Text, the Composition, and the Interpretation of the Gospels* (New York: Doubleday, 1999), p. 147.
10. J. Edward Wright, *The Early History of Heaven* (Oxford: Oxford University Press, 2000), p. 33.
11. Ibid., p. 54.
12. Robert W. Funk, *Honest to Jesus: Jesus for a New Millennium* (New York: HarperSanFrancisco, 1996), p. 75.
13. Walter Fink, *The Powers That Be: Theology for a New Millennium* (New York: Doubleday, 1998), p. 15.
14. Ibid., p. 16.
15. Victor H. Matthews and Don C. Benjamin, *Old Testament Parallels: Laws and Stories from the Ancient Near East* (Mahwah, NJ: Paulist Press, 1991), p. 22 fig. 10.
16. Robert Naeye, *Through the Eyes of Hubble: The Birth, Life and Violent Death of Stars* (Bristol and Philadelphia: Institute of Physics Publishing, 1998), p. 7.
17. Lee Smolin, *The Life of the Cosmos* (London: Weidenfeld & Nicholson, 1997), p. 24.
18. See Ian G. Barbour, *Religion and Science: Historical and Contemporary Issues* (London: SCM Press, 1998), p. 57; and Peter Atkins, *Galileo's Finger: The Ten Great Ideas of Science* (Oxford: Oxford University Press, 2003), p. 247.
19. Peter Barrett, *Science and Technology since Copernicus* (London and New York: T & T Clark International, 2004), pp. 81–2.
20. Robert Doran, *Birth of a Worldview: Early Christianity in Its Jewish and Pagan Context* (Boulder, CO: Westview Press, 1995), p. 1.
21. Gordon Kaufman, *In Face of Mystery: A Constructive Theology* (Cambridge MA: Harvard University Press, 1993), p. 113.
22. Ibid., p. 74.
23. Ibid., p. 90.
24. Paul Davies, *God and the New Physics* (New York: Touchstone, Simon & Schuster, 1983), p. 229.
25. Ibid.
26. Paul Brockelman, *Cosmology and Creation: The Spiritual Significance of Contemporary Cosmology* (New York and Oxford: Oxford University Press, 1999), p. 15.
27. Joseph Campbell, 'The Mythological Dimension', *Historical Atlas of the World*, vol. 1 (New York: Perennial Library, 1988), p. 8.
28. Barbour, *Religion and Science*, pp. 281–2.
29. Ibid.
30. For Barbour's own more explicit explanation, see ibid., pp. 283–4.
31. Daniel C. Dennett, *Darwin's Dangerous Idea: Evolution and the Meaning of Life* (London: Penguin Books, 1995), p. 21.
32. J. Wentzel van Hussteen, *Duet or Duel? Theology and Science in a Postmodern World* (London: SCM Press, 1998), p. 87.
33. John F. Haught, *God after Darwin: A Theology of Evolution* (Boulder, CO, and Oxford: Westview Press, 2000), p. 11.
34. Owen Chadwick, *The Victorian Church, Part Two: 1860–1901* (London: SCM Press, 1972), p. 1.
35. Ibid., p. 2.
36. *Catechism of the Catholic Church*, p. 87 n390.
37. Ibid., no. 400, p. 90.
38. Günther Weber, *I Believe, I Doubt: Notes on Christian Experience* (London: SCM Press, 1998), p. 106.
39. Explained in John Gribbin, *Companion to the Cosmos* (London: Phoenix, 1996), p. 62.
40. Ibid., pp. 61–2.
41. Brockelman, *Cosmology and Creation*, p. 56.
42. Ibid., p. 54.
43. Ibid., p. 53.
44. Gribbin, *Companion to the Cosmos*, p. 582.
45. Kaufman, *In Face of Mystery*, ch. 19.

twelve

1. Wayne Ellwood, *The No-Nonsense Guide to Globalization* (London: Verso, 2001), p. 12. See, too, Martin Albow, *The Global Age* (Cambridge: Polity Press, 1996); Ulrich Beck, *What Is Globalization?* (Cambridge: Polity Press, 2000); Zygmunt Bauman, *Globalization: The Human Consequences* (Cambridge: Polity Press, 1998); and Jan Aart Scholte, *Globalization: A Critical Introduction* (London: Palgrave, 2000).
2. Hans Küng, *Judaism: The Religious Situation of Our Time* (London: SCM Press, 1992), p. ii.
3. Harold Coward, *Pluralism in the World Religions* (Oxford: Oneworld, 2000), p. vii.
4. John Hick, *The Rainbow of Faiths: Critical Dialogues in Religious Pluralism* (London: SCM Press, 1995), p. ix.
5. Ibid.
6. Ibid.
7. Ibid.
8. John Hick, *The Metaphor of God Incarnate* (London: SCM Press, 1993), p. ix.
9. Paul Knitter, *No Other Name: A Critical Survey of Christian Attitudes Toward the World Religions* (Maryknoll, NY: Orbis Books, 1985), p. 219.
10. Raymond Brown, *The Death of the Messiah: From Gethsemene to the Grave: A Commentary on the Passion Narratives in the Four Gospels* (New York: Doubleday, 1994), p. 831.
11. Ibid., p. 831 n22. See, too, John Dominic Crossan, *Who Killed Jesus? The Roots of Anti-Semitism in the Gospel Story of the Death of Jesus* (New York: HarperSanFrancisco, 1995), pp. x–xi.
12. Quoted in Edward Schillebeeckx, *Church: The Human Story of God*, trans. John Bowden (London: SCM Press, 1990), p. xvii.
13. 'Dogmatic Constitution on the Church' (*Lumen Gentium*, 21 November, 1964), in Austin Flannery, ed., *Vatican Council II* (Northport, NY: Costello, and Dublin: Dominican Publications, 1996), no. 16, p. 22.
14. Anthony Giddens, *Runaway World: How Globalization is Reshaping Our Lives* (London: Routledge, 1999), pp. 10–11.
15. John Hick, *God Has Many Names* (Philadelphia: Westminster Press, 1982), p. 14.
16. For the details of John Hick's life and works, see Chester Gillis, 'John Harwood Hick', in Donald W. Musser and Joseph L. Price, eds, *A New Handbook of Christian Theologians* (Nashville: Abingdon Press, 1996), pp. 221–8.
17. L. Miller and Stanley J. Grenz, eds, *Fortress Introduction to Contemporary Theologies* (Minneapolis, MN: Fortress Press, 1998), p. 180.
18. Ibid., p. 181.
19. John Hick, *The Fifth Dimension: An Exploration of the Spiritual Realm* (Oxford: Oneworld, 1999), p. 5. See, as well, John Hick, *An Interpretation of Religion: Human Responses to the Transcendent* (London: Macmillan Press, 1989), ch. 2.
20. Hick, *The Fifth Dimension*, p. 5.
21. Miller and Grenz, *Fortress Introduction to Contemporary Theologies*, p. 184
22. Thomas Aquinas, *Summa Theologiae*, II/II, Q. 1, art. 2.
23. Hick, *The Rainbow of Faiths*, p. 29.
24. Karl Rahner, *Theological Investigations*, vol. V: *Later Writings*, trans. Karl-H. Kruger (Baltimore: Helicon Press, and London: Darton, Longman & Todd, 1969), pp. 115–34.
25. Ibid., p. 118.
26. Ibid., p. 121.
27. Ibid., p. 131.
28. Ibid., p. 133.
29. Jacques Dupuis, *Toward a Christian Theology of Religious Pluralism* (Maryknoll, NY: Orbis Books, 1997), p. 6.
30. Edward Schillebeeckx, *Jesus in Our Western Culture* (London: SCM Press, 1987), p. 9.

conclusion

1. Umberto Eco, *The Name of the Rose* (London: Vintage, 1998), p. 399.
2. Rudolf Bultmann, 'New Testament and Mythology: The Problem of Demythologizing the New Testament Proclamation', in *New Testament and Mythology and Other Basic Writings*, ed. Schubert M. Ogden (Philadelphia, PA: Fortress Press, 1989 [1941]), pp. 1–43; pp. 4–5.
3. A typical example of the latter appears at the end of Pope John Paul II's apostolic letter, *Mane Nobiscum Dominum* ('Abide with Us Lord'), signed on 7 October 2004 to inaugurate the Year of the Eucharist 2004–2005. The letter concludes with these words: 'In this Year of grace, sustained by Mary, may the Church discover new enthusiasm for her

mission and come to acknowledge ever more fully that the Eucharist is the source and summit of her entire life' (London: Catholic Truth Society, 2004), p. 32. Consult John Cornwell, *The Pope in Winter: The Dark Face of John Paul's Papacy* (London: Viking, 2004).

4. Ziauddin Sardar, *The A to Z of Postmodern Life: Essays on Global Culture in the Noughties* (London: Vision, 2002), p. 21. Sardar is here describing life in the United States of America.

5. Ibid., p. 9.

6. Ibid., pp. 48–9.

7. Ibid., p. 15.

8. Gordon D. Kaufman, *Theology for a Nuclear Age* (Manchester: Manchester University Press, 1985), p. 16.

9. United Nations Development Programme, *Global Environment Outlook 2000* (London: Earthscan, 1999), p. xx.

10. Ibid., p. xxi.

11. Gordon D. Kaufman, 'Reconceiving God and Humanity in Light of Today's Evolutionary-Ecological Consciousness', in Raymond F. Bulman and Frederick J. Parrella, eds, *Religion in the New Millennium: Theology in the Spirit of Paul Tillich* (Macon, GA: Mercer University Press, 2001), pp. 235–50; p. 236.

12. Ibid., p. 237.

13. Ibid.

further reading

Peter Barrett, *Science and Theology since Copernicus: The Search for Understanding* (London: T & T Clark International, 2004).

Deborah Brown, ed., *Christianity in the 21st Century* (New York: Crossroad, 2000).

Louis Dupré, *The Enlightenment and the Intellectual Foundations of Modern Culture* (New Haven and London: Yale University Press, 2004).

Roger Haight, *Jesus: Symbol of God* (Maryknoll, NY: Orbis Books, 1999).

John H.S. Kent, *The End of the Line? The Development of Christianity in the Last Two Centuries* (London: SCM Press, 1982).

Hans Küng, *Theology for the Third Millennium: An Ecumenical View* (New York: Doubleday, 1998).

Gaspar Martinez, *Confronting the Mystery of God: Political, Liberation, and Public Theologies* (New York and London: Continuum, 2001).

Hugh McCleod and Werner Ustorf, *The Decline of Christendom in Western Europe, 1750–2000* (Cambridge: Cambridge University Press, 2003).

Peter McEnhill and George Newlands, *Fifty Key Christian Thinkers* (London and New York: Routledge, 2004).

John Thornhill, *Modernity: Christianity's Estranged Child* (Grand Rapids, MI: Eerdmans, 2000).

Keith Ward, *What the Bible Really Teaches: A Challenge for Fundamentalists* (London: SPCK, 2004).

Günther Weber, *I Believe, I Doubt: Notes on Christian Experience* (London: SCM Press, 1998).

index